RSF: The Russell Sage Foundation Journal of the Social Sciences

Opportunity, Mobility, and Increased Inequality

VOLUME 2 • NUMBER 2 • MAY 2016

RSF: The Russell Sage Foundation Journal of the Social Sciences ISSN 2377-8261

The Russell Sage Foundation

The Russell Sage Foundation, one of the oldest of America's general purpose foundations, was established in 1907 by Mrs. Margaret Olivia Sage for "the improvement of social and living conditions in the United States." The foundation seeks to fulfill this mandate by fostering the development and dissemination of knowledge about the country's political, social, and economic problems. While the foundation endeavors to assure the accuracy and objectivity of each book it publishes, the conclusions and interpretations in Russell Sage Foundation publications are those of the authors and not of the foundation, its trustees, or its staff. Publication by Russell Sage, therefore, does not imply foundation endorsement.

Board of Trustees

Sara S. McLanahan, *Chair*
Larry M. Bartels
Karen S. Cook
W. Bowman Cutter III
Sheldon H. Danziger
Kathryn Edin
Lawrence F. Katz
David Laibson
Nicholas Lemann
Martha Minow
Peter R. Orszag
Claude M. Steele
Shelley E. Taylor
Richard H. Thaler
Hirokazu Yoshikawa

Mission Statement

RSF: The Russell Sage Foundation Journal of the Social Sciences is a peer-reviewed, open-access journal of original empirical research articles by both established and emerging scholars. It is designed to promote cross-disciplinary collaborations on timely issues of interest to academics, policymakers, and the public at large. Each issue is thematic in nature and focuses on a specific research question or area of interest. The introduction to each issue will include an accessible, broad, and synthetic overview of the research question under consideration and the current thinking from the various social sciences.

RSF Journal Editorial Board

Elizabeth O. Ananat, Duke University
Annette Bernhardt, University of California, Berkeley
Karen S. Cook, Stanford University
Sheldon H. Danziger, RSF President
Janet C. Gornick, The CUNY Graduate Center
Jennifer Hochschild, Harvard University
Douglas S. Massey, Princeton University
Mary E. Pattillo, Northwestern University
James Sidanius, Harvard University
Mary C. Waters, Harvard University
Bruce Western, Harvard University

Copyright © 2016 by Russell Sage Foundation. All rights reserved. Printed in the United States of America. No part of this publication may be reproduced, stored in a retrieval system, or transmitted in any form or by any means, electronic, mechanical, photocopying, recording, or otherwise, without the prior written permission of the publisher. Reproduction by the United States Government in whole or in part is permitted for any purpose.

Opinions expressed in this journal are not necessarily those of the editors, editorial board, trustees, or the Russell Sage Foundation.

We invite scholars to submit proposals for potential issues through the *RSF* application portal: https://rsfjournal.onlineapplicationportal.com/. Submissions should be addressed to Suzanne Nichols, Director of Publications.

To view the complete text and additional features online please go to **www.rsfjournal.org**.

Russell Sage Foundation
112 East 64th Street
New York, NY 10065

ISSN (print): 2377-8253
ISSN (electronic): 2377-8261
ISBN: 978-0-87154-991-4

RSF: The Russell Sage Foundation
Journal of the Social Sciences
VOLUME 2 NUMBER 2
MAY 2016

Opportunity, Mobility, and Increased Inequality

ISSUE EDITORS
Katharine Bradbury, Federal Reserve Bank of Boston
Robert K. Triest, Federal Reserve Bank of Boston

CONTENTS

Introduction: Inequality of Economic Opportunity **1**
Katharine Bradbury and Robert K. Triest

Perspectives on Inequality and Opportunity from the Survey of Consumer Finances **44**
Janet L. Yellen

Modeling Equal Opportunity **60**
Isabel V. Sawhill and Richard V. Reeves

Multiple Barriers to Economic Opportunity for the "Truly" Disadvantaged and Vulnerable **98**
Timothy M. Smeeding

Can Early Childhood Interventions Decrease Inequality of Economic Opportunity? **123**
Katherine Magnuson and Greg J. Duncan

Rising Inequality in Family Incomes and Children's Educational Outcomes **142**
Greg J. Duncan and Richard J. Murnane

Neighborhoods, Cities, and Economic Mobility
Patrick Sharkey **159**

Inequality of Opportunity and Aggregate Economic Performance **178**
Katharine Bradbury and Robert K. Triest

Introduction: Inequality of Economic Opportunity

KATHARINE BRADBURY AND ROBERT K. TRIEST

In the United States, inequality in the distribution of economic rewards, such as income and wealth, has widened greatly in recent decades. This has led to a spirited debate regarding the causes and consequences of increased economic inequality. A fundamental area of contention is whether the increase is evidence of underlying economic problems that need correction. Increased inequality may result from increased risk taking and entrepreneurship in an environment of rapid technological change, with some entrepreneurs producing better, or just luckier, innovations than others, and reaping greater rewards. It may also result from increased disparities in work effort, with more industrious individuals earning higher incomes as a result of their greater effort. In both these cases, one could argue convincingly that the increase in inequality is justified and that no remedial changes in public policy are needed. On the other hand, if the increase in inequality results mostly from factors largely beyond the ability of individuals to control or counteract, then a strong case can be made for a public policy response.

In other words, the extent to which economic inequality is viewed as an appropriate matter for public policy concern depends, in part, on the underlying causal mechanisms. *Inequality of economic opportunity*, a contributing factor to overall economic inequality, reflects inequality in an individual's innate characteristics and the circumstances of birth and early environment. It is generally regarded much more negatively than inequality of economic outcomes, because it is associated with characteristics and circumstances that are beyond an individual's ability to control. Although a degree of inequality in economic outcomes can have the positive effect of providing incentives for entrepreneurship and work effort, inequality of economic opportunity cannot be defended on these grounds. And few, if any, would claim that inequality of opportunity is desirable on moral grounds.

The articles in this issue examine the causes of inequality of economic opportunity and analyze the potential for public policy to reduce it. This essay provides an overview of the topic and aims to integrate the analyses provided in the other articles. Several major themes emerge from our reading of the research on inequality of opportunity:

- Inequality of economic outcomes is both a consequence and a cause of inequality of

Katharine Bradbury is senior economist and policy advisor at the Federal Reserve Bank of Boston. **Robert K. Triest** is vice president and economist at the Federal Reserve Bank of Boston.

The views expressed in this article are those of the authors and do not necessarily represent the positions of the Federal Reserve Bank of Boston or the Federal Reserve System. The authors thank Suzanne Lorent and two anonymous reviewers for very helpful comments and Stephanie Bonds and Sam Richardson for expert research assistance. Direct correspondence to: Katharine Bradbury at katharine.bradbury@bos.frb.org, Research Department, Federal Reserve Bank of Boston, 600 Atlantic Ave., Boston, MA 02210; and Robert K. Triest at robert.triest@bos.frb.org, Research Department, Federal Reserve Bank of Boston, 600 Atlantic Ave., Boston, MA 02210.

opportunity. Children growing up in low-income families lack many of the developmental and educational advantages enjoyed by children growing up in more affluent families. The barriers to opportunity that disadvantaged children face are often amplified by the effects of other barriers to schooling and labor market success later in life, leading to a perpetuation of inequality of economic outcomes across generations.

- Intergenerational economic mobility, the ability of children to enjoy higher economic status than that of their parents, is closely linked to equality of opportunity. Intergenerational mobility appears to be relatively low in the United States and shows no sign of improvement in recent history. Empirical studies point to a substantial risk of continued stagnation of intergenerational mobility unless public policy changes in ways that break down barriers to economic opportunity. Rates of intergenerational mobility vary substantially by the geographic location where one grows up, suggesting that policies that change the economic and social environment may be effective in promoting economic opportunity and mobility.

- Barriers to economic opportunity occur throughout life, but many of the most damaging obstacles to opportunity appear at very young ages. Some children are born into environments of economic deprivation and risk falling behind before they even enter preschool or kindergarten.

- Additional barriers appear as children age, often amplifying the effects of disadvantages first encountered at very young ages. Disadvantaged children tend to live in areas with relatively low-quality public schools and face obstacles to attaining postsecondary degrees. Barriers to opportunity in the labor market further amplify the effects of unequal access to opportunity during childhood and adolescence.

- Public policy has the potential to reduce substantially the effects of barriers to opportunity. Some policies, such as targeted, high-quality preschool, can compensate at least partly for early-life disadvantages. Other policies may improve the quality of schools and neighborhood environments encountered by disadvantaged children, limiting the extent to which their environment hinders their educational attainment and early labor market outcomes. Labor market policies that offer opportunities for skill development and career development for workers with relatively modest formal credentials may also attenuate the negative effects of earlier disadvantages.

- Reducing inequality of opportunity need not come at the expense of economic growth or efficiency. Barriers to economic opportunity generally interfere with the efficient operation of the economy and result in suboptimal development of human talent and resources. Empirical evidence shows a positive association between equality of opportunity and aggregate economic growth.

CONCEPTS AND MEASURES OF INEQUALITY OF ECONOMIC OPPORTUNITY

Although the term *inequality of economic opportunity* is broadly understood to refer to inequality associated with an individual's circumstances at birth and during childhood, the way the term is operationalized varies across researchers and commentators, and a wide range of measures are used to quantify its magnitude.

To measure inequality of opportunity, and to develop polices to promote it, a common understanding of the term, at least conceptually, is critical. A key difficulty in arriving at a workable definition lies in specifying the circumstances and outcomes for which individuals are not considered responsible. Equality of opportunity intuitively requires that circumstances beyond one's control, such as parents' education, should not affect one's economic outcomes, but allows other factors that are under one's control, such as one's own educational attainment, to affect one's economic outcomes. But parents' educational attainment has been found to influence, although not completely determine, the educational attainment of their children. So how can we separate the effects of circumstances beyond one's control from those that are influenced by these circumstances but still at least partly under one's control?

Circumstances and "Effort"

John Roemer (1993, 1998) has been especially influential among economic researchers and has spawned a growing research literature on the measurement of inequality of opportunity (for a clear exposition, see also Roemer and Trannoy, forthcoming). Roemer's approach separates the population of interest into types defined by circumstances beyond one's control, such as parental education, parental economic status, race, ethnicity, gender, the neighborhood or labor market where one grew up, and one's family structure while growing up. Within the group of people who experience a specific set of circumstances, there will be a distribution of an outcome variable of interest, such as income in adulthood. The distribution of the outcome for a given circumstance type is assumed to depend on responsible actions (such as the effort exerted in the labor market) taken by individuals of that type. For example, suppose that the only circumstance variable we choose to treat as not under one's control is parental education. There will be some distribution of income among people whose parents did not graduate from high school as well as other distributions for other circumstance types, such as those whose parents both received four-year college degrees. The distribution of income within a circumstance type is taken to be driven by differences in the responsible actions (which we often refer to as effort) taken by people of that type, whereas differences in the distribution of income between types are taken to be the result of differences in opportunities available to people of different types.

In Roemer's approach, complete equality of opportunity requires equality of outcomes for people of a given percentile rank in the effort distributions of each type. In other words, equality of opportunity is attained when the chance of achieving a given outcome depends not on one's circumstances but instead on position in the distribution of effort. This captures the notion that effort is influenced by circumstances, but still under individuals' control. In our example, when parental education is the only circumstance and income is the outcome of interest, the income of someone at the 75th percentile of the effort distribution among people whose parents did not graduate from high school would equal that of someone at the 75th percentile of the effort distribution among people whose parents both graduated from four-year colleges.[1] The responsible actions taken by someone at the 75th percentile of the effort distribution of these two types would generally differ. Consider one specific type of responsible action, investing in one's schooling. Educational attainment of people whose parents did not graduate from high school tends to be lower than educational attainment of people whose parents graduated from college. This difference in the effort distribution across circumstance types is taken to be due to the influence of circumstances on effort, and full equality of opportunity in Roemer's approach requires eliminating (or compensating for) differences in outcomes associated with differences in the distribution of effort across circumstance types.

Marc Fleurbaey and Vito Peragine (2013) distinguish this approach, which they call the ex post perspective, from a somewhat different approach to defining and measuring equality of opportunity, which they call the ex ante perspective. In the ex ante perspective, equality of outcomes is not needed between people of different circumstance types at the same point in the effort distribution; instead, it requires only that the average outcomes of people of different circumstance types be equated. In our example, equality of opportunity would require that the average income of people whose parents did not complete high school would be equal to the average income of people whose parents both graduated from four-year colleges. This is an ex ante perspective on equality of opportunity in the sense that it is based on information available before we know where

---

1. This would hold true for any given percentile of the income distribution comparing any two circumstance types.

people stand in the effort distribution for their circumstance type. In contrast, Roemer's approach is an ex post perspective in the sense that equality of opportunity requires that outcomes for people of different circumstance types be equated for people with the same rank in their effort distributions, which means that we need to know where people stand in the effort distribution.

Whether one adopts the ex ante or the ex post approach to defining and measuring inequality of opportunity, specifying what range of factors are to be included in the set of circumstances over which one has no control is critical. Parental income is an obvious candidate and is often used in empirical applications. This variable is a proxy for the differing opportunities available to children growing up in high-income families compared with the opportunities of children growing up in low-income families. Parental education is another relevant circumstance. It is closely related to parental income, but it also captures how more educated parents may promote educational attainment and economic success in their offspring. Other family characteristics, such as the number of parents living with the child, also play an important role in children's development and the economic opportunities open to them later in life. The possible effect of discrimination on opportunities suggests that race, ethnicity, and gender should be included in defining the set of circumstance types. Childhood geographic location is another important circumstance that affects economic opportunity in several ways. City and state play a large role in determining the availability and quality of preschool programs open to low-income families and determine the quality of public K–12 education; the local labor market also plays an important role in creating economic opportunities and providing incentives for investment in education and training. At a finer-grained level of geographic demarcation, one's neighborhood while growing up affects factors such as exposure to crime and drugs, peer and role models, and often the specific schools that one attends.

Xavier Ramos and Dirk Van de Gaer (2012) and Paolo Brunori, Francisco Ferreira, and Vito Peragine (2013) review empirical applications of the approaches outlined, as well as some other methods. Because of data limitations, the set of circumstance variables specified in empirical studies is much more limited than the complete set discussed previously (and one could argue convincingly that even that set is incomplete). In practice, only a small subset of the full range of potential circumstance variables is observed and specified in defining circumstance types. As a result, the portion of overall inequality of outcomes attributed to inequality of opportunity is undoubtedly an underestimate of what a more complete set of circumstance variables would yield. Of the Brunori, Ferreira, and Peragrine country estimates, the share of total income inequality attributed to inequality of opportunity ranges from 2 percent to 34 percent.

Intergenerational Mobility and Equality of Opportunity

Much of the empirical research related to inequality of opportunity focuses on measures of intergenerational mobility rather than using the approaches described. Intergenerational income mobility is closely related to measures of inequality of opportunity in which parental income is the only variable used to classify people into circumstance types and income is the outcome variable of interest. High intergenerational income mobility implies that one's childhood family income plays only a modest role in determining one's income as an adult. One would intuitively expect an increase in intergenerational income mobility to be associated with a decrease in inequality of opportunity. However, although intergenerational income mobility is closely related to inequality of opportunity, the two concepts differ in important respects.

One distinction is that measures of intergenerational income mobility typically do not capture the relationship between inequality in parental income and the extent of inequality in adult children's income. However, this relationship is central to the concept of inequality of opportunity. If variance in parental income is minimal, then income inequality associated with parental income types (inequality of opportunity) will also be minimal, even when intergenerational income mobility is low. Conversely, a high degree of parental income inequality may be a source of a substantial inequality of opportunity even if intergenerational income mobility is reasonably high.

A second potential distinction between intergenerational income mobility and equality of opportunity revolves around whether we are considering absolute or relative income mobility. Absolute income mobility refers to the relationship between the amount of income received by someone as an adult and the inflation-adjusted income received by his or her parents a generation earlier. In contrast, relative income mobility refers to the relationship between a person's position in the income distribution and the position of his or her parents in the income distribution a generation earlier. It is possible for a high degree of absolute income mobility to be present even when income rankings change little across generations. Consider an extreme hypothetical case in which every adult's income is exactly double that of his or her parents. In this example, absolute mobility is high, but everyone occupies the same position in the income distribution as their parents a generation earlier. If we take parental income as an exogenous circumstance, then all of the income inequality of the children's generation represents inequality of opportunity, because it is fully determined by parental income. In general, no consistent theoretical relationship exists between absolute income mobility and equality of opportunity.

In contrast, an increase in relative income mobility will generally be associated with an increase in equality of opportunity. As relative income mobility increases, parental income becomes a less important determinant of one's position in the income distribution. Suppose that members of the children's generation are classified into types according to their parents' income (treating parental income as the sole circumstance variable). As relative income mobility increases, more of the income inequality in the children's generation income will be within circumstance types rather than between types, so measured inequality of opportunity will decrease.

Another potential distinction between intergenerational income mobility and equality of opportunity concerns whether parental income is a comprehensive summary measure of circumstances, and also whether income is the outcome measure of greatest interest. Income certainly may be used to convey advantages to one's children, but some parents choose to forgo earnings opportunities and instead use more of their time for parenting activities. Such choices are facilitated by the availability of financial wealth or the presence of a second parent. Thus, a case can be made that parental income must be supplemented by other variables, including parental education and family structure, to capture adequately the circumstances that determine the opportunities open to children. One can make a somewhat similar case for why income is not the only outcome variable of interest, and for the analysis of broader measures of well-being.

Isabel Sawhill and Richard Reeves (in this issue) discuss the distinction between relative and absolute income mobility, and reach the same conclusion: relative intergenerational mobility is more closely related to equality of opportunity than absolute intergenerational mobility is. They also discuss the question of "mobility of what?" and note that it is instructive to examine mobility across a broad range of outcomes beyond just income, including education, well-being, and educational status. However, they also note that income is a powerful indicator of other outcomes and of special interest.

In recent research, Brunori and his colleagues (2013) compute an ex ante measure of inequality of opportunity and a measure of intergenerational earnings mobility (the intergenerational earnings elasticity) for a large number of countries and find a robust cross-country negative correlation between intergenerational earnings mobility and the share of overall income inequality that is attributed to inequality of opportunity. Thus, despite important conceptual differences between the two concepts, intergenerational mobility has a strong empirical association with equality of opportunity.

KEY FACTS: INTERGENERATIONAL MOBILITY IN THE UNITED STATES

Sawhill and Reeves provide in this issue an overview of current patterns of relative intergenerational income mobility, and Timothy Smeeding, also in this issue, examines which subgroups of the population appear to face particularly severe obstacles to economic advancement. (For comprehensive reviews of the research literature on intergenerational mobility, see Solon 1999; Black and Devereux 2011; and Jäntti and Jenkins 2015.)

Drawing on both their research and that of others, Sawhill and Reeves document that in the United States the position of one's parents in the income distribution strongly predicts one's own place in the income distribution in adulthood. This is especially true for those born to families at the top and bottom of the income distribution: one set of estimates suggests that 60 percent of those born into a bottom-quintile family will themselves be in the bottom two quintiles of the income distribution at age forty, and that 56 percent of those born into a top-quintile family will be in the top two quintiles of the distribution at age forty. Other researchers have estimated qualitatively similar relationships. For example, using a different data source, Susan Urahn and her colleagues (2012) find that 70 percent of those growing up in families in the bottom two quintiles of the income distribution will also be in the bottom two quintiles as adults.

Contrary to popular impression, measured intergenerational income mobility in the United States tends to be less than that in many other advanced economies. Jo Blanden (2013) provides a recent compilation of estimates of intergenerational mobility across countries. Although sampling variance makes it difficult to draw definitive conclusions, point estimates of the intergenerational income elasticity (one measure of intergenerational income persistence) are greater for the United States than for Australia and several countries in western Europe. Of the twelve countries for which Blanden is able to identify comparable estimates, only Brazil has greater intergenerational income persistence (and so less intergenerational income mobility) than the United States.

U.S. Trends

The trend in intergenerational income mobility in the United States over recent decades and especially its implications for changes in equality of opportunity are somewhat controversial. The data requirements for analyzing changes over time in intergenerational mobility are daunting, resulting in a paucity of studies on this topic. Using census data on adults matched to synthetic parents in the previous generation, Daniel Aaronson and Bhashkar Mazumder (2008) find evidence that intergenerational income mobility decreased in the late twentieth century. Deirdre Bloome and Bruce Western (2011) document a similar decline in mobility based on data from two cohorts in the National Longitudinal Survey, and David Levine and Mazumder (2007) use data on brothers to come to a similar conclusion. In contrast, both Chul-In Lee and Gary Solon (2009) and Raj Chetty, Nathaniel Hendren, Patrick Kline, Emmanuel Saez, and Nicholas Turner (2014), using two different sources of intergenerational longitudinal data, find little evidence of changes over time in intergenerational income mobility, at least for recent adult cohorts.

As discussed earlier, changes in intergenerational mobility may be only loosely connected to changes in inequality of opportunity. If we consider parental income a circumstance variable, then any measure of inequality of opportunity would increase as inequality of parents' income increases. Increasing income inequality and largely unchanged intergenerational income mobility would combine to produce a trend of increasing inequality of opportunity. This appears to have been the pattern in late twentieth-century America.

Population Subgroups

Particular subgroups of the population appear to be especially vulnerable to lack of mobility. Examination of differences in mobility across subgroups is of interest in its own right and can also give us insight into the mechanisms that may underlie barriers to opportunity.

Smeeding reports in this issue that among people born into bottom-quintile families, blacks, children of never-married mothers, and children of parents lacking a high school diploma are especially likely to be in the bottom quintile of the income distribution in adulthood. Mazumder (2011) cites earlier studies and offers as well new evidence that blacks experience both lower rates of upward mobility and higher rates of downward mobility than whites do. Chetty, Hendren, Kline, and Saez (2014a) present estimates showing that intergenerational mobility varies greatly across geographic areas of the United States. The variability in rates of intergenerational mobility raises the question of what underlies differences in mobility. To what extent are characteristics such as race and geographic location causal factors affecting mobility, and to what extent are they instead proxies for other less easily measured characteristics, such as limited access to quality schooling, that are the more direct causal factors? We return to this question in our discussion of mechanisms.

Membership in the subgroups discussed can be considered beyond one's control. In the context of the measures of inequality of opportunity discussed earlier in this essay, it is not differences in intergenerational mobility across circumstance types that are most relevant, but instead the extent to which inequality of outcomes is explained by circumstance types. Inequality between circumstance types defined by factors beyond an individual's control, such as race, parents' education, family structure, or place where one lives while growing up, forms the basis of the ex ante measures of inequality of opportunity. That intergenerational mobility is especially low among specific subgroups that are already overrepresented in the bottom quintile of the income distribution suggests that barriers to economic opportunity are especially severe for these groups.

DYNAMICS: INEQUALITY OF OUTCOMES AND INEQUALITY OF OPPORTUNITY

The close connection between intergenerational mobility and equality of opportunity raises the question of the impact inequality of outcomes has on inequality of opportunity. In simple terms, the outcomes-affect-opportunity hypothesis is that as the overall distribution of outcomes becomes more unequal it reduces low-income children's access to education and to other opportunities to accumulate human capital and move up the income ladder, and it increases high-income children's access to enrichment beyond schooling, in turn enhancing the ability of advantaged children to stay at the top. Both these changes tie individuals' economic prospects more tightly to their parents' economic success.

Several research papers explore this question, focusing on how unequal outcomes lead to unequal opportunity or how unequal outcomes reduce mobility, which is interpreted as indicating unequal opportunity. Miles Corak explores a variety of mechanisms that link income inequality, equality of opportunity, and intergenerational mobility.[2] Introducing his analysis, he notes that "an emerging body of evidence suggests that more inequality of incomes in the present is likely to make family background play a stronger role in the adult outcomes of young people, with their own hard work playing a commensurately weaker role" (2013a, 79). Corak first establishes the empirical regularity—labeled the Great Gatsby curve by Alan Krueger—that countries with greater inequality of incomes at a point in time also "tend to be countries in which a greater fraction of economic advantage and disadvantage is passed on between parents and their children" (80).

To understand the causal links, Corak then investigates the various channels through which parents' income can influence their children's accumulation of human capital and their adult outcomes, influences that he notes are mediated by the different balance struck between family, labor market, and public policy in determining outcomes across countries. For example, high returns to education not only make the income distribution more unequal and thereby provide rich families with relatively more resources to invest in their children, but also increase the incentive for the

---

[2]. In his *Journal of Economic Perspectives* article of that title.

rich to make such investments. Corak argues that parents with high incomes create advantages for their children both through monetary investments (better schools, enrichment experiences) and by passing along nonmonetary advantages—behavior, motivation, aspirations, and connections. One example of nonmonetary advantage is the guidance and culture supportive of college attendance.

Corak also discusses public policies that can either exacerbate or blunt inequality of outcomes, such as public provision of early childhood education: he notes that public policies outside of education, such as in health care and fiscal (tax and transfer) policy, can also intervene or not between parental income and children's outcomes. He argues that public policies in the United States, including even public K–12 schooling, are particularly tilted toward the advantaged. He also notes that public provision of health care, as in most other developed nations, helps level the playing field, leading to more preventive care for those with low incomes and hence to fewer negative health shocks that could have longer-term consequences" (2013a, 97).

Corak concludes by pointing out that "inequality lowers mobility because it shapes opportunity. It heightens the income consequences of innate differences between individuals; it also changes opportunities, incentives, and institutions that form, develop, and transmit characteristics and skills valued in the labor market; and it shifts the balance of power so that some groups are in a position to structure policies or otherwise support their children's achievement independent of talent" (2013a, 98). Regarding policies to address inequality of opportunity, he reminds us of Roemer's argument that policy should offset only those aspects of differential success that relate to circumstances, and argues that different nations may well make different judgment calls regarding which circumstances are appropriate to offset.

In a sense, Brunori, Ferreira, and Peragine (2013) begin their analysis here, citing behavioral economics experiments indicating that people do distinguish between factors over which individuals have control and those they do not, when evaluating the fairness of the distribution of outcomes. They use these findings to argue that inequality should be evaluated not only from the point of view of its direct impact on growth or other aspects of the economy but also in terms of fairness. They note that inequality reflecting circumstances beyond the individual's control is widely viewed as unfair. Their paper focuses on an ex ante measure of inequality of opportunity used by others in the literature (including Ferreira et al. 2014; Marrero and Rodriguez 2013), which quantifies the extent of inequality between groups of people defined in terms of circumstances beyond their control (see Bradbury and Triest later in this issue).

Brunori and his colleagues (2013) examine the cross-sectional correlations between the inequality of opportunity measure and other country characteristics, including per capita output, inequality of outcomes, and intergenerational mobility. Like Corak, they find a positive relationship between inequality of opportunity and income inequality. They also note a positive correlation between this between-group inequality of opportunity measure and the standard intergenerational mobility measure (the intergenerational elasticity of income) as well as the intergenerational correlation of education, even when the measures come from different papers and are based on different data sources. They conclude by saying

> inequality of opportunity is the missing link between the concepts of income inequality and social mobility. If higher inequality makes intergenerational mobility more difficult, it is likely because opportunities for economic advancement are more unequally distributed among children. Conversely, the way lower mobility may contribute to the persistence of income inequality is through making opportunity sets very different among the children of the rich and the children of the poor. (2013, 17)

Pablo Mitnik, Erin Cumberworth, and David Grusky "eke out as much evidence on [whether opportunities to get ahead are growing more unequal] as the available data will allow" (2013, 1). They focus on measuring the trend in intergenerational *social-class* mobility and find evidence of recent rigidification in the U.S. class structure.[3] The negative trend in class mobility is especially pronounced among younger cohorts, for whom the rise in inequality would have had maximum influence during childhood, and is focused on professional and managerial parents, who have increasingly been successful in passing along status to their children.

Along similar lines, Smeeding (2013) argues that existing empirical work on U.S. intergenerational mobility cannot tell us much about the impact of rising inequality of outcomes on mobility because the recent and current young adults whose mobility can be examined were born and mostly grew up before inequality widened considerably beginning in the 1980s. We should look for evidence of growing divergence in success at early life stages between children raised in rich and poor families, Smeeding maintains. He notes that most developed nations show differences in school readiness associated with parental socioeconomic status (SES) and that some nations' education institutions succeed in reducing these differences somewhat, but most do not. Lane Kenworthy (2012) points to specific early-life indicators that have worsened, citing Sean Reardon's (2011) work on growing school performance gaps between high- and low-SES children and Martha Bailey and Susan Dynarski's (2011) research showing rising SES gaps in college completion.

Bloome (2015) provides a comprehensive and careful recent addition to this literature by examining how intergenerational mobility varies with inequality of outcomes in the geographic area where people grew up. Using individual data from two longitudinal surveys, she regresses children's adult incomes on their parents' incomes interacted with inequality observed in their state of residence when the children were growing up.[4] She finds that "the best available data cannot confirm the hypothesis that inequality and mobility are systematically linked in the United States" (22). Given that she has improved considerably on the precision of earlier estimates, if a relationship exists, she argues that it must be quite small. She also notes that the estimated relationship may reflect countervailing trends; for example (much as Corak noted), inequality-associated higher barriers to college completion among the poor may be partly offset by the increased incentives for those at the bottom of the income or wealth distribution to attempt a college degree.

We next present new empirical evidence in favor of the Great Gatsby curve, and show that this relationship holds up, though in somewhat attenuated fashion, when other factors are controlled for. Our analysis begins where Corak's does, by establishing the empirical relationship, in our case within the United States. Figures 1 and 2 plot inequality of income and intergenerational income mobility across commuting zone (CZ) areas.[5] The vertical axes are transformed versions of Chetty, Hendren, Kline, and Saez relative mobility and absolute mobility measures (2014b).[6] The horizontal axes are a measure of inequality of income in

---

3. They define social class mobility in occupational terms, professionals/managers at the top and unskilled workers at the bottom.

4. In addition to simple interaction terms, she allows the intergenerational coefficient to vary with inequality through the use of state fixed effects and random coefficients estimates. She examines inequality when the children were teens and, alternatively, when they were around age four.

5. Commuting zones generally coincide with metropolitan areas in urban locations, but also include combinations of counties in rural areas, so as to exhaust the territory of the United States.

6. Chetty et al.'s measure of relative (im)mobility is the elasticity of child income rank at age thirty to thirty-one with respect to parent rank when the child was in his or her teens. We have inverted that measure (by subtracting from one, and also multiplied the result by 100) so that it is larger—more positive—where intergenerational mobility is higher; we refer to the result as "adjusted relative mobility" to call attention to this transformation. Chetty et al.'s absolute mobility measure indicates the expected adult rank of a child whose parents were at the 25th income percentile when the child was growing up.

Figure 1. Relative Mobility and Inequality of Parental Income

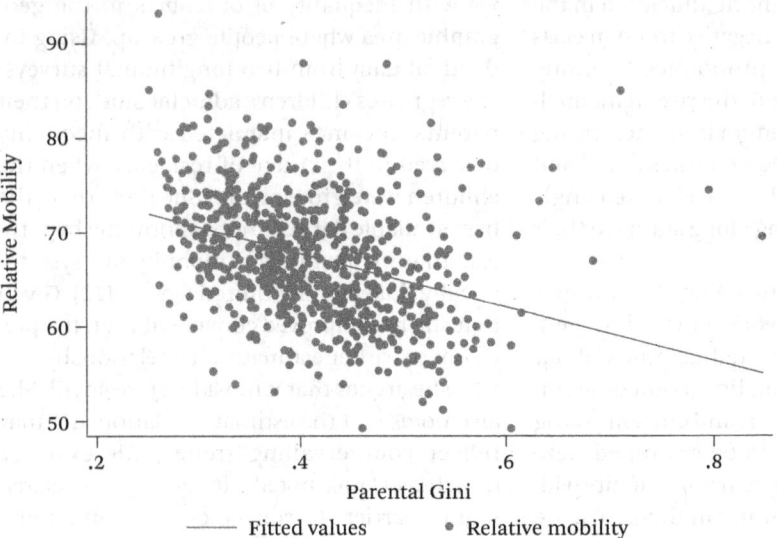

Source: Authors' calculations based on Chetty, Hendren, Kline, and Saez 2014b.
RM = 79.07*** −28.28***Gini (***$p<0.001$) R^2 = 0.12

Figure 2. Absolute Mobility and Inequality of Parental Income

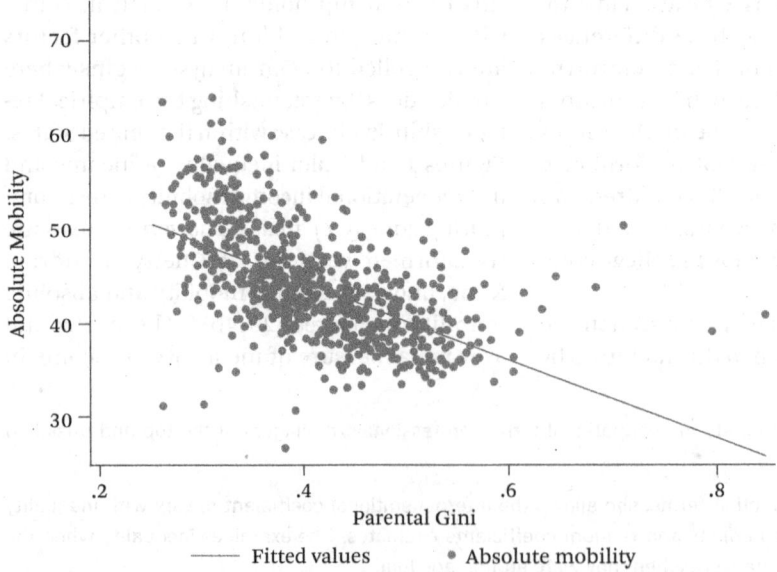

Source: Authors' calculations based on Chetty, Hendren, Kline, and Saez 2014b.
AM = 60.93*** −41.56***Gini (***$p<0.001$) R^2 = 0.33

the parental generation, the Gini coefficient.[7] As in Corak's depiction, both figures indicate that places with greater inequality of income also display less mobility, both relative and ab-

7. The Gini coefficient may take on values ranging from 0, indicating that all incomes are equal, to 1, indicating maximal inequality.

Figure 3. Relative Mobility and Size of the Middle Class While Growing Up

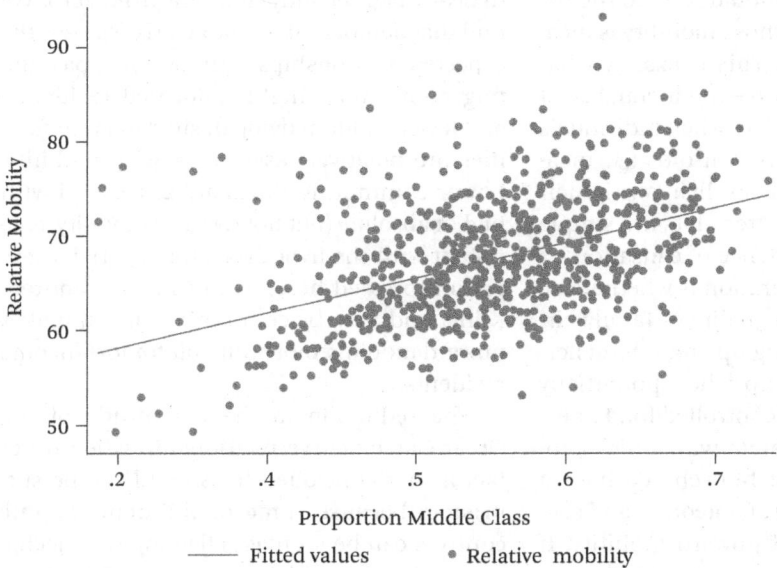

Source: Authors' calculations based on Chetty, Hendren, Kline, and Saez 2014b.
AM = 16.95*** + 49.08***middle class (***$p<0.001$) $R^2 = 0.20$

Figure 4. Absolute Mobility and Size of the Middle Class While Growing Up

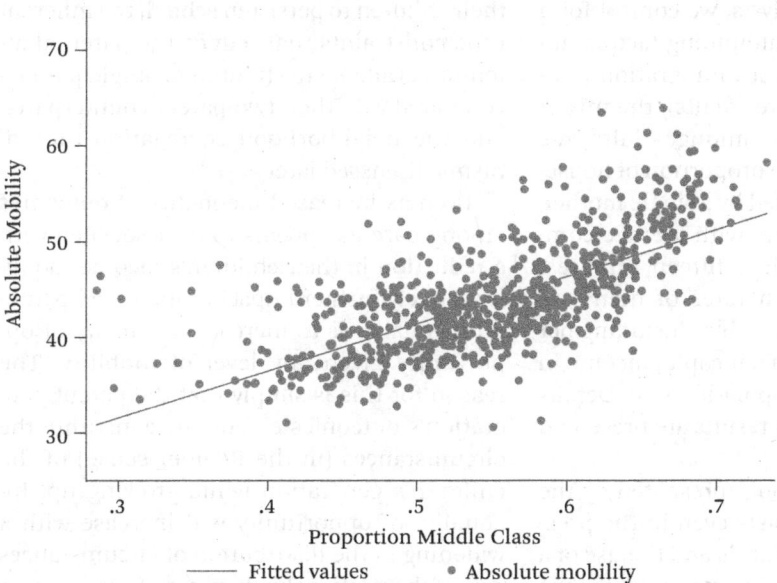

Source: Authors' calculations based on Chetty, Hendren, Kline, and Saez 2014b.
AM = 16.95*** + 49.08***middle class (***$p<0.001$) $R^2 = 0.46$

solute. Figures 3 and 4 use the size of the middle class (proportion of CZ parents whose incomes are between the 25th and 75th percentiles of the national income distribution) as the indicator of inequality. The size of the middle class is inversely related to inequality and fairly strongly related to mobility—places with a larger middle class display more mobility.

One of the issues raised by those who have challenged the import of Corak's empirical relationship relates to timing: critics argue that the inequality measure should refer to the period when the children whose mobility is measured were growing up. This is exactly what these scatter plots refer to—the inequality of parental income, by location, when individuals whose outcomes as thirty-year-olds are measured were in their mid-teens, living with their parents. Nonetheless, scatter plots are simple correlations and not evidence of causation.[8]

An additional consideration is whether the relationship between inequality of family circumstances while growing up and intergenerational mobility holds up when potentially confounding factors are controlled for. For example, it might be that areas with a high proportion of single-parent households have a high degree of inequality of outcomes and also generate a lower rate of upward mobility. If this is true, and if we do not statistically control for single-parent households, then we might mistakenly attribute low upward mobility to general inequality, rather than to the prevalence of single-parent households. Using multiple regression analysis, we control for a variety of potentially confounding factors, including a measure of past immigration (percentage of foreign-born residents), the mix of educational attainment among adults age twenty-five and older, the proportion of households with children headed by a single mother, the proportion of workers with average commuting times of less than fifteen minutes, labor force participation rates of men and women, and economic variables including per capita income, growth in per capita income in the prior decade, and population size. Details and complete regression results are presented in the appendix.

The simple correlation represented by the Great Gatsby curve persists even in the presence of demographic controls and the use of a parental inequality measure that predates the period during which the adult children's mobility is measured. The estimated association between inequality of circumstances while growing up and economic mobility is considerably smaller when controlling for potentially confounding factors, although it is mostly statistically significantly different from zero. We find that demographic characteristics have the expected relationships with mobility: past immigration, more highly educated residents, and fewer children living in single-parent families are positively associated with mobility. Lower commuting times are associated with higher absolute (but not relative) mobility, consistent with the hypothesis that spatial segregation (proxied here, as in Chetty, Hendren, Kline, and Saez by commuting times) makes upward mobility more difficult for low-income residents.

The reduction in the magnitude of the Great Gatsby curve relationship when other factors are controlled for should not be surprising, because some of the demographic controls can be seen as reflecting the mechanisms through which inequality among parents is likely to be passed along to their children. These mechanisms include support (financial as well as via encouragement and expectations) by more-educated parents for their children to persist in school, the inherent time constraints that reduce the parental attention available to children of single parents compared with their two-parent counterparts, and the neighborhood segregation mechanisms discussed later.

Even as increased inequality of outcomes among parents appears to be associated with a reduction in their children's income mobility, a likely further impact of increased parental inequality is to increase inequality of opportunity given any level of mobility. The reason for this is simply that the parent generation's outcomes essentially constitute the circumstances (in the Roemer sense) of the children's generation while growing up. Inequality of opportunity will increase with a widening of the distribution of circumstances even if the relationship between circumstances and outcomes (intergenerational mobility) does not change. As Bloome notes, although rising inequality of (parental) outcomes may not *cause* a reduction in mobility, "the economic consequences of growing up rich or

---

8. Chetty, Hendren, Kline, and Saez (2014a) report the same look at the Great Gatsby curve across the 709 CZs, except via regression coefficients (their table V) rather than scatter plots.

poor have risen, simply because the distance between the rich and poor has increased" (2015, 29).[9] Furthermore, the ongoing rise in inequality of outcomes in the United States (and other nations) heightens the need for further research to understand the mechanisms that underlie the observed relationships.

MECHANISMS
Factors that enhance or diminish opportunities for economic advancement are present throughout the life cycle. Circumstances beyond the control of children affect their social and cognitive development and their opportunities for education and training from conception through early adulthood. Institutions and policies interact with circumstances and individual behavior in ways that may either hinder or promote opportunities for education and advancement and also affect other outcomes, such as conviction for criminal activity. In adulthood, exogenous circumstances continue to impinge on opportunities, both directly and through their effect on investments and outcomes earlier in life.

The Social Genome Model (SGM) developed by the Brookings Institution (Sawhill and Reeves in this issue; Winship and Owen 2013) models the mechanisms through which opportunities for economic mobility cascade over the life cycle and is used by researchers to study the factors affecting intergenerational mobility. The model simulates the progression of individuals through the stages of life, starting by specifying circumstances at birth. Initial circumstances—such as family structure, maternal education, and birth weight—directly affect the probability of successful outcomes throughout childhood and adolescence and, through these early stage outcomes, have indirect effects on outcomes later in life. Income in adulthood is influenced by the cumulative effects of outcomes at earlier ages. For example, circumstances at birth affect school readiness, which in turn affects academic and social development in middle childhood, which then affects final educational attainment, which affects income in adulthood.

Circumstances, behavior, institutions, and policies may interact in complex ways to create or hinder economic opportunity. Joseph Fishkin (2014, 2016) notes that opportunities for economic mobility may be limited by bottlenecks one must pass through to reach the next stage in the pursuit of a goal. Analyzing inequality of opportunity as due to a set of bottlenecks that are difficult to negotiate or circumvent is useful in thinking about the obstacles to economic opportunity at different stages of the life cycle and in thinking about the effects of institutions and policies on economic opportunity. In the sections that follow, we survey the main findings of the research literature on the effects of bottlenecks and barriers to opportunity facing individuals as they progress through life.

EARLY CHILDHOOD INFLUENCES ON MOBILITY AND ECONOMIC OPPORTUNITY
A large and growing research literature documents the important role of early childhood development, when many of the barriers to economic mobility first arise, in shaping opportunities and outcomes later in life. Comprehensive reviews of this literature are provided in Douglas Almond and Janet Currie (2011a) and Currie and Maya Rossin-Slater (2015). Here, citing only a sampling of the most relevant studies, we provide a more limited review of the main themes and findings emerging from this research. This topic is especially pertinent to understanding the mechanisms through which inequality of opportunity arises. Factors associated with early childhood development are circumstances beyond the ability of young children to control, and so clearly represent inequality of opportunity.

Moreover, early childhood factors may have an especially important influence on the opportunities open to children in adolescence and adulthood. In a series of papers, Flavio

---

9. Chetty, Hendren, Kline, Saez, and Turner (2014) make a similar comment: "children entering the labor market today have the same chances of moving up in the income distribution (relative to their parents) as children born in the 1970s. *However, because inequality has risen, the consequences of the 'birth lottery'—the parents to whom a child is born—are larger today than in the past*" (2014, online abstract [emphasis added]).

Cunha and James Heckman (2007, 2008) and later with Susanne Schennach (2010) develop a model of human capital development and provide empirical evidence showing that early childhood development increases an individual's capacity to benefit from investment at later stages of the life cycle. In another study, Cunha and his colleagues (2006) survey earlier research on skill development over the life cycle. A key feature of human capital investment that underlies the importance of early childhood investments is the tendency for skills acquired at one stage of life to augment the skills acquired later in life, which some refer to as *dynamic complementarity* (see Cunha and Heckman 2007). Early-life skills not only persist, but also increase children's capacity to develop further. For example, basic language acquisition in infancy allows a young child to progress in further cognitive development. A closely related phenomenon is the ability of investments at one stage of life to increase the productivity of investments at later stages, or *self-productivity* (see Cunha and Heckman 2007). For example, the efficacy of investment in elementary and secondary school education programs may be greater for a child who has attended a high-quality preschool than for the same child had she or he not attended preschool. In the words of Cunha and Heckman, these two features of human capital investment "produce multiplier effects which are the mechanisms through which skills beget skills and abilities beget abilities" (2007, 6).

Investments made early in childhood will generally have larger multiplier effects than those made later in life for the simple reason that early childhood investment can affect more stages of subsequent development. Conversely, bottlenecks interfering with development and opportunity early in life are likely to be especially damaging to children's future opportunities and outcomes.

Prenatal and Neonatal Factors
The earliest bottlenecks interfering with economic opportunity and mobility occur *in utero*. Currie (2011) and Almond and Currie (2011a, 2011b) synthesize the evidence on the role of prenatal health factors in health and economic outcomes later in life. Evidence is substantial that prenatal and neonatal health is affected by environmental factors such as maternal nutrition, maternal health, and exposure to pollution. Neonatal health, in turn, affects child development and outcomes later in life. Some of the environmental factors associated with poor neonatal health are borne disproportionately by relatively low-income women, and therefore this is a mechanism by which inequality of outcomes in the parents' generation leads to inequality of opportunity among children.

A surprisingly robust relationship exists between indicators of prenatal health and outcomes later in life. Birth weight is an indicator of prenatal health that has received much attention, in part because it is very widely measured. It is well documented that low birth weight is associated with reduced wages in adulthood (see, among others, Currie 2011). Research supports the hypothesis that this relationship is causal, rather than being due simply to the correlation between birth weight and other unobserved factors affecting outcomes. For example, Sandra Black, Paul Devereux, and Kjell Salvanes (2007) examine a sample of twins to control for other factors related to a child's circumstances and find that the estimated long-term effects of low birth weight hold up to the controls for these factors. Much of the effect of birth weight on economic outcomes appears to operate through its effect on cognitive development. David Figlio and his colleagues (2014) estimate a positive relationship between birth weight and standardized test scores in a sample of twins (to control for unobserved factors). Interestingly, they also find that family background is more strongly associated with test performance than neonatal health is; low-birth-weight children with highly educated parents outscore high-birth-weight children with relatively poorly educated parents. This suggests that, in principle, the disadvantages associated with low birth weight can be offset by other factors. However, in practice, low birth weight and poor health in childhood tend to be associated with being born to low-income parents (Case, Lubotsky, and Paxson 2002; Currie and Moretti 2007). Thus, in the absence of public intervention, compensatory measures may not be available to low-income families and this mechanism may contribute to low rates of intergenerational income mobility.

The inequality of outcomes associated with prenatal health represents inequality of opportunity whether or not a causal relationship runs from prenatal health to outcomes. An alternative possibility is that prenatal health serves as a proxy for unobserved early life circumstances. Nevertheless, to design effective programs and policies to reduce inequality of opportunity associated with early life circumstances, the causal relationships between early life circumstances and outcomes need to be understood.

Researchers have used natural experiments to identify causal links from prenatal health to outcomes later in life. For example, Almond and his colleagues (2010) examine the long-term effects of being subjected in utero to the 1959 to 1961 Chinese famine and find substantial reductions in literacy and employment for this birth cohort in the 2000 Chinese census. Similarly, in other research, Almond (2006) examines long-term effects of prenatal exposure to the 1918 influenza pandemic and finds the effects to be increased risk of adult disability and reduced educational attainment and earnings. Adam Isen, Maya Rossin-Slater, and Reed Walker (2014) use geographic variation in changes in air pollution concentration following implementation of the Clean Air Act of 1970 to identify the effect of exposure to air pollution in the year of birth. They find that greater exposure to pollution leads to lower earnings in adulthood, driven mostly by decreased labor force participation.

Overall, it is now well established that health in early childhood affects outcomes later in life. Although health risks are correlated with other factors such as low family income that may also be associated with barriers to development and opportunity, the role of early child health in affecting outcomes is a mechanism distinct from the more general contribution of other associated factors.

Compensatory Programs and Policies

Programs that improve maternal and early life health and nutrition have the potential to improve child health outcomes, with concomitant gains in later life outcomes. In the United States, the Special Supplemental Program for Women, Infants, and Children (WIC) is the public program most directly targeted at improving maternal and early childhood nutrition. Currie and Rossin-Slater survey research on the effects of WIC, and conclude that although identifying effects of the program on child health outcomes is difficult, "recent work that carefully attempts to identify the causal effects of WIC nevertheless points to positive and relatively large effects of the program" (Currie and Rossin-Slater 2015, 222).

The Supplemental Nutrition Assistance Program (SNAP), formerly known as the Food Stamp Program (FSP), provides means-tested payments to households to be used for food expenditures, although many analysts have concluded that SNAP/FSP is effectively an income support program. Almond, Hilary Hoynes, and Diane Schanzenbach (2011) use geographic variation in the initial rollout of the FSP to identify causal effects of potential prenatal participation in the FSP on birth weight and find that the program increased birth weights, especially at the low end of the birth-weight distribution.

Given the success of the FSP in improving birth weight, one would expect other policies that boost family income to also result in improved neonatal health outcomes and eventual improvements in adult economic outcomes. The Earned Income Tax Credit (EITC) has become a significant source of income for families with low earnings. Hoynes, Douglas Miller, and David Simon (2012) use variation in EITC generosity due to tax reforms to identify the causal effect of EITC payments on birth outcomes and find that an increase in EITC income is associated with a reduction in the incidence of low birth weight and an increase in average birth weight. Using a similar identification strategy, Gordon Dahl and Lance Lochner (2012) estimate that an increase in EITC income causes a substantial increase in children's standardized test scores.

Early Childhood Education

The policy instrument with arguably the greatest potential to increase equality of opportunity in early childhood is the provision of high-quality early childhood education (ECE). Katherine Magnuson and Greg Duncan provide in this issue an overview of the evidence on the overall effectiveness of ECE and an analysis of the extent to which expanded ECE can promote equality of opportunity.

The way in which ECE combines with children's classroom readiness to promote learning and development, and its implications for how ECE might be most effectively targeted, has provoked some controversy. Magnuson and Duncan note that developmentalists tend to hold a view of the role of ECE that differs from the "skills-beget-skills" model of human capital investment described earlier. That model predicts that the productivity of ECE will be greatest for children who start preschool equipped with the cognitive and socioemotional skills needed to take full advantage of preschool learning opportunities. Developmentalists instead view the productivity as driven by how well an ECE program matches the developmental needs of the child in question. Children who enter preschool with relatively low skill levels due to factors associated with economic disadvantage may especially benefit from high-quality preschool programs designed to compensate for their economic disadvantage. In this example, the ECE program would substitute for skill development outside school rather than largely complement skills developed before entering the program. Of course, it is possible that the skills-beget-skills model might hold over broader phases of the life cycle even if the developmentalists' view is more accurate with regard to early childhood education. Furthermore, compensatory programs at young ages, such as with preschool programs, would be especially important if the skills-beget-skills phenomenon holds for human capital investments at later ages.

Magnuson and Duncan document in this issue that measures of children's prekindergarten skills differ greatly by socioeconomic status. These differences are especially pronounced for math and reading skills, and smaller for attention skills. The large differences in pre-kindergarten skills across socioeconomic strata point to the possibility of reducing inequality of opportunity by expanding high-quality compensatory preschool education targeted to economically disadvantaged children. The evidence on the efficacy of ECE in improving school readiness is generally favorable, Magnuson and Duncan write, though variation is considerable in the magnitude of the effects across programs and test score gains associated with preschool attendance fade as students age.

Of perhaps greater relevance to the topic of inequality of opportunity, several research studies have found favorable long-term impacts of preschool attendance. One of the most studied preschool programs is Head Start, a large federally funded U.S. program targeted at economically disadvantaged children. Using comparisons with siblings who did not attend Head Start to control for confounding factors, Eliana Garces, Duncan Thomas, and Currie (2002) find that Head Start attendance results in increased earnings and educational attainment among whites and decreased probability of being booked or charged with a crime among blacks. David Deming (2009) also uses siblings who did not attend Head Start as controls and finds that Head Start attendance results in a substantial increase in a summary index of young adult outcomes, including high school graduation, college attendance, and reductions in crime and teen parenthood. Strikingly, Head Start participation closes one-third of the gap in this index between children with median and bottom-quartile family income. Two high-quality preschool programs targeted at disadvantaged children, the Perry Preschool and the Abecedarian Project, randomly assigned potential participants into enrollment and control groups and have been extensively studied. Research has documented substantial positive effects on a variety of long-term outcomes for both programs.

Magnuson and Duncan document in their article in this issue that participation in ECE programs is higher among children in top-income-quintile families than among their counterparts from lower in the income distribution. This suggests that expanding preschool enrollment among children from relatively low-income families is likely to be an effective way to reduce inequality of opportunity.

EDUCATION AND INEQUALITY OF OPPORTUNITY

The widespread American prescription to ameliorate rising inequality is to advance education. However, if the education system reinforces existing differences rather than leveling the playing field, we cannot expect more education to cure inequality. This section reviews evidence on the degree to which the education system in the United States mitigates or amplifies the cumulative effects on children entering school of current and past advantages and disadvantages.

Primary and Secondary Education: Kindergarten Through Twelfth Grade

As discussed, substantial differences in school readiness exist between children of poor and rich parents, reflecting a wide range of influences, including prenatal health, child care arrangements, and number of books in a child's home. Sawhill and Reeves report in this issue that 66 percent of children born more advantaged begin school with acceptable prereading and math skills and generally school-appropriate behavior, whereas only 46 percent of less advantaged children do.[10] A key question is whether primary schools, once children come under their care, level the playing field and reduce these disparities. Most research findings suggest that they do not, for a variety of reasons.

One part of the answer has to do with the fact that most primary and secondary education is provided as a local government service in the United States; that is, to the extent that rich and poor families live in different communities, their children will go to different schools. And to the extent that K–12 education relies on local financing, those schools' available resources are likely to be correlated with parental income. Even without local financing, if peers influence the quality of education, living in a poorer community may negatively affect the quality of education a child receives. Caroline Hoxby (1998) shows a positive relationship (statistically significantly different from zero) between per-pupil district spending and district per capita income in the representative states of Massachusetts and Illinois from 1900 through 1980, controlling for per-pupil property valuation and selected demographic variables. Several studies examine school finance reforms and show that as spending becomes more equal across districts, so does student performance (Hoxby 2001; Card and Payne 2002; Chaudhary 2009; Jackson, Johnson, and Persico 2014). These studies provide evidence that when funding depends at least in part on local parental resources, both spending and test scores will be higher (and dropout rates lower) in districts where parents are relatively better off. School finance reforms in many states have reduced dependence on local tax bases, but they have not eliminated the relationship between school spending and local wealth.

Furthermore, even within local school districts, individual schools typically have neighborhood catchment areas, so income segregation among neighborhoods within a community may translate into lower-quality education for poor children either in the presence of peer effects or because within-district school-level per-pupil spending is not adjusted to compensate for differences in the costs of educating children from advantaged versus disadvantaged backgrounds. Kendra Bischoff and Sean Reardon (2014) document significant growth in the last forty years in neighborhood segregation of families by socioeconomic status. Similarly, Joseph Altonji and Richard Mansfield (2011) find that neighborhoods and high schools have become increasingly segregated by socioeconomic status, even as racial segregation has decreased. Annette Lareau and Kimberly Goyette note the prevalence of neighborhood schools, examine the links between choice of residential location and school, and argue that differential access to information (or access to different information sources) and institutional/structural and financial constraints imply that richer families "may be more easily and freely able to enact their ideal

---

10. Sawhill and Reeves distinguish disadvantaged and advantaged not just on the basis of parental income or socioeconomic status. The Social Genome Model they use in their analysis defines *advantaged* as being born at normal birth weight to a nonpoor married mother with at least a high school diploma.

preferences," while poorer families face more trade-offs and operate within a more limited choice set (2014, xiv–xv). Although school choice programs are often seen as a way to reduce socioeconomic or racial segregation of schools, Lareau and Goyette argue that they "may not always reduce inequalities in school quality across families from different social backgrounds, but instead may reproduce or even exacerbate them" (xv).

Another link in the chain is provided by Bruce Sacerdote (2011), who cites studies that find significant effects of peer ability on students' academic achievement, though some disagree about the magnitude of these effects. William Duncombe, Phuong Nguyen-Hoang, and John Yinger (2015) document substantial additional costs associated with educating disadvantaged students. Bruce Baker (2009) summarizes a number of studies that examine cost differentials related to student characteristics among schools within districts and adds to that literature, emphasizing that equal per-pupil spending does not provide equal educational opportunity when student-body composition, such as poverty incidence, varies across schools.

Even without unequal school districts or unequal schools within districts, children with rich parents benefit from greater enrichment expenditures than children with poor parents do. These benefits include music and art lessons, books and toys, trips, and tutoring (Kaushal, Magnuson, and Waldfogel 2011; Duncan and Murnane, this issue).

Tallying the impact of a full range of factors, Sean Reardon documents a growing school achievement gap between low and high socioeconomic status students over the last fifty years (Reardon 2011).[11] He finds, in addition, that the relationship between parents' educational attainment and their children's achievement has been relatively stable even as the relationship with parental income has strengthened.[12] Reardon reports that the income achievement gap is large when children enter school and does not appear to change appreciably during K–12 school attendance.

To the degree that children benefit from inheriting innate abilities from their parents as well as from exposure to parental attitudes and the advantages that money can buy, these relationships between parental income and school achievement overstate the influence of opportunity. However, even controlling for math achievement, low-SES children disproportionately fail to complete high school: among children with top-quartile eighth grade math scores in 1988, 10.7 percent of low-SES children had not completed high school by 2000, whereas "rounds to 0" percent of high-SES children had dropped out; for those in the middle two quartiles of math scores, 12.4 percent of low-SES children and 0.6 percent of high-SES children had not completed high school twelve years later (Fox, Connolly, and Snyder 2005, table 21).

Duncan and Murnane describe later in this issue the mechanisms by which these growing educational gaps have been developing: some operate through the family and some via schools. They point to differences that arise in early childhood before children begin formal schooling, differential enrichment expenditures, and parental time investments before and throughout the school-age years that amplify the advantages of high-income children, plus increasing segregation by income of U.S. schools and the associated concentration in lower-income districts of children whose behavioral problems negatively affect classmates' ability to learn. Sawhill and Reeves report, also in this issue, that 66 percent of more-advantaged children graduate high school with a GPA of 2.5 or better and without having been convicted of a crime or having become a parent, but only 37 percent of less-advantaged children do so. The Social Genome Model in-

---

11. Reardon combines results from many previous cross-sectional studies and measures the test-score gap between children with parents at the 90th and at the 10th income percentiles; test score differences are measured in standard deviation units.

12. In recent years, Reardon notes, the income achievement gap has approached the size of the parental-education achievement gap, but parental education remains somewhat more important.

volves gross flows in both directions at each transition. However, the success rate for those born advantaged (66 percent) is the same at adolescence and in early childhood (being school-ready when they begin school), whereas the success rate of those born disadvantaged (46 percent in early childhood) deteriorates between these two transitions (37 percent at the end of adolescence), which suggests that the K–12 schooling years do not erase—and may worsen—the disparities that children present when entering school.

Completing high school—or not—and the quality of high school education are critical determinants, together with parental educational attainment and parental income, of the next stage in the lives of youth. Some enter the workforce, some go on to additional training, and others continue their education in more academic settings, beginning two- or four-year college programs. Many of the factors that play a role in high school graduation and performance have independent effects also on college enrollment and completion. Returning to the issue of socioeconomic segregation between districts and between schools, Gregory Palardy, for example, finds that "socioeconomic segregation has a strong association with high school graduation and college enrollment. Controlling for an array of student and school factors, students who attend high socioeconomic composition (SEC) schools are 68 percent more likely to enroll at a four-year college than students who attend low SEC schools. . . . The results indicate the association between SEC and attainment is due more to [socioeconomic-based] peer influences" than to other school effects that reflect resource disparities and practices, such as rigor of curriculum and disciplinary practices (2013, 714).

Postsecondary Education

Martha Bailey and Susan Dynarski (2011) help elaborate the issue of postsecondary education gaps and trends; they use panel data to compare higher education enrollment, persistence, and completion for high-income and low-income members of the National Longitudinal Survey of Youth (NLSY) 1979 cohort (born between 1961 and 1964) and the NLSY 1997 cohort (born between 1979 and 1982). They find that college-entry rates were higher for the later cohort, regardless of income, but enrollment of students who grew up in the richest quartile of families rose faster than enrollment of those in the poorest quartile. A 40 percentage-point gap in college enrollment of students born in the early 1960s between poorest-quartile and richest-quartile students expanded to a 51 point gap for the later cohort; similarly, the earlier cohort's 31 point gap in college completion between rich and poor grew to a 45 point gap for the later cohort.[13] A 2015 paper by Greg Duncan, Kenneth Lee, Ariel Kalil, and Kathleen Ziol-Guest uses similar NLSY data and also includes data from the Panel Study of Income Dynamics (PSID) on same-age cohorts to estimate educational gaps between children growing up in low-income versus high-income families. Like Bailey and Dynarski (2011), they find that educational attainment was measurably higher for later cohorts than for earlier ones at all income levels, but the gap between high- and low-income students between the two cohorts grew larger.[14] Their data, like Bailey and Dynarski's, show further increases over time (between cohorts) in the fraction of students

13. Bailey and Dynarski (2011) find that it is especially among women that the income gap in college entry and college completion increased between the two cohorts; women with high-income parents saw the steepest increases in both college entry and completion between the two cohorts.

14. Duncan and colleagues' data show that students who grew up in the poorest income quintile in the late 1970s completed 11.7 to 12.0 years of school, on average, compared with 13.9 to 14.0 years for richest-quintile students in the early cohort; later-cohort students from low-income families completed from 12.1 to 12.3 years versus the 15.0 years for the richest-quintile students, implying that the gap between rich and poor expanded from between 2.0 and 2.3 years to between 2.7 and 2.9 years. The year ranges reported in this sentence represent data from the NLSY79 and NLSY97 compared with corresponding cohorts in the PSID (fourteen- to sixteen-years-old in the late 1970s and fourteen- to sixteen-year-olds in the late 1990s); it is remarkable how close these educational attainment estimates from the two data sources are.

of all income levels who complete college, and expanding gaps between those who grew up in richest-quintile and poorest-quintile families.[15]

Although these average attainment data reflect all the influences on and behaviors of low-income versus high-income students and hence overstate the opportunity disparities, data including eighth grade math test scores on a cross-sectional snapshot of students halfway between the late 1970s and late 1990s cohorts indicate that a substantial part of the completion gap reflects inequality of opportunity. Mary Anne Fox, Brooke Connolly, and Thomas Snyder (2005) report that among low-income students with top-quartile eighth-grade mathematics scores in 1988, 74 percent continued their education beyond high school and 29 percent completed a bachelor's degree or higher by 2000.[16] By contrast, virtually all high-SES high-scorers continued in school beyond high school graduation and 74 percent obtained a bachelor's degree or higher by 2000. High-SES students with low eighth-grade test scores (scores in the bottom quartile) continued beyond high school and graduated from college at higher rates (83 percent and 30 percent, respectively) than low-SES children with the *highest* test scores did. Thus, even attaining top-quartile 8th grade math test scores did not earn low-income children as much access to higher education as their rich classmates with the poorest test scores enjoyed. Philippe Belley and Lochner (2007) report higher gaps in college attendance between students with low and high family income for a cohort born in 1979–1982 (NLSY97) than for a cohort born in 1961–1964 (NLSY 79).[17] In their regression analysis, Belley and Lochner conclude that although "ability is equally important for both cohorts, family income plays a substantially more important role in determining college attendance for the NLSY97 youth" than for the earlier cohort (14).

Obstacles to Postsecondary Education

Considerable research has examined the nature of the obstacles facing low-income students in pursuing higher education. Some concern the attitudes, expectations, and aspirations regarding postsecondary education that surround rich versus poor children among parents, peers, and teachers during their earlier years of schooling; some reflect the quality of the education (or the quality of the credential) that students receive in high school. Because many low-income parents did not go beyond high school and some high schools serving concentrated-poverty populations do not have college-focused guidance departments, lack of information about the benefits of degree attainment or the process of applying to postsecondary schools can hinder low-income students. Furthermore, high and rising college costs can create substantial perceived and actual financial barriers, even in the presence of need-responsive financial aid programs.

Brian Jacob and Tamara Linkow (2011) present data showing a strong link between tenth graders' expectations about attending college and their parents' educational attainment or income level.[18] Although SES-associated gaps in expectations decreased between the early 1970s and mid-2000s, tenth graders in the mid-

---

15. Only 2 to 6 percent of students who grew up in the poorest income quintile in the late 1970s completed college, on average, versus 36 to 38 percent for richest-quintile students in the early cohort; 8 to 9 percent of low-income later-cohort children completed college versus 54 to 59 percent for the richest quintile. Thus, the college-completion gap between rich and poor students increased from 32 to 34 percentage points for the late 1970s cohort to 45 to 51 points for the later cohort: (Duncan et al. 2015, table 1).

16. Continuing beyond high school graduation includes some college, received certificate or license, received associate's degree, and received bachelor's degree or higher.

17. They use the Armed Forces Qualifying Test as the measure of ability and group students into quartiles; they also group family incomes into quartiles. College attendance by the age of twenty-one is measured because of the youth of the NLSY97 sample.

18. The intergenerational transmission of educational attainment is a widely researched topic (for a review of recent literature, see Black and Devereux 2011).

2000s with college-educated parents were still roughly 10 percentage points (girls) to 16 percentage points (boys) more likely than tenth graders whose parents did not complete college to expect to obtain a bachelor's themselves. The college-expectations gap between tenth graders with parents in the richest and poorest quintiles of family income remained high in the early 2000s at 40 percentage points (girls) to 48 percentage points (boys). These authors also show that expectations "have an important influence on college enrollment and persistence" (159). Data for high school seniors similarly show that students whose parents were more highly educated or had higher SES expected to obtain more education themselves (Aud, KewalRamani, and Frohlich 2011, table 52; Aud et al. 2012, table A-35-1). Joshua Goodman (2008) looks at college-going intentions of Massachusetts 2003 and 2004 public high school graduates and similarly finds substantial differences between low- and high-income students; these differences shrink but do not disappear when he controls for skills (test scores). He finds specifically that "low income students in the middle and upper parts of the skill distribution appear the most constrained, particularly with respect to four-year public colleges" (Goodman 2008, 5).

One issue in college-going for low-income students is the academic preparation they receive in high school. Course offerings sometimes differ between low- and high-income schools and districts, and a student's course taking can differ depending on college-attendance intentions, which are partly a function of income even controlling for ability, as noted in the previous paragraph. Students in high-poverty schools take fewer high-level math and science courses than students in low-poverty schools: National Center for Education Statistics data show that 80 percent of 2009 high school graduates from low-poverty schools completed algebra II–trigonometry and 23 percent took calculus, while only 71 percent and 7 percent, respectively, of graduates from high-poverty schools did.[19] Similarly, 40 percent of graduates from low-poverty high schools completed biology, chemistry, and physics, compared to only 23 percent of graduates from high-poverty schools.

Advanced placement (AP) course taking also differs between schools. Brett Lane and Phomdaen Souvanna (2013) report much lower AP participation rates and lower overall success rates in high-need schools than in low-need schools in the absence of the Mass Math + Science Initiative, a program implemented in some schools in Massachusetts to increase low-income students' participation and success in AP courses.[20] Schools that participated in the program saw immediate and dramatic increases in AP participation and success rates and have sustained those gains over the four-plus years that the program has run.[21] The success of this program implies that barriers unrelated to their abilities prevent students at low-income schools from getting ahead in this

---

19. Low-poverty schools are those in which 0 to 25 percent of students qualify for free or reduced-price lunches, while 76 to 100 percent of students receive free or reduced-price lunches in high-poverty schools. See Aud et al. 2012, Appendix A, table A-31-1, pp. 234–35.

20. Their data show participation rates (the number of AP exams taken divided by the number of juniors and seniors in the school) of 21 percent for the 2011–2012 school year at low-need schools not participating in the program as compared with 13 percent in high-need non-participating schools; low need means fewer than 35 percent of students qualify for free or reduced-price lunch while high need indicates the school has more than 50 percent of its students eligible for free or reduced-price lunch or has been classified as level 3 or 4 in terms of school accountability status. The overall success rate (number of exams scoring 3 or better divided by the number of juniors and seniors) was 14 percent for low-need schools and less than 6 percent in high-need non-participating schools. Authors' calculations based on Lane and Souvanna 2013, table 3, p. 11.

21. Students in participating schools were more than 2.5 times as likely to take an AP course as students in otherwise similar comparison group schools, and overall success rates were also about twice as high as those in comparison schools. The simple success rate—test scores of 3 or better per test—is lower for participating schools, as would be expected when broadening the pool of test-takers.

way. Taking AP courses and completing them successfully is said to increase college applications, enrollment, and persistence.

The availability of college counselors varies considerably between high- and low-income high schools, reducing the chances that low-income children receive useful advice about college-going. Christopher Avery, Jessica Howell, and Lindsay Page document less availability of college counseling for low-income high school students, which they attribute largely to "inadequate school finances, insufficient counselor training programs, and a lack of clarity about how school counselors should allocate their time" (2014, 1). They conclude, "Armed with less information about colleges than their higher-income peers, students from modest backgrounds may be at greater risk of selecting a postsecondary alternative that is not a good fit" (2). Hoxby and Avery document that many low-income, high-achieving high school students fail to apply to high-quality selective colleges that would be a better academic fit than the much less selective colleges they typically attend. They note that these students lack access to appropriate college counseling because they "come from districts too small to support selective public high schools, are not in a critical mass of fellow high achievers, and are unlikely to encounter a teacher who attended a selective college" (2013, 1).

Recent studies and experiments have shed light on additional information problems that impede low-income students in the college-going process. Carrell and Sacerdote report on an inexpensive intervention involving cash bonuses and coaching for high school seniors identified by guidance counselors and find large effects on college enrollment and persistence for young women but no effect for men; in addition, "offering cash bonuses alone without mentoring has no effect" (2013, 1). Eric Bettinger and his colleagues (2012) offered low-income adults who received tax-preparation help simultaneous assistance filling out the lengthy Free Application for Federal Student Aid (FAFSA) along with estimates of aid (and tuition) at nearby colleges. They find the combined treatment increased significantly the proportion of students who had completed two years of college three years after receiving services, but find no effect of aid and tuition information without filling out the FAFSA.

Some low-income individuals, however, lack both the necessary information and the financial resources to pay for college. Although net tuition at public and private nonprofit four-year institutions is typically lower for low-income students than for their high-income counterparts because grants and scholarships are higher, net tuition still represents a considerably higher proportion of income for low-income students or their parents.[22] As a result, many students and families borrow to meet college costs. Belley and Lochner, as noted earlier, document a substantial increase in the effects of family income on college attendance between the NLSY79 and NLSY97 cohorts. They develop a model that includes credit constraints and conclude, "Overall, it is likely that borrowing constraints have become more stringent over the past few decades and that this is at least partially responsible for the increase in college attendance gaps by family income" (2007, 32). Janet Yellen shows in this issue much higher student loan debt burdens for families in the lower half of the wealth distribution than for richer families and reports that these disparities increased between 1995 and 2013.

All in, children of affluent parents graduate from college at substantially higher rates than children of low-income parents, and the gap persists even when controlling for ability in the form of test scores. A variety of mechanisms serve to prepare poor children less well for college in addition to making it more difficult for them to attend and persist through graduation even with equal preparation. The consequences of these parental-income gaps in schooling are enormous, as educational attainment is a key determinant of labor market suc-

---

22. For 2011–2012 data on average net price of tuition at public and private nonprofit four-year institutions by income group (net price nets out all grants and scholarships but does not take account of loan aid), see the 2014 study by Grace Kena and her colleagues (indicator 35, figures 2 and 4).

cess. Four-year college graduates have higher labor force participation rates, lower unemployment rates (that is, higher employment rates given participation), and higher pay for full-time, full-year employment than high school graduates or individuals with some college or AA degrees. As discussed in the next section, Jo Blanden and her colleagues (2014) document a dominant role for educational attainment as a factor contributing to the correlation between an adult's earnings and his parents' family income when he was growing up. Thus, unequal education is both an effect and a cause of unequal opportunity.

INEQUALITY OF OPPORTUNITY IN THE LABOR MARKET

It seems likely that much of the intergenerational transmission of labor market success is accomplished via educational attainment, both because education is an important determinant of labor earnings and because research shows strong intergenerational correlations in educational attainment. This section investigates the degree to which labor market opportunities may differ among people who grow up in different circumstances beyond disparities in education. That is, to what extent do the children of low-income parents see lower earnings as adults than children of high-income parents, even controlling for educational attainment? Given the disparities in educational attainment documented earlier and elsewhere in this issue, any disparities added on in the labor market will compound the degree of inequality of opportunity and inequality of outcomes.

What mechanisms could cause labor market opportunities to be distributed unequally among young workers with similar education? Children of low-income parents may be less healthy, have different noncognitive skills and attitudes (including, for example, lower expectations of labor market success) and have inferior access to personal networks, connections, and internships that are instrumental in the job search and advancement processes, resulting in access to less prestigious and less remunerative positions. In addition, labor market institutions and processes may widen or reduce the degree of inequality associated with any educational disparities. Here, we provide an overview of research on the role of barriers to opportunity in the labor market, and the role of the labor market in amplifying the effects of barriers encountered earlier in life.

Some parents can provide their children with especially useful employment information and networks when they seek a job. Research indicates that friends and family are an important source of referrals or information on job openings during job search (Holzer 1988; Ionnides and Loury 2004). Explicit nepotism would amplify the effects of more benign information disparities. Moreover, some parents may be able to pay for (or support their children during) work internships and other forms of work enrichment or work experience beyond education that enhance job prospects, providing support that poorer parents or poorer young labor market entrants cannot afford. In addition, Miles Corak (2013a) and others have written about intergenerational transmission of attitudes, values, preferences, aspirations, and soft skills that can enhance or hurt workers' labor market prospects.

An extensive literature examines intergenerational earnings elasticities or correlations, especially between fathers and sons (for recent reviews, see Solon 1999, 2002; Bjorklund and Jäntti 2009; Black and Devereux 2011; on daughters, see Chadwick and Solon 2002; for intergenerational elasticity estimates on daughters, see Solon 1999, table 6). This literature does not generally control for education because it seeks to quantify the full relationship, including the contribution of education. Nonetheless, some authors do shed light on the net-of-education question. For example, in his *Labor Handbook* article, Solon (1999) lays out a simplified version of the theoretical model posited by Gary Becker and Nigel Tomes (1979), in which a child's earnings in adulthood reflect parental investments in his/her human capital (education) as well as his/her endowment of earnings capacity and market luck (a stochastic element). That endowment, in turn, is determined "by the reputation and 'connections' of their families, the contribution to the ability, race, and other characteristics of children from the genetic constitutions of their families, and the learning, skills, goals, and other 'family commodities' acquired through belonging to a particular family culture" (Becker and Tomes quoted in Solon 1999, 1764).

Solon (1999) goes on to note several "crucial" aspects of the intergenerational transmission of earnings status implied by the simple model, including that intergenerational transmission occurs through a multitude of processes and that parental income is not the only intergenerational influence on child's earnings. Thus, to go beyond education, as we want to do here, we need to think about children's endowments and about how the various processes determining earnings interact. Regarding that interaction, a child's endowment is correlated with the parental endowment; in addition, some elements of the child's endowment may help determine the degree to which parental investments translate into educational attainment and the degree to which they have a direct impact on earnings, even after controlling for education.

Solon concludes that the intergenerational earnings elasticity, a measure of the relationship between parents' earnings and that of their children in adulthood, for U.S. men is "somewhere around 0.4" (1999, 1795) and notes that this estimate is higher than similar estimates for Canada, Finland, and Sweden; an elasticity of zero would indicate no relationship between the earnings of children and parents, and an elasticity of one would indicate a near-exact correspondence. In a later paper, Solon (2004) also includes the influence of government investments in human capital (public financing of education), which can be redistributive or not. That is, to the degree that publicly funded education is focused on poorer children or public funds are inversely related to parental income, the intergenerational earnings elasticity will be lower. Corak notes that "we can expect the intergenerational elasticity [of earnings] to differ across countries for reasons associated with the costs and returns of investing in a child's human capital, the way in which the labor market works and how 'good jobs' are obtained, and the income inequalities between parents." (2013b, 114).

Another aspect of interaction among the processes determining outcomes is that the influence of educational attainment on earnings depends on the rate of return to education in the labor market; that rate of return—or educational wage premium—is a labor market characteristic. Nations or eras with greater disparities in pay levels according to educational attainment will, other things equal, have higher intergenerational earnings elasticities (hence, lower mobility) because any level of intergenerational correlation in education translates into greater differences in earnings and, hence, higher correlation of parent and child earnings.

Jo Blanden, Paul Gregg, and Lindsey Macmillan group the key factors or mechanisms in intergenerational earnings persistence—"those variables that are related to family incomes and that have a return in the [labour] market"—into four categories: noncognitive skills, cognitive ability, early labor market experiences, and educational attainment (2007, 1).[23] Although it is impossible to separate these influences (because, for example, cognitive ability helps to determine educational attainment as well as later earnings), it is still instructive to delve into them one by one to learn what we can infer about labor market influences net of education; indeed, Blanden, Gregg, and Macmillan argue that "many of the associations operate in a sequential way" (4).

In their initial examination of intergenerational persistence for a 1970 British cohort, they find the intergenerational elasticity of earnings to be 0.32.[24] They then decompose that elasticity by examining the relationships among the factors and family background / parental income and success-rewards in the labor market. They find that "better off children have better noncognitive traits and perform better in all cognitive tests . . . achieve more at all lev-

---

23. The title of Blanden, Gregg, and Macmillan's paper mentions only three, but in the text they explore early labor market experience as well.

24. The intergenerational elasticity is derived from the estimated relationship between child earnings at age thirty and parental family income.

els of education and have greater [labour] market attachment in their teens and 20s" (8). Furthermore, the cognitive variables are generally more strongly associated with parental income than the noncognitive traits. After analyzing how these factors are related to earnings at age thirty, they use both sets of regression results to decompose the estimated earnings elasticity into components explained by each of the factors and an unexplained component, which amounts to 46 percent of the elasticity. In this analysis, they find educational attainment to be the most important factor, accounting for 31 percent of the total estimated elasticity.[25] Early labor market attachment comes in a distant second among the explanatory factors, explaining 9 percent of the elasticity; noncognitive and cognitive factors explain only 6 to 7 percent, largely because their influence appears to work mostly through education. If we attribute the entire earnings elasticity excluding the education component to what goes on in the labor market, we obtain an upper-bound estimate of the importance of variations in labor market opportunity of close to 70 percent. The direct influence of early labor market experience, together with the effects of cognitive and noncognitive skills not operating via education, yields a lower-bound estimate of 23 percent for this British cohort of sons. They undertake a similar decomposition to understand the sources of a drop in mobility observed between 1958 and 1970 cohorts and find that a strengthening relationship between parental income and both educational attainment and early labor market attachment accounts for most of the change.

A 2014 paper by Blanden, Robert Haveman, Smeeding, and Kathryn Wilson compares intergenerational transmission for men in the United States and Great Britain using decompositions that lack the measures of noncognitive traits and cognitive ability (because they are not available in the U.S. Panel Study of Income Dynamics), and add in early marriage, marital status and health at age thirty, and measures of occupation at ages thirty and thirty-four. This study retains the pathways of education and early labor market attachment. Overall, they find higher mobility in the British sample than in the U.S. sample. They report that "the linkage between parental income and offspring earnings [in the United States] is largely accounted for by the offspring-education pathway, whereas in Great Britain, offspring occupation plays a much stronger role. The difference in the strength of the education pathway is due to relative differences in the returns to education in the two countries rather than to relative differences in the influence of parental income on educational attainments" (Blandon et al. 2014, 442). Note that labor market returns to education reflect the operation of the labor market rather than the heritability of education. Quantifying the contributions, their data indicate that education accounts for 26 percent of the persistence in the United States and 12 percent in Great Britain, even when controlling for occupation. The other pathways between parental income and an offspring's earnings—early marriage, early labor force attachment, and marital status and health at age thirty—account for only 6 percent of persistence in both the United States and Great Britain.[26] Occupational choices account for 24 percent in the United States and 34 percent in Great Britain. Interestingly, a simulation exercise indicates that education's contribution to the overall U.S. elasticity would be roughly cut in half if the returns to education in the United States were at the lower, British level.

Other relevant literature examines the transmission of employers between fathers and sons (see, for example, Bingley, Corak, and Westergard-Nielsen 2011; Corak and Piraino 2011). The transmission of employers is part of a broader mechanism regarding parental provision of both information and social networks that can enhance the labor market prospects of their offspring; parents may also invest in firm-specific types of human capital. Miles

---

25. They measure educational attainment at and after age sixteen, as number of O-levels at age sixteen, number of A-levels, staying in school after sixteen, earning a degree, and staying in school after eighteen.

26. Missing variables "explain" 4 percent of U.S. persistence and less than 1 percent in Great Britain.

Corak and Patrizio Piraino (2011) also note that transmission of employers may reflect fathers' possible direct role in the hiring process, including nepotism. They measure inherited employers in two ways: whether the son has ever worked for an employer that ever employed their father; whether the son's main employer at age thirty-three was also the father's main employer when the son was in his teens. They find that about 40 percent of a cohort of Canadian young men meet the first criterion, largely reflecting early jobs (in the teen years and early twenties), and that 6 percent to 9 percent have the same main employer in adulthood. Although Corak and Piraino are unable to infer causality, their findings are consistent with all of these hypothesized mechanisms. Intergenerational transmission of employers is higher when the father has self-employment income and is at or near the top of the fathers' earnings distribution. They also find that transmission of employers contributes to nonlinearities in intergenerational earnings elasticities: high elasticities in the middle and at the upper tail of the fathers' distribution reflect the pattern of those who inherit an employer from their father. Similar research using Canadian and Danish data yields similar findings (Bingley, Corak, and Westergard-Nielsen 2011). Regarding the correlation with father's earnings level, the study notes that "mobility out of the bottom has little to do with inheriting an employer from the father, while the preservation of high income status is distinctly related to this tendency" (1).

One example of recent U.S. labor market institutions that may be contributing to unequal opportunity, even among those with a college education, is internships. Unpaid internships are said to provide important job experience and connections to young graduates and sometimes lead to offers of paid employment. But low-income labor market entrants, with or without college debt, often cannot afford to work without pay and therefore lose out on these opportunities. Some court decisions have limited employers' exploitation of young workers and some colleges have raised funds to provide scholarships to provide living stipends to low-income students who want to serve as interns, but these remedies are unlikely to have made a serious dent in the prevalence of the practice and its disparate impact.[27] As Ross Eisenbrey of the Economic Policy Institute observes, "It's hard to quantify the impact of this phenomenon [internships] on the decline in economic mobility, but I suspect it has been substantial and will continue to grow until the Department of Labor cracks down on what is, in many cases, illegal exploitation" (2012).[28]

Existing research finds an important role for parental income and other family-related factors in determining labor market earnings, even beyond parental influence on educational attainment. These effects occur via transmission (by both nature and nurture) of attitudes, skills, preferences, and social networks, and even nepotism. Depending on one's interpretation of the unexplained portion of intergenerational earnings elasticities, noneducation factors account for one-quarter to three-quarters of U.S. earnings transmission from parents to sons.[29] These numbers are higher when taking account that part of the education portion reflects returns to educational attainment determined in the labor market; indeed, much of the difference in intergenerational

---

27. Data are generally lacking on the prevalence of unpaid internships. In promoting a 2011 event to discuss internships in the U.S. labor market, and the book *Intern Nation* by Ross Perlin, the Economic Policy Institute noted, "Internships have become a principal point of entry for young people seeking white-collar careers, and it is estimated that half of all college students will do an internship before graduating. Between 1 and 2 million people overall will work as interns this year in the United States, saving firms $600 million dollars."

28. Two key criteria in determining the legality of an internship at a for-profit private sector employer is that "the internship experience is for the benefit of the intern," "the intern does not displace regular employees, but works under close supervision of existing staff," and "the employer . . . derives no immediate advantage from the activities of the intern" (U.S. Department of Labor 2010).

29. These figures are based on reported U.S. estimates (Blanden et al. 2014, table 6, column 1).

transmission between the United States and Great Britain represents differences between the two nations in education returns.

Do these findings suggest policy interventions that might reduce parental influence in the labor market? Although rules exist to limit outright nepotism—at least in public employment, many interventions aimed directly at reducing parental influence would be seen as impinging on parents' autonomy in raising their children. However, policies that enhance opportunities for all children to succeed, as discussed earlier would have two positive impacts on the labor market: More disadvantaged children would attain higher education, thereby directly improving their labor market outcomes, and the resulting increase in the supply of educated workers would moderate the high returns to education that still prevail in U.S. labor markets and contribute, as documented, to the heritability of earnings.

Additional policies in the labor market could further equalize opportunities. Jared Bernstein (2014), for example, argues that after education, the next most important policy actions governments must undertake are to level the playing field for workers who seek to form or join unions, and to increase the minimum wage to counter the lack of bargaining power of many in the workforce. Raising the minimum wage and promoting unions is likely to reduce the labor market returns to education (and occupation) relative to less-regulated market outcomes. Furthermore, labor regulations and policies that nudge firms toward adopting human resource practices that result in opportunities for workers to learn by doing and to acquire occupation- and firm-specific human capital (perhaps by creating career ladders in positions with relatively modest educational requirements) may reduce the association between parental income and early labor market attachment and advance the interests of employers by reducing worker turnover. As noted, action to limit the prevalence and exploitative aspects of internships or to provide more equitable access to internships would also reduce inequality of opportunity in the labor market.

THE ROLE OF GEOGRAPHY IN INEQUALITY OF OPPORTUNITY

Children have no choice over the geographic area where they are born and raised, so geography is clearly a dimension of circumstance that should be considered in evaluating the extent of inequality of opportunity. Research on the role of geography in economic opportunity, which we survey in this section, shows that economic opportunity varies substantially across geographic areas, though the mechanisms underlying this relationship are not yet fully understood.

Branko Milanovic (2015) summarizes the degree of inequality of opportunity associated with geography globally by decomposing total global income inequality into inequality of opportunity (between-country inequality) and residual inequality. He finds that inequality of opportunity constitutes a "huge but decreasing" share of overall inequality between 1988 and 2008, amounting to almost 70 percent of total interpersonal inequality in 2008. He reports that a measure of intercountry inequality, the mean log deviation of income, was 0.68 in 2008, down from 1998 and 1988, and that the global interpersonal mean log deviation was 0.98 in 2008, also lower than in 1998 and 1988 (see the top panel of table 1).[30]

Milanovic provides a metaphor for his analytical framework: he suggests seeing the world income distribution as a long pole and each country's distribution as being represented by a plaque on that pole. An individual's income lies within the range covered by the plaque representing his or her home country, and that home country substantially circumscribes the person's economic prospects. The plaque represents two "circumstances beyond individual control: level of development of one's country of residence, proxied by its GDP per capita or average number of years of education, and inequality of distribution within that country" (2015, 456). Milanovic uses the term *circum-*

---

30. The mean log deviation measure is often referred to as Theil L. Milanovic's dataset includes 118 countries in 2008, representing 92 percent of the world population. This inter-country inequality measure depends only on average income in each nation.

Table 1. Geographic Inequality of Opportunity
Inequality is measured as mean log deviation (Theil L) of income

Geography, Income Unit, and Year	Total Inequality[a]	Inter-Area[b] (Geographic)	Between-Area Percentage of Total
Global, across countries (Milanovic)			
1988	1.070	0.862	80.6
1998	1.035	0.764	73.8
2008	0.983	0.677	68.9
United States households			
1988	0.401		
1998	0.488		
1999	0.476		
2008	0.541		
U.S. commuting zones, cohort families[c]			
1996–2000	0.492	0.031	6.3
U.S. counties, cohort families[c]			
1996–2000	0.492	0.055	11.2
U.S. census tracts, households			
1999		0.081	17.0

Source: Authors' compilation based on Milanovic 2015 and U.S. Census Bureau 2014a; authors' calculations based on Chetty, Hendren, Kline, and Saez 2014b and U.S. Census Bureau 2014b.
[a]Total measures inequality between individuals, households, or cohort families. For cohort families, total is inequality across centiles of the distribution, not individual families.
[b]Inter-area measures inequality between areas, assuming area mean income applies to all units in an area.
[c]Cohort families are tax filing units that claimed children born in 1980–1982 on tax returns in 1996–2000.

stances in the Roemerian sense, as elements of "fate, decided at birth" (as he puts it) or public goods reflecting the country in which they reside. To improve her lot, an individual has three options: she can rely on hard work or luck to rise within her country's distribution; she can hope for her country to experience strong growth and have its plaque move up the pole; or she can migrate to a higher-income country.

Milanovic notes that "the topic of inequality of opportunity is traditionally studied at the national level" at least in part because of "the unstated view that equality of opportunity is something that ought to hold at the national level or for which only national governments can be held responsible" (2015, 452–53). Geographic aspects of inequality of opportunity within the United States are the focus of the remainder of this section, but Milanovic's global measures (for comparison) and his pole metaphor also prove useful in what follows.

Looking within the United States, overall interhousehold income inequality is, of course, considerably smaller than Milanovic reports among global individuals and across nations.[31] The Census Bureau reports a mean log deviation of household income equal to 0.54 in 2008, up from 1998 and 1988 (see second panel of table 1). Data on family income for parents re-

---

31. If the U.S. data were those that Milanovic included for the United States in his global measures, they would necessarily show less inequality within the United States than globally, given that the United States is one nation among many.

ported by Chetty, Hendren, Kline, and Saez (2014b) show a mean log deviation across centile means of 0.49 during the 1996 to 2000 period.[32] With these data, we can also follow Milanovic and decompose total inequality into the part associated solely with geography and the residual. This exercise applied to commuting zones as the geographic unit within the United States yields a between-area mean log deviation of 0.03 during the 1996–2000 period, which amounts to only 6 percent of total inequality (measured across centiles for the same tax-filing population of parents). Repeating the same exercise across counties, the smaller geographic building blocks of commuting zones, yields a mean log deviation of 0.06, or 11 percent of total inequality.

Given the prevalence of economic segregation in residential location, one might expect that a higher share of inequality would be explained by a more-detailed geography. That is, in fact, the case: if we go down to the neighborhood level, we find somewhat greater interarea disparities, with a mean log deviation of 1999 household incomes across census tracts nationwide of 0.08, or 17 percent of the 0.48 nationwide 1999 mean log deviation of household incomes published by the census (see table 1). Although this represents greater interarea disparities than the CZ or county figures, it is still small compared with Milanovic's intercountry differences. Differences in mean incomes across commuting zones, across counties, or even across census tracts do not explain much of the total inequality of incomes in the nation; within the United States, the length of the "pole" in Milanovic's metaphor is shorter and the area "plaques" are wider and have much greater overlap. Moreover, the measures of geographic location used in the decompositions are for current location, not where people grew up. Given the prevalence of geographic migration, especially between neighborhoods, one should not necessarily interpret the interarea component as measuring inequality of opportunity, although it may indicate inequality of circumstances for the generation currently growing up.

Inequality of Opportunity Across U.S. Commuting Zones and Counties

Chetty, Hendren, Kline, and Saez (2014a) explore the geography of inequality of opportunity in the United States, using commuting zones as their geographic units; they analyze data on 709 commuting zones covering virtually all U.S. territory and population.[33] Using measures of relative and absolute intergenerational mobility, they document wide variations in mobility across commuting zones within the United States. Moreover, they note that relative mobility patterns across CZs are highly correlated with absolute mobility.[34] They provide a much-cited heat-map of absolute mobility variations across CZs nationwide, showing broad regional patterns of mobility as well as variations within regions and differences between rural and urban areas. Even though variation within regions is substantial, the map shows concentrations of low mobility across the southern United States. This is quite consistent with the finding of Gustavo Marrero and Juan Rodriguez (2013) that southern U.S. states exhibit high inequality of opportunity

---

32. This mean log deviation figure is remarkably close to the U.S. Census Bureau figure cited above for all households in 1998. This is surprising, given that 0.49 from Chetty, Hendren, Kline, and Saez is an underestimate of total household inequality for at least two reasons. First, the inequality of incomes across individual households or filing units should be higher than inequality across centile means of households or filing units. (Milanovic's analysis, however, also used centiles for each country and computed the (weighted) mean log deviation among those values.) Probably more important, the Chetty data are tax-filing-unit incomes of a subset of the population that is undoubtedly more homogeneous than the set of all tax filers; their 1996 to 2000 sample is parents with children born between 1980 and 1982.

33. The 709 CZs with data contained 99.96 percent of the U.S. population in 2000.

34. Their measure of relative mobility is the slope coefficient from the child-rank on parent-rank regression, which indicates the difference in expected ranks between children in the richest versus poorest families. Their primary measure of absolute mobility is the mean percentile income rank of children whose parents were at the 25th percentile of the national income distribution.

when measured across circumstance groups defined by race and parental education (see especially figures 2a, 2b, and table 1).

What mechanisms might be at work to cause such substantial differences in opportunity—and hence differences in intergenerational mobility—among commuting zone areas? Chetty, Hendren, Kline, and Saez explore a number of covariates of mobility at the CZ level. These explorations do not attempt to establish causation, but they do suggest some geography-related forces that may be at work. Discussing such factors may help us sort out circumstances, as Milanovic uses the term (based on Roemer), that are mediated by physical nearness versus those that are not, even though they may exhibit geographic patterns.

One of Chetty, Hendren, Kline, and Saez's five important covariates of income mobility across CZs is the degree of income inequality in the CZ (2014a). We explored this factor in discussing the Great Gatsby curve—the relationship between inequality of outcomes and subsequent inequality of opportunity or intergenerational mobility.

The most important covariates of income mobility across CZs in the Chetty, Hendren, Kline, and Saez analysis relate to family structure, specifically the fraction of families with children that are headed by single mothers (2014a).[35] CZs in which a substantial fraction of children are living in single-parent families display lower absolute mobility. Analysts offer many links, both causal and associational, between single motherhood and low family income that explain why more children in CZs with a high proportion of single mothers start at the bottom (of the national income distribution)—and hence are likely to be nearer the bottom as adults. In addition, hypotheses about why, given parental income, children in single-parent households may have less opportunity to advance, focus on factors such as parental education and associated aspirations for children, as well as parental time available to devote to interacting with children. Chetty, Hendren, Kline, and Saez note, however, that low mobility in CZs characterized by high prevalence of single-parent households is not simply a compositional result; children of married-couple families show lower mobility, on average, in CZs with high fractions of single parents (2014a).

A third strong correlate of mobility across CZs is the quality of local schools. We discussed earlier the importance of K–12 school quality and the U.S. pattern of local public school provision in generating opportunity.

Chetty, Hendren, Kline, and Saez find measures of social capital strongly related to mobility outcomes across commuting zones, citing earlier studies that establish the importance of social networks and engagement in community organizations in determining social and economic outcomes (2014a). They measure social capital with indicators of violent crime rates, religiosity, and a social capital index constructed by other researchers, which they aggregate to the CZ level. To the degree that social capital has a geographic aspect, it is presumably at a considerably smaller geographic unit than the commuting zone. For example, Robert Putnam's work focuses on the community and neighborhood level, investigating people's interaction, trust, and cooperation with neighbors and their social peers (2000, 2015, 2016). His discussion comments accompanying this issue examine the interaction between propinquity (geographic nearness) and social networks in various contexts. It is among the traditional working classes that neighborhood ties have tended to be most important, and researchers have documented greater success for those living in neighborhoods with what the literature calls collective efficacy. Putnam notes that the nongeographic networks characteristic of higher-income parents and children appear to provide access to broader opportunity.

The last of Chetty, Hendren, Kline, and Saez's five most important covariates is the degree of geographic segregation—by income or by race—within a CZ (2014a). Measures of segregation likely capture shared versus separate experiences of children raised in rich and poor

---

35. In the family structure category, they also examine the fractions of CZ adults who are divorced and who are married, and they find similar results, but not as strong as for single mothers

families within a CZ and their exposure to families in the other group. Partly because spatial residential segregation is often associated with separate schools and other public institutions from parks to libraries, it is likely to limit favorable peer effects and positive economic role models for low-income children in addition to reducing the funding and quality of the public services to which they have access. Like social capital measures, these segregation indicators point to smaller geographies as important loci in which opportunity takes shape.

In a 2015 paper, Chetty and Hendren explore another path for improving one's situation highlighted by Milanovic—moving to a new area (geographic mobility) to achieve upward mobility. The authors find that children gain the positive outcomes of destination counties in proportion to how young they were when their parents moved there from a county with poorer outcomes.[36] Unlike Milanovic's scenario, however, Chetty and Hendren do not find that the positive effects of moving extend to adults (twenty-four and older at the time of the move). They identify causal effects of residence location (county) when growing up and estimate these effects for every county nationwide, interpreting them as neighborhood exposure effects. They also explore county characteristics associated with better outcomes, as indicated by more positive causal effects and find better outcomes for children who grow up in counties with "less concentrated poverty, less income inequality, better schools, a larger share of two-parent families, and lower crime rates" (Chetty and Hendren 2015, 1).

Covariates such as family structure or school quality, though they have geographic patterns, are not inherently related to physical adjacency in the way that social capital, crime rates, and segregation are, because the latter depend at least in part on neighborhood proximity. Thus, isolating geography's role might require controlling for (subtracting out) geographic disparities that are not based on propinquity.[37]

Inequality of Opportunity Across Neighborhoods

Inequality of opportunity across neighborhoods potentially involves different mechanisms than inequality of opportunity associated with coarser measures of geography. Although causality has been difficult to pin down, the association between the characteristics of the neighborhoods children grow up in and the economic outcomes of those children as adults is clear.

William Julius Wilson (1987) is credited with being among the first to hypothesize that neighborhood environment has an important role in shaping opportunity. In particular, he focused on the potentially negative consequences of growing up in inner-city areas of concentrated poverty after both manufacturing jobs and the black middle class had largely moved out. Socially isolated, with few positive (employed) role models and few jobs available locally, children growing up in severely disadvantaged neighborhoods were likely to be scarred in terms of educational attainment and eventual employment.

Patrick Sharkey's paper in this issue summarizes key research on the role of neighborhoods in enhancing or limiting access to opportunity. As noted, many of the mechanisms at work at the neighborhood level relate to spatial segregation, which limits exposure of members of different income groups, racial groups, cultural groups, or other dimension of segregation to each other. This can in turn perpetuate the disadvantages suffered by one generation, passing them on to their children. These arguments are based on the idea that neighborhoods are more than just the combination of individuals who live there and in-

---

[36]. "Better" destination counties are those with more positive outcomes for children who live there throughout childhood compared with outcomes for children who live in the origin county throughout childhood. The outcome on which they focus is income as a young adult (age twenty-four or twenty-six), but they find similar "exposure" effects on college attendance, teenage birth rates, and marriage rates.

[37]. Julia Burdick-Will and her colleagues (2011), for example, report the conclusion of Dobbie and Fryer that test scores are unresponsive to changes in neighborhood environments in the absence of school-quality changes.

stead also depend on peer effects, role models, social networks, and the like being important aspects of access to opportunity.

Sharkey notes in this issue that observational studies find strong correlations between child neighborhood conditions and adult economic outcomes and that the consequences in terms of academic performance and educational attainment of growing up in a disadvantaged environment appear to be cumulative; that is, outcomes worsen with length of exposure. Sharkey also summarizes his joint work with Bryan Graham (2013), which examines the links between spatial segregation and economic mobility, noting that the tight connection between family economic status and neighborhood economic status that segregation creates will increase the transmission of family economic status across generations. Their paper confirms a relationship between mobility and spatial economic segregation using three data sets, but notes that the association does not provide evidence of causation.

As Julia Burdick-Will and her colleagues (2011) point out, many nonexperimental studies find substantial effects of neighborhood on children's life chances—findings that admittedly include some bias from selection effects—yet the Moving to Opportunity (MTO) experiment found no discernable neighborhood effects. Burdick-Will and her colleagues attempt to reconcile experimental, quasi-experimental, and observational studies of neighborhood influence, and come out in the middle, concluding that some neighborhood circumstances do matter for children's outcomes. In particular, they argue that what seems to matter is whether children live in the most economically distressed or dangerous neighborhoods. They find little support for either neighborhood differences in school quality or racial composition playing a key role in children's differential school performance outcomes. By contrast, they see concentrated neighborhood disadvantage as an important influence, and also find that crime rates and exposure to violence are negatively related to children's test scores.[38] They note, however, that this evidence is mostly circumstantial, based on large differences in levels of violent crime and neighborhood disadvantage between the MTO cities of Baltimore and Chicago (where test score improvements did occur among the MTO treatment group) and the other three MTO cities of Boston, New York, and Los Angeles.

Chetty, Hendren, and Lawrence Katz (2015) bring new data to bear and successfully reconcile the all-cities experimental MTO results with observational studies, finding substantial neighborhood "exposure" effects on adult outcomes (earnings and college-going) of children whose families were offered the MTO voucher requiring they move to a low-poverty neighborhood when they were young (younger than thirteen). They combine Internal Revenue Service data with MTO data to look at recent (young adult) outcomes (through 2012) and differentiate by age of the child when the family was randomly assigned to one of the MTO treatments or to control group status. They find negative effects, sometimes significantly different from zero for children who were older when the MTO moves occurred, a finding that, they argue, may reflect disruption effects; these would be offset for younger children by positive exposure effects proportional to the length of exposure to lower-poverty neighborhoods.

In summing up existing research on the role of neighborhoods in access to opportunity, Sharkey (this issue) notes the wide variation in opportunity and economic mobility across geographic areas in the United States. Investigating sources of that variation, the research mostly identifies correlations but has not succeeded in establishing causal relationships or even pinned down key mechanisms; as a result, he notes, "as a whole, however, the research explaining geographic variation in economic mobility remains at a very early stage."

---

38. They measure "concentrated neighborhood disadvantage" following Sampson, Sharkey, and Raudenbush (2008), as a weighted average of neighborhood poverty, percentage of residents who are black, percentage of adults who are unemployed, percentage of households with a female head, percentage of residents on welfare, and percentage of residents under age eighteen.

THE RELATIONSHIP BETWEEN INEQUALITY OF OPPORTUNITY AND ECONOMIC GROWTH

Our focus has been on the mechanisms through which barriers to opportunity arise and how they affect economic outcomes for individuals, along with potential policy remedies. This raises the question of what effect policies that reduce barriers to opportunity would likely have on aggregate economic performance. If removing barriers to opportunity promotes economic growth, these spillovers reduce the overall cost of such policies.

The literature relating inequality of opportunity and aggregate economic performance is extremely limited and most of it was developed out of the considerably more extensive literature relating overall inequality (that is, inequality of outcomes) and growth. Hypotheses regarding the effects of overall inequality on growth lay out plausible effects with both positive and negative signs and the empirical literature is correspondingly inconclusive. By contrast, theory suggests that inequality of opportunity will be a drag on economic growth, because individuals who lack opportunity will not be able to produce to their full potential and thus some capital will not be put to its most productive use.

Evidence on Effects of Unequal Opportunity on Growth

Two papers that directly investigate the influence of inequality of opportunity on growth decompose total inequality into two parts, inequality of opportunity and a residual inequality labeled inequality of effort, and include the two parts in a growth regression in place of a total inequality measure (Ferreira et al. 2014; Marrero and Rodriguez 2013). They measure inequality of opportunity as the between-group dispersion in outcomes, where groups are defined in terms of circumstances individuals face that are not within their control, as in Roemer's framework, summarized earlier. Francisco Ferreira and his colleagues (2014) use a set of circumstance variables observed only selectively for individuals in an international panel analysis. They fail to find negative effects of inequality of opportunity on growth, perhaps because their circumstance groups are unevenly measured or possibly because such effects are not detectable or do not operate across nations with different cultural and institutional contexts. By contrast, Marrero and Rodriguez (2013) analyze inequality of opportunity and growth across U.S. states and time and use eight circumstance groups, defined on the basis of four categories of parental educational attainment, cross-classified by two racial groups. They find significant and negative effects of inequality of opportunity on growth, effects that persist through various robustness checks. They argue that "returns to effort may encourage people to invest in education and to exert an effort, while inequality of opportunity may not favor human and physical capital accumulation in the more talented individuals" (120).

Bradbury and Triest measure inequality or equality of opportunity in a different way in this issue; they use indicators of relative and absolute intergenerational mobility at the commuting-zone level of geography within the United States that were developed and published by Chetty, Hendren, Kline, and Saez (2014a, 2014b). Intergenerational mobility measures reflect how equal or unequal opportunity is by indicating how tied a child's adult income is to the (parental-income) circumstances in which he or she grew up. Bradbury and Triest find positive effects of intergenerational mobility, especially absolute mobility, on income growth between 2000 and 2013 in a cross-section of commuting zones, indicating that inequality of opportunity, as proxied by low intergenerational mobility, acts as a drag on local-area growth.

A fourth paper takes an entirely different approach, investigating the addition to output associated with the reduction over the last several decades in the inequality of access to high-level occupations suffered earlier by women and blacks compared with white men in the United States. Chang-Tai Hsieh and his colleagues (2013) do not directly estimate the effect of inequality of opportunity on growth. Instead, they mark the stark differences in occupations in the United States in 1960 between white men, on one hand, and white women, black women, and black men, on the other. They argue that, because these differences were so great, they cannot possibly be random or the result of unequal talent—white men, for example, accounted for 94 percent of U.S. physicians and 96 percent of lawyers in 1960—and instead largely reflect unequal opportunity. They then estimate the addition to U.S. output made by the degree to which those differences shrank in the ensuing years and attribute that contribution—a remarkable 15 to 20 percent of U.S. economic growth—to equalization of opportunity via great reductions in the barriers women and blacks face in their access to skilled professions, encouraging members of these formerly severely disadvantaged groups to invest in their own human capital and gain the ability to contribute more fully to the national output.

These various approaches to measuring the impact of inequality of opportunity on growth point to negative effects, at least in the United States. (The international panel analysis by Ferreira and his colleagues [2014] failed to find negative effects.) As noted earlier, this is not surprising, given that theory consistently suggests negative effects to the degree that unequal opportunity prevents individuals from performing to their full potential and prevents capital from being invested in the most high-value projects. Although not unexpected, these findings imply that the economic effects of unequal opportunity are large enough to be measurable at the macro level of output or economic growth and hence that policymakers have an additional impetus to reduce inequality of opportunity.

Policies to Improve both Economic Opportunity and Aggregate Performance

The empirical evidence reviewed suggests that removing barriers to economic opportunity may also improve aggregate economic performance. Certain policies may have the potential to achieve both of these objectives.

Bernstein (2014) points toward policies that have positive output effects via enhancing opportunities without negative side-effects from reducing incentives for others to achieve or invest. His first policy recommendation is that governments should enhance their investments aimed at helping disadvantaged children overcome barriers in the U.S. educational system. As noted earlier, a rapidly growing empirical literature indicates that early childhood interventions targeted at disadvantaged populations have high social rates of return; this topic is also addressed by Magnuson and Duncan in their paper in this issue. Health, nutrition, and preschool programs help to lessen the effect of poverty in early childhood on long-term outcomes. Payoffs would also be positive for policies to lessen the link between the quality of elementary and secondary schooling and parental income or wealth, as discussed earlier. The Duncan and Murnane paper in this issue focuses on specific policies to raise K–12 educational quality for disadvantaged children.

Beyond high school, policies are also needed to break the link between family economic status and college attendance. Children of low-income parents are much less likely than their high-income counterparts to enroll in and graduate from four-year college programs, even conditional on standardized test scores. Better-targeted financial aid programs, greater outreach to disadvantaged students, and more widespread and effective compensatory programs to guide disadvantaged students through college have the potential to reduce the effect of parents' income on postsecondary schooling investment.

Other policies are needed to provide more opportunities for people to get back on track after suffering the effects of being born disadvantaged. Children from disadvantaged backgrounds are more likely to fall off standard academic and career tracks, and do not enjoy the same degree of insurance more affluent families offer. Enhanced opportunities for adult education and degree completion, and programs to improve labor market and educational opportunities for people with criminal records would attenuate some of the obstacles facing those who have slipped off track.

SUMMARY

The research reviewed offers grounds for both optimism and pessimism regarding prospects for addressing inequality of opportunity in the United States. Barriers to economic opportunity are pervasive, and the growth in inequality of outcomes has both increased the stakes associated with confronting barriers and increased the difficulty in overcoming these obstacles. Absent substantial increases in the scope and scale of policy interventions, inequality of opportunity is likely to persist, along with stagnation or deterioration of economic mobility. On the other hand, research has made great strides in identifying and understanding the mechanisms relating barriers to opportunity to economic outcomes. Although detailed research and analysis are required to evaluate the success of specific policies in breaking down barriers to opportunity and improving labor market outcomes, such policies clearly exist and some have already been implemented. In considering whether the future will bring improvements in economic opportunity and mobility, the most problematic question and thus the largest area of uncertainty may be in whether the political will exists to enact policies of sufficient scale and scope to address the problem.

APPENDIX

This appendix reports the results of the multiple regression analysis discussed earlier. The regression results underlie our analysis of whether the Great Gatsby curve relationship between intergenerational mobility and inequality of outcomes for the older generation holds up when one controls for other factors that arguably might also affect intergenerational mobility. Descriptive statistics (variable means, etc.) for the variables used in the regressions are presented in table A1.

Tables A2 and A3 report regression results in a cross-section of commuting zones, with relative and absolute mobility as the dependent variables, measures of inequality as

Table A1. Summary Statistics

	Mean	SD
Absolute mobility	43.94	5.681
Relative mobility	67.49	6.479
Gini (inequality) of parental income	0.410	0.0792
Parental middle class	0.550	0.0786
Top 1 percent income share	10.84	5.049
Per capita income, 1980	8.538	1.777
Per capita income, 1990	15.88	2.989
Per capita income growth, 1970–1980	149.2	26.42
Per capita income growth, 1980–1990	87.68	20.83
Foreign born, 1980	0.0252	0.0318
Foreign born, 1990	0.0275	0.0391
Workers with commute < fifteen minutes, 1980	0.508	0.142
Workers with commute < fifteen minutes, 1990	0.489	0.139
Households with kids headed by single mom, 1980	0.0491	0.0168
Households with kids headed by single mom, 1990	0.0582	0.0194
Less than high school, 1980	0.381	0.110
Less than high school, 1990	0.287	0.0907
More than high school, 1980	0.399	0.0809
More than high school, 1990	0.441	0.0912
Male labor force participation rate, 1980	72.27	6.050
Male labor force participation rate, 1990	70.62	5.787
Female labor force participation rate, 1980	46.07	5.966
Female labor force participation rate, 1990	52.87	6.206
Logarithm of population, 1980	11.57	1.406
Logarithm of population, 1990	11.60	1.454
Observations	709	

Source: Authors' calculations based on U.S. Census Bureau 2014c, U.S. Bureau of Economic Analysis 2014, and Chetty, Hendren, Kline, and Saez 2014b.

Table A2. Mobility Regressions, 1990 Demographics

	Absolute Mobility			Relative Mobility		
	(1)	(2)	(3)	(4)	(5)	(6)
Gini (inequality) of parental income	-8.082***		-16.057***	-2.806		-16.735**
	(2.148)		(3.780)	(3.133)		(5.576)
Parents middle class		16.581***	11.903***		12.154**	7.905+
		(2.910)	(3.090)		(4.276)	(4.559)
Top 1 percent income share			0.143***			0.214***
			(0.041)			(0.060)
Per capita income growth, 1980–1990	0.009	0.007	0.011+	0.007	0.008	0.010
	(0.007)	(0.006)	(0.006)	(0.010)	(0.009)	(0.009)
Per capita income, 1990	-0.089	-0.036	-0.074	-0.460***	-0.409***	-0.481***
	(0.063)	(0.064)	(0.065)	(0.092)	(0.093)	(0.095)
Foreign born, 1990	17.775***	20.535***	21.656***	53.898***	56.814***	57.243***
	(3.576)	(3.590)	(3.569)	(5.215)	(5.275)	(5.264)
Workers with commute < fifteen minutes, 1990	12.199***	10.821***	11.080***	3.997	2.584	3.515
	(1.727)	(1.736)	(1.733)	(2.519)	(2.551)	(2.557)
Households with kids headed by single mom, 1990	-122.617***	-96.319***	-89.355***	-137.107***	-114.768***	-105.832***
	(7.036)	(8.945)	(9.010)	(10.262)	(13.146)	(13.291)
Less than high school, 1990	-2.648	3.380	2.564	-8.714+	-3.584	-5.165
	(3.616)	(3.797)	(3.768)	(5.275)	(5.581)	(5.558)
More than high school, 1990	7.000*	10.147**	10.493**	14.188**	17.475***	16.639***
	(3.188)	(3.234)	(3.227)	(4.649)	(4.752)	(4.759)
Male labor force participation rate, 1990	0.221***	0.226***	0.215***	0.001	-0.002	-0.004
	(0.032)	(0.031)	(0.031)	(0.046)	(0.046)	(0.046)
Female labor force participation rate, 1990	-0.250***	-0.249***	-0.267***	-0.009	-0.011	-0.032
	(0.034)	(0.033)	(0.033)	(0.049)	(0.049)	(0.049)
Logarithm of population, 1990	0.149	-0.023	0.119	-0.453+	-0.571*	-0.402
	(0.165)	(0.165)	(0.166)	(0.240)	(0.242)	(0.245)
Constant	41.513***	26.052***	33.224***	83.439***	72.856***	79.590***
	(3.635)	(4.271)	(4.558)	(5.302)	(6.277)	(6.723)
Regional fixed effects	Yes	Yes	Yes	Yes	Yes	Yes
Observations	709	709	709	709	709	709
R^2	0.781	0.787	0.792	0.642	0.646	0.652

Source: Authors' calculations based on U.S. Census Bureau 2014c, U.S. Bureau of Economic Analysis 2014, and Chetty, Hendren, Kline, and Saez 2014b.
+$p < 0.10$; *$p < 0.05$; **$p < 0.01$; ***$p < 0.001$

explanatory variables, and various other commuting-zone characteristics as exogenous and predetermined control variables that help explain mobility. These regressions build on those reported elsewhere in this issue (Bradbury and Triest, table 4). Table A2 uses 1990 measures of those characteristics—when the children whose mobility is observed were about age ten, and table A3 uses measures from 1980, just before they were born (1980 to 1982). Columns 1 through 3 (absolute mobility as dependent variable) and 4 through 6 (relative mobility) of tables A2 and A3 include alternative measures of inequality; specifically, columns 1 and 4 include the Gini coefficient to measure inequality (as in figure 1), columns 2 and 5 the proportion middle class (as in figure 2), and columns 3 and 6 include the Gini, the

Table A3. Mobility Regressions, 1980 Demographics

	Absolute Mobility			Relative Mobility		
	(1)	(2)	(3)	(4)	(5)	(6)
Gini (inequality) of parental income	-5.855**		-14.972***	-3.459		-16.073**
	(1.845)		(3.444)	(2.930)		(5.487)
Parents middle class		11.530***	7.000**		14.966***	11.141**
		(2.438)	(2.694)		(3.867)	(4.293)
Top 1 percent income share			0.153***			0.218***
			(0.036)			(0.058)
Per capita income growth, 1970–1980	0.014**	0.015***	0.017***	0.025***	0.027***	0.028***
	(0.005)	(0.005)	(0.004)	(0.007)	(0.007)	(0.007)
Per capita income, 1980	-0.397***	-0.339**	-0.420***	-0.890***	-0.820***	-0.917***
	(0.105)	(0.104)	(0.104)	(0.166)	(0.165)	(0.166)
Foreign born, 1980	28.319***	32.071***	32.006***	67.457***	73.760***	73.178***
	(3.672)	(3.787)	(3.744)	(5.832)	(6.009)	(5.965)
Workers with commute < fifteen minutes, 1980	11.413***	10.540***	11.188***	3.251	1.760	2.818
	(1.586)	(1.591)	(1.581)	(2.518)	(2.524)	(2.518)
Households with kids headed by single mom, 1980	-162.948***	-140.580***	-133.013***	-154.203***	-121.291***	-109.104***
	(7.775)	(9.547)	(9.648)	(12.348)	(15.146)	(15.372)
Less than high school, 1980	-3.853	-1.263	-2.034	-12.532**	-8.713*	-9.649*
	(2.740)	(2.794)	(2.763)	(4.352)	(4.433)	(4.403)
More than high school, 1980	9.468**	10.542***	10.278**	16.325**	18.828***	17.659***
	(3.159)	(3.143)	(3.122)	(5.017)	(4.987)	(4.974)
Male labor force participation rate, 1980	0.278***	0.279***	0.272***	0.103**	0.097*	0.09*
	(0.025)	(0.024)	(0.024)	(0.039)	(0.039)	(0.039)
Female labor force participation rate, 1980	-0.245***	-0.248***	-0.262***	-0.077+	-0.079+	-0.101*
	(0.026)	(0.026)	(0.026)	(0.042)	(0.041)	(0.041)
Logarithm of population, 1980	0.526***	0.378*	0.519***	-0.204	-0.368	-0.228
	(0.149)	(0.149)	(0.151)	(0.236)	(0.236)	(0.240)
Constant	31.422***	21.541***	27.994***	74.786***	63.204***	68.971***
	(3.455)	(3.792)	(4.095)	(5.488)	(6.017)	(6.524)
Regional fixed effects	Yes	Yes	Yes	Yes	Yes	Yes
Observations	709	709	709	709	709	709
R^2	0.815	0.818	0.823	0.641	0.648	0.655

Source: Authors' calculations based on U.S. Census Bureau 2014c, U.S. Bureau of Economic Analysis 2014, and Chetty, Hendren, Kline, and Saez 2014b.

+p < 0.10; *p < 0.05; **p < 0.01; ***p < 0.001

proportion middle class, and the income share of the top 1 percent in the CZ.

The control variables include a rough measure of past immigration (percentage of foreign-born residents), the mix of educational attainments among adults ages twenty-five and older in the CZ, the proportion of single-mother households, labor force participation rates for men and women, the proportion of workers with average commuting times of less than fifteen minutes, and economic variables including per capita income, growth in per capita income in the prior decade, and population size. The regressions also include fixed effects for census divisions.

The strong negative coefficient on the Gini

coefficient in the scatter plot lines persists into column 1 in the two tables (with 1990 or 1980 controls) for absolute mobility but is not statistically significant for relative mobility (column 4). In both cases, the slope coefficient is much smaller when controls are added; in the relative mobility case, the estimate is so small that it is dwarfed by the standard error. However, columns 2 and 5 indicate that even for relative mobility, the size of the (parental) middle class has a statistically significant positive relationship with children's mobility. And both estimated relationships show up in columns 3 and 6, where the Gini and proportion middle class obtain coefficient estimates significantly different from zero, as does the size of the income share of the richest 1 percent of families in the commuting zone. The latter coefficient is opposite in sign to that of the Gini, even though they are both indicators of inequality; this sign reversal for the top 1 percent income share suggests that while inequality in the lower parts of the CZ income distribution constrains mobility, inequality at the very top does not. The use of 1980 measures (table A3) versus 1990 (table A2) for the control variables makes little difference to the coefficients on the inequality measures.

REFERENCES

Aaronson, Daniel, and Bhashkar Mazumder. 2008. "Intergenerational Economic Mobility in the United States, 1940 to 2000." *Journal of Human Resources* 43(1): 139–72.

Almond, Douglas. 2006. "Is the 1918 Influenza Pandemic Over? Long-Term Effects of in Utero Influenza Exposure in the Post-1940 U.S. Population." *Journal of Political Economy* 114(4): 672–712.

Almond, Douglas, and Janet Currie. 2011a. "Human Capital Development Before Age Five." In *Handbook of Labor Economics*, vol. 4B, edited by David Card and Orley Ashenfelter. Philadelphia, Pa.: Elsevier.

———. 2011b. "Killing Me Softly: The Fetal Origins Hypothesis." *Journal of Economic Perspectives* 25(3): 153–72.

Almond, Douglas, Lena Edlund, Hongbin Li, and Junsen Zhang. 2010. "Long-Term Effects of Early-Life Development: Evidence from the 1959 to 1961 China Famine." In *The Economic Consequences of Demographic Change in East Asia*, NBER-EASE vol. 19. Chicago: University of Chicago Press.

Almond, Douglas, Hilary W. Hoynes, and Diane Whitmore Schanzenbach. 2011. "Inside the War on Poverty: The Impact of Food Stamps on Birth Outcomes." *Review of Economics and Statistics* 93(2): 387–403.

Altonji, Joseph G., and Richard K. Mansfield. 2011. "The Role of Family, School, and Community Characteristics in Inequality in Education and Labor-Market Outcomes." In *Whither Opportunity? Rising Inequality, Schools, and Children's Life Chances*, edited by Greg J. Duncan and Richard J. Murnane. New York: Russell Sage Foundation.

Aud, Susan, William Hussar, Frank Johnson, Grace Kena, Erin Roth, Eileen Manning, Xiaolei Wang, and Jijun Zhang. 2012. *The Condition of Education 2012*. NCES 2012-045. Washington: U.S. Department of Education.

Aud, Susan, Angelina KewalRamani, and Lauren Frohlich. 2011. *America's Youth: Transitions to Adulthood*. NCES 2012-026. Washington: U.S. Department of Education.

Avery, Christopher, Jessica S. Howell, and Lindsay Page. 2014. "A Review of the Role of College Counseling, Coaching, and Mentoring on Students' Postsecondary Outcomes." College Board Research, Research Brief (October). New York: The College Board. Accessed January 3, 2016. http://research.collegeboard.org/sites/default /files/publications/2015/1/college-board -research-brief-role-college-counseling-coach ing-mentoring-postsecondary-outcomes.pdf.

Baker, Bruce D. 2009. "Within-District Resource Allocation and the Marginal Costs of Providing Equal Educational Opportunity: Evidence from Texas and Ohio." *Education Policy Analysis Archives* 17(3): 1–31. Accessed January 3, 2016. http://files.eric.ed.gov/fulltext/EJ83 5083.pdf.

Bailey, Martha J., and Susan M. Dynarski. 2011. "Inequality in Postsecondary Education." In *Whither Opportunity? Rising Inequality, Schools, and Children's Life Chances*, edited by Greg J. Duncan and Richard J. Murnane. New York: Russell Sage Foundation.

Becker, Gary, and Nigel Tomes. 1979. "An Equilibrium Theory of the Distribution of Income and Intergenerational Mobility." *Journal of Political Economy* 87(6): 1153–89.

Belley, Philippe, and Lance Lochner. 2007. "The Changing Role of Family Income and Ability in Determining Educational Achievement." NBER working paper 13527. Cambridge, Mass.: National Bureau of Economic Research.

Bernstein, Jared. 2014. "The Impact of Inequality on Growth." Washington, D.C.: Center for American Progress.

Bettinger, Eric P., Bridget Terry Long, Philip Oreopoulos, and Lisa Sanbonmatsu. 2012. "The Role of Application Assistance and Information in College Decisions: Results from the H&R Block FAFSA Experiment." Quarterly Journal of Economics 127(3): 1205–42.

Bingley, Paul, Miles Corak, and Niels Westergard-Nielsen. 2011. "The Intergenerational Transmission of Employers in Canada and Denmark." IZA discussion paper series no. 5593 (March). Bonn: Institute for the Study of Labor.

Bischoff, Kendra, and Sean F. Reardon. 2014. "Residential Segregation by Income 1970–2009." In Diversity and Disparities: America Enters a New Century, edited by John Logan. New York: Russell Sage Foundation.

Bjorklund, Anders, and Markus Jäntti. 2009. "Intergenerational Income Mobilty and the Role of Family Background." In The Oxford Handbook of Economic Inequality, edited by Wiemer Salverda, Brian Nolan, and Timothy M. Smeeding. Oxford: Oxford University Press.

Black, Sandra E., and Paul J. Devereux. 2011. "Recent Developments in Intergenerational Mobility." In Handbook of Labor Economics, edited by David Card and Orley Ashenfelter. Philadelphia, Pa.: Elsevier.

Black, Sandra E., Paul J. Devereux, and Kjell G. Salvanes. 2007. "From the Cradle to the Labor Market? The Effect of Birth Weight on Adult Outcomes." Quarterly Journal of Economics 122(1): 409–39.

Blanden, Jo. 2013. "Cross-Country Rankings in Intergenerational Mobility: A Comparison of Approaches from Economics and Sociology." Journal of Economic Surveys 27(1): 38–73.

Blanden, Jo, Paul Gregg, and Lindsey Macmillan. 2007. "Accounting for Intergenerational Income Persistence: Noncognitive Skills, Ability, and Education." Economic Journal 117(519) (March): C43-60.

Blanden, Jo, Robert Haveman, Timothy Smeeding, and Kathryn Wilson. 2014. "Intergenerational Mobility in the United States and Great Britain: A Comparative Study of Parent-Child Pathways." Review of Income and Wealth 60(3) (September): 425–49.

Bloome, Deirdre. 2015. "Income Inequality and Intergenerational Income Mobility in the United States." Social Forces 93(3): 1047–80.

Bloome, Dierdre, and Bruce Western. 2011. "Cohort Change and Racial Differences in Educational and Income Mobility." Social Forces 90(2): 375–95.

Brunori, Paolo, Francisco H.G. Ferreira, and Vito Peragine. 2013. "Inequality of Opportunity, Income Inequality and Economic Mobility: Some International Comparisons." Policy Research working paper no. 6304. Washington, D.C.: The World Bank.

Burdick-Will, Julia, Jens Ludwig, Stephen W. Raudenbush, Robert J. Sampson, Lisa Sanbonmatsu, and Patrick Sharkey. 2011. "Converging Evidence on Neighborhood Effects on Children's Test Scores: An Experimental, Quasi-Experimental, and Observational Comparison." In Whither Opportunity? Rising Inequality, Schools, and Children's Life Chances, edited by Greg J. Duncan and Richard J. Murnane. New York: Russell Sage Foundation.

Card, David, and A. Abigail Payne. 2002. "School Finance Reform, the Distribution of School Spending, and the Distribution of Student Test Scores." Journal of Public Economics 83(1): 49–82.

Carrell, Scott, and Bruce Sacerdote. 2013. "Late Interventions Matter Too: The Case of College Coaching in New Hampshire." Cambridge, Mass.: National Bureau of Economic Research.

Case, Anne, Darren Lubotsky, and Christina Paxson. 2002. "Economic Status and Health in Childhood: The Origins of the Gradient." American Economic Review 92(5): 1308–34.

Chadwick, Laura, and Gary Solon. 2002. "Intergenerational Income Mobility Among Daughters." American Economic Review 92(1)(March): 335–44.

Chaudhary, Latika. 2009. "Education Inputs, Student Performance and School Finance Reform in Michigan." Economics of Education Review 28(1): 90–98.

Chetty, Raj, and Nathaniel Hendren. 2015. "The Impacts of Neighborhoods on Intergenerational Mobility: Childhood Exposure Effects and County-Level Estimates." Cambridge, Mass.: Harvard

University. Accessed January 3, 2016. http://scholar.harvard.edu/files/hendren/files/nbhds_paper.pdf?m=1430722623.

Chetty, Raj, Nathaniel Hendren, and Lawrence F. Katz. 2015. "The Effects of Exposure to Better Neighborhoods on Children: New Evidence from the Moving to Opportunity Experiment." *NBER* working paper no. 21156. Cambridge, Mass.: National Bureau of Economic Research.

Chetty, Raj, Nathaniel Hendren, Patrick Kline, and Emmanuel Saez. 2014a. "Where Is the Land of Opportunity? The Geography of Intergenerational Mobility in the United States." *Quarterly Journal of Economics* 129(4): 1553–623.

———. 2014b. "Data from Chetty, Hendren, Kline, and Saez (2014): Descriptive Statistics by County and Commuting Zone." Data downloaded from the Equality of Opportunity Project. Accessed February 2, 2016. http://equality-of-opportunity.org/index.php/data.

Chetty, Raj, Nathaniel Hendren, Patrick Kline, Emmanuel Saez, and Nicholas Turner. 2014. "Is the United States Still a Land of Opportunity? Recent Trends in Intergenerational Mobility." *American Economic Review: Papers and Proceedings* 104(5): 141–47.

Corak, Miles. 2013a. "Inequality from Generation to Generation: The United States in Comparison." In *The Economics of Inequality, Poverty, and Discrimination in the 21st Century*, edited by Robert S. Rycroft. Santa Barbara, Calif.: ABC-CLIO.

———. 2013b. "Income Inequality, Equality of Opportunity, and Intergenerational Mobility" *Journal of Economic Perspectives* 27(3): 79–102.

Corak, Miles, and Patrizio Piraino. 2011. "The Intergenerational Transmission of Employers." *Journal of Labor Economics* 29(1): 37–68.

Cunha, Flavio, and James Heckman. 2007. "The Technology of Skill Formation." *American Economic Review Papers and Proceedings* 97(2): 31–47.

———. 2008. "Formulating, Identifying and Estimating the Technology of Cognitive and Noncognitive Skill Formation." *Journal of Human Resources* 43(4): 738–82.

Cunha, Flavio, James J. Heckman, Lance Lochner, and Dimitriy V. Masterov. 2006. "Interpreting the Evidence on Life Cycle Skill Formation." In *Handbook of the Economics of Education*, edited by Eric Hanushek and Finis Welch, vol. 1. Philadelphia, Pa.: Elsevier.

Cunha, Flavio, James J. Heckman, and Susanne M. Schennach. 2010. "Estimating the Technology of Cognitive and Noncognitive Skill Formation." *Econometrica* 78(3): 883–931.

Currie, Janet. 2011. "Inequality at Birth: Some Causes and Consequences." *American Economic Review: Papers and Proceedings* 101(3): 1–22.

Currie, Janet, and Enrico Moretti. 2007. "Biology as Destiny? Short-and Long-Run Determinants of Intergenerational Transmission of Birth Weight." *Journal of Labor Economics* 25(2): 231–63.

Currie, Janet, and Maya Rossin-Slater. 2015. "Early-Life Origins of Life-Cycle Well-Being: Research and Policy Implications." *Journal of Policy Analysis and Management* 34(1): 208–42.

Dahl, Gordon B., and Lance Lochner. 2012. "The Impact of Family Income on Child Achievement: Evidence from the Earned Income Tax Credit." *American Economic Review* 102(5): 1927–56.

Deming, David. 2009. "Early Childhood Intervention and Life-Cycle Skill Development: Evidence from Head Start." *American Economic Journal: Applied Economics* 1(3): 111–34.

Duncan, Greg. J., Kenneth T. H. Lee, Ariel Kalil, and Kathleen M. Ziol-Guest. 2015. "Parent Income-Based Gaps in Schooling, Earnings and Family Income: Cross-Cohort Trends in the NLSYs and the PSID." Accessed February 2, 2016. http://sites.uci.edu/gduncan/files/2013/06/RSF-Memo-Duncan-et-al-010815.pdf.

Duncombe, William, Phuong Nguyen-Hoang, and John Yinger. 2015. "Measurement of Cost Differentials" In *Handbook of Research in Education and Policy*, edited by Helen F. Ladd and Margaret E. Goertz. New York: Routledge.

Economic Policy Institute. 2011. "Unpaid and Exploited? Examining Interns in the U.S. Labor Market." *EPI* forum and discussion, May 18. Washington, D.C.: Economic Policy Institute. Accessed December 27, 2015. http://www.epi.org/event/unpaid-and-exploited-examining-interns-in-the-u-s-labor-market.

Eisenbrey, Ross. 2012. "Unpaid Internships Hurt Mobility." *Economic Policy Institute* blog post, January 12. Accessed April 7, 2016. http://www.epi.org/blog/unpaid-internships-economic-mobility/.

Ferreira, Francisco H. G., Christoph Lakner, Maria Ana Lugo, and Berk Ozler. 2014. "Inequality of Opportunity and Economic Growth: A Cross-Country Analysis." *Policy Research* working paper no. 6915. Washington, D.C.: The World Bank.

Figlio, David, Jonathan Guryan, Krzysztof Karbownik, and Jeffrey Roth. 2014. "The Effects of Poor Neonatal Health on Children's Cognitive Development."*American Economic Review* 104(12): 3921–55.

Fishkin, Joseph. 2014. *Bottlenecks: A New Theory of Equal Opportunity*. Oxford: Oxford University Press.

———. 2016. "From Subgroups to Bottlenecks: New Directions for the Empirical Study of Intergenerational Mobility: Comments on 'Multiple Barriers to Economic Opportunity in the United States.'" In *Additional Materials. RSF: The Russell Sage Journal of the Social Sciences*, volume 2, issue 2. Available at: http://www.rsfjournal.org.

Fleurbaey, Marc, and Vito Peragine. 2013. "Ex Ante Versus Ex Post Equality of Opportunity." *Economica* vol. 80(317): 118–30.

Fox, Mary Anne, Brooke A. Connolly, and Thomas D. Snyder. 2005. *Youth Indicators 2005: Trends in the Well-Being of American Youth*. NCES 2005-050. Washington: U.S. Department of Education.

Garces, Eliana, Duncan Thomas, and Janet Currie. 2002. "Longer-Term Effects of Head Start." *American Economic Review* 92(4): 999–1012.

Goodman, Joshua. 2008. "Skills, Schools, and Credit Constraints: Evidence from Massachusetts." *Department of Economics* discussion paper series no. 0809-03. New York: Columbia University.

Graham, Bryan, and Patrick Sharkey. 2013. "Mobility and the Metropolis: The Relationship between Inequality in Urban Communities and Economic Mobility." Washington, D.C.: The Pew Charitable Trusts.

Holzer, Harry J. 1988. "Search Method Use by Unemployed Youth" *Journal of Labor Economics* 6(1): 1–20.

Hoxby, Caroline M. 1998. "How Much Does Spending Depend on Family Income? The Historical Origins of the Current School Finance Dilemma." *Papers and Proceedings of the American Economic Association* 88(2): 309–14.

———. 2001. "All School Finance Equalizations Are Not Created Equal." *Quarterly Journal of Economics* 116 (November): 1189–231.

Hoxby, Caroline M., and Christopher Avery. 2013. "'The Missing "One-Offs": The Hidden Supply of High-Achieving, Low Income Students." *Brookings Papers on Economic Activity* (Spring): 1–65.

Hoynes, Hilary W., Douglas L. Miller, and David Simon. 2012. "Income, the Earned Income Tax Credit, and Infant Health." *NBER* working paper no. 18206. Cambridge, Mass.: National Bureau of Economic Research.

Hsieh, Chang-Tai, Eric Hurst, Charles I. Jones, and Peter J. Klenow. 2013. "The Allocation of Talent and U.S. Economic Growth." *NBER* working paper no. 18693. Cambridge, Mass.: National Bureau of Economic Research.

Ionnides, Yannis M., and Linda Datcher Loury. 2004. "Job Information Networks, Neighborhood Effects, and Inequality." *Journal of Economic Literature* 42(4): 1056–93.

Isen, Adam, Maya Rossin-Slater, and Reed Walker. 2014. "Every Breath You Take—Every Dollar You'll Make: The Long-Term Consequences of the Clean Air Act of 1970." *NBER* working paper no. 19858. Cambridge, Mass.: National Bureau of Economic Research.

Jackson, C. Kirabo, Rucker Johnson, and Claudia Persico. 2014. "The Effect of School Finance Reforms on the Distribution of Spending, Academic Achievement, and Adult Outcomes." *NBER* working paper no. 20118. Cambridge, Mass.: National Bureau of Economic Research.

Jacob, Brian A., and Tamara Wilder Linkow. 2011. "Educational Expectations and Attainment." In *Whither Opportunity? Rising Inequality, Schools, and Children's Life Chances*, edited by Greg J. Duncan and Richard J. Murnane. New York: Russell Sage Foundation.

Jäntti, Markus, and Stephen P. Jenkins. 2015. "Income Mobility." In *Handbook of Income Distribution*, edited by Anthony B. Atkinson and François Bourguignon, vol. 2A. Philadelphia, Pa.: Elsevier.

Kaushal, Neeraj, Katherine Magnuson, and Jane Waldfogel. 2011. "How Is Family Income Related to Investments in Children's Learning?" In *Whither Opportunity? Rising Inequality, Schools, and Children's Life Chances*, edited by Greg J. Duncan and Richard J. Murnane. New York: Russell Sage Foundation.

Kena, Grace., Susan Aud, Frank Johnson, Xiaolei Wang, Jujun Zhang, Amy Rathbun, Sidney Wilkinson-Flicker, and Paul Kristapovich. 2014. *The Condition of Education 2014*. NCES 2014-083. Washington: U.S. Department of Education.

Kenworthy, Lane. 2012. "It's Hard to Make It in America: How the United States Stopped Being the Land of Opportunity." *Foreign Affairs* 91(6): 97–109.

Lane, Brett, and Phomdaen Souvanna. 2013. "Mass Math + Science Initiative 2013 High School Impact Study." Boston, Mass.: Institute for Strategic Leadership and Learning.

Lareau, Annette, and Kimberly Goyette. 2014. Preface. In *Choosing Homes, Choosing Schools*. New York: Russell Sage Foundation.

Lee, Chul-In, and Gary Solon. 2009. "Trends in Intergenerational Income Mobility." *Review of Economics and Statistics* 91(4): 766–72.

Levine, David E., and Bhashkar Mazumder. 2007. "The Growing Importance of Family: Evidence from Brothers' Earnings." *Industrial Relations* 46(1): 7–21.

Marrero, Gustavo A., and Juan G. Rodriguez. 2013. "Inequality of Opportunity and Growth." *Journal of Development Economics* 104 (September): 107–22.

Mazumder, Bhashkar. 2011. "Black-White Differences in Intergenerational Economic Mobility in the United States." Working paper no. 2011-10. Chicago: Federal Reserve Bank of Chicago.

Milanovic, Branko. 2015. "Global Inequality of Opportunity: How Much of Our Income Is Determined by Where We Live?" *Review of Economics and Statistics* 97(2): 452–60.

Mitnik, Pablo A., Erin Cumberworth, and David B. Grusky. 2013. "Social Mobility in a High Inequality Regime." Stanford Center for the Study of Poverty and Inequality. Stanford, Calif: Stanford University.

Palardy, Gregory J. 2013. "High School Socioeconomic Segregation and Student Attainment." *American Education Research Journal* 50(4): 714–54.

Putnam, Robert D. 2000. *Bowling Alone: The Collapse and Revival of American Community*. New York: Simon & Schuster.

———. 2015. *Our Kids: The American Dream in Crisis*. New York: Simon & Schuster.

———. 2016. "Social Networks and Geography: Comments on 'How Does Geography Affect Equality of Opportunity.'" In *Additional Materials. RSF: The Russell Sage Journal of the Social Sciences*, volume 2, issue 2. Available at: http://www.rsfjournal.org.

Ramos, Xavier, and Dirk Van de Gaer. 2012. "Empirical Approaches to Inequality of Opportunity: Principles, Measures, and Evidence." *IZA* discussion paper no. 6672. Bonn: Institute for the Study of Labor.

Reardon, Sean F. 2011. "The Widening Academic Achievement Gap Between the Rich and the Poor: New Evidence and Possible Explanations." In *Whither Opportunity? Rising Inequality, Schools, and Children's Life Chances*, edited by Greg J. Duncan and Richard J. Murnane. New York: Russell Sage Foundation.

Roemer, John E. 1993. "A Pragmatic Theory of Responsibility for the Egalitarian Planner." *Philosophy and Public Affairs* 22(2): 144–66.

———. 1998. *Theories of Distributive Justice*. Cambridge, Mass.: Harvard University Press.

Roemer, John E., and Alain Trannoy. Forthcoming. "Equality of Opportunity: Theory and Measurement." *Journal of Economic Literature*.

Sacerdote, Bruce. 2011. "Peer Effects in Education: How Might They Work, How Big Are They and How Much Do We Know Thus Far?" In *Handbook of the Economics of Education*, vol. 3, edited by Eric A Hanushek, Stephen J. Machin, and Ludger Woessmann. Philadelphia, Pa.: Elsevier.

Sampson, Robert J., Patrick Sharkey, and Stephen Raudenbush. 2008. "Durable Effects of Concentrated Disadvantage on Verbal Ability Among African-American Children." *Proceedings of the National Academy of Sciences* 105(3): 845–53.

Smeeding, Timothy M. 2013. "On the Relationship Between Income Inequality and Intergenerational Mobility." *GINI* discussion paper no. 89. Madison: University of Wisconsin. Accessed April 7, 2016. http://gini-research.org/system/uploads/589/original/89.pdf?1385131374.

Solon, Gary. 1999. "Intergenerational Mobility in the Labor Market." In *Handbook of Labor Economics*, edited by Orley Ashenfelter and David Card. Philadelphia, Pa.: Elsevier.

———. 2002. "Cross-Country Difference in Intergenerational Earnings Mobility." *Journal of Economic Perspectives* 16(3): 59–66.

———. 2004. "A Model of Intergenerational Mobility Variation over Time and Place." In *Generational Income Mobility in North America and Europe*, edited by Miles Corak. Cambridge: Cambridge University Press.

U.S. Bureau of Economic Analysis. 2014. "Regional Data: GDP and Personal Income," tables CA1–3 (Personal income summary), CA4 (Personal income and employment summary), CA25 (Total full-time and part-time employment by SIC industry), and CA25N (Total full-time and part-time employment by NAICS industry). Washington: U.S. Government Printing Office. Accessed September 17, 2014. http://bea.gov/itable/iTable.cfm?ReqID=70&step=1#reqid=70&step=1&isuri=1.

U.S. Census Bureau. 2014a. "Selected Measures of Household Income Dispersion: 1967 to 2014." Washington: U.S. Government Printing Office. Accessed December 15, 2014. https://www.census.gov/hhes/www/income/data/historical/inequality/Table%20IE-1.pdf.

———. 2014b. Census tract data accessed via Minnesota Population Center. *National Historical Geographic Information System: Version 2.0*. Minneapolis, Minn.: University of Minnesota. Accessed December 19, 2014. https://nhgis.org/.

———. 2014c. Data from decennial censuses accessed via Minnesota Population Center. *National Historical Geographic Information System: Version 2.0*. Minneapolis, Minn.: University of Minnesota. Accessed August 27, 2014. https://nhgis.org/.

U.S. Department of Labor, Wage and Hour Division. 2010. "Fact Sheet #71: Internship Programs under the Fair Labor Standards Act." Washington: U.S. Government Printing Office. Accessed December 2, 2015. http://www.dol.gov/whd/regs/compliance/whdfs71.pdf.

Urahn, Susan K., Erin Currier, Dana Elliott, Lauren Wechsler, Denise Wilson, and Daniel Colbert. 2012. *Pursuing the American Dream: Economic Mobility Across Generations*. Washington, D.C.: Pew Charitable Trusts.

Wilson, William Julius. 1987. *The Truly Disadvantaged: The Inner City, the Underclass, and Public Policy*. Chicago: University of Chicago Press.

Winship, Scott, and Stephanie Owen. 2013. "Guide to the Brookings Social Genome Model." Washington, D.C.: Brookings Institution.

Perspectives on Inequality and Opportunity from the Survey of Consumer Finances

JANET L. YELLEN

During the past several decades, the United States has experienced its most sustained rise in inequality since the nineteenth century. The U.S. distribution of income and wealth is now wider than in most other advanced countries. To provide a factual basis for further discussion, this paper reviews trends in income and wealth inequality over the past several decades, and then discusses four significant sources of economic opportunity in the United States: the resources available for children in their most formative years, affordable higher education, private business ownership, and inheritances.

Keywords: income, inequality, inherited wealth, United States, wealth

The distribution of income and wealth in the United States has been widening more or less steadily for several decades, to a greater extent than in most advanced countries (Morelli, Smeeding, and Thompson 2015). This trend paused during the Great Recession because of larger wealth losses for those at the top of the distribution and because increased safety-net spending helped offset some income losses for those below the top. But widening inequality resumed in the recovery as the stock market rebounded, wage growth and the healing of the labor market have been slow, and the increase in home prices has not fully restored the housing wealth lost by the large majority of households for which it is their primary asset.

The extent of and continuing increase in inequality in the United States greatly concern me. The past several decades have seen the most sustained rise in inequality since the nineteenth century after more than forty years of narrowing inequality following the Great Depression. By some estimates, income and wealth inequality are near their highest levels in the past hundred years, much higher than the average during that time and probably higher than for much of American history before then (for income inequality, see Atkinson, Piketty, and Saez 2011; for wealth inequality, see Saez and Zucman 2014; for income inequality before 1913, see Lindert and Williamson 2012). It is no secret that the past few decades of widening inequality can be summed up as significant income and wealth gains for those at the very top and stagnant living standards for the majority. I think it is appropriate to ask whether this trend is compatible with values rooted in our nation's history, among them the high value Americans have traditionally placed on equality of opportunity.

Some degree of inequality in income and wealth, of course, would occur even with completely equal opportunity because variations in effort, skill, and luck will produce variations in outcomes. Indeed, some variation in outcomes arguably contributes to economic growth be-

Janet L. Yellen is chair of the Board of Governors of the Federal Reserve System.

This article was presented as the keynote address at the fifty-eighth economic conference at the Federal Reserve Bank of Boston on October 17, 2014. Direct correspondence to: Janet L. Yellen at 20th Street and Constitution Ave. NW, Washington, D.C. 20551.

cause it creates incentives to work hard, get an education, save, invest, and undertake risk. However, to the extent that opportunity itself is enhanced by access to economic resources, inequality of outcomes can exacerbate inequality of opportunity, thereby perpetuating a trend of increasing inequality. Such a link is suggested by the Great Gatsby curve, the finding that, among advanced economies, greater income inequality is associated with diminished intergenerational mobility (Kreuger 2012). In such circumstances, society faces difficult questions of how best to fairly and justly promote equal opportunity. My purpose is not to provide answers to these contentious questions, but rather to provide a factual basis for further discussion. This volume more broadly focuses on equality of economic opportunity and on ways to better promote it.

In this paper, I review trends in income and wealth inequality over the past several decades, then identify and discuss four sources of economic opportunity in America—think of them as building blocks for the gains in income and wealth that most Americans hope are within reach of those who strive for them. The first two are widely recognized as important sources of opportunity: resources available for children and affordable higher education. The second two may come as more of a surprise: business ownership and inheritances. Like most sources of wealth, family ownership of businesses and inheritances are concentrated among households at the top of the distribution. But both of these are less concentrated and more broadly distributed than other forms of wealth, and there is some basis for thinking that they may also play a role in providing economic opportunities to a considerable number of families below the top.

In focusing on these four building blocks, I do not mean to suggest that they account for all economic opportunity, but I do believe they are all significant sources of opportunity for individuals and their families to improve their economic circumstances.

INCOME AND WEALTH INEQUALITY IN THE SURVEY OF CONSUMER FINANCES

I start with the basics about widening inequality, drawing heavily on a trove of data generated by the Federal Reserve's triennial Survey of Consumer Finances (SCF), the latest of which was conducted in 2013 and published in September 2014 (see Bricker et al. 2014).[1] The SCF is broadly consistent with other data that show widening wealth and income inequality over the past several decades, but I use the SCF because it offers the added advantage of specific detail on income, wealth, and debt for each of six thousand households surveyed.[2] This detail from family balance sheets provides a glimpse of the relative access to the four sources of opportunity I discuss.

Although the recent trend of widening income and wealth inequality is clear, the implications for a particular family partly depend on whether that family's living standards are rising as its relative position changes. There have been some times of relative prosperity, where income has grown for most households but inequality has widened because the gains were proportionally larger for those at the top; widening inequality might not be as great a concern if living standards improve for most families. That was the case for much of the 1990s, when real incomes were rising for most households. At other times, however, inequality has widened because income and wealth grew for those at the top and stagnated or fell for others. At still other times, inequality has widened when incomes were falling for most

---

1. In the SCF, questions about assets are based on these values at the time of the survey. Because most interviews were completed between April and December 2013, some of the asset values do not reflect price increases experienced in late 2013, and none reflect increases in 2014. Income questions in the SCF refer to the prior calendar year, so the 2013 survey reports 2012 income. More complete data and documentation pertaining to the SCF is available at the Federal Reserve website (see http://www.federalreserve.gov/econresdata/scf/scf index.htm).

2. *Households* and *families* are used interchangeably in these remarks because the SCF uses both interchangeably to describe its respondents.

Figure 1. Income Share by Income Group

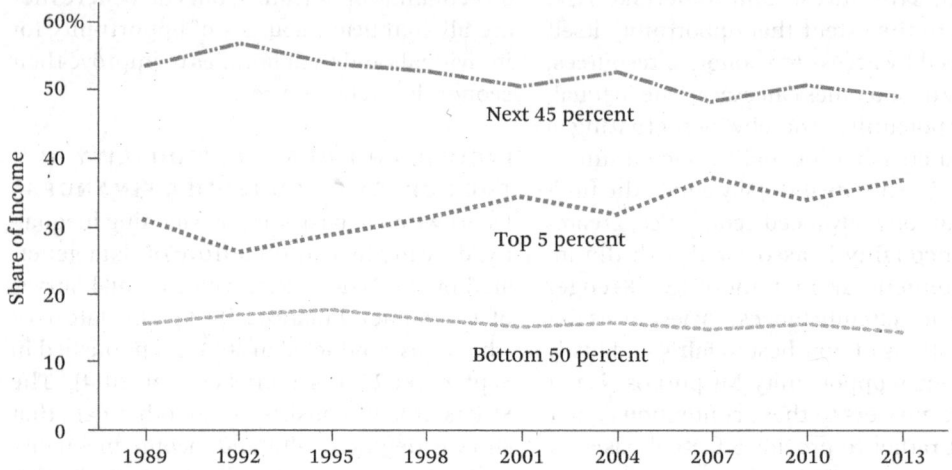

Source: Bricker et al. 2014

Figure 2. Mean Income by Income Group

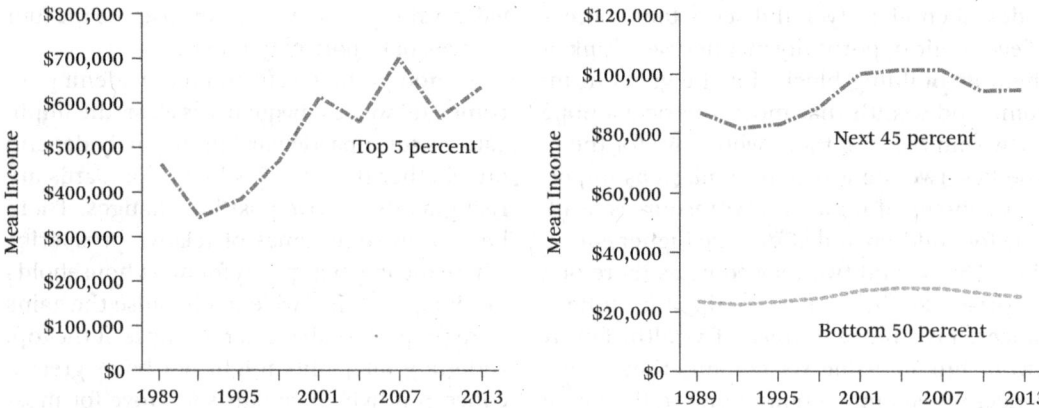

Source: Bricker et al. 2014.
Note: Inflation-adjusted 2013 dollars.

households, but the declines toward the bottom were proportionally larger. Unfortunately, the past several decades of widening inequality has often involved stagnant or falling living standards for many families.

Since the survey began in its current form in 1989, the SCF has shown a rise in the concentration of income in the top few percent of households, as shown in figure 1.[3] By definition, of course, the share of all income held by the rest, the vast majority of households, has fallen by the same amount.[4] This concentra-

3. The share of income that went to the top 5 percent of households—a threshold of $230,000 in gross income in 2013—rose from 31 percent of income reported by all respondents in 1989 to 37 percent in 2007. The income share for this group fell in the financial crisis, to 34 percent in 2010, then rose in the recovery, regaining a 37 percent share in 2013.

4. The top half of the distribution, except for the top 5 percent, earned 53 percent of all income in 1989 but only 51 percent in 2010. In 2013, households in the next 45 percent had incomes between $47,000 and $230,000.

Figure 3. Net Worth Share by Net Worth Group

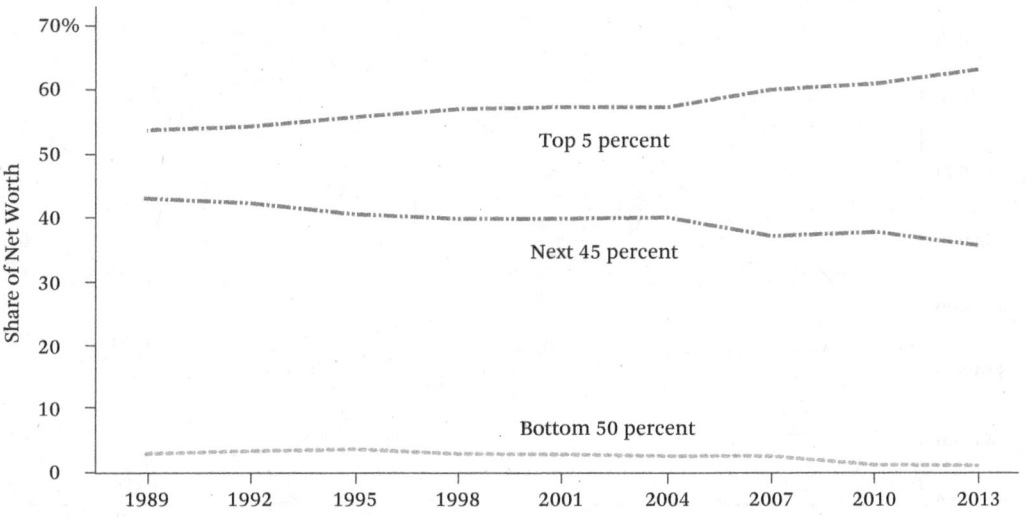

Source: Bricker et al. 2014.

tion was the result of income and living standards rising much more quickly for those at the top. After adjusting for inflation, the average income of the top 5 percent of households grew by 38 percent from 1989 to 2013, as depicted in figure 2. By comparison, the average real income of the other 95 percent of households grew less than 10 percent. Income inequality narrowed slightly during the Great Recession, because income fell more for the top than for others, but resumed widening in the recovery, and by 2013 had nearly returned to the pre-recession peak.[5]

The distribution of wealth is even more unequal than that of income, and the SCF shows that wealth inequality has increased more than income inequality since 1989. As shown in figure 3, the wealthiest 5 percent of American households held 54 percent of all wealth reported in the 1989 survey. Their share rose to 61 percent in 2010 and reached 63 percent in 2013. By contrast, the rest of those in the top half of the wealth distribution—families that in 2013 had a net worth between $81,000 and $1.9 million—held 43 percent of wealth in 1989 and only 36 percent in 2013.

The lower half of households by wealth held just 3 percent of wealth in 1989 and only 1 percent in 2013. To put that in perspective, figure 4 shows that the average net worth of the lower half of the distribution, representing 62 million households, was $11,000 in 2013.[6] About one-fourth of these families reported zero wealth or negative net worth, and a significant fraction of those said they were "underwater" on their home mortgages, owing more than

---

Although income has rebounded for the top 5 percent in the recovery, the share that went to the next 45 percent declined further to 49 percent in 2013. The bottom half of the distribution saw their share of income fall from 16 percent in 1989 to 15 percent in 2007, edge up in 2010, and then reach a new low for the 2013 survey at 14 percent.

5. Largely because of losses in income from financial holdings, the share of total income received by the top 5 percent of households fell 3 percentage points from 2007 to 2010, with the next 45 percent and lower half of households each gaining about half of that share. Some of the nominal income losses for households below the top 5 percent were offset by larger-than-normal transfer payments during the recession.

6. All SCF income and wealth data prior to the 2013 survey are adjusted for inflation by expressing the values in 2013 dollars.

Figure 4. Mean Net Worth for Bottom 50 Percent Net Worth Group

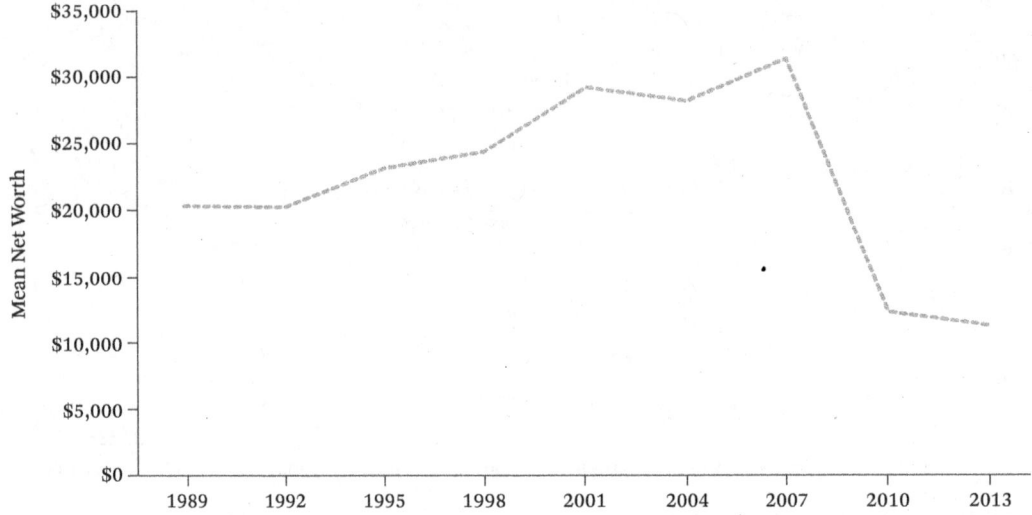

Source: Bricker et al. 2014.
Note: Inflation-adjusted 2013 dollars.

Figure 5. Mean Net Worth by Net Worth Group

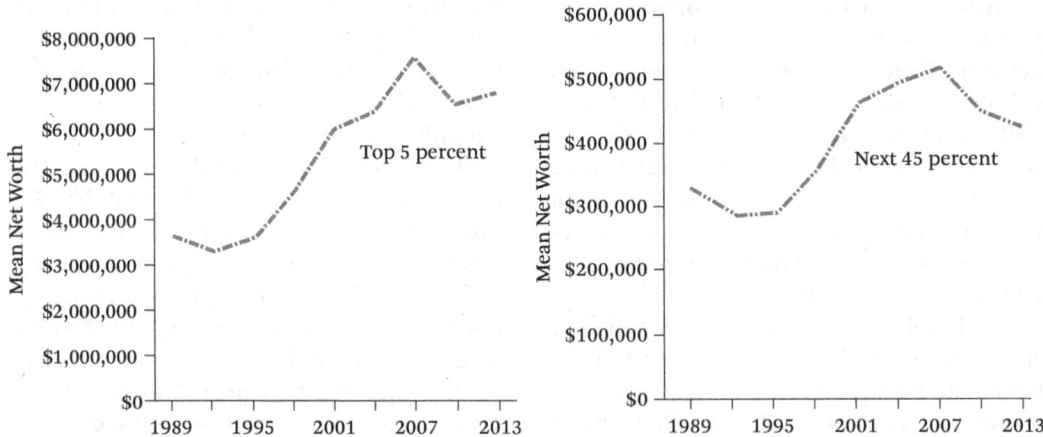

Source: Bricker et al. 2014.
Note: Inflation-adjusted 2013 dollars.

the value of the home.[7] This $11,000 average is 50 percent lower than the average wealth of the lower half of families in 1989, adjusted for inflation. Average real wealth rose gradually for these families for most of those years, then dropped sharply after 2007. Figure 5 shows that average wealth also grew steadily for the next 45 percent of households before the crisis but did not fall nearly as much afterward. Those next 45 percent of households saw their wealth, measured in 2013 dollars, grow from an average of $323,000 in 1989 to $516,000 in 2007 and

---

7. In the 2013 SCF, 17 percent of all families reporting zero or negative net worth also reported they were underwater on their home mortgages.

Figure 6. Homeowners' Equity by Net Worth Group

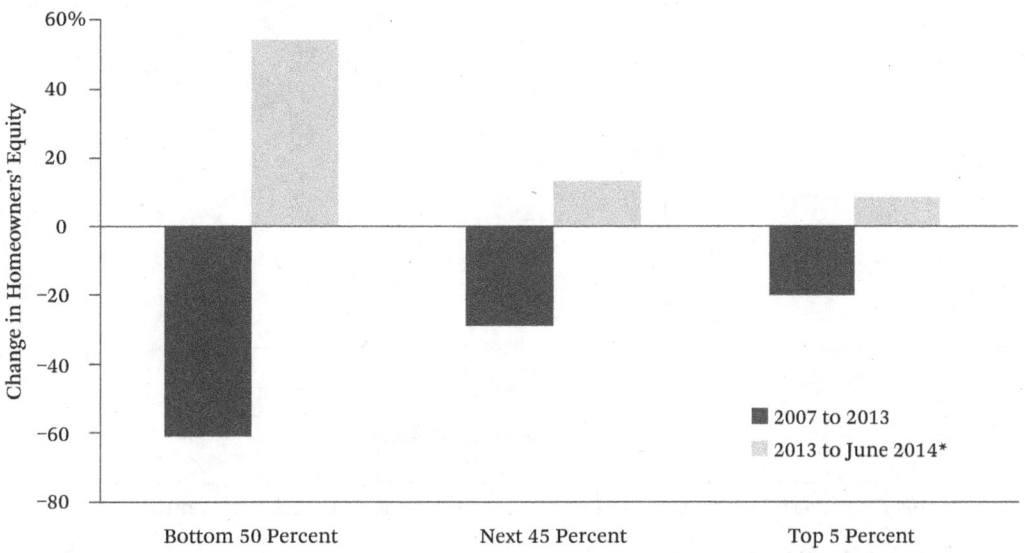

Source: Bricker et al. 2014.
*indicates this estimate is based on projections by staff of the Federal Reserve Board.

then fall to $424,000 in 2013, a net gain of about one-third over twenty-four years. Meanwhile, the average real wealth of families in the top 5 percent has nearly doubled, on net—from $3.6 million in 1989 to $6.8 million in 2013.

Housing wealth—the net equity held by households, consisting of the value of their homes minus their mortgage debt—is the most important source of wealth for all but those at the very top.[8] It accounted for three-fifths of wealth in 2013 for the lower half of families and two-fifths for the next 45 percent, but only one-fifth for the top 5 percent. The share of housing in total net worth for all three groups has not changed much since 1989.

Given that housing accounts for a larger share of wealth for those in the bottom half of the wealth distribution, their overall wealth is affected more by changes in home prices. Furthermore, homeowners in the bottom half have been more highly leveraged on their homes, amplifying this difference. As a result, although the SCF shows that all three groups saw proportionally similar increases and subsequent declines in home prices from 1989 to 2013, the effects on net worth were greater for those in the bottom half of households by wealth. Foreclosures and the dramatic fall in house prices affected many of these families severely, pushing them well down the wealth distribution. Figure 6 shows that homeowners in the bottom half of households by wealth reported 61 percent less home equity in 2013 than in 2007. The next 45 percent reported a 29 percent loss of housing wealth, and the top 5 percent lost 20 percent.

Fortunately, rebounding housing prices in 2013 and 2014 have restored a good deal of the loss in housing wealth, with the largest gains for those toward the bottom. Based on rising home prices alone and not counting possible changes in mortgage debt or other factors, Federal Reserve staff estimate that between 2013 and mid-2014, average home equity rose 49 percent for the lowest half of families by wealth that own homes.[9] The estimated gains are

---

8. Housing wealth includes the net equity in primary residences and other residential real estate.

9. The house price data used are from CoreLogic, and data track price changes at the Core Based Statistical Area level between the survey month in 2013 and June 2014. The average increase in home prices over this period was 8 percent. No adjustments are made to account for possible changes in mortgage leverage.

Figure 7. Share of All Financial Assets by Net Worth Group

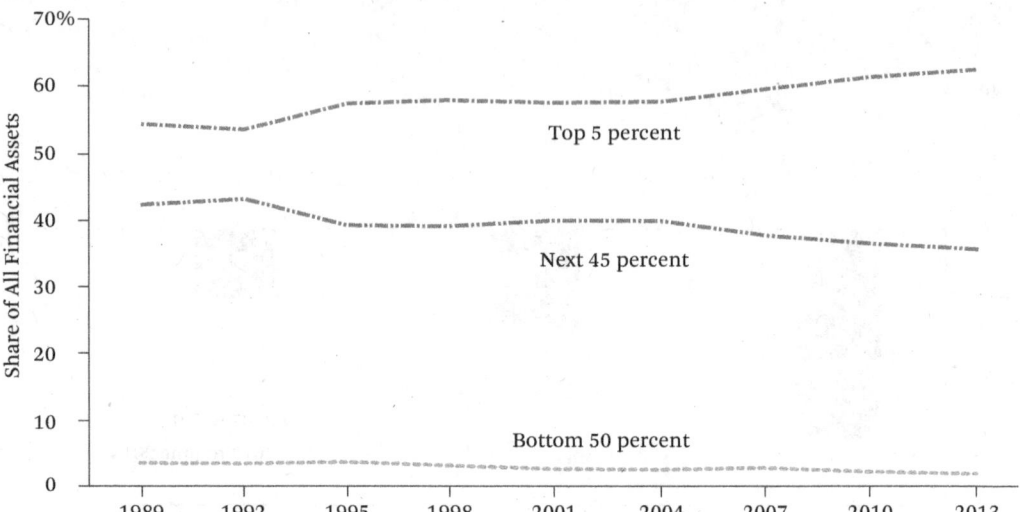

Source: Bricker et al. 2014.

somewhat less for those with greater wealth.[10] Homeowners in the bottom 50 percent, who had an average overall net worth of $25,000 in 2013, would have seen their net worth increase to an average of $33,000 due solely to home price gains since 2013, a 32 percent increase.

Another major source of wealth for many families is financial assets, including stocks, bonds, mutual funds, and private pensions.[11] Figure 7 shows that the wealthiest 5 percent of households held nearly two-thirds of all such assets in 2013, the next 45 percent of families held about one-third, and the bottom half of households, just 2 percent. Note that the distribution of financial wealth has concentrated at the top since 1989 at rates similar to those for overall wealth, as shown in figure 3.[12]

Those are the basics on wealth and income inequality from the SCF. Other research tells us that inequality tends to persist from one generation to the next. For example, one study that divides households by income found that four in ten children raised in families in the lowest-income fifth of households remain in that quintile as adults (see Pew Charitable Trusts 2012). Fewer than one in ten children of families at the bottom later reach the top quintile. The story is flipped for children raised in the highest-income households: when they grow up, four in ten stay at the top and fewer than one in ten fall to the bottom.

Research also indicates that economic mobility in the United States has not changed much in the last several decades; that mobility is lower in the United States than in most other advanced countries; and, as noted earlier, that economic mobility and income inequality among advanced countries are negatively cor-

---

10. Home price gains in 2013 and 2014 are estimated to have raised the home equity of home-owning households in the next 45 percent of households in the wealth distribution by 12 percent, and by 9 percent for home-owning households in the top 5 percent.

11. The SCF defines financial assets as liquid assets, certificates of deposit, directly held pooled investment funds, stocks, bonds, quasi-liquid assets (including retirement accounts), savings bonds, whole life insurance, other managed assets, and other financial assets.

12. In 1989, the top 5 percent of households held 54 percent of financial assets, the next 45 percent (that is, home-owning households in the 50th through 95th percentiles of the wealth distribution) held 42 percent, and the bottom half held 4 percent.

related (see Chetty et al. 2014; see also OECD 2010; Krueger 2012).

FOUR BUILDING BLOCKS OF OPPORTUNITY

An important factor influencing intergenerational mobility and trends in inequality over time is economic opportunity. We can measure overall mobility and inequality, but summarizing opportunity is harder, which is why I focus on some important sources of opportunity—the four building blocks mentioned earlier.

Two of those are so significant that you might call them cornerstones of opportunity, and both are largely related to education. The first of these cornerstones I would describe more fully as "resources available to children in their most formative years." The second is higher education that students and their families can afford.

Two additional sources of opportunity are evident in the SCF. They affect fewer families than the two cornerstones I have just identified, but enough families and to a sufficient extent that I believe they are also important sources of economic opportunity.

The third building block, as shown by the SCF, is ownership of a private business.[13] This usually means ownership and sometimes direct management of a family business. The fourth source of opportunity is inherited wealth. As one would expect, inheritances are concentrated among the wealthiest families, but the SCF indicates they may also play an important role in the opportunities available to others.

Resources Available for Children

In households with children, family resources can pay for things that research shows enhance future earnings and other economic outcomes—homes in safer neighborhoods with good schools, for example, better nutrition and health care, early childhood education, intervention for learning disabilities, travel and other potentially enriching experiences (see, for example, Almond and Currie 2011). Affluent families have significant resources for things that give children economic advantages as adults, and the cited SCF data indicate that many other households have very little to spare for this purpose. These disparities extend to other household characteristics associated with better economic outcomes for offspring, such as homeownership rates, educational attainment of parents, and a stable family structure.[14]

According to the SCF, the gap in wealth between families with children at the bottom and the top of the distribution has been growing steadily over the past twenty-four years, but that pace has accelerated recently. Figure 8 shows that the median wealth for families with children in the lower half of the wealth distribution fell from $13,000 in 2007 to $8,000 in 2013, after adjusting for inflation, a loss of 40 percent.[15] These wealth levels look small alongside the much higher wealth of the next 45 percent of households with children. But these families also saw their median wealth fall dramatically—by one-third in real terms—from $344,000 in 2007 to $229,000 in 2013. The top 5 percent of families with children saw their me-

---

13. Business assets in the SCF include both actively and non-actively managed businesses but do not include ownership of publicly traded stock.

14. Homeownership by parents is strongly associated with economic success for children (see Boehm and Schlottmann 1999). Ninety-seven percent of top-earning families with children own a home, compared with fewer than half of the bottom 50 percent; educational attainment of parents is strongly predictive of outcomes for children that determine earnings (see Douglas-Hall and Chau 2007). A considerable body of literature establishes the correlation between educational attainment of parents and their children. Other research has identified that this relationship is causal (see, for example, Oreopoulos, Page, and Stevens 2006). Eighty-six percent of top-earning households in the SCF with children are headed by a college graduate, compared with 12 percent in the bottom half of households with children; children raised by a single parent earn less as adults (see Powell and Parcel 1997). Only 4 percent of top-earning households with children are headed by unmarried parents, compared with 47 percent for the lower half of households with children.

15. Distributional statistics for families with children are based on a sorting of only families with children.

Figure 8. Median Net Worth for Households with Children by Net Worth Group

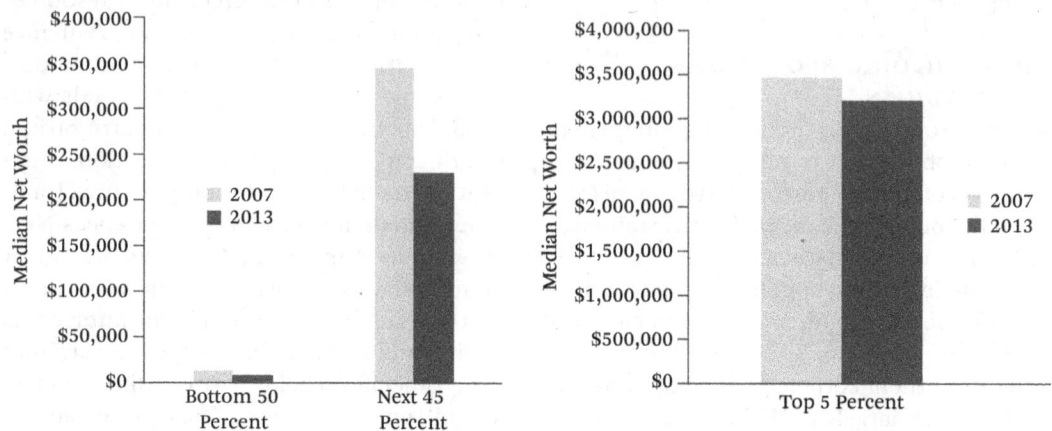

Source: Bricker et al. 2014.
Note: Inflation-adjusted 2013 dollars.

dian wealth fall only 9 percent, from $3.5 million in 2007 to $3.2 million in 2013, after inflation.

For families below the top, public funding plays an important role in providing resources to children that influence future levels of income and wealth. Such funding has the potential to help equalize these resources and the opportunities they confer.

Social safety-net spending is an important form of public funding that helps offset disparities in family resources for children. Spending for income security programs since 1989 and until recently was fairly stable, ranging between 1.2 and 1.7 percent of gross domestic product (GDP), with higher levels in this range related to recessions. However, such spending rose to 2.4 percent of GDP in 2009 and 3 percent in 2010.[16] Researchers estimate that the increase in the poverty rate because of the recession would have been much larger without the effects of income security programs (see Thompson and Smeeding 2013).

Public funding of education is another way governments can help offset the advantages some households have in resources available for children. One of the most consequential examples is early childhood education. Research shows that children from lower-income households who get good-quality prekindergarten education are more likely to graduate from high school and attend college as well as hold a job and have higher earnings, and they are less likely to be incarcerated or receive public assistance (see Heckman et al. 2010, and Belfield et al. 2006). Figure 9 shows that access to quality early childhood education has improved since the 1990s, but it remains limited—41 percent of children were enrolled in state or federally supported programs in 2013. Gains in enrollment have stalled since 2010, as has growth in funding, in both cases because of budget cuts related to the Great Recession. These cuts have reduced per-pupil spending in state-funded programs by 12 percent after inflation, and access to such programs, most of which are limited to lower-income families, varies considerably from state to state and within states, because local funding is often important.[17] In 2010, the United States ranked

---

16. Figures derived from Congressional Budget Office historic budget data. Income security programs include UI, SSI, SNAP EITC, and other family support and nutrition programs.

17. The share of four-year-olds in state-funded pre-K programs increased from 14 percent in 2002 to 27 percent in 2010 but has been 28 percent since. Head Start enrollments have been fairly steady since 2005. Forty-one

Figure 9. Share of Four-Year-Olds Enrolled in Publicly Funded Pre-K

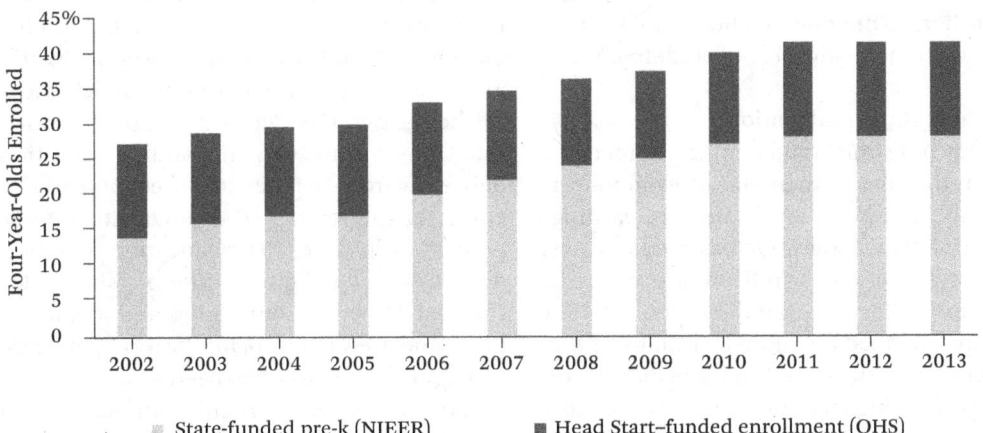

Sources: Annie E. Casey Foundation 2014a; U.S. Census Bureau 2015; Barnett et al. 2013.

twenty-eighth out of thirty-eight advanced countries in the share of four-year-olds enrolled in public or private early childhood education (see OECD 2013b).

Similarly, the quality and the funding levels of public education at the primary and secondary levels vary widely, and this unevenness limits public education's equalizing effect. The United States is one of the few advanced economies in which public education spending is often lower for students in lower-income households than for students in higher-income households (see OECD 2013a). Some countries strive for more or less equal funding, and others actually require higher funding in schools serving students from lower-income families, expressly for the purpose of reducing inequality in resources for children.

A major reason the United States is different is that we are one of the few advanced nations that funds primary and secondary public education mainly through subnational taxation. Half of U.S. public school funding comes from local property taxes, a much higher share than in other advanced countries, and thus the inequalities in housing wealth and income I have described enhance the ability of more-affluent school districts to spend more on public schools. Some states have acted to equalize spending to some extent in recent years, but there is still significant variation among and within states. Even after adjusting for regional differences in costs and student needs, there is wide variation in public school funding in the United States (Education Week 2014).

Spending is not the only determinant of outcomes in public education. Research shows that higher-quality teachers raise the educational attainment and the future earnings of students (see Hanushek 2011; for estimates of the future earnings students gain by having a better teacher, see Chetty, Friedman, and Rockoff 2014). Better-quality teachers can help equalize some of the disadvantages in opportunity faced by students from lower-income households, but here, too, certain forces work against raising teacher quality for these students. Research shows that, for a variety of reasons, including inequality in teacher pay, the best teachers tend to migrate to and concentrate in schools in higher-income areas (see Isenberg et al. 2013; Haycock and Hanushek 2010). Even within districts and in individual schools, where teacher pay is often uniform

---

percent of four-year-olds were enrolled in federally funded Head Start or state-funded pre-K education programs in 2013 (see Barnett et al. 2013; for analysis of Head Start enrollment by age, see Annie E. Casey Foundation 2014b).

based on experience, factors beyond pay tend to lead more-experienced and better-performing teachers to migrate to schools and to classrooms with more-advantaged students.[18]

Affordable Higher Education

For many individuals and families, higher education is the other cornerstone of economic opportunity. The premium in lifetime earnings because of higher education has increased over the past few decades, reflecting greater demand for college-educated workers. By one measure, the median annual earnings of full-time workers with a four-year bachelor's degree are 79 percent higher than the median for those with only a high school diploma (see Baum 2014). The wage premium for a graduate degree is significantly higher than the premium for a college degree. Despite escalating costs for college, the net returns for a degree are high enough that college still offers a considerable economic opportunity to most people.[19]

Along with other data, the SCF shows that most students and their families are having a harder time affording college. College costs have risen much faster than income for the large majority of households since 2001 and have become especially burdensome for households in the bottom half of the earnings distribution.

Rising college costs, the greater numbers of students pursuing higher education, and the recent trends in income and wealth have led to a dramatic increase in student loan debt. Outstanding student loan debt quadrupled from $260 billion in 2004 to $1.1 trillion in 2014. Sorting families by wealth, the SCF shows that the relative burden of education debt has long been higher for families with lower net worth, and that this disparity has grown much wider in the past couple decades. Figure 10 shows that from 1995 to 2013, outstanding education debt grew from 26 percent of average yearly income for the lower half of households to 58 percent of income.[20] The education debt burden was lower and grew a little less sharply for the next 45 percent of families and was much lower and grew not at all for the top 5 percent.[21]

Higher education has been and remains a potent source of economic opportunity in America, but I fear the large and growing burden of paying for it may make it harder for many young people to take advantage of the opportunity higher education offers.

Opportunities to Build Wealth Through Business Ownership

For many people, the opportunity to build a business has long been an important part of the American dream. The SCF shows that ownership of private businesses—in addition to housing and financial assets—is a significant source of wealth and can be a vital source of opportunity for many households to improve their economic circumstances and position in the wealth distribution.

Although business wealth is highly concentrated at the top of the distribution, it also represents a significant component of wealth for some other households.[22] Figure 11 shows that

---

18. Better and more-experienced teachers tend to move to better-resourced schools, including those with more active outside funding, or those with more-advantaged students, such as magnet schools. Even within schools, more-experienced and higher-performing teachers are more likely to teach Advanced Placement classes which tend to serve more-advantaged students. The result is that lower-income and lower-achieving students are more likely to be taught by less experienced and lower-performing teachers (see Clotfelter et al. 2007; Clotfelter, Ladd, and Vigdor 2005; Lankford, Loeb, and Wyckoff 2002).

19. Taking into account the cost of paying for education and years spent in college and not working, economists at the Federal Reserve Bank of New York estimate that the lifetime return to a college degree is 15 percent (see Abel and Deitz 2014).

20. Education debt in the SCF reflects the total amount of debt outstanding at the time of the survey.

21. Education debt-to-income ratio is calculated based on what SCF respondents reported as their usual income. Numbers are for families with education debt.

22. The SCF does not ask households whether they started businesses that closed, so reported business ownership and wealth is largely related only to those businesses that succeed.

Figure 10. Ratio of Mean Education Debt to Mean Income by Net Worth Group (for Families with Education Debt)

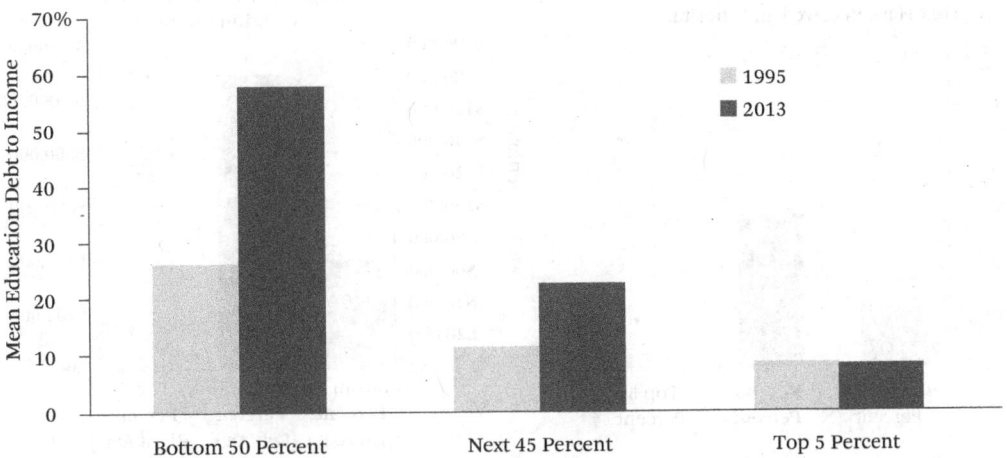

Source: Bricker et al. 2014.

Figure 11. Business Holdings and Values in 2013 by Net Worth Group

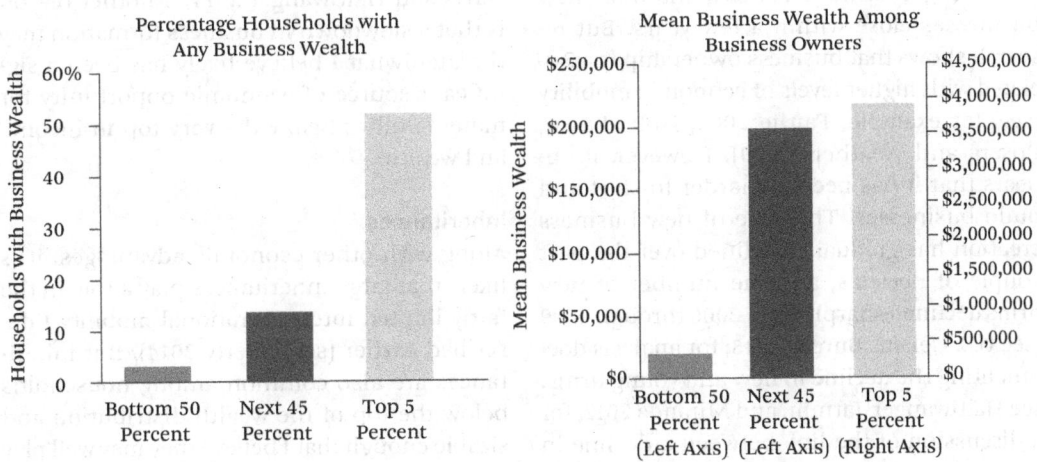

Source: Bricker et al. 2014.

slightly more than half of the top 5 percent of households have a share in a private business. The average value of these holdings is nearly $4 million. Only 14 percent of families in the next 45 percent have ownership in a private business, but for those that do, this type of wealth constitutes a substantial portion of their assets—the average amount of this business equity is nearly $200,000, representing more than one-third of their net worth. Only 3 percent of the bottom half of households hold equity in a private business, but it is a big share of wealth for those few.[23] The average amount of this wealth is close to $20,000, 60

---

23. Distributional statistics for business ownership and assets exclude outliers with large negative net worth.

Figure 12. Inheritance Receipt and Values in 2013 by Net Worth Group

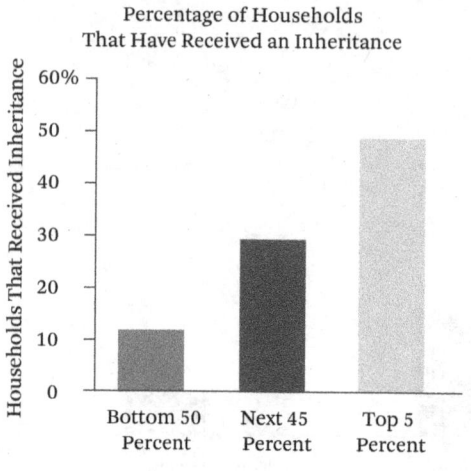
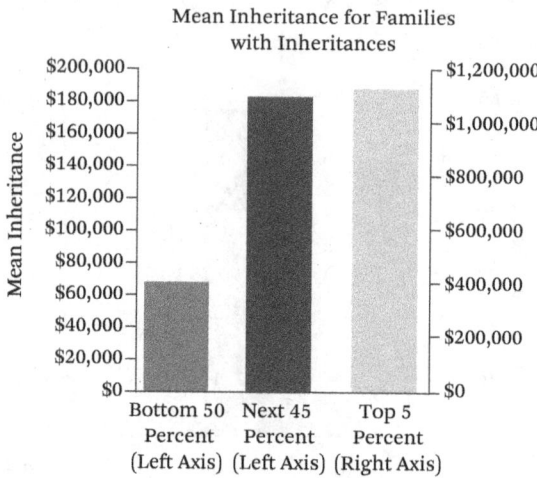

Source: Bricker et al. 2014.

percent of the average net worth for these households.[24]

Owning a business is risky, and most new businesses close within a few years. But research shows that business ownership is associated with higher levels of economic mobility (see, for example, Fairlie 2004; Holtz-Eakin, Rosen, and Weathers 2000). However, it appears that it has become harder to start and build businesses. The pace of new business creation has gradually declined over the past couple of decades, and the number of new firms declined sharply from 2006 through 2009 (see U.S. Census Bureau 2015; for analysis documenting the decline in new and young firms, see Haltiwanger, Jarmin, and Miranda 2012; for a discussion of the link between a decline in young firms and constrained credit access, see Siemer 2014). The latest SCF shows that the percentage of the next 45 percent who own a business has fallen to a twenty-five-year low, and equity in those businesses, adjusted for inflation, is at its lowest point since the mid-1990s. One reason to be concerned about the apparent decline in new business formation is that it may serve to depress the pace of productivity, real wage growth, and employment (see Davis and Haltiwanger 2014). Another reason is that a slowdown in business formation may threaten what I believe likely has been a significant source of economic opportunity for many families below the very top in income and wealth.

Inheritances

Along with other economic advantages, it is likely that large inheritances play a role in the fairly limited intergenerational mobility I described earlier (see Piketty 2014). But inheritances are also common among households below the top of the wealth distribution and sizable enough that I believe they may well play a role in helping these families economically.

Figure 12 shows that half of the top 5 percent of households by wealth reported receiving an inheritance at some time, but a considerable number of others did as well—almost 30 percent of the next 45 percent and 12 percent of the bottom 50 percent. Inheritances are concentrated at the top of the wealth distribu-

---

24. Business wealth took a big hit due to the recession and has only partly recovered for most families. For the bottom half of the distribution, the $20,000 average in business wealth in 2013 was down from $29,000, after adjusting for inflation, in 2007. The nearly $200,000 held by the next 45 percent with businesses was down from $228,000 in 2007. The $4 million in business wealth of the top 5 percent in 2013 was down, in real terms, from $4.4 million in 2007.

tion but less so than total wealth. Just over half of the total value of inheritances went to the top 5 percent and 40 percent went to households in the next 45 percent. Seven percent of inheritances were shared among households in the bottom 50 percent, a group that together held only 1 percent of all wealth in 2013.[25]

The average inheritance reported by those in the top 5 percent who had received them was $1.1 million. That amount dwarfs the $183,000 average among the next 45 percent and the $68,000 reported among the bottom half. But compared with the typical wealth of these households, the additive effect of bequests of this size is significant for the millions of households below the top 5 percent that receive them.

The average age for receiving an inheritance is forty, when many parents are trying to save for and secure the opportunities of higher education for their children, move up to a larger home or one in a better neighborhood, launch a business, switch careers, or perhaps relocate to seek more opportunity. Considering the overall picture of limited resources for most families I have described, I think the effects of inheritances for the sizable minority below the top that receive one are likely a significant source of economic opportunity.

CONCLUSION

These examples only just touch the surface of the important topic of economic opportunity, and other papers in this volume address additional aspects. Research about the causes and implications of inequality is ongoing, and I hope that this volume helps spur further study of economic opportunity and its effects on economic mobility. Using the SCF and other sources, I have offered some observations about how access to four specific sources of opportunity may vary across households, but I cannot offer any conclusions about how much these factors influence income and wealth inequality. I do believe that these are important questions, and I hope that further research will help answer them.

REFERENCES

Abel, Jaison R., and Richard Deitz. 2014. "Do the Benefits of College Still Outweigh the Costs?" *Current Issues in Economics and Finance* 20(3): 1–9. Accessed December 8, 2015. http://www.newyorkfed.org/research/current_issues/ci20-3.pdf.

Administration for Children and Families (ACF). 2014. "Head Start Program Facts Fiscal Year 2013." Washington: U.S. Department of Health and Human Services. Accessed December 8, 2015. http://eclkc.ohs.acf.hhs.gov/hslc/data/factsheets/docs/hs-program-fact-sheet-2013.pdf.

Almond, Douglas, and Janet Currie. 2011. "Human Capital Development before Age Five." In *Handbook of Labor Economics*, vol. 4B, edited by David Card and Orley Ashenfelter. Amsterdam: North Holland.

Annie E. Casey Foundation. 2014a. *2014 KIDS COUNT Data Book*. Baltimore, Md.: The Annie E. Casey Foundation. Accessed January 8, 2016. http://www.aecf.org/m/resourcedoc/aecf-2014kidscountdatabook-2014.pdf.

———. 2014b. "KIDS COUNT Data Center." Baltimore, Md.: The Annie E. Casey Foundation. Accessed January 8, 2016. http://datacenter.kidscount.org.

Atkinson, Anthony B., Thomas Piketty, and Emmanuel Saez. 2011. "Top Incomes in the Long Run of History." *Journal of Economic Literature* 49(1): 3–71.

Barnett, W. Steven, Megan E. Carolan, James H. Squires, and Kirsty Clarke Brown. 2013. *The State of Preschool 2013: State Preschool Yearbook*. New Brunswick, N.J.: National Institute for Early Education Research. Accessed December 8, 2015. http://www.nieer.org/sites/nieer/files/yearbook2013.pdf.

Baum, Sandy. 2014. "Higher Education Earnings Premium: Value, Variation, and Trends." Washington, D.C.: The Urban Institute. Accessed December 8, 2015. http://www.urban.org/UploadedPDF/413033-Higher-Education-Earnings-Premium-Value-Variation-and-Trends.pdf.

Belfield, Clive R., Milagros Nores, Steve Barnett, and Lawrence Schweinhart. 2006. "The High/Scope

---

25. Reported inheritances can have been received at any point in the respondent's life. As with other forms of wealth cited in these remarks, inheritances have been adjusted for inflation and are expressed in 2013 dollars.

Perry Preschool Program: Cost-Benefit Analysis Using Data from the Age-40 Followup." *Journal of Human Resources* 41(1): 162-90.

Boehm, Thomas P., and Alan M. Schlottmann. 1999. "Does Home Ownership by Parents Have an Economic Impact on Their Children?" *Journal of Housing Economics* 8(3): 217-32.

Bricker, Jesse, Lisa J. Dettling, Alice Henriques, Joanne W. Hsu, Kevin B. Moore, John Sabelhaus, Jeffrey Thompson, and Richard A. Windle. 2014. "Changes in U.S. Family Finances from 2010 to 2013: Evidence from the Survey of Consumer Finances." *Federal Reserve Bulletin* 100 (September): 1-41. Accessed December 8, 2015. http://www.federalreserve.gov/pubs/bulletin/2014/articles/scf/scf.htm.

Chetty, Raj, John N. Friedman, and Jonah E. Rockoff. 2014. "Measuring the Impacts of Teachers II: Teacher Value-Added and Student Outcomes in Adulthood." *American Economic Review* 104(9): 2633-79.

Chetty, Raj, Nathaniel Hendren, Patrick Kline, Emmanuel Saez, and Nicholas Turner. 2014. "Is the United States Still a Land of Opportunity? Recent Trends in Intergenerational Mobility." *American Economic Review* 104(5): 141-47.

Clotfelter, Charles T., Helen F. Ladd, and Jacob Vigdor. 2005. "Who Teaches Whom? Race and the Distribution of Novice Teachers." *Economics of Education Review* 24(4): 377-92.

Clotfelter, Charles, Helen F. Ladd, Jacob Vigdor, and Justin Wheeler. 2007. "High Poverty Schools and the Distribution of Teachers and Principals." *North Carolina Law Review* 85(2): 1345-79.

Davis, Steven J., and John Haltiwanger. 2014. "Labor Market Fluidity and Economic Performance." *NBER* working paper no. 20479. Cambridge, Mass.: National Bureau of Economic Research.

Douglas-Hall, Ayana, and Michelle Chau. 2007. "Parents' Low Education Leads to Low Income, Despite Full-Time Employment." Fact Sheet, November. New York: National Center for Children in Poverty. Accessed December 8, 2015. http://www.nccp.org/publications/pub_786.html.

Education Week. 2014. *Quality Counts 2014: District Disruption and Revival*. Bethesda, Md.: Editorial Projects in Education. Accessed December 8, 2015. http://www.edweek.org/ew/toc/2014/01/09/index.html.

Fairlie, Robert W. 2004. "Earnings Growth Among Young Less-Educated Business Owners." *Industrial Relations* 43(3): 634-59.

Haltiwanger, John, Ron Jarmin, and Javier Miranda. 2012. "Where Have All the Young Firms Gone?" Business Dynamics Statistics Briefing. Washington: U.S. Census Bureau. Accessed December 8, 2015. http://www.census.gov/ces/pdf/BDS_StatBrief6_Young_Firms.pdf.

Hanushek, Eric A. 2011. "The Economic Value of Higher Teacher Quality." *Economics of Education Review* 30(3): 466-79.

Haycock, Kati, and Eric A. Hanushek. 2010. "An Effective Teacher in Every Classroom: A Lofty Goal, But How to Do It?" *Education Next* 10(3): 46-52.

Heckman, James J., Seong Hyeok Moon, Rodrigo Pinto, Peter A. Savelyev, and Adam Yavitz. 2010. "The Rate of Return to the HighScope Perry Preschool Program." *Journal of Public Economics* 94 (1-2): 114-28.

Holtz-Eakin, Douglas, Harvey S. Rosen, and Robert Weathers. 2000. "Horatio Alger Meets the Mobility Tables." *Small Business Economics* 14(4): 243-74.

Isenberg, Eric, Jeffrey Max, Philip Gleason, Liz Potamites, Robert Santillano, Heinrich Hock, and Michael Hansen. 2013. *Access to Effective Teaching for Disadvantaged Students*. NCEE Report 2014-4001. Washington: U.S. Department of Education. Accessed December 8, 2015. http://ies.ed.gov/ncee/pubs/20144001/pdf/20144001.pdf.

Krueger, Alan B. 2012. "The Rise and Consequences of Inequality in the United States." Speech delivered at the Center for American Progress. Washington, D.C. (January 12, 2012). Accessed December 8, 2015. http://www.whitehouse.gov/sites/default/files/krueger_cap_speech_final_remarks.pdf.

Lankford, Hamilton, Susanna Loeb, and James Wyckoff. 2002. "Teacher Sorting and the Plight of Urban Schools: A Descriptive Analysis." *Education Evaluation and Policy Analysis* 24(1): 37-62.

Lindert, Peter H., and Jeffrey G. Williamson. 2012. "American Incomes 1774-1860." *NBER* working paper no. 18396. Cambridge, Mass: National Bureau of Economic Research.

Morelli, Salvatore, Timothy Smeeding, and Jeffrey Thompson. 2015. "Post-1970 Trends in Within-Country Inequality and Poverty: Rich and Middle-

Income Countries." In *Handbook of Income Distribution*, vol. 2A, edited by Anthony B. Atkinson and François Bourguignon. Amsterdam: North Holland.

Oreopoulos, Philip, Marianne E. Page, and Ann Huff Stevens. 2006. "The Intergenerational Effects of Compulsory Schooling." *Journal of Labor Economics* 24(4): 729–60.

Organization for Economic Cooperation and Development (OECD). 2010. "A Family Affair: Intergenerational Social Mobility Across OECD Countries." In *Economic Policy Reforms: Going for Growth 2010*. Paris: OECD. Accessed December 8, 2015. http://www.oecd.org/tax/public-finance/chapter%205%20gfg%202010.pdf.

———. 2013a. *Education at a Glance 2013: OECD Indicators*. Paris: OECD. Accessed December 8, 2015. http://dx.doi.org/10.1787/eag-2013-en.

———. 2013b. "How Do Early Childhood Education and Care (ECEC) Policies, Systems and Quality Vary Across OECD Countries?" *Education Indicators in Focus* 11 (February). Paris: OECD. Accessed December 8, 2015. http://www.oecd.org/education/skills-beyond-school/EDIF11.pdf.

Pew Charitable Trusts. 2012. "Pursuing the American Dream: Economic Mobility Across Generations." Washington, D.C.: Pew Charitable Trusts. Accessed December 8, 2015. http://www.pewtrusts.org/~/media/legacy/uploadedfiles/pcs_assets/2012/PursuingAmericanDreampdf.pdf.

Piketty, Thomas. 2014. *Capital in the 21st Century*. Translated by Arthur Goldhammer. Cambridge, Mass.: Harvard University Press.

Powell, Mary Ann, and Toby L. Parcel. 1997. "Effects of Family Structure on the Earnings Attainment Process: Differences by Gender." *Journal of Marriage and Family* 59(2): 419–33.

Saez, Emmanuel, and Gabriel Zucman. 2014. "Wealth Inequality in the United States Since 1913: Evidence from Capitalized Income Tax Data." *NBER* working paper no. 20625. Cambridge, Mass.: National Bureau of Economic Research.

Siemer, Michael. 2014. "Firm Entry and Employment Dynamics in the Great Recession." *Finance and Economics Discussion Series* no. 2014–56. Washington, D.C.: Board of Governors of the Federal Reserve System. Accessed December 8, 2015. http://www.federalreserve.gov/pubs/feds/2014/201456/201456pap.pdf.

Thompson, Jeffrey P., and Timothy M. Smeeding. 2013. "Inequality and Poverty in the United States: The Aftermath of the Great Recession." *Finance and Economics Discussion Series* no. 2013–51. Washington, D.C.: Board of Governors of the Federal Reserve System. Accessed December 8, 2015. http://www.federalreserve.gov/pubs/feds/2013/201351/201351pap.pdf.

U.S. Census Bureau. 2015. "Business Dynamics Statistics." Washington: U.S. Department of Commerce. Accessed December 8, 2015. http://www.census.gov/ces/dataproducts/bds/data.html.

Modeling Equal Opportunity

ISABEL V. SAWHILL AND RICHARD V. REEVES

We examine the themes of equal opportunity, intergenerational mobility, and inequality. We address the normative and definitional questions of selecting measures of mobility and summarize the current state of intergenerational mobility in the United States and abroad. We introduce a new microsimulation model, the Social Genome Model (SGM), which provides a framework for measuring success in each stage of the life cycle. We show how the SGM can be used not only to understand the pathways to the middle class, but also to simulate the impact of policy interventions on rates of mobility.

Keywords: Social Genome Model, mobility, opportunity

The Horatio Alger ideal of upward mobility has a strong grip on the American imagination (Reeves 2014). But recent years have seen growing concern about the distance between the rhetoric of opportunity and the reality of intergenerational mobility trends and patterns.

The related issues of equal opportunity, intergenerational mobility, and inequality have all risen up the agenda, for both scholars and policymakers. A growing literature suggests that the United States has fairly low rates of relative income mobility, by comparison to other countries, but also wide variation within the country. President Barack Obama has described the lack of upward mobility, along with income inequality, as "the defining challenge of our time." Speaker Paul Ryan believes that "the engines of upward mobility have stalled."

But political debates about equality of opportunity and social and economic mobility often provide as much heat as light. Vitally important questions of definition and motivation are often left unanswered. To what extent can "equality of opportunity" be read across from patterns of intergenerational mobility, which measure only outcomes? Is the main concern with absolute mobility (how people fare compared to their parents)—or with relative mobility (how people fare with regard to their peers)? Should the metric for mobility be earnings, income, education, well-being, or some other yardstick? Is the primary concern with upward mobility from the bottom, or with mobility across the spectrum?

In this paper, we discuss the normative and definitional questions that guide the selection of measures intended to capture "equality of opportunity"; briefly summarize the state of knowledge on intergenerational mobility in the United States; describe a new microsimulation model designed to examine the process of

Isabel V. Sawhill and **Richard V. Reeves** are senior fellows in Economic Studies at the Brookings Institution, Washington, D.C. 20036.

The authors thank Katharine Bradbury and Robert Triest for their very helpful comments on an earlier draft. Direct correspondence to: Isabel V. Sawhill at isawhill@brookings.edu, Brookings Institution, 1775 Massachusetts Ave., Washington, D.C. 20036; and Richard V. Reeves at rreeves@brookings.edu, Brookings Institution, 1775 Massachusetts Ave., Washington, D.C. 20036.

mobility—the Social Genome Model (SGM); and how it can be used to frame and measure the process, as well as some preliminary estimates of the simulated impact of policy interventions across different life stages on rates of mobility.

The three steps being taken in mobility research can be described as the what, the why, and the how. First, it is important to establish what the existing patterns and trends in mobility are. Second, to understand why they exist—in other words, to uncover and describe the "transmission mechanisms" between the outcomes of one generation and the next. Third, to consider how to weaken those mechanisms—or, put differently, how to break the cycles of advantage and disadvantage.

CONCEPTS AND DEFINITIONS

Amartya Sen, the Nobel Prize-winning economist, famously argued that since everyone favors equality of one sort or another, the key question is: equality of what (Sen 1979)? In particular, what do we mean by *equality of opportunity*? Assuming we can approximate opportunity in some way, do we really want equality of it, or just more equality than we have right now? And how will we determine the acceptable level? Should we focus on opportunities or outcomes, on intergenerational or intragenerational mobility, on absolute or relative mobility, on incomes or some other measure of adult outcomes?

Opportunities or Outcomes?

First, are we interested in opportunities or outcomes? It hardly needs saying that the two are not the same. Individuals are born with different initial endowments and into different family environments that, in the absence of radical social engineering, constrain or enhance their opportunities. Individual preferences matter as well. An opportunity—say, for a college education—may be equally available to Fred and Bob. If Fred chooses to take up the opportunity and Bob chooses not to, their life outcomes—say, in earnings—may differ too.

Understanding how far inequalities of outcome reflect inequalities of opportunity or merely inequalities of abilities or preferences is, of course, a difficult task. For one thing, we need a robust way to measure whether an opportunity is within an individual's opportunity set. More difficult still, we need a way to determine whether an individual's abilities and preferences—say, to go to college—are a reflection of their background, rather than fixed, individually based attributes.

In short, "perfect" mobility rates—with no statistical association at all between background and outcomes—would be an unreasonable as well as unrealistic goal for a number of reasons. On the other hand, we are a long way from worrying about the problems related to perfect mobility. In our view, it is safe to say that current mobility patterns reflect real differences in substantive opportunities which ought to be tackled.

Intragenerational or Intergenerational?

Individuals will move up and down the income ladder during their own lifetime, especially during the prime working-age years. Typically, incomes will rise during the course of one's career and taper down during retirement. Positive and negative income shocks are also possible along the way, especially from unemployment. The movement of an individual along the income distribution during his or her lifetime is defined as intragenerational mobility.

By contrast, intergenerational mobility compares the outcome of an individual with the outcome of their parents, in terms of rank position, income, or another measure. Typically, the comparison is between the parents' income at midlife and the child's adult income at roughly the same point, say the mid-thirties.

Our focus in this paper is on intergenerational mobility, but we recognize that both are important. The two kinds of mobility are also empirically related: the extent to which parental outcomes influence the adult outcomes of their children will depend in part on the ability of each generation to move up during their lifetimes.

Relative or Absolute Mobility?

A related and important distinction is between relative and absolute mobility. Relative mobility is a measure of how far the income rank of parents influences the income rank of children. A society with high relative mobility is

Figure 1. American Children Whose Family Income Exceeds Parents' Family income

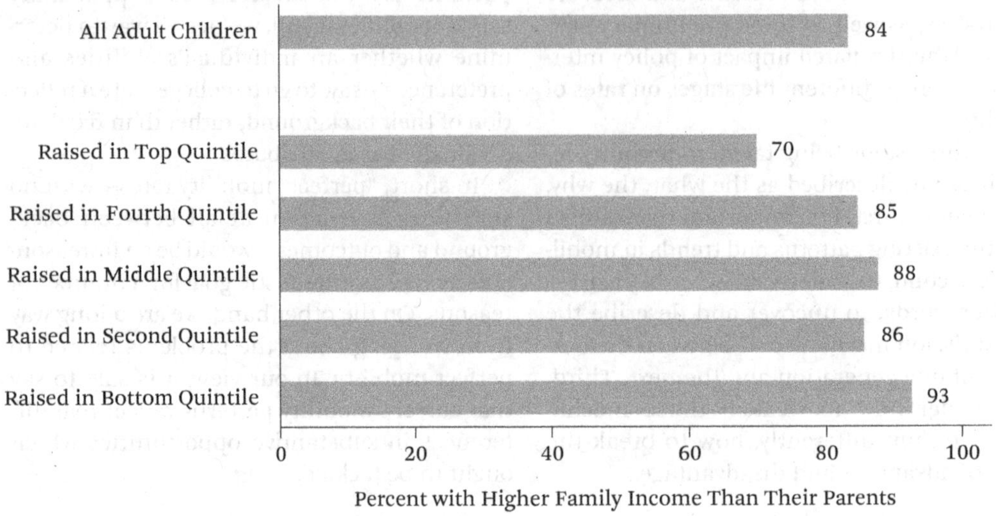

Category	Percent
All Adult Children	84
Raised in Top Quintile	70
Raised in Fourth Quintile	85
Raised in Middle Quintile	88
Raised in Second Quintile	86
Raised in Bottom Quintile	93

Percent with Higher Family Income Than Their Parents

Source: Economic Mobility Project 2012.

one with a limited association between the income rank of parents and the (adult) income rank of their children. By contrast, absolute mobility rates are all about real dollar amounts, rather than rank positions (on the distinction between relative and absolute mobility, see Katharine Bradbury and Robert Triest in this volume).

Most people have been upwardly mobile in the absolute sense: 84 percent of U.S. adults, according to the latest estimates, based on an analysis of the Panel Study of Income Dynamics (PSID) for the Economic Mobility Project at the Pew Charitable Trusts (Economic Mobility Project 2012). Those raised in families toward the bottom of the income distribution are the most likely to overtake their parents' income status, as figure 1 shows.

Of course both kinds of mobility matter, though for somewhat different reasons. One version of the American Dream is of growing prosperity for the overwhelming majority, and this is captured well by absolute mobility rates. The two key drivers here are the rates of economic growth and the distribution of that growth.

In theory at least, it is possible to have a society with high relative mobility but low absolute mobility, or vice versa. In practice, societies will display a different mix. Postwar America, for example, was an engine of absolute mobility, fueled by strong and broadly shared economic growth (Economic Mobility Project 2012). But relative mobility rates remained flat, as we discuss.

Policymakers will likely balance the need to promote both kinds of mobility, and some scholars are exploring innovative ways to combine aspects of both kinds of mobility into a single measure (Genicot and Ray 2013). But it is important to be clear which kind of mobility a particular policy is attempting to improve, so that the efficacy of the policy can be judged against the appropriate benchmark. In the end, most people want both growth and shared prosperity but also fluidity and meritocratic fairness.

Mobility of What?

The array of possibilities here is kaleidoscopic: income, wages, education, well-being, and occupational status. The truth is that all of them matter, and it is instructive to examine mobility patterns in each, and indeed on other dimensions (Graham and Nikolova 2013). An important item on the mobility research agenda is deepening our understanding of the interactions between mobility on these different dimensions. We also need to keep a range of successful outcomes in mind. For instance, a person from an affluent background might receive a great education and choose a career that is stimulating to them, high in status but low in earnings: they become the curator of a small arts museum, perhaps. In income terms, they may be downwardly mobile, but in all the other dimensions they may have risen up the ladder.

It is important to bear this diversity in mind, but at the same time we need to select some concrete dimensions to focus our research efforts. And though achievements on the various dimensions do not go together lock-step, they do cluster together quite strongly. In most cases, education, wages, income, status, and well-being will point in the same direction (Haskins and Sawhill 2009).

We follow most researchers in the field by focusing on income as an outcome and, in particular, on household income. Income is a powerful predictor of other outcomes in terms of health, employment, housing, family formation, and so on. It is also what Joseph Fishkin describes as an "instrumental good"—in other words, one that can be fairly easily converted into other goods, including opportunity-enhancing ones such as education (2014). Income is also easier to measure on a comparable basis than many other constructs.

Because most recent research, including our own, has focused on relative intergenerational income mobility (RIIM), we now briefly review the evidence for this particular measure of opportunity.

RELATIVE INTERGENERATIONAL INCOME MOBILITY: THE EVIDENCE

Taken as a whole, the United States has fairly low rates of RIIM. Rates appear to have been flat for at least the last few decades (Chetty, Hendren, Kline, and Saez 2014). However, there is significant geographical variation within the United States in mobility patterns—as least as much, it seems, as between the United States and other nations (Chetty, Hendren, Kline, Saez, and Turner 2014). These geographical variations are visible both between fairly large areas, such as commuting zones, but also at a smaller, neighborhood level.

There are sharp differences in mobility patterns by race, with African Americans in particular having a much worse mobility pattern than white Americans (Mazumder 2012, 2014). There are modest differences in mobility patterns for women and men, which we do not address here but are examined by a number of scholars (Isaacs, Sawhill, and Haskins 2008).

There are also marked gaps in mobility patterns at different levels of education, as well as for different family structures experienced during childhood. Other papers in this collection provide a detailed picture of these patterns (see articles in this volume by Timothy Smeeding, Katherine Magnuson, Patrick Sharkey, and Eric Rosengren).

Current Overall Picture on Mobility

A standard technique for assessing intergenerational mobility is sorting children and their parents into their respective income distributions and plotting the results. This procedure generates a social mobility transition matrix. Such matrices can then be conditioned to capture differences by individual characteristics, for example, race, gender, education, etc. If a society has "perfect" mobility, then—regardless of conditioning—children whose parents are in the lowest quintile of the parent income distribution are as likely to end up in the lowest quintile of the child income distribution as they are to end up in any other quintile. An alternative approach—developed in particular by the economist Bhashkar Mazumder—is rank directional mobility, which tracks an individual's position on the whole income rank compared to their parents' rank (Bhattacharya and Mazumder 2011).

Still another way to measure the degree of mobility is to estimate the relationship between parental and child incomes or earnings around age thirty-five or forty, a measure referred to as intergenerational elasticity (IGE). It reflects both the correlation between the economic status of parent and child and any change in the distribution of these economic outcomes between the two generations.

In addition, different sources of data can be

Figure 2. Social Mobility Matrix, United States Overall

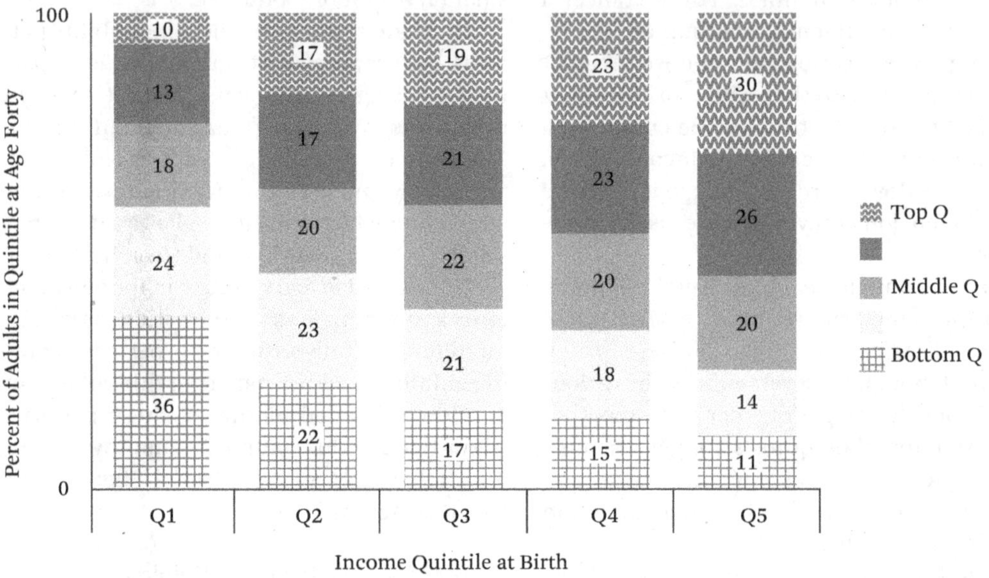

	Q1	Q2	Q3	Q4	Q5
Top Q	10	17	19	23	30
	13	17	21	23	26
Middle Q	18	20	22	20	20
	24	23	21	18	14
Bottom Q	36	22	17	15	11

Y-axis: Percent of Adults in Quintile at Age Forty
X-axis: Income Quintile at Birth

Source: Reeves 2014.

used, including longitudinal surveys such as the PSID or the National Longitudinal Survey of Youth (NLSY), Social Security data, or tax records. Again, each has its strengths and weaknesses (Winship and Owen 2013).

The United States exhibits a high degree of intergenerational income "stickiness," especially at the top and the bottom of the income distribution. Using the dataset constructed from the NLSY79 for the SGM, figure 2 shows that children born to families at the bottom of the income distribution (that is, whose parents' income falls in the bottom quintile) have a 36 percent probability of remaining stuck there in adulthood—far more than the "ideal" 20 percent. Likewise, children on the opposite end of the spectrum have a 30 percent chance of remaining in the highest income quintile. The difference is similarly more than twofold between the odds of a child born in the top quintile ending up in one of the top two quintiles (the "comfortable middle class") as an adult and one born in the bottom quintile (56 percent versus 23 percent). Other studies using different datasets find similar results; most of those using the PSID find lower rates of mobility (Isaacs, Sawhill, and Haskins 2008).

International Variations

Comparing cross-generation trends across countries is inevitably difficult. However, the broad picture that emerges from these comparisons is fairly clear and consistent: within economically developed countries, mobility rates are highest in Scandinavia and lowest in the United States, UK, and Italy, with Australia, Western Europe, and Canada lying somewhere in between. Table 1 provides a list of the most recent, reliable income elasticity coefficients for a range of nations (Blanden 2014).

Given the huge differences on a whole range of factors between nations—not least population size and diversity—these comparisons can only take us so far. It is instructive to look at close neighbors, too, and scholars such as the economist Miles Corak have conducted a number of studies comparing the United States to Canada. Overall, Canadian rates of mobility appear to be higher. One analysis compares intergenerational earnings persistence by earnings decile in the United States and Canada and finds greater persistence in the United States, especially at the top and bottom of the distribution (see figures 3 and 4) (Corak 2010).

Table 1. Preferred Estimates of Income Mobility

Country	Elasticity	Country	Elasticity
Brazil	0.52 (0.011)	New Zealand	0.25 (0.09)
United States	0.341 (0.0004)	Germany	0.24 (.053)
UK	0.37 (0.05)	Sweden	0.24 (0.011)
Italy	0.33 (0.026)	Canada	0.23 (0.01)
France	0.32 (0.045)	Finland	0.20 (.020)
Spain	0.29 (0.03)	Denmark	0.14 (0.004)
Norway	0.25 (0.006)	Japan	0.31 (0.043)
Australia	0.25 (.080)	South Africa	0.48 (0.045)

Source: Blanden 2014.

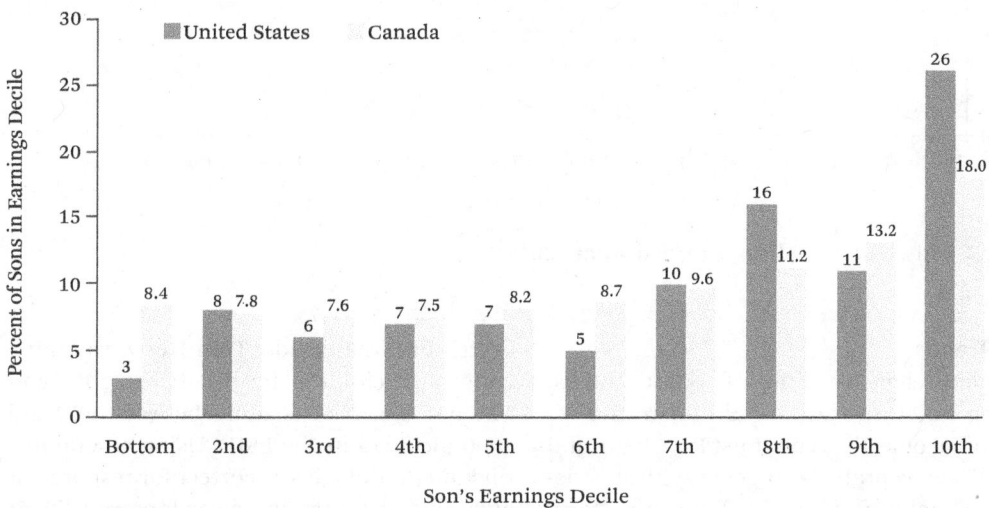

Figure 3. Earnings Decile of Sons Born to Top-Decile Fathers

Source: Corak 2010.

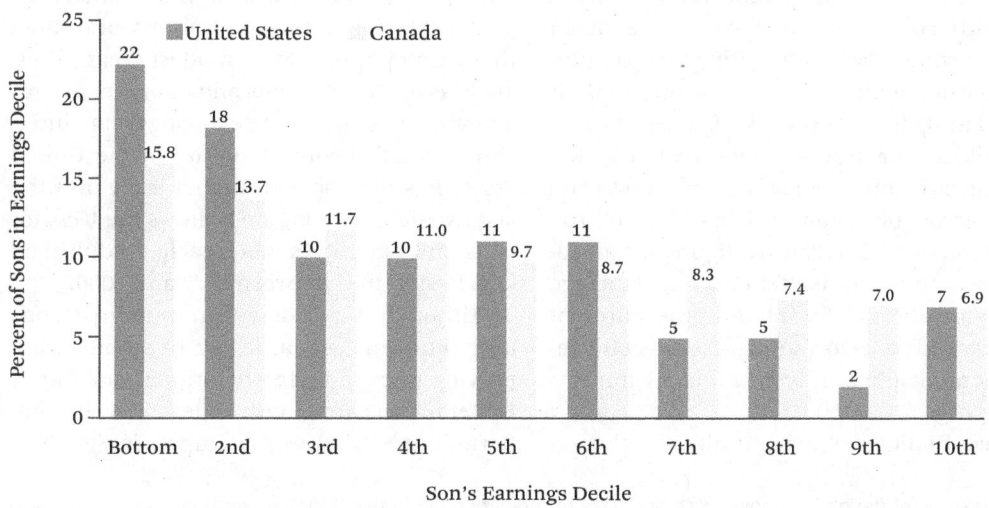

Figure 4. Earnings Decile of Sons born to Bottom-Decile Fathers

Source: Corak 2010.

Figure 5. Intergenerational Mobility Estimates

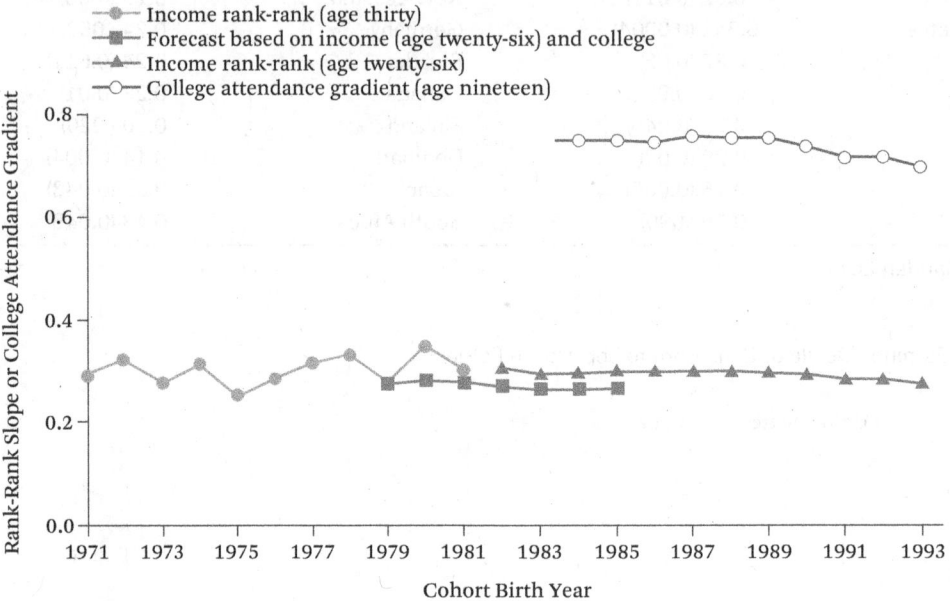

Source: Chetty, Hendren, Kline, Saez, and Turner 2014.

Time Trends

In a comprehensive series of recent studies, making innovative use of administrative records of income, the economist Raj Chetty and his colleagues probe both geographical variations in mobility (see below) and long-term trends. Their conclusion is that RIIM rates are flat (Chetty, Hendren, Kline, and Saez 2014).

Raj Chetty and coauthors estimate a rank-rank specification, each child ranked within their birth cohort according to his or her mean family income at age twenty-nine to thirty, and each set of parents ranked according to their mean family income over the five years when the child is fifteen to nineteen years old. Regressing child rank on parent rank shows "no trend" across birth cohorts (that is, 1971–1974, 1975–1978, or 1979–1982); see figure 5. The authors also use college attendance and college quality as alternative outcome measures of mobility and come to a similar conclusion: "Intergenerational mobility is stable (or improving slightly)."

These findings echo the results of earlier research on time trends. Tom Hertz examined cohorts of children born between 1952 and 1975 and observed as adults between 1977 and 2000 included in the PSID. Using several distinct methodologies to correct for respondent attrition, he found "no clear long-run linear trends in the IGE of family income or family income per person" (Hertz 2007, 46). Chul-In Lee and Gary Solon used the same underlying dataset and come to a similar conclusion (2009). Although data limitations prevented them from ruling out a modest trend, their analysis of IGEs for sons and daughters—they analyze the two separately—suggests "intergenerational income mobility in the United States has not changed dramatically over the last two decades." Figure 6 shows the IGEs for sons and daughters who reached adulthood (age twenty-five) between 1977 and 2000.[1]

Although the evidence on mobility trends over time suggests a degree of stability, improving rates of intergenerational mobility is by definition a long-term endeavor. So it is important to be alert to contemporary signals of

---

1. The results for daughters show some decrease in mobility early in the 1980s, in contrast to the discussed findings, but this result may be anomalous.

Figure 6. Intergenerational Income Elasticities

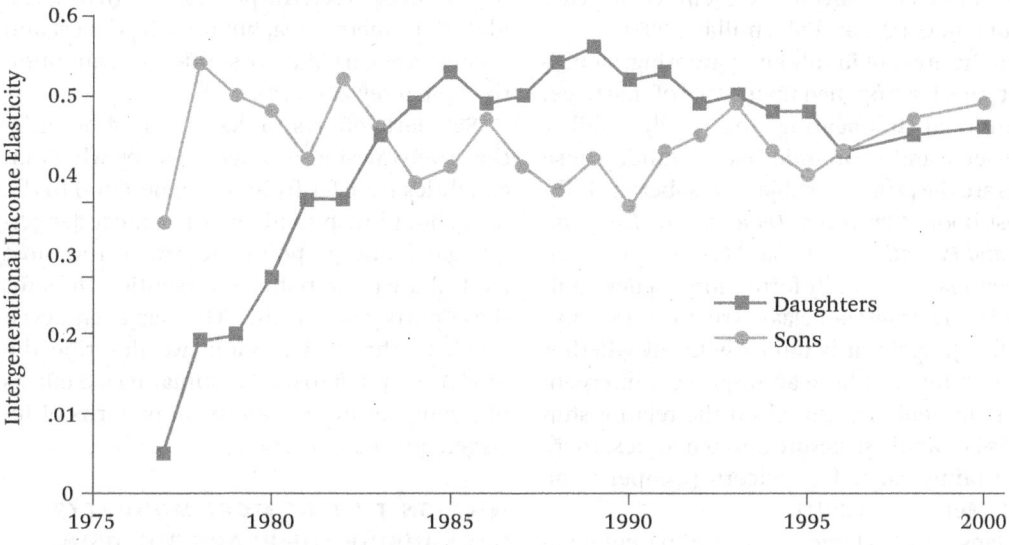

Source: Lee and Solon 2009.

a potential improvement or worsening in mobility rates in the decades ahead. In particular, it is worth looking at growing inequalities in income, educational attainment, family structure and parenting, and by neighborhood. Most of these are covered in other papers in this volume, so our treatment here is brief.

Income inequality has been rising in recent decades. The extent of the rise is strongly determined by the selection of income measure (in particular, the difference between pre-tax and pre-transfer income and post-tax and post-transfer income). There is certainly a strong intuitive claim in the idea of a positive relationship between inequality and immobility, not least because, as Isabel Sawhill has said elsewhere, "when the rungs of the ladder are far apart, it becomes more difficult to climb the ladder.... Inequality in one generation may mean less opportunity for the next generation to get ahead and thus still more inequality in the future" (quoted in Froomkin 2010; quoted also in Krueger 2012).

So far, however, no definitive evidence suggests that rising inequality has led to declining intergenerational mobility (Chetty, Hendren, Kline, and Saez 2014). This could be because the primary driver of income inequality is the gap between the top of the distribution and the majority of the population, which may not influence mobility rates in the population more broadly (Burtless 2014). It is also possible that income inequality has been pulling downwards on mobility rates, but that other forces—such as declining teen pregnancy or crime rates, or rising high school graduation rates—have been pulling in the opposite direction. Or, it could simply be a matter of time.

Some evidence does exist for growing gaps in levels of educational attainment by parental income background, in the early years, through K–12, and into higher education (see articles by Katherine Magnuson, Greg Duncan, and Richard Murnane in this volume; see also Reardon 2011; Bailey and Dynarski 2011). Most of these are covered by other contributors to this collection; suffice for us to say that to the extent that educational attainment predicts adult outcomes, rising gaps by background could, prima facie, result in lower rates of intergenerational mobility. From the perspective of relative mobility, gaps in attainment are of course more important than the overall levels. If higher education rates rise, but rise disproportionately among the affluent, the effects on RIIM are likely to be negative. Evidence is good, for example, that differences in higher educational attainment by income background have had a strong, negative influence on intergenerational mobility in the UK in recent years (Blanden, Gregg, and Macmillan 2007).

In the areas of family and parenting, significant gaps have opened up in rates of marriage, intentional childbearing, and family stability by social and economic background. These gaps are the principal subject of Isabel Sawhill's latest book, *Generation Unbound: Drifting into Sex and Parenthood Without Marriage*, in which she writes that "family formation is a new fault line in the American class structure" (Sawhill 2014, 76). Again, it is too early to say whether these trends will have an impact on intergenerational mobility. But given the relationship between family structure and outcomes, there is certainly cause for concern (Cooper et al. 2011; McLanahan 2011).

Gaps are also large in terms of parental engagement and parenting skills along income, race, and educational axes. Work by the economist James Heckman and colleagues shows that parents provide vital "scaffolding" around the skill development of their children (Cunha and Heckman 2008; Cunha, Heckman, and Schennach 2010). Research by the psychologists Ross Thompson, Ariel Kalil, and others shows how supportive, nurturing parenting styles can blunt the impact of poverty and underpin the development of positive skills and outlook (Kalil 2014; Thompson 2014). Our own research suggests that narrowing parenting gaps would have a positive impact on certain outcomes, including high school graduation rates (Reeves and Howard 2013a).

In addition to growing gaps in income, education, family structure, and parenting, individuals are increasingly sorting themselves into different communities in America. Neighborhoods have become somewhat less segregated along race lines in recent decades, though from high levels, but rates of segregation by economic status have risen (Sharkey 2013a). The sociologist Patrick Sharkey provides suggestive evidence that cities with higher rates of economic segregation have lower rates of intergenerational mobility. As he concludes: "The degree to which the poor live apart from the rich is a more robust predictor of economic mobility than the overall amount of inequality within a metropolitan area. In other words, what matters is not just the size of the gap between the poorest and richest residents of a metro area, but how the richest and poorest are sorted across different communities" (Sharkey 2013b, 1).

Scholarly efforts to discover and describe the "transmission mechanisms" by which inequalities transfer from one generation to the next should help to identify the most dangerous gaps, and so point the way to the most fruitful areas for policy intervention. It is for these purposes that the SGM has been developed. In the next section, we describe the model and put it to work, estimating the effects of a range of interventions on patterns of intergenerational mobility.

WHY ISN'T THERE MORE MOBILITY? A LOOK INSIDE THE BLACK BOX USING THE SOCIAL GENOME MODEL

Much of the literature on intergenerational mobility has relied on a simple mobility matrix or a summary statistic such as the IGE. The most common measure of mobility is the relationship between the income of a parent and the income of the child as an adult. This research literature leaves unanswered a number of important questions that work using the SGM is beginning to address:

1. Is income a sufficient measure of a child's early background and later "success"?
2. Can we fill in the black box and show the pathways to adult success?
3. What might be done to improve social mobility?
4. How do we measure the effectiveness of alternative programs and policies aimed at this goal?

The SGM—originally developed at Brookings and now a partnership between Brookings, the Urban Institute, and Child Trends—is a first attempt to answer such questions.

The Conceptual Framework

The SGM is a life cycle model with five life stages (after circumstances at birth) with a corresponding set of success measures at the end of each life stage, as illustrated in figure 7. A

Figure 7. Stages of the Social Genome Model

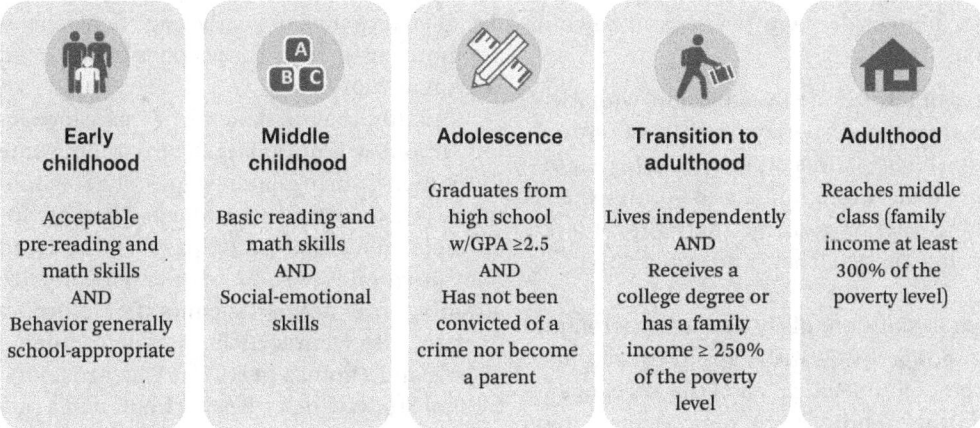

Source: Sawhill and Karpilow 2014.

few brief points are worth making about the construction of the model.

First, the SGM is theoretically motivated by the long literature on human capital formation. Gaps in skills, in particular, help explain mobility patterns. An ongoing debate over the relative contribution of cognitive and "noncognitive" skills (variously labeled grit, persistence, prudence, conscientiousness, and so on) aside, agreement exists that both sets of skills matter, that the two sets are strongly interrelated, and that both are malleable—with noncognitive skills more malleable later, and certainly well into adolescence (Roberts et al. 2007; Heckman, Stixrud, and Urzua 2006).

The SGM includes measures of both cognitive and noncognitive skill acquisition at the end of middle childhood (ages ten to eleven) and at the end of adolescence (ages eighteen to nineteen). We also look at both achievement (for example, test scores, GPA) and attainment (for example, graduation from high school or college). Other measures of skill acquisition could, of course, be added, and factor analysis could be used to hunt for important latent variables (Heckman, Pinto, and Savelyev 2013). New work by James Heckman and others on character or noncognitive skills suggests that self-control (prudence) and persistence (grit) also matter for later success (Reeves and Howard 2013b). Currently, the model includes some direct measures of social-emotional development in childhood, and some rough behavioral proxies for these skills, such as involvement in crime, having a baby as a teenager, or being suspended from school.

Although the model attempts to measure human capital broadly, the core relationship is the one between education and earnings, in the tradition of the economists Gary Becker, Jacob Mincer, and later contributors to the human capital literature. Lessons from that literature include the following:

- The rate of return on education is in the neighborhood of 6 to 10 percent.

- Most of the results from ordinary least squares regressions (finding rates of return of around 6 percent) reflect a causal effect and not an ability bias (the ability bias in such estimates is small and likely compensated for by a bias in the opposite direction due to measurement error) (Card 2001; Ashenfelter and Rouse 1999).

- Rates of return have increased for recent cohorts, probably because of a lag in the response of supply to demand (Goldin and Katz 2008).

- Marginal returns may differ from average returns and depend on who is being targeted by an intervention (Carneiro, Heckman, and Vytlacil 2011).

- The "rate of return to education" is heterogeneous across skill sets, and depends on labor market demand (Owen and Sawhill 2013).
- Rates of return vary by subgroup, with African Americans experiencing higher returns than whites, natives experiencing higher returns than immigrants, and youth experiencing higher returns than the elderly (Henderson, Polachek, and Wang 2011).

Gaps in skills are likely to overlap strongly, though not perfectly, with gaps in educational achievement. Indeed, much of the effect of education on mobility rates may be mediated through cognitive ability, and vice versa. Higher levels of education are clearly associated with significantly higher rates of upward mobility. Children who go on to achieve a college degree regardless of their parents' income are more likely to make it to the top income quintile, whereas those who complete only high school have significantly worse mobility patterns (see paper by Timothy Smeeding in this volume).

Another ongoing debate is over the extent to which skills are heritable, rather than learned. For the purposes of the present discussion, it is enough to endorse Jo Blanden's view that "genes play an important role in generating intergenerational transmissions. But they... are not the whole story" (2014, 20).

Second, the SGM is a dynamic model, allowing changes in one life stage to be passed through to the next. As James Heckman has famously stated, success begets success. The process of human capital formation is cumulative, and rates of return vary with the level of prior skill development. Although the process of human development begins in the home and is greatly influenced by the quality of parenting, the process continues through the school years (Garcia and Heckman 2014). Also, cognitive and noncognitive skills may be complementary. The children in the Perry Preschool Project, for example, did better in high school because the noncognitive skills they acquired early on helped them focus and stay out of trouble. James Heckman calls this capacity-building "self-productivity." It is one reason why the economists Flavio Cunha and James Heckman find that later-stage interventions designed to remediate early-stage deficiencies are more costly than earlier ones (Cunha and Heckman 2008).

Relatedly, the full benefits of early-stage interventions will not materialize without some investment during later stages. The economists Janet Currie and Duncan Thomas, for example, show that participants in the Head Start program lose some of their performance advantage over nonparticipants after returning to their disadvantaged home environments (Currie and Thomas 1995). The Chicago Longitudinal Study, which tracked children in a preschool program, also found that adolescent and adult-stage benefits were greater for children that received extended interventions through sixth grade; later investment helped the children capitalize on earlier investment (Reynolds et al. 2011). As noted in more detail later in this paper, one advantage of the SGM's life-cycle, cumulative approach is that it can capture the effects of sustained intervention throughout childhood and adolescence.

Third, the SGM incorporates multiple social, personal, and economic indicators, as suggested by research evidence, into each life stage. Circumstances at birth provide the most vivid illustration of the need for this multidimensional approach. Parents determine not only a child's genetic endowment but also the early home environment—and this is not merely, or even mostly, a question of income. The literature in sociology that has used a multiple measure of "class" or of various advantages and disadvantages at birth is extensive. Child's birth weight is included as a proxy for prenatal environment, which recent literature suggests can be critical to future development (Glover 2011). Maternal education plays a strong role in the model and gets at some mixture of genetic endowment and home environment. In addition, the model includes direct measures of the quality of parenting using the Home Observation for Measurement of the Environment Revisited (HOME) scale, which scores parents on the level of cognitive stimulation and emotional support they provide to their children. In the SGM, we sometimes use such a multidimensional measure, looking at a child's family income, maternal education, marital status, and weight at birth. At other times, we use conventional measures of family income.

Fourth, although individual earnings are a function of human capital accumulation, broadly defined, they do not, of course, depend only on human capital. Imperfections in the labor market (for example, discrimination or high rates of unemployment induced by a recession) may also determine how much a person can earn. In addition, many unobserved characteristics affect earnings. For these kinds of reasons, the ability of even well-specified earnings equations to explain a lot of the variance in individual earnings is limited.

Fifth, the SGM operationalizes a series of success measures for each life stage. These were selected after a review of the literature on child development and human capital, with particular attention paid to empirical evidence suggesting which measures were predictive of later success. Our other selection criteria were the availability of data on the measure and the advice of experts in the field.[2] Our final success measure is family income at age forty, in particular the proportion who become "middle class by middle age." For our purposes, if an individual's family income at age forty (middle age) is 300 percent or more of the family-size adjusted poverty threshold—roughly $68,000 for a family of four—they have cleared our adult success benchmark. This is necessarily a heavily normative formulation of what defines success. Some scholars prefer a measure of capacities (health and education, for example), or even of adult happiness over a measure of income (Sen 1992). The model could of course be used to explore a wide variety of outcomes: this is the one we have selected for our purpose of examining patterns of intergenerational mobility.

Sixth, the SGM must still be considered a work in progress. A number of improvements, additions, and extensions are currently being worked on or considered, including the following:

- a more detailed structural model for the long and critical life stage between ages ten and nineteen;[3]
- a labor market module based on an earnings function and several identities (relating, for example, income to earned and unearned sources and to the earnings and employment experience of different family members), as well as a series of equations that relate employment and earnings to the state of the labor market; and
- a family formation module, possibly by connecting the SGM to another model, FamilyScape, which is now a partnership between Brookings and Child Trends. FamilyScape models the process of family formation in detail, including the formation of a dyad, whether a couple has sex, whether they use birth control, become pregnant, have an abortion, marry or divorce, and whether a birth occurs and to what kind of parents. By linking the two—or by using the Urban Institute's Dynasim model—it might become possible to create a two-generation model.

Structure of the SGM

With the previously discussed conceptual framework in mind, we turn to a description of the model. The model is structured as a series of regression equations in which outcomes in each life stage are treated as dependent on outcomes in all prior life stages, plus some more contemporaneous variables. More specifically,

$$Outcome = \beta_0 + \beta_1 CAB + \beta_2 Previous\ Stage\ Outcomes + \varepsilon$$

where $\beta 1$ and $\beta 2$ are vectors of coefficients, CAB is the set of *Circumstances at Birth* variables, *Previous Stage Outcomes* is the set of outcomes

---

[2]. Some measures strongly suggested by theory or by other experts were simply not available or were not well measured enough to include in the model. Examples include paternal education and child health outcomes, which were poorly measured in our dataset.

[3]. Child Trends is developing the model, breaking the adolescent stage into multiple more detailed stages, and adding variables that capture additional information on peer relationships and educational progress.

from temporally prior stages (see figure 7), and ε is a random error term.[4] For all variables and equations used in the model, as well as an explanation of the model's structure, see the appendix.

The relationships between variables across life stages were estimated using ordinary least squares regression for continuous outcomes and a linear probability model for dichotomous outcomes. Other functional forms were tried and did not significantly affect the results.

The model tries to capture both the direct and indirect effects, via their effects on intermediate outcomes, of all prior outcomes in a child's life. For this reason, the equations for the later stages often contain many variables. For example, the equation predicting high school graduation contains twenty-five independent variables, representing a core set of demographic variables, measures of a child's birth circumstances (family structure, birth weight, income, maternal education), early childhood outcomes (cognitive and noncognitive), and middle childhood outcomes (cognitive and noncognitive). Because of the nested or recursive structure of the model, the coefficients capture both the direct effect of a variable and its indirect or mediated effect through its impact on some earlier life outcome. For example, the coefficient on school readiness reflects the effects of that variable (or any intervention affecting it) on later outcomes (for example, adult income) due to its effects on some earlier outcome (for example, reading at age ten) but also its effects on some less measurable aspect of a child's development that has a direct effect on incomes even after accounting for all of the intermediate outcomes. These direct effects are sometimes called sleeper effects. Because of this structure, it is possible to explore not only how much early outcomes are correlated with later ones but also through which paths.

Efforts are under way to test alternative specifications that allow for more interactions or better measures of these outcomes and to benchmark the parameters against external research findings from the most sophisticated literature on these topics. Not only does each equation include a different set of variables, but sixteen equations representing the many different outcomes are included in the model (see figure 7). These outcomes, or benchmarks of success, were selected based on a year-long review of the literature, the advice of other experts and practitioners, the availability of data, and sometimes an explicitly normative framing of desirable goals at each life stage (for example, a crime-free adolescence).

Regression models do not, of course, provide causal estimates of the kind of long-term relationships hypothesized in our model. For these reasons, but also because of measurement error and difficult specification issues, we do not want to argue that the model's parameters and any predictions based on them are necessarily correct or that one can make causal inferences based on them. Instead we hope that this fledgling effort to create a framework in which the process of mobility is made more explicit and some data attached to that process will lead to a better understanding of mobility that will encourage others to improve on our efforts.

Data

The SGM is constructed using two data sets from the Bureau of Labor Statistics' National Longitudinal Surveys. Our primary data set is the Children of the NLSY79 (CNLSY). It represents children born mainly in the 1980s and 1990s and is the source of our data for the birth, early and middle childhood, and adolescent stages. No respondent in the CNLSY is yet old enough to track through adulthood, so we impute their adult values with help from a second dataset, NLSY79.[5]

---

[4]. Because of the need to impute data for the two adult stages of the model, the actual specification for these two stages is different than in the case of the childhood stages. For a complete list of the variables used to measure outcomes at each life stage and some of the other control variables used in the model, see Winship and Owen 2013.

[5]. The NLSY79 followed Americans from the generation just before the CNLSY sample. To impute the adult-stage outcomes for the CNLSY respondents, we follow a two-step process. First, we use regression analysis of

The result is a longitudinal dataset in which synthetic individuals, part actual CNLSY data and part imputed data, pass through five life stages from birth to adulthood. This includes 5,783 children from the CNLSY, born between 1971 and 2009.[6]

SOCIAL GENOME MODEL AS A POLICY TOOL

The SGM has a number of advantages as a policy tool for studying social mobility. First, it provides an explicit framework for considering pathways to the middle class (Sawhill, Winship, and Grannis 2012). As noted earlier, the model divides the life cycle into five stages and identifies outcomes in each stage that are predictive of later outcomes and eventual economic success. This framework allows us to assess not only whether children are likely to be successful as adults but also whether they are likely to be successful middle schoolers, adolescents, or young adults. Allowing for these intermediate outcomes and the transitions between them, as the SGM does, is critical to understanding downward and upward mobility; we can test whether and how gaps in success persist or cumulate over time.

Second, although the model relies on certain metrics of success, it allows for flexibility in how success is defined. We currently use a family income of at least 300 percent of poverty by age forty, but other measures could be used. In addition, a user interested in a specific question, such as the proportion of African American children who are reading at grade level by age ten, or the number of poor children who graduate from college, or the number of adolescent boys who have ever been involved with the juvenile justice system, will be able to use the model to answer these and numerous similar questions.

Third, the SGM can take the results of rigorous evaluations of social programs, typically randomized controlled trials (RCTs), and estimate their simulated impact on longer-term outcomes. This allows for the "test driving" of policy experiments without the significant delay and expense of a real-world evaluation. For example, if we know how a preschool program affects school readiness at age five, we can use the SGM to estimate its effects on later outcomes, such as high school graduation rates or adult earnings, without having to wait thirty years and spend millions of dollars on a real-world evaluation of the program.

Fourth, the SGM enables decision-makers to compare the relative predicted effectiveness of different interventions using a standardized metric, such as discounted lifetime income, and then compare those results to the costs of the program. For instance, we show later in this paper that the predicted positive impact on lifetime income of a multistage intervention targeted at children living in families with incomes below 200 percent of the poverty line would more than pay for the intervention. The use of such cost-benefit analyses may lead to more informed decisions on where to invest the marginal dollar of public or philanthropic funds.

Fifth, the SGM can be used to look at the cumulative impacts of intervening not just once but multiple times and in multiple domains over a child's life. By design, many evaluations are limited to quantifying the short-run effect of a single, isolated intervention. But disadvantaged children may need more than a one-time boost whose effects may fade over

---

the NLSY79 to estimate the relationships between birth and adolescent values, and adult outcomes. Then we apply the regression coefficients, which summarize those relationships, to the birth and adolescent values in the CNLSY sample. This plug-in approach gives us predicted adult outcomes for each CNLSY respondent. This assumes that the CNLSY respondents will follow a similar life-trajectory to the older, NLSY79 respondents. As a result, our model does not incorporate possible cohort effects. Both the CNLSY and the NLSY79 also suffer from missingness because of attrition, nonresponse, and data entry error. We use imputation to fill in these gaps.

6. Because the CNLSY children were born to mothers who were living in the United States in 1978, we exclude children who immigrated after 1978, or were born to mothers who immigrated after 1978. Our data and model, then, are best viewed as applying to the entire set of children born to women living in the U.S. Child Trends, in conjunction with Brookings, retooled the model to use data from the 1997 National Longitudinal Survey of Youth (see Moore et al. 2014).

Figure 8. Success at Each Life Stage, Circumstances at Birth

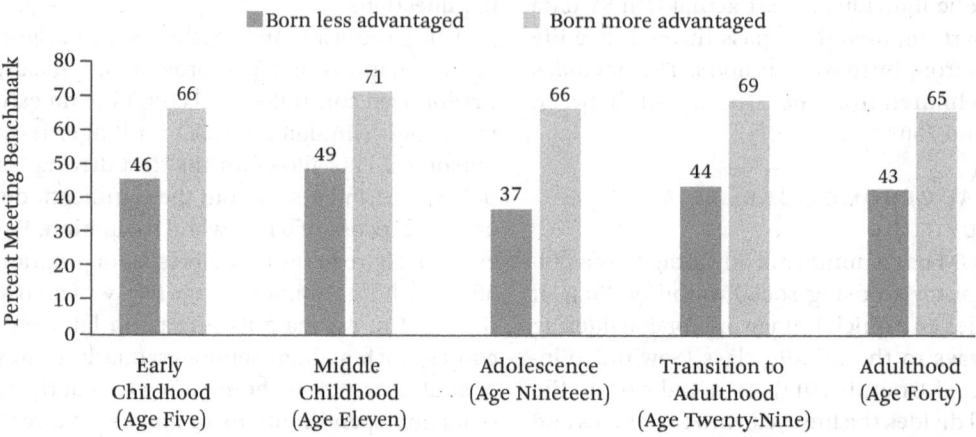

Source: Authors' update to Sawhill, Winship, and Grannis 2012.

time. Perhaps they need a parenting program in infancy, a preschool experience as a toddler, a reading program in elementary school, and so forth (Sawhill and Karpilow 2014). The SGM can be, and—as will be discussed—has already been, used to evaluate such multiple intervention efforts.

Sixth, the SGM allows for examinations of the distributional implications of different policies. For many years, researchers have documented persistent gaps in success between men and women, whites and African Americans, and children of high-income parents and low-income parents. Because the SGM is based on a detailed representation of the demographic and economic characteristics of the U.S. population, it will allow us to measure and monitor these gaps not only at baseline but also after a targeted intervention. For example, we can simulate the predicted effect of a middle childhood education initiative on the black-white gap in success at adulthood.

Finally, the SGM can be used to set research priorities. Where the model's parameters or data are weak (discussed later in this paper), it is usually because insufficient resources have been devoted to collecting the right data or estimating the most important parameters. Currently, in characterizing the birth circum-

stances of children, we rely on data on the mother only, for example, her education attainment, age at child's birth, and so on. Ideally, we would include analogous data on the father, but the NLSY79 does not contain good data on such questions. This is just one example of a research gap that may be worth filling.

Use of the SGM

The SGM has been put to work as a policy tool in several previous papers (see, for instance, Sawhill and Karpilow 2014; Sawhill, Karpilow, and Venator 2014; and Moore et al. 2014).[7] Some of this work has been descriptive and documents how pathways to success vary systematically for different groups of children. Of particular concern, we document a significant and persistent gap between children born into disadvantaged and advantaged circumstances (Sawhill, Winship, and Grannis 2012).

As shown in figure 8, among children born of normal birth weight to married mothers who were not poor and had at least a high school education at the time of their child's birth (advantaged-at-birth), 66 percent can be expected to be ready to start kindergarten, versus only 46 percent otherwise. This gap never narrows—even by the end of adolescence, children who are less advantaged at birth are 29

---

[7]. For a full list, see the Social Genome Project website (http://www.social-genome.org).

Figure 9. Probability of Being On or Off Track

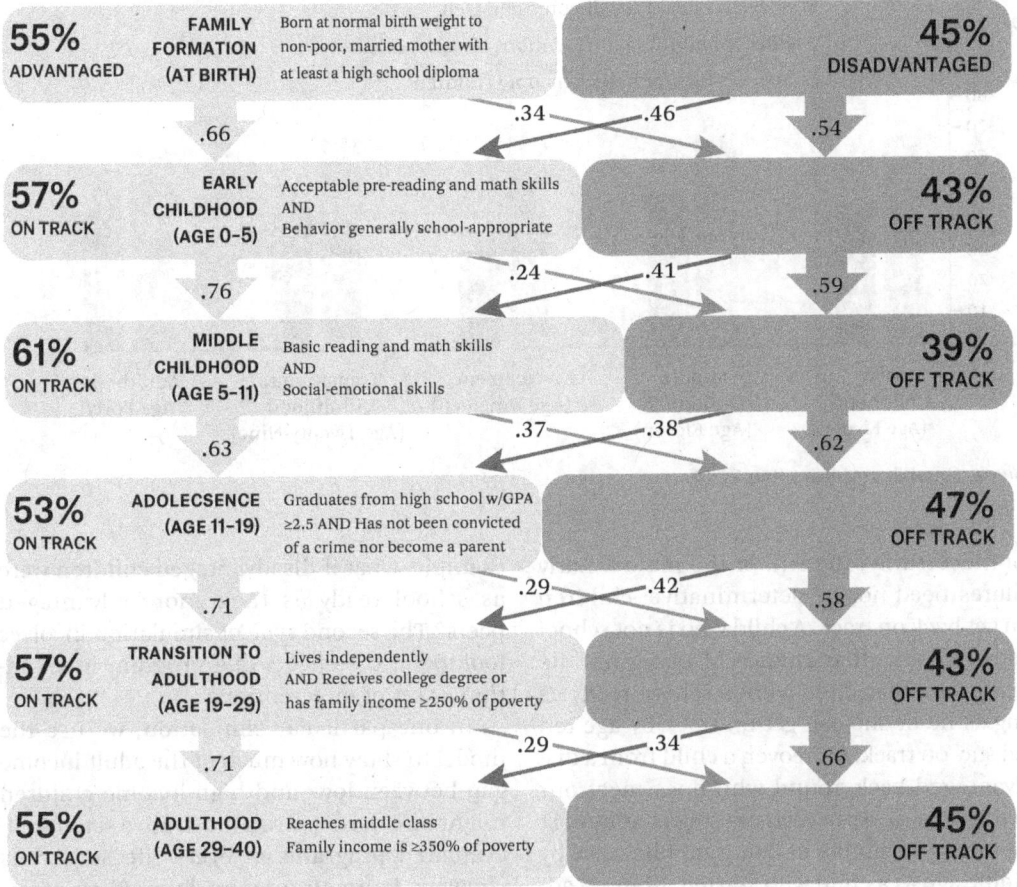

Source: Authors' update to Sawhill, Winship, and Grannis 2012.

percentage points less likely to succeed as adults.[8] At age forty, the gap in the likelihood of being middle class between advantaged-at-birth and disadvantaged-at-birth children is 22 percentage points.

The model also confirms that success begets further success. Not only do children born advantaged retain a large advantage at the end of early childhood, but the pattern also persists in subsequent stages. In middle childhood, adolescence, and adulthood, those who succeeded in the previous stage are much more likely than those who did not to succeed again. For example, we find that 76 percent of children in our sample who are well prepared to start school are able to master basic skills by age eleven, compared with just 41 percent of children who were ill prepared (see figure 9). Acquiring these basic academic and social skills by age eleven further increases a child's chances of completing high school with good grades and risk-free behavior by a similar magnitude—which, in turn, further increases the chances that a young person acquires a college degree or the associated income. Success by age twenty-nine doubles the chances of being middle class by middle age.

Nevertheless, falling off the success track is

---

8. Here, we define success in adulthood as being middle class (income of at least 300 percent of poverty line) by middle age (age forty).

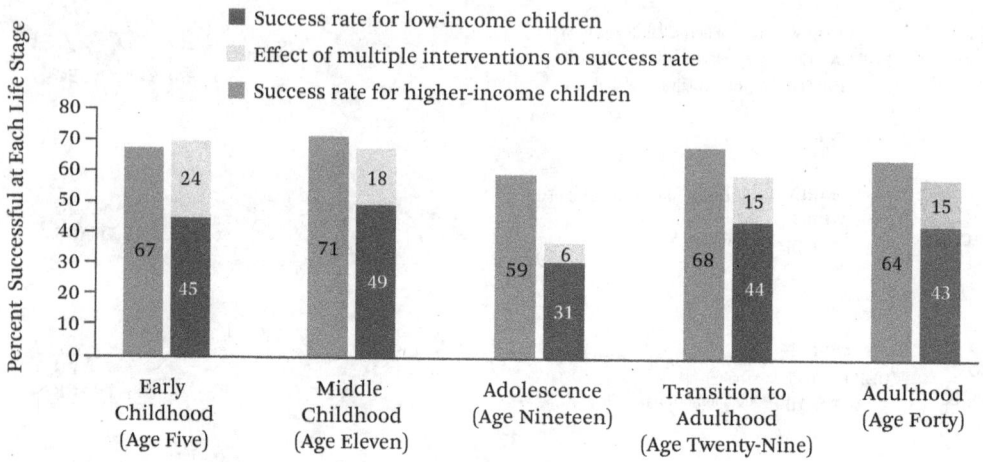

Figure 10. Success at Each Life Stage, Income at Birth

Source: Sawhill and Karpilow 2014.

not (necessarily) the end of the matter. Early failures need not be determinative; children can get back on track. A child who is not school ready has a similar chance of being middle class as another child who is school ready as long as he or she can get on track by age ten and stay on track. Moreover, a child from a disadvantaged background who does meet our metrics of success in each life stage has almost the same probability of being middle class by middle age as a child who started off more advantaged. The problem is that there are relatively few such children. These findings point to the importance of early interventions by government or parents that keep children on the right track.

Beyond these descriptive analyses, we have used the SGM to conduct two types of simulations. The first involves analyzing the effects of changing a particular set of parameters or variables to explore certain what-if questions. For example, what if disadvantaged children were as school ready as their more advantaged peers? The second type of simulation involves looking at the effects of a program intervention or set of interventions.

In one particular simulation, we use the model to show how much of the adult income gap between low- and high-income children might be closed with an illustrative set of well-evaluated programs at every life stage.[9] As shown in figure 10, we model the effects of five interventions targeted on children born to families with incomes less than 200 percent of the federal poverty line by adjusting outcome variables from early childhood to adolescence (see table 2).[10] Although each program has been evaluated independently, their cumulative and long-term impact has not. The program evaluation literature is extensive, but most of this literature only provides estimates of short-term impacts and does not permit

9. We define low-income as family income below 200 percent of the poverty line. High-income is defined as the complement—at least 200 percent of the poverty line (Sawhill and Karpilow 2014).

10. Only children born to families with incomes less than 200 percent of the federal poverty line receive the treatment—they make up the bottom two quintiles and approximately one-third of the middle quintile of the income distribution. This threshold was chosen because it was used as a means test for many of the programs on which we base our simulation. Modifying the targeting threshold (up to a point) does not yield substantively different results. Eliminating targeting completely—that is, allowing all children to reap benefits from each intervention—is inappropriate given that many higher-income children may already benefit from the programs included in our simulation, for example, high-quality preschool.

Table 2. Summary of Postbirth Interventions

Life Stage	Intervention Model	Description	Adjusted Variable	Effect Size
Early childhood	Home Instruction for Parents of Preschool Youngsters (HIPPY)	Biweekly home visits and group meetings to instruct and equip parents to be effective teachers for their children	Reading Hyperactivity	0.75 SD −0.68 SD
	Preschool	High-quality center-based preschool programs that provide educational services to children directly	Reading Math Antisocial Behavior	0.45 SD 0.45 SD −0.20 SD
Middle childhood	Social Emotional Learning (SEL)	Broad range of interventions that focus on improving behavioral, emotional, and relationship competencies	Reading Math	0.36 SD 0.27 SD
	Success for All (SFA)	School-wide reform program with a strong emphasis on early detection and prevention of reading problems	Antisocial Behavior	−0.22 SD
Adolescence	Talent Development (TD)	Comprehensive high school reform initiative aimed at reducing student dropout rates	Reading Math	0.32 SD 0.65 SD

Source: Sawhill and Karpilow 2014.

comparison of different intervention strategies based on their predicted effects on lifetime incomes. Our rationale for pursuing such a simulation is that if we want to see larger and longer lasting effects on adult outcomes, we may have to combine early childhood initiatives with interventions in elementary school, adolescence, and beyond.

The predicted results of intervening early and often are impressive. The baseline 20 percentage point gap in the share of low-income and high-income children reaching middle class by middle age shrinks to 6 percentage points after the multi-stage intervention, as shown in figure 10. When we measure the impact of the same set of interventions, targeted on low-income children, but look at how they affect racial gaps in success rates later in life, the results are less dramatic but still encouraging.[11] White-black gaps in success narrow in every stage of the life cycle, although large disparities still persist, especially in adolescence and adulthood (see figure 11).

These interventions also pass muster under a simple cost-benefit test. Table 3 shows the marginal lifetime income effect of each program, as well as its cost per child. We estimate the total cost per child for all of these programs is just over $20,000. The discounted lifetime income of the average participant in these programs would increase by more than $200,000. Looked at from a society-wide perspective, this much additional income would likely produce sufficient additional revenues

---

11. Again, success here is defined as reaching the middle class by middle age.

Figure 11. Gap in White-Black Success Rate

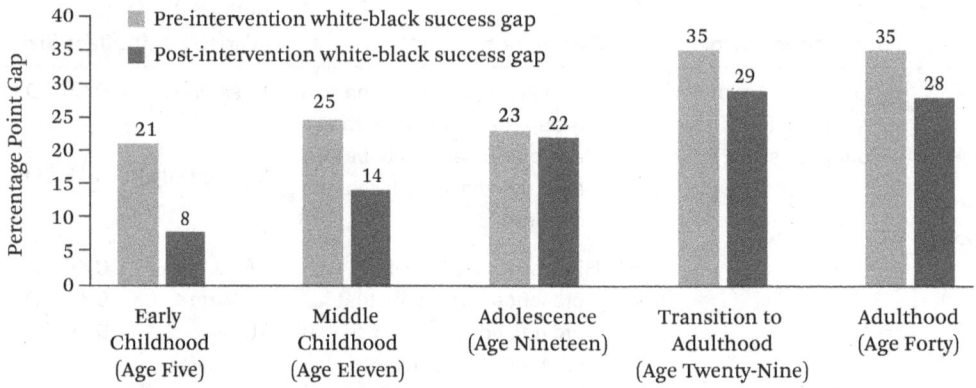

Source: Sawhill and Karpilow 2014.

Table 3. Costs and Estimated Benefits of Simulated Interventions

	Marginal Lifetime Income Effect	Cost per Child
HIPPY (ages three through five)	$43,371	$3,500
Preschool (ages three through five)	$45,651	$8,100
SFA and SEL (ages six through eleven)	$47,594	$8,100
Talent development (ages fourteen through eighteen)	$68,574	$1,400
Total	$205,190	$21,100

Source: Sawhill and Karpilow 2014.

to offset the costs of the programs. We caution once more that these predictions are only that. They are based on a model that is still quite primitive and has many limitations, as detailed in the following section.

Limitations of the SGM

These results suggest the SGM's utility to evaluators and policymakers. That said, the model has certain limitations, reflecting both the availability of data and the state of research in the field.

On the data front, no longitudinal data set follows children from birth to age forty and includes a rich set of variables about their outcomes at each life stage. This has necessitated a significant amount of imputation or simulation of outcomes, which has added to measurement error.

The model also lacks a module devoted explicitly to family formation and childbearing. Although marriage and childbearing are at work behind the scenes of our regressions, an improved model would make these factors explicit. In addition, good measures of childhood health are lacking in our data set.

With respect to the accuracy of the model parameters, the biggest concern is whether the regression coefficients can be considered causal estimates of the effects of different variables on the outcomes being measured. We make no claims to this effect. However, we investigated the reasonableness of the model by looking in particular at whether the returns to education predicted by the model are similar to those in the best external literature and found that they are. On the other hand, when we try to benchmark the model against some of the RCT evidence from long-term follow ups (for example, Perry Preschool), the model tends to underestimate some effects and overestimate others. This is likely due to an insufficiently specified model of child development and the limited variables available in the NLSY79 datasets. But it could also reflect the fact that the Perry Preschool Program was given to a particularly disadvantaged group that has no counterpart in today's environment, in which mothers are more educated and many children receive some form of out-of-home care. More work to benchmark the model against the best evidence available from external research is needed.

The Social Genome Model: Lessons and Next Steps

The SGM provides a tool for learning more about how—and why—a child's circumstances at birth are related to his or her eventual success in life, including adult incomes. It can also be used to simulate the potential effects of a variety of interventions designed to help less advantaged children climb the ladder. We find it encouraging that a set of well-evaluated programs appear, according to the current model at least, to make it possible to close a substantial portion of the gap in the lifetime incomes between children born into lower- and higher-income families. We stress, however, that the predicted effects do not represent causal estimates. The only way to get truly causal estimates is to do a RCT over thirty to forty years. This approach has three disadvantages. First, it bypasses an entire cohort of children while one waits for the results. Second, it assumes that the impacts of an intervention on today's children are the same as those found for a much earlier cohort of children growing up in a different historical period. Third, it does not permit one to aggregate the results of different evidence-based policies in one consistent framework or model. We believe a model-based prediction of the likely effects of multiple interventions in different life stages is better than nothing. We further believe that research is an evolutionary or cumulative process. The question is whether others in the field will find these predicted effects of some interest and whether this will catalyze new efforts to find better sources of data and more adequate models that better capture the complexity of childhood development and the potential of various interventions to change childhood trajectories. The current model has many inadequacies but it will take years, and the efforts of many different researchers, to improve on the kind of data and modeling that we hope will undergird the policy choices of the future.

CONCLUSION

The issue of intergenerational mobility is likely to be on the public agenda for the foreseeable future, especially against a background of weak growth rates in the economy and in median earnings and rising income inequality. In recent years, scholars have made considerable progress in describing the patterns of mobility in the United States. The main challenges now are to increase our understanding of the transmission mechanisms between the status of one generation and the next and to develop a policy agenda for promoting greater mobility.

APPENDIX

As explained, the Social Genome Model is a recursive set of equations of the form:

$$Outcome = \beta_0 + \beta_1 CAB + \beta_2 Previous\ Stage\ Outcomes + \varepsilon$$

The variables included and their definitions are presented in table A1, the regression coefficients in tables A2 through A4. As an example, take the equation predicting reading ability by age nine or ten:

$$mcRead = -0.199 + .039 gender - .220 black + .017 hispanic - .083 otherRace + .062 matEd2 + .125 matEd3 + .128 matEd4 - .005 cabMatAge + .005 cabMatAge1 - 0.021 cabMarried - .007 cabLbw + .037 cabFamIncFpl + .067 cabPpvt + .003 cabParEmoSup + .015 cabParCogStim + .004 cabMomAfqt + .111 ecMath + .360 ecRead + .016 ecAnti + .067 ecHyper$$

The variables at earlier stages work directly and indirectly to affect middle childhood reading. (The indirect effects cannot be read directly from the regression coefficients but can be calculated.) The predicted effect of early childhood reading on reading in middle childhood is substantial, even after controlling for a large number of background variables and other measures of early childhood readiness for school. To be exact, 1 standard deviation improvement in early childhood reading scores predicts a 0.36 standard deviation improvement in individual middle childhood reading scores.

To fully appreciate the way in which these regression coefficients are used it is important to understand the simulation process. As explained in greater detail in the *Guide to the Social Genome Model*, a number of steps are taken when doing a simulation. Briefly,

> We first take the effect sizes from a rigorous evaluation and apply them to the appropriate target population and relevant independent variable or variables in our model.
>
> We then compare a baseline run of the model with a postintervention run of the model in which, say, an enhanced reading score is allowed to affect subsequent outcomes. Because the predicted effect on later outcomes such as educational attainment or income are the difference between a preintervention baseline run and a postintervention run of the model, errors in the levels of the variables cancel out. However, the coefficients that are used to propagate an initial experimentally estimated effect size (for example, a change in reading scores) through the remainder of the model could be biased because the parameters used to predict later outcomes are estimated using conventional multivariate regression techniques. Most of the variables we shift as the result of an intervention are either an educational achievement or attainment variable. That fact led us to worry most about whether our coefficients were a biased estimate of the effect of some measure of education on earnings. The best external research suggests that the conventional regression-estimated effect of education on earnings does not include a lot of bias and that what bias exists may be compensated for by measurement error (see, for example, Ashenfelter and Rouse 1999). Our model predicts roughly a 7 percent rate of return on years of education.

The coefficients in tables A2 through A4 need to be interpreted with caution. They are used only to update an individual child's characteristics after an intervention has shifted one or more of that child's characteristics. As is typical in all large microsimulation models, the updating is done iteratively within the model *at the level of an individual observation with adjustment for individual errors postsimulation*. Given the iterative or recursive nature of the model, many of the individual coefficients are not readily interpretable because they work through multiple channels to affect a predicted value downstream from the intervention, typically with attenuated effects. In addition, given the large number of control variables in the model, many turn out to be insignificant and noisy. To understand the way in which they are used you need to fully understand the simulation process. Here, in a little more detail, is how it works (as explained in the technical guide to the model).

The Model's Structure

SGM predicts the thirty-three outcomes from early childhood through adulthood listed in table A1. Through adolescence, it does so using the *Circumstances at Birth* variables in table A1 plus all outcomes from intervening stages. So, for example, if we were predicting high school graduation, one of the outcomes in adolescence, the regression equation would include all of the *CAB* variables and all of the outcomes in early childhood (EC) and middle childhood (MC). The equation we estimate for each outcome through adolescence (*ADOL*) is as follows:

$$Outcome = \beta_0 + \beta_1 CAB + \beta_2 Previous\ Stage\ Outcomes + \varepsilon \quad \text{Equation 1}$$

where β_1 and β_2 are vectors of coefficients, *CAB* is the set of *Circumstances at Birth* variables in table A1, *Previous Stage Outcomes* is the set of outcomes from temporally prior stages, and ε is the error term containing unobserved characteristics.

Beginning with *Transition to Adulthood* (*TTA*) outcomes, however, we must estimate different equations because of our reliance on NLSY79-

based imputations for measures in *TTA* and in adulthood. We are limited to predictor variables that are common to both datasets, which come from the *CAB* and *ADOL* stages. For *TTA* outcomes, we estimate using this calculation:

$$TTA\ Outcome = \beta_0 + \beta_1 CAB^* + \beta_2 ADOL + \varepsilon \quad \text{Equation 2}$$

where the asterisk following *CAB* indicates the subset of *CAB* variables available in the NLSY79 and where *ADOL* is the set of adolescent outcomes.[12] For adulthood income, we estimate using this calculation:

$$Adult\ Income = \beta_0 + \beta_1 CAB^* + \beta_2 ADOL + \beta_3 TTA + \varepsilon \quad \text{Equation 3}$$

where *TTA* is the set of *Transition to Adulthood* outcomes. EC and MC outcomes cannot directly affect *TTA* outcomes and adulthood income in these specifications, though they may indirectly affect them through the *ADOL* variables. The SGM may be shown in graphically as in figure 1 in the guide.

Process for Doing Simulations

To simulate the effect of any policy intervention, we use the following procedure:

1. Estimate coefficients for our regression equations.
2. Use those coefficients to create a synthetic baseline.
3. Adjust one or more variables to reflect the policy intervention.
4. Propagate the effects of that intervention through the model using the coefficients estimated in Step 1.
5. Calculate the effect of the intervention on later outcomes.
6. Calculate the effect on lifetime income.

Step 1. Estimating Coefficients

We estimate coefficients on our entire nationally representative samples of children in the CNLSY and adults in the NLSY79.[13] We conduct substantial imputation of missing values in both surveys, and we include cases with imputed values in these estimation samples. Continuous outcomes (all early and middle childhood outcomes, GPA, and the income measures) are estimated using OLS.[14] To account for the long right tail of income variables, we estimate them in logged forms which are converted back to their original metric when we report the results. Binary outcomes are estimated using a linear probability model.[15]

Step 2. Creating the Synthetic Baseline

Once we have estimated the model, we use the estimated coefficients and the actual values for the baseline characteristics to predict each of the outcomes for every individual in the target population. The target population can be defined either by the limited applicability of an intervention (for example, children who al-

---

12. The subset of CAB variables in the NLSY79 includes race, gender, maternal age, and maternal education.

13. We might prefer to newly estimate the coefficients on simulation-specific target populations each time. However, because our TTA and adulthood income equations must be estimated on NLSY79 data, and only limited pre-adolescent information is available in that data, it is not generally possible to restrict this data to target populations defined with respect to at-birth characteristics or early outcomes.

14. Continuous measures include all early and middle childhood outcomes, GPA, all income measures, and a number of adolescent variables including math and reading scores, self-esteem, frequency of religious service, and gender role attitudes.

15. Binary measures include high school graduation, teen birth, conviction, college graduation, marijuana use, other drug use, early sex, suspension, fighting, hitting, damaging property, participation in school clubs, and independence in ADOL and TTA. We confirmed that our results were similar using logistic regression models and chose linear probability models for the greater flexibility they have in the context of structural equation modeling.

ready attend preschool cannot be affected by an intervention that enrolls children in preschool) or because the effect size we use for a given policy is taken from a rigorous evaluation of a specific population and would require unacceptable assumptions to generalize (for example, the Nurse Family Partnership home visiting program generally has been available only to poor, first-time mothers).

For the fifteen continuous outcomes in EC, MC, and ADOL, we add the residual terms back to individuals' predicted values, which leaves each person's baseline value the same as their actual value.[16] We do so because we reassign each person the same residual when we implement the intervention later on. Doing so ensures that the only thing that changes between the baseline and policy estimates is the value of the outcome or outcomes that the policy intervention affects, and it leaves the simulated counterfactual as consistent with the actual baseline as possible. It also incorporates into the policy estimates potentially valuable information about individuals' unobserved characteristics.

For the twelve binary outcomes in adolescence, the linear probability models are used to produce predicted probabilities for each individual. These estimates are bound such that no individual may have a predicted probability less than 0 or greater than 1. To assign each person a dichotomous value, he or she is randomly assigned a number between 0 and 1. If their random number is less than their predicted probability, then the outcome is predicted to occur. If their random number is greater than or equal to their predicted probability, then their outcome is predicted not to occur. We retain the random number drawn for each person for the simulated counterfactual, again, in order to keep everything as consistent as possible with the baseline.

For TTA and adulthood outcomes, the creation of baseline values is somewhat different because of the necessity of relying on the NLSY79 to estimate coefficients. To impute TTA outcomes, we use actual CAB values from the CNLSY with the corresponding coefficients estimated from the NLSY79, but we use the *baseline* adolescent values rather than the actual values in the CNLSY data. For continuous adolescent outcomes, the baseline values are exactly the same as the actual values because we add residuals to the predicted values, but for dichotomous adolescent outcomes, the baseline values are those predicted from the procedure just described.[17]

To impute adult income, we again use actual CAB values from the CNLSY and baseline adolescent values, and we also use the baseline TTA values just estimated. All of these values are combined with the coefficients estimated from the NLSY79. Because we do not have actual TTA and adulthood outcomes, we do not have actual residual terms for each individual after estimating continuous baseline outcomes. We instead give everyone a residual that is randomly drawn from a normal distribution with mean zero and with standard deviation taken as the standard error of regression from the applicable NLSY79 equation. As with earlier stages, after predicting dichotomous outcomes using a linear probability model, we take a random draw to determine whether to assign individuals a 0 or a 1.

Step 3. The Intervention
To implement a policy intervention or what-if scenario, we must first make three important decisions: which metric or metrics are affected, for whom, and by how much. For what-if scenarios, this is simply a matter of specifying the change, such as "what if we equalized the middle childhood reading scores of poor and non-

---

16. GPA is restricted to be between 0 and 4 after prediction.

17. Those baseline values need not equal the actual values in the CNLSY because our predictions of dichotomous outcomes are imperfect. It might seem preferable to use the actual values here, but doing so would create inconsistencies in the postintervention run of the model—we might predict, in the postintervention run, some actual high school graduates, for instance, to be dropouts, which would mean that an intervention could be estimated to worsen outcomes among some youth.

poor children?" In that case we would just increase every poor child's reading score by the amount of the poor-nonpoor reading gap. For a policy intervention, we rely on the best-practice evaluations, preferably randomized controlled trials, of others to generate effect sizes. When determining an effect size, we err on the conservative side or simulate a range of possible effects to avoid a false sense of precision and to account for differences between metrics in our model and the evaluation studies.

We also use the data in the evaluation literature to determine which portion of our model's population should receive the effects of the program, looking at whether the evidence shows heterogeneous effects on particular subgroups. The comprehensive school reform program, Success for All, for example, was implemented in a variety of schools nationwide and showed a high degree of homogeneity of its effects in different schools; on the other hand, a program like Nurse Family Partnership, for which only low-income, first-time mothers are eligible, requires that we narrow our treatment group in the model.

After deciding on the target population and the appropriate effect size, we apply the intervention differently depending on whether it affects a continuous or dichotomous variable. If it is a continuous variable, we simply add the effect size to everyone in the target group. For interventions on dichotomous variables, we come up with effect sizes as a percentage change from baseline. For example, if some intervention increases high school graduation by 15 percent, we calculate how many extra individuals (N) in our data would need to graduate to increase the rate within the target population by 15 percent, randomly sort the individuals who were in the target group and had not graduated from high school, and then change the top N people from nongraduates to graduates.

Step 4. Propagating the Effects Through the Model

To simulate the effect of the changes we make in step 3 on subsequent life stages, we apply the estimated coefficients from step 1 to the simulated data, which have now been adjusted according to the effect size of the intervention being evaluated. In doing so, we implicitly assume that the only thing an intervention changes is a person's measured outcomes, and not the relationship between the different outcomes or unmeasured outcomes.

Every outcome prior to the intervention stage is unaffected, as is every outcome in the intervention stage we did not perturb directly as part of the intervention. We iterate though the subsequent stages and predict outcomes for each stage using earlier outcomes, which have been adjusted by the intervention. This ensures that the effect of the intervention is carried though the entire life course. For example, if we improved middle childhood reading, our postintervention data through middle childhood would be exactly the same as the preintervention baseline (except for middle childhood reading) but our adolescent data would be predicted using the increased reading scores and would reflect that change. To predict the *Transition to Adulthood* outcomes, we would use the newly predicted adolescent outcomes that include the effect of the intervention, and adulthood income would be predicted from these new adolescent outcomes as well the newly predicted *Transition to Adulthood* outcomes. As noted, to ensure that our effect size reflects only the impact of the intervention, continuous outcomes are assigned their same residual from step 2, and dichotomous outcomes are assigned a 0 or 1 based on the same random number from step 2.

Step 5. Calculating the Impact of the Intervention

When reporting how outcomes have changed based on an intervention which alters one or more earlier outcomes, we compare the preintervention simulated outcomes from step 2 to the postintervention simulated outcomes from step 4. For most outcomes, the pre- and post-values are used to calculate a percent change in each outcome as a result of the intervention. If a middle childhood intervention increases the high school graduation rate from 75 percent to 80 percent, then the effect size is to increase graduation by $(80-75)/75 = 6.7$ percent.

For our early and middle childhood outcomes, which are all measured in terms of standard deviations, we simply subtract the pre-value from the post-value.

Next, we assess how the intervention affected general measures of "success" at each life stage. The success measures are dichotomous variables corresponding to the definitions presented in table A1. We estimate success rates using the preintervention simulated outcomes for the individual components of success, and do the same using the postintervention simulated outcomes.[18]

Step 6. Calculating the Impact on Lifetime Income

Along with the effects on our outcomes and success measures, we also report the effect of our interventions on lifetime income. To get a preintervention estimate for lifetime family income, we first find the sample average family income at ages twenty-nine and forty. We calculate the slope between these two ages as follows:

$$\text{29-to-40 slope} = (\overline{Income_{40}} - \overline{Income_{29}})/11 \quad \text{Equation 4}$$

Assuming linear income growth for simplicity, we use an individual's family income at age twenty-nine and forty, with the average slope calculated in equation 4, to interpolate average income at every age between twenty-nine and forty. For example, the estimated mean income value at age thirty is $(\overline{Income_{29}}) + 1 * (29\text{--}40\ slope)$.[19]

The process of estimating income at ages before age twenty-nine and after age forty is slightly more complicated, but uses a similar approach. Each income (age twenty-two, age twenty-three, ..., age sixty) is discounted from birth using a real discount rate of 3 percent. So discounted age forty income is $(\overline{Income_{40}})/1.03^{40}$. Finally, lifetime family income is the sum of every discounted income:

$$\text{discounted lifetime income} = \sum_{i=22}^{62} (\overline{Income_i})/1.03^i \quad \text{Equation 5}$$

To estimate the *change* in lifetime income that results from an intervention or what-if, this process is done with both pre- and post-income values. We subtract discounted lifetime income *pre* from discounted lifetime income *post* to get the mean change in lifetime income.

Caveats

As also explained in the *Guide to the Social Genome Model*, the researchers who built the model dealt with numerous methodological and data issues and attempted to validate the results against independent sources of data. It is worth noting that our predictions of adult household incomes accord very well with data from the CPS although both our values and CPS values are a little low relative to the PSID.

The model's choice of age ranges and life stage outcomes is motivated by human capital theory and some of the other literature on child development, including a literature review on the determinants of education and earnings, and consultations with other experts in the field. The predictions should not be interpreted as causal estimates of the long-term effects of an intervention.

The biggest data issue has been a seam in the data at the end of adolescence, requiring us to find variables capable of linking the CNLSY to the NLSY79 and imputing values for

---

18. Note that we do policy simulations that include income-to-needs at age twenty-nine and age forty separately from the simulations that include income measured continuously in dollars. We consider income-to-needs solely to construct the success measures for TTA and adulthood. The basic simulation equations do not include income-to-needs, and the simulation equations to predict income-to-needs do not include income.

19. We use mean incomes to compute the slope—as opposed to using individual incomes to compute individual-specific slopes—because some individual slopes are negative, which would complicate the estimation of stylized lifetime income effects. At the same time, our spline estimation prevents us from having to assume a linear growth rate, which would involve substantial under- and over-prediction of income at different points in the age profile.

the adult period. Many of the adolescent variables included in the model were imported to improve the linking of the CNLSY and the NLSY (that is, they are variables in both data sets that earlier analysis had showed were predictive of adult outcomes). This is the weakest part of the model, but our benchmarking of the model's predicted adult outcomes, such as college graduation and family income, against independent sources of data (for detailed tables of results, see the guide), reassured us that the model was doing an adequate job of making these predictions.

The Social Genome Model, originally developed at Brookings, is now a partnership between Brookings, the Urban Institute, and Child Trends. Anyone interested in an update to this work should check the SGM website (http://www.social-genome.org). Research teams at both the Urban Institute and Child Trends have recalibrated some of the parameters in the model and also run it on the NLSY97 in addition to the NLSY79. The results vary depending on the parameterization and the data used but are similar, giving us some confidence that the model's predictions are reasonably stable and not overly dependent on the exact specification and data used. We welcome ideas for further improvements. The current model should be viewed as a framework within which to look at the process of social mobility, and its limitations should be seen as a challenge to the research community to find better theory, data, and methods with which to estimate the longer-term effects of various interventions. Although RCTs are now the gold standard for estimating the causal impact of an intervention on some outcome of interest, for some purposes RCTs are simply not practical or feasible given the very long follow-up periods required to measure long-term outcomes and the ethical issues involved in bypassing an entire generation of children or relying on even cruder assumptions about likely long-term effects.

Table A1. Variable Definitions

Stage	Variable	
Circumstances at birth	Gender	A dichotomous variable indicating the sex of the individual. Males are the omitted category.
	Race	Dichotomous variables indicating whether the child is black, Hispanic, or other. The omitted category consists of white children.
	Maternal Educational Attainment	Dichotomous variables are included to indicate whether the individual's mother graduated from high school, attended some college, or obtained a bachelor's degree or more advanced degree. The omitted category is mothers who did not finish high school.
	Maternal Age at Time of Child's Birth	A continuous variable measuring the age of the mother (in years) at the time of the child's birth.
	Maternal Age at First Birth	A continuous variable measuring the age of the mother (in years) at the time of her first child's birth.
	Marital Status of Child's Parents at Time of Birth	A dichotomous variable indicating whether the child's mother was married when he or she was born. The omitted category includes those children whose mothers were not married, even if cohabitating, at the time of their birth.
	Family Income at Birth	This continuous variable is the log-transformed measure of the family's income as a percent of the federal poverty line in the year that the child was born.
	Low Birth Weight	A dichotomous variable indicating whether a child weighed 5.5 pounds or less when he or she was born. The omitted category consists of children who weighed more than 5.5 pounds at the time of birth.
	Mother's AFQT Score	The age-normed percentile score of the child's mother on the Armed Forces Qualifying Test, a general achievement test taken when the mothers were between sixteen and twenty-three.
	Parenting: Cognitive Stimulation	Standardized score on the HOME Inventory Cognitive Stimulation scale, measured when the child is younger than two.
	Parenting: Emotional Support	Standardized score on the HOME Inventory Emotional Support scale, measured when the child is younger than two.
	Early Verbal Ability	The age-standardized score of the child on the Peabody Picture Vocabulary Test (PPVT), measured when the child is three or four.
Early childhood (age five)	Math	Age-standardized scores from the math section of the Peabody Individual Achievement Test (PIAT)
	Reading	Age-standardized scores from the reading recognition section of the Peabody Individual Achievement Test (PIAT)
	Antisocial Behavior	Age-standardized antisocial behavior subscale from the Behavior Problems Index (BPI). Scores are reverse coded so that higher is better.
	Hyperactivity	Age-standardized hyperactivity subscale from the Behavior Problems Index (BPI). Scores are reverse coded so that higher is better.

Table A1. (*cont.*)

Stage	Variable	
Middle childhood (age eleven)	Math	Age-standardized scores from the math section of the Peabody Individual Achievement Test (PIAT)
	Reading	Age-standardized scores from the reading recognition section of the Peabody Individual Achievement Test (PIAT)
	Antisocial Behavior	Age-standardized antisocial behavior subscale from the Behavior Problems Index (BPI). Scores are reverse coded so that higher is better.
	Hyperactivity	Age-standardized hyperactivity subscale from the Behavior Problems Index (BPI). Scores are reverse coded so that higher is better.
Adolescence (age nineteen)	High School Graduation Status	A dichotomous variable indicating whether the individual received a high school diploma by age nineteen. GED earners are not counted as high school graduates.
	Grade Point Average (GPA)	A continuous variable of average grade in the last year of high school. Ranges from 0 to 4.
	Criminal Conviction	A dichotomous variable indicating whether the individual was convicted of any charges other than minor traffic violations by age nineteen.
	Teen Parent	A dichotomous variable indicating whether the individual reported having a child by age nineteen.
	Lives Independently from parents	A dichotomous variable indicating whether the individual was living independently from his or her parents at age nineteen.
	Math	Age-standardized score on a test measuring mathematical ability: math section of the Peabody Individual Achievement Test (PIAT) at age thirteen or fourteen in the CNLSY and arithmetic reasoning section of the Armed Services Vocational Aptitude Battery (ASVAB), taken between ages fifteen and twenty-three, in the NLSY79.
	Reading	Age-standardized score on a test measuring verbal ability: reading recognition section of the Peabody Individual Achievement Test (PIAT) at age thirteen or fourteen in the CNLSY and word knowledge section in the Armed Services Vocational Aptitude Battery (ASVAB), taken between ages fifteen and twenty-three, in the NLSY79.
	Family Income	This continuous variable is the log-transformed measure of the family's income during early adolescence (ideally measured at age thirteen, fourteen, fifteen, or sixteen).
	Marijuana Use	This dichotomous variable indicates whether the individual reports having ever used marijuana (CNLSY) or having used marijuana in the past year (NLSY79).
	Other Drug Use	This dichotomous variable indicates whether the individual reports having ever used drugs other than marijuana or amphetamines (CNLSY) or having used drugs other than marijuana in the past year (NLSY79).
	Early Sex	This dichotomous variable indicates whether the individual reports having had sexual intercourse before age fifteen.

Table A1. (cont.)

Stage	Variable	
Adolescence (age nineteen) (cont.)	Suspension	This dichotomous variable indicates whether the individual was ever suspended from school.
	Fighting	This dichotomous variable indicates whether the individual reported getting in a fight at school or work in the past year.
	Hitting	This dichotomous variable indicates whether the individual reported hitting or seriously threatening to hit someone in the past year.
	Damaging Property	This dichotomous variable indicates whether the individual reported intentionally damaging the property of others in the past year.
	Self-Esteem Index	Age-standardized IRT score on the Rosenberg Self-Esteem Scale.
	Religious Service Attendance	This variable measures frequency of religious service attendance on a scale of 0 (none) to 5 (more than once a week).
	Gender Role Attitudes	This continuous variable is the mean of the individual's answers to five questions about how he or she views women.
	Participation in School Clubs	Dichotomous variable indicating whether the individual participated in clubs in high school such as band, choir, or sports.
Transition to adulthood (age twenty-nine)	Family Income	This continuous variable is the log-transformed measure of the family's income during the year the individual was twenty-nine years old.
	Family Income to Needs	This continuous variable is the log-transformed measure of the family's income as a percentage of the federal poverty during the year the individual was twenty-nine years old.
	College Completion	Dichotomous variable indicating whether the individual obtained a four-year degree or higher.
	Lives Independently from Parents	A dichotomous variable indicating whether the individual was living independently from his or her parents at age twenty-nine.
Adulthood (age forty)	Family Income	This continuous variable is the log-transformed measure of the family's income during the year the individual was forty years old.
	Family Income to Needs	This continuous variable is the log-transformed measure of the family's income as a percentage of the federal poverty during the year the individual was forty years old.

Source: Authors' compilation.

Outcome Prediction Regressions

Table A2. Early Childhood and Middle Childhood Outcomes

	ecMath (Math Scores at Age Five–Six)	ecRead (Reading Scores at Age Five–Six)	ecAnti (Antisocial Behavior at Age Five–Six)	ecHyper (Hyperactivity at Age Five–Six)	mcMath (Math Scores at Age Ten–Eleven)	mcRead (Reading Scores at Age Ten–Eleven)	mcAnti (Antisocial Behavior at Age Ten–Eleven)	mcHyper (Hyperactivity at Age Ten–Eleven)
gender	0.018904	0.121959	0.243874	0.250316	-0.17521	0.038797	0.199664	0.188864
black	-0.1297	0.189867	0.029594	0.138353	-0.21887	-0.22049	-0.13755	0.025035
hispanic	-0.05345	0.138821	0.17328	0.131733	-0.05843	0.016657	0.016501	0.108351
otherRace	-0.07385	0.014875	0.18553	0.206544	-0.04437	-0.083	-0.00747	0.079038
matEd2	0.045286	0.068779	0.159832	0.177408	0.021086	0.061652	0.097754	0.049561
matEd3	0.085451	0.16224	0.256458	0.218371	0.040429	0.125366	0.100238	0.062428
matEd4	0.27233	0.22564	0.225497	0.389272	0.106163	0.12769	0.131283	0.078281
cabMatAge	-0.00665	-0.00327	0.011978	0.028064	0.006491	-0.00462	0.009855	-0.00079
cabMatAge1	0.015769	0.016885	-0.0036	-0.01541	0.004796	0.004839	0.00236	-0.00238
cabMarried	0.01958	0.060694	0.057067	0.049981	-0.00469	-0.02089	0.070576	0.022167
cabLbw	-0.08772	-0.12214	-0.0041	-0.06236	-0.06551	-0.0069	-0.02757	-0.04688
cabFamIncFpl	0.028034	0.033313	0.04041	0.030402	0.014259	0.03694	0.028568	0.003854
cabPpvt	0.131849	0.120464	0.044706	0.086152	0.049762	0.067198	-0.00572	0.007036
cabParEmoSup	0.021463	-0.00431	0.079571	0.068624	0.006263	0.002864	0.024663	0.015364
cabParCogStim	0.035558	0.032731	0.087209	0.069281	0.022479	0.015397	0.03053	0.018971
cabMomAfqt	0.005807	0.006634	7.18E-05	0.000941	0.005355	0.004378	-0.00014	0.000926
ecMath					0.235293	0.111101	0.00483	0.054423
ecRead					0.210429	0.35917	0.034448	0.022756
ecAnti					0.021075	0.015506	0.37923	0.116345
ecHyper					0.061383	0.067465	0.116996	0.390312
intercept	-0.62215	-0.94848	-0.60819	-0.83881	-0.38751	-0.19916	-0.50863	-0.0991
R^2	0.1859	0.1609	0.0883	0.1245	0.3765	0.3788	0.312	0.2767

Source: Authors' compilation.

Table A3. Adolescent Outcomes

	adolHs (High School Graduation)	adolBirth (Teen Birth)	adolGpa (GPA)	adolConvict (Criminal Conviction)	adolMath (Math)
gender	0.024803	0.115033	0.170925	−0.10442	−0.11648
black	0.049503	0.058792	−0.01763	−0.06543	−0.11373
hispanic	−0.02278	0.105756	−0.02298	0.005076	−0.11182
otherRace	−0.07757	0.055014	0.101019	0.062903	−0.04973
matEd2	0.126889	−0.09987	0.058885	−0.04808	0.011075
matEd3	0.143189	−0.10562	0.11241	−0.06002	−0.02041
matEd4	0.135164	−0.0945	0.259241	−0.09323	0.04453
cabMatAge	0.00237	0.001717	0.008021	0.006745	−0.00376
cabMatAge1	0.002094	−0.00641	0.007525	−0.00116	0.012525
cabMarried	0.030465	−0.03232	0.065373	−0.07217	0.035966
cabLbw	0.016286	−0.02504	0.018336	0.001026	0.003882
cabFamIncFpl	0.024128	−0.01149	−0.00956	−0.00712	0.005731
cabPpvt	0.008314	0.004532	0.00468	0.001613	0.028337
cabParEmoSup	0.001671	−0.01433	0.001501	0.007185	−0.00818
cabParCogStim	0.001944	0.00096	0.003384	−0.00714	0.007666
cabMomAfqt	−8.20E−05	−0.00036	0.002433	−0.0005	0.002587
ecMath	0.015206	−0.00381	0.038993	−0.01095	0.092228
ecRead	0.017872	0.001541	0.019973	−0.01334	0.019441
ecAnti	0.028669	−0.00988	0.006853	−0.00909	−0.02211
ecHyper	−0.02054	−0.00268	0.002504	0.015657	0.022601
mcMath	0.019686	−0.01795	0.052673	0.015953	0.434562
mcRead	0.010927	−0.00848	0.025361	−0.00924	0.1378
mcAnti	0.041416	−0.0084	0.06057	−0.04414	0.033526
mcHyper	0.010812	0.001607	0.059541	−0.00964	0.029367
intercept	0.590778	0.277945	2.217064	0.213027	−0.2176
R^2	0.1853	0.1569	0.2041	0.08	0.5227

adolRead (Read)	adolInc (Family Income)	adolIndep (Lives Independently from Parents)	adolEarlySex (Early Sex)	adolSelfEsteem (Self-Esteem Index)	adolDamageProperty (Damaging property)
−0.00163	−0.07568	0.076161	−0.02195	−0.18152	−0.105427
−0.0536	−0.31361	−0.10737	0.0992123	0.37306	−0.002235
0.037953	−0.1913	−0.07389	0.0853673	−0.00244	0.0671071
−0.00326	−0.10793	0.00178	0.0072385	0.146987	0.0437333
0.060458	0.442045	−0.06683	−0.088935	0.090241	−0.013457
0.009684	0.525166	−0.04445	−0.090589	0.057126	−0.028812
−0.03386	0.637487	−0.08816	−0.097125	0.061526	−0.032128
−0.00508	−0.00254	−0.00356	0.0037966	−0.01467	−0.002869
0.002046	0.006047	−0.00628	−0.005946	0.000783	−0.001133
−0.02153	0.208944	0.012382	−0.090126	−0.02737	−0.018247
0.027088	−0.14555	−0.01927	0.0118362	−0.10647	0.0268664
0.011076	0.133832	−0.01639	−0.005894	0.050184	0.0039734
0.03287	−0.00106	−0.00222	0.0029939	0.068538	0.0010607
0.023159	0.017604	−0.01239	−0.011289	0.00163	0.0049936
0.007751	0.049571	−0.01573	0.0079626	0.033712	0.0172399
0.002345	0.007374	0.000167	−1.86E−05	−0.00154	0.000091
0.032299	0.031245	0.019216	−0.006427	0.055409	−0.009233
0.034626	0.049732	0.000647	0.0040184	−0.04187	0.0129152
−0.01699	0.047093	−0.00669	−0.000107	0.047196	0.0119009
0.008579	−0.02883	−0.00272	−0.001576	−0.00662	−0.001028
0.086172	0.031922	0.009537	−0.002214	0.056294	0.0164869
0.602254	−0.01854	−0.00531	−0.007706	0.094175	−0.007475
0.066184	0.002686	−0.03289	−0.038062	0.031148	−0.057882
0.010334	0.090584	−0.00867	−0.01155	0.039719	0.004114
0.004803	9.758433	0.476732	0.3637962	0.40817	0.3053755
0.5929	0.1902	0.0684	0.1051	0.064	0.0677

Table A3. (*Cont.*)

	adolFight (Fighting)	adolHit (Hitting)	adolSuspend (Suspension)	adolMarijuana (Marijuana Use)
gender	−0.04138	−0.10642	−0.072998	−0.03425
black	−0.00352	0.0006636	0.1908452	−0.112427
hispanic	−0.0023	0.0139355	0.0489738	0.0049473
otherRace	0.025721	0.0299238	0.0099518	0.0076051
matEd2	−0.03882	−0.029353	−0.010075	−0.05498
matEd3	−0.0335	−0.040134	−0.018638	−0.061095
matEd4	−0.03702	−0.076669	−0.030907	−0.111039
cabMatAge	−0.00883	−0.000381	−0.00161	−0.010786
cabMatAge1	−0.00018	−0.004298	−0.003171	−0.005836
cabMarried	−0.03439	−0.049229	−0.041558	−0.062936
cabLbw	0.00082	−0.003774	−0.020341	0.0163089
cabFamIncFpl	0.013045	0.0115596	0.0056989	−0.001649
cabPpvt	−0.00283	0.0039814	0.0064589	0.0098538
cabParEmoSup	0.004944	0.0102301	−0.013869	0.0108683
cabParCogStim	0.003752	0.0009732	−0.005689	0.0005094
cabMomAfqt	−0.00036	−0.000729	−8.83E-05	−0.000132
ecMath	0.000515	−0.012903	−0.004682	−0.00199
ecRead	−0.00317	0.0075674	0.0032331	−0.002805
ecAnti	0.000396	0.0061965	−0.016683	−0.01725
ecHyper	0.00228	−0.010879	0.0039318	0.0078014
mcMath	−0.00141	0.0164909	0.0201491	0.0206738
mcRead	−0.0039	0.0135147	−0.020177	0.0266279
mcAnti	−0.03497	−0.047741	−0.075529	−0.040784
mcHyper	−0.00433	−0.010546	−0.014604	−0.013897
intercept	0.411634	0.477741	0.3103284	0.9011838
R^2	0.0951	0.0667	0.1976	0.0851

Source: Authors' compilation.

adolOtherDrug (Other Drug Use)	adolHsClub (Participation in School Clubs)	adolRelServ (Religious Service Attendance)	adolGenderRole (Gender Role Attitudes)
−0.014831	0.0684602	−0.07729	0.2767102
−0.066028	0.0070092	−0.79484	0.087795
−0.029821	−0.040038	−0.29228	0.0179912
−0.039281	0.0539026	−0.19409	0.0577652
−0.003287	0.0769293	−0.22507	0.047796
0.0003134	0.0961848	−0.43521	0.0438276
−0.003107	0.1309736	−0.81985	0.0202436
−0.002775	−0.004496	0.002255	−0.007052
−0.000932	0.0027287	−0.01928	−0.000659
−0.01737	0.0087148	−0.39536	−0.060999
−0.012992	−0.101763	0.052724	0.0169083
0.0004384	0.0055832	0.009163	0.0118431
0.0013941	0.0242737	−0.02238	0.0243812
0.002561	−0.006408	0.08725	0.0040863
0.0040535	0.0150972	−0.04354	0.0058304
−1.64E-05	0.0011134	−0.00259	0.000722
0.0003128	0.0113636	0.0115	0.0054753
2.71E-06	0.0052319	−0.02538	−0.001583
−0.00195	0.0241237	−0.03895	0.0195944
0.002099	0.0008716	−0.00886	−0.000809
−0.009427	0.033854	0.073772	0.060716
0.0123686	−0.008071	−0.02128	0.0199537
−0.006421	0.0144231	0.00384	0.020834
−0.004974	0.033202	−0.08656	−0.017218
0.1918993	0.571242	4.240868	2.054974
0.0202	0.1117	0.0812	0.1235

Table A4. Transition to Adulthood and Adulthood Outcomes

	ttaIndep (Lives Independently from Parents)	ttaCollege (College Completion)	ttaFamIncC (Family Income)	ttaFamIncFpl (Family Income to Needs)	adFamIncC (Family Income)
gender	0.04271	-0.03504	-0.08409	-0.16236	-0.23956
black	-0.11764	0.055169	-0.29146	-0.28963	-0.2712
hispanic	-0.04498	0.021398	-0.0982	-0.1277	-0.11214
otherRace	0.011492	-0.05978	-0.16864	-0.18659	-0.19334
matEd2	-0.00915	0.003588	0.004699	0.039108	-0.01949
matEd3	0.006378	0.096953	0.007874	0.056443	-0.10301
matEd4	-0.00728	0.225878	0.036273	0.135453	-0.1517
cabMatAge	-0.00058	0.000358	-0.00266	-0.00344	0.002026
cabMatAge1	-0.00331	0.005675	0.002064	0.007334	-0.00263
adolHs	0.033018	-0.0336	0.250706	0.263997	0.324467
adolBirth	0.045465	-0.08679	0.000906	-0.14592	-0.00997
adolGpa	0.001137	0.047492	0.081715	0.077736	0.04358
adolConvict	-0.05633	-0.02659	-0.19122	-0.20671	-0.09461
adolMath	0.01032	0.083265	0.052919	0.049799	0.043631
adolRead	0.015016	0.004866	0.113087	0.136859	0.131804
adolInc	-0.00419	0.019118	0.099275	0.100026	0.057776
adolIndep	0.030774	0.083104	0.018737	0.02049	0.022916
adolEarlySex	-0.00747	-0.00807	-0.03016	-0.01835	-0.17068
adolSelfEsteem	0.005002	0.003086	0.035861	0.042474	-0.03015
adolDamageProp	0.000882	0.011632	0.036656	0.037795	-0.07891
adolFight	-0.00501	-0.02303	-0.04587	-0.06577	-0.03509
adolHit	0.011168	-0.02403	-0.02336	-0.01143	0.009642
adolSuspend	-0.01521	-0.03724	-0.08369	-0.07554	-0.04886
adolMarijuana	0.021901	-0.00993	0.03847	0.049251	0.062612
adolOtherDrug	-0.01063	-0.02059	0.030263	0.083292	-0.01885
adolHsClub	0.012369	0.072895	0.076333	0.079283	0.142804
adolRelServ	-0.00671	-0.01362	-0.03142	-0.02083	-0.02751
adolGenderRole	-0.01075	0.041859	0.022461	0.042922	0.152489
ttaIndep					0.382121
ttaCollege					0.13012
ttaFamIncC					0.377835
intercept	1.00811	-0.3200115	9.311073	-0.58669	5.287203
R^2	0.0553	0.2966	0.1623	0.2107	0.2351

Source: Authors' compilation.

REFERENCES

Ashenfelter, Orley, and Cecilia Rouse. 1999. "Schooling, Intelligence, and Income in America: Cracks in the Bell Curve." NBER working paper no. 6902. Cambridge, Mass.: National Bureau of Economic Research.

Bhattacharya, Depobam, and Bhashkar Mazumder. 2011. "A Nonparametric Analysis of Black-White Differences in Intergenerational Income Mobility in the United States." *Quantitative Economics* 2(3): 335–79.

Blanden, Jo. 2014. "Concepts, Measures and Mechanisms: An Overview of Empirical Evidence on Intergenerational Social Mobility in the U.S. and UK." Unpublished paper. University of Surrey and London School of Economics.

Blanden, Jo, Paul Gregg, and Lindsey Macmillan. 2007. "Accounting for Intergenerational Income Persistence: Noncognitive Skills, Ability, and Education." *Economic Journal* 117(519): C43–60.

Burtless, Gary. 2014. "Income Growth and Income Inequality: The Facts May Surprise You." Washington, D.C.: Brookings Institution. Last modified January 6, 2014. http://www.brookings.edu/research/opinions/2014/01/06-income-gains-and-inequality-burtless.

Card, David. 2001. "Estimating the Return to Schooling: Progress on Some Persistent Econometric Problems." *Econometrica* 69(5): 1127–60.

Carneiro, Pedro, James J. Heckman, and Edward J. Vytlacil. 2011. "Estimating Marginal Returns to Education." *American Economic Review* 101(6): 2754–81.

Chetty, Raj, Nathaniel Hendren, Patrick Kline, and Emmanuel Saez. 2014. "Where Is the Land of Opportunity: The Geography of Intergenerational Mobility in the United States." *Quarterly Journal of Economics* 129(4): 1553–623.

Chetty, Raj, Nathaniel Hendren, Patrick Kline, Emmanuel Saez, and Nicholas Turner. 2014. "Is the United States Still a Land of Opportunity? Recent Trends in Intergenerational Mobility." *American Economic Review* 104(5): 141–47.

Cooper, Carey E., Cynthia A. Osborne, Audrey N. Beck, and Sara S. McLanahan. 2011. "Partnership Instability, School Readiness, and Gender Disparities." *Sociology of Education* 84(3): 246–59.

Corak, Miles. 2010. "Chasing the Same Dream, Climbing Different Ladders: Economic Mobility in the United States and Canada." *Economic Mobility Project* report. Washington, D.C.: The Pew Charitable Trusts.

Cunha, Flavio, and James J. Heckman. 2008. "Formulating, Identifying, and Estimating the Technology of Cognitive and Noncognitive Skill Formation." *Journal of Human Resources* 43(4): 738–82.

Cunha, Flavio, James J. Heckman, and Susanne M. Schennach. 2010. "Estimating the Technology of Cognitive and Noncognitive Skill Formation." *Econometrica* 78(3): 883–931.

Currie, Janet, and Duncan Thomas. 1995. "Does Head Start Make a Difference?" *American Economic Review* 85(3): 341–64.

Economic Mobility Project. 2012. *Pursuing the American Dream: Economic Mobility across Generations*. Washington, D.C.: The Pew Charitable Trusts.

Fishkin, Joseph. 2014. *Bottlenecks: A New Theory of Equal Opportunity*. Oxford: Oxford University Press.

Froomkin, Dan. 2010. "Social Immobility: Climbing the Economic Ladder Is Harder in the U.S. than in Most European Countries." *Huffington Post*, March 17. Last modified May 25, 2011. http://www.huffingtonpost.com/2010/03/17/social-immobility-climbin_n_501788.html.

García, Jorge Luis, and James J. Heckman. 2014. "Ability, Character, and Social Mobility." Unpublished paper. University of Chicago.

Genicot, Garance, and Debraj Ray. 2013. "Measuring Upward Mobility." Unpublished paper. Georgetown University and New York University.

Glover, Vivette. 2011. "Annual Research Review: Prenatal Stress and the Origins of Psychopathology: An Evolutionary Perspective." *Journal of Child Psychology and Psychiatry* 52(4): 356–67.

Goldin, Claudia, and Lawrence F. Katz. 2008. *The Race Between Education and Technology*. Cambridge, Mass.: Belknap Press for Harvard University Press.

Graham, Carol, and Milena Nikolova. 2013. "Happy Peasants and Frustrated Achievers? Agency, Capabilities, and Subjective Well-Being." HCEO working paper no. 13. Chicago: Human Capital and Economic Opportunity Global Working Group.

Haskins, Ron, and Isabel Sawhill. 2009. *Creating an Opportunity Society*. Washington, D.C.: Brookings Institution Press.

Heckman, James, Rodrigo Pinto, and Peter Savelyev. 2013. "Understanding the Mechanisms through Which an Influential Early Childhood Program Boosted Adult Outcomes." *American Economic Review* 103(6): 2052-86.

Heckman, James, Jora Stixrud, and Sergio Urzua. 2006. "The Effects of Cognitive and Noncognitive Abilities on Labor Market Outcomes and Social Behavior." *Journal of Labor Economics* 24(3): 411-82.

Henderson, Daniel J., Solomon W. Polachek, and Le Wang. 2011. "Heterogeneity in Schooling Rates of Return." *Economics of Education Review* 30(6): 1202-14.

Hertz, Tom. 2007. "Trends in the Intergenerational Elasticity of Family Income in the United States." *Industrial Relations* 46(1): 22-50.

Isaacs, Julia B., Isabel V. Sawhill, and Ron Haskins. 2008. *Getting Ahead or Losing Ground: Economic Mobility in America*. Washington, D.C.: Brookings Institution and the Pew Charitable Trusts.

Kalil, Ariel. 2014. "Addressing the Parenting Divide to Promote Early Childhood Development for Disadvantaged Children." In *Policies to Address Poverty in America*, edited by Melissa S. Kearney and Benjamin H. Harris. Washington, D.C.: Brookings Institution Press.

Krueger, Alan B. 2012. "The Rise and Consequences of Inequality." Lecture at the Center for American Progress. Washington, D.C. (January 12, 2012).

Lee, Chul-In, and Gary Solon. 2009. "Trends in Intergenerational Income Mobility." *Review of Economics and Statistics* 91(4): 766-72.

Mazumder, Bhashkar. 2012. "Black-White Differences in Intergenerational Economic Mobility in the United States." *Economic Perspectives* 38(1): 1-18.

———. 2014. "Upward Intergenerational Mobility in the United States." Washington, D.C.: The Pew Charitable Trusts.

McLanahan, Sara. 2011. "Family Instability and Complexity after a Nonmarital Birth: Outcomes for Children in Fragile Families." In *Social Class and Changing Families in an Unequal America*, edited by Marcia J. Carlson and Paula England. Stanford, Calif.: Stanford University Press.

Moore, Kristin A., Vanessa H. Sacks, Jennifer Manlove, and Isabel Sawhill. 2014. "What If You Earned a Diploma and Delayed Parenthood? Intergenerational Simulations of Delayed Childbearing and Increased Education." Research brief no. 27. Bethesda, Md.: Child Trends.

Owen, Stephanie and Isabel V. Sawhill. 2013. "Should Everyone Go to College?" *CCF* brief no. 50. Washington, D.C.: Brookings Institution.

Reardon, Sean. 2011. "The Widening Academic Achievement Gap Between the Rich and the Poor: New Evidence and Possible Explanations." In *Whither Opportunity? Rising Inequality, Schools, and Children's Life Chances*, edited by Greg J. Duncan and Richard J. Murnane. New York: Russell Sage Foundation.

Reeves, Richard. 2014. "Saving Horatio Alger: Equality, Opportunity, and the American Dream." *The Brookings Essay* series, August. Washington, D.C.: Brookings Institution.

Reeves, Richard V., and Kimberly Howard. 2013a. "The Parenting Gap." Center on Children and Families paper. Washington, D.C.: Brookings Institution.

———. 2013b. "The Glass Floor: Education, Downward Mobility, and Opportunity Hoarding." Center on Children and Families paper. Washington, D.C.: Brookings Institution.

Reynolds, Arthur J., Judy A. Temple, Suh-Ruu Ou, Irma A. Arteaga, and Barry A. B. White. 2011. "School-Based Early Childhood Education and Age-28 Well-Being: Effects by Timing, Dosage, and Subgroups." *Science* 333(6040): 360-64.

Roberts, Brent W., Nathan R. Kuncel, Rebecca Shiner, Avshalom Caspi, and Lewis R. Goldberg. 2007. "The Power of Personality: The Comparative Validity of Personality Traits, Socioeconomic Status, and Cognitive Ability for Predicting Important Life Outcomes." *Perspectives on Psychological Science* 2(4): 313-45.

Sawhill, Isabel V. 2014. *Generation Unbound: Drifting into Sex and Parenthood Without Marriage*. Washington, D.C.: Brookings Institution Press.

Sawhill, Isabel V., and Quentin Karpilow. 2014. "How Much Could We Improve Children's Life Chances by Intervening Early and Often? *CCF* brief no. 54. Washington, D.C.: Brookings Institution.

Sawhill, Isabel V., Quentin Karpilow, and Joanna Venator. 2014. "The Impact of Unintended Childbearing on Future Generations." *Center on Children and Families* paper. Washington, D.C.: Brookings Institution.

Sawhill, Isabel V., Scott Winship, and Kerry Searle Grannis. 2012. "Pathways to the Middle Class:

Balancing Personal and Public Responsibilities." *Social Genome Project* paper. Washington, D.C.: Brookings Institution.

Sen, Amartya. 1979. "Equality of What?" Lecture, Stanford University. Stanford, Calif. (May 22, 1979).

———. 1992. *Inequality Reexamined*. New York and Cambridge, Mass.: Russell Sage Foundation and Harvard University Press.

Sharkey, Patrick. 2013a. "Mobility and the Metropolis: How Communities Factor into Economic Mobility." *Economic Mobility Project* report. Washington, D.C.: The Pew Charitable Trusts.

———. 2013b. "Rich Neighborhood, Poor Neighborhood: How Segregation Threatens Social Mobility." *Social Mobility Memos*, December 5, 2013. Accessed January 8, 2015. http://www.brookings.edu/blogs/social-mobility-memos/posts/2013/12/04-how-segregation-threatens-mobility.

Thompson, Ross A. 2014. "Stress and Child Development." *Future of Children* 24(1): 41–59.

Winship, Scott, and Stephanie Owen. 2013. "Guide to the Brookings Social Genome Model." *Social Genome Project* paper. Washington, D.C.: Brookings Institution.

Multiple Barriers to Economic Opportunity for the "Truly" Disadvantaged and Vulnerable

TIMOTHY M. SMEEDING

This article answers several questions: Which subgroups of the U.S. population—designated by race, ethnicity, family structure, educational status, income, wealth, consumption, or other characteristics—appear to be particularly vulnerable to a lack of economic opportunity based on household characteristics of the family and its children? To what degree does poor access to economic advancement appear to reflect low income or wealth, or do additional barriers contribute substantially to some subgroups' limited opportunities? Similarly, what advantages accrue to high-income and other privileged groups, such as those born into a well-established married family? What does current research tell us about the mechanisms through which barriers operate and policies that might be effective in reducing them?

Keywords: opportunity, black, high school dropout, unmarried mother, income, wealth, consumption

Economic opportunity and mobility are not the same thing. But without more opportunity, we are unlikely to see a systematic increase in social and economic intergenerational mobility (IGM) (see Jencks and Tach 2006; Smeeding 2014). Policymakers concerned about these issues should be thinking both about how to overcome barriers to create more opportunity for those left behind, and about how to overcome barriers to make greater opportunity translate into more mobility. Not everyone takes advantage of opportunities and often personal agency leads to less mobility, even when better opportunities are available, for example, when young, unmarried partners have a baby (see Sawhill 2014). Social scientists therefore need a framework to trace out progress against reducing barriers that inhibit increases in opportunity and IGM, especially for groups who have multiple disadvantages.

The traditional literature on the study of IGM does not help us much in creating such a framework. Most scholarly discussions focus on the inheritance of income mobility in past decades. In other words, they ask how the relative economic status of grown children (ages

---

Timothy M. Smeeding is Lee Rainwater Distinguished Professor of Public Affairs and Economics at the La Follette School of Public Affairs and Institute for Research on Poverty, University of Wisconsin–Madison.

The author thanks the Boston Federal Reserve Bank for its support in completing this paper, and the Russell Sage Foundation for support for parts of it. Emily Cuddy and Jonathan Fisher helped with data preparation; Deborah Johnson, David Chancellor, and Dawn Duren provided additional editorial help. Angela Glover Blackwell, Joseph R. Fishkin, Katharine Bradbury, Robert Triest, two referees, and the participants at the Boston Federal Reserve Bank Conference on *Inequality of Economic Opportunity* held October 17–18, 2014, are thanked for comments on an earlier draft and presentation. All errors of commission and omission are the responsibility of the author alone. Direct correspondence to: Timothy M. Smeeding at smeeding@lafollette.wisc.edu, Institute for Research on Poverty, University of Wisconsin–Madison, 3464 Sewell Social Sciences Bldg., Madison, WI 53706.

thirty-five to forty) compares with their parents' status when they were young (between 1966 and 1979). Some of these studies tell us that overall mobility has not declined in recent decades, which is not surprising for an economy where income gains were widespread across the population and living standards rose across the distribution up until the 1980s. We also know from national and cross-national research the great deal of stickiness at both the top and bottom of the relative IGM matrix of parental and child incomes: the children of the rich tend to remain rich and the children of the poor, poor. Further, we know that the resource levels separating poor from rich have grown in magnitude since the inequality generation was born in the 1980s, and that absolute mobility for the children of the bottom quintile has fallen since 1980 as returns to education and assortative mating have strengthened the differences between the top and bottom of the family income distributions (Autor 2014; Schwartz 2013; McLanahan and Jacobsen 2014). Although the economic landscape has changed since the 1970s, the experiences of older cohorts still may be important—even if the intergenerational mobility of older baby boomers may look very different from that of the post–baby boom Generation X or Millennials (those born between 1980 and 2000), and the generation born since—because they are the parents of today's children.

If we are to push for policies to enhance opportunity and improve IGM for the next generation, we need to look at the factors that are affecting today's and tomorrow's children's chances at upward mobility. Borrowing from William Julius Wilson (1987), we are concerned here with upward mobility among only truly disadvantaged families with multiple obstacles facing them and their children. In our analyses, we sometimes refer to the *truly advantaged* at the top of the social and economic heap. A life cycle approach can help us assess trajectories by setting up markers of success or failure along the road to greater IGM from birth through adulthood. As we view IGM from this perspective, we are able to observe factors that affect parents and children's opportunities and mobility. It allows us to identify the obstacles that vulnerable groups face and to focus on policies to aid them across the life course to reach the American Dream of a stable middle-class lifestyle.

In this article, I set out to apply the life cycle model to determine which subgroups of the U.S. population—designated by race, family structure, and education, as well as by income, consumption, and wealth—appear to be particularly vulnerable to a lack of economic opportunity. I assess the social and economic circumstances that create barriers to opportunity and mobility and examine how they contribute to limit opportunities for the vulnerable. These barriers are not just low economic resources, but also include a set of mechanisms and processes that either discourage or encourage opportunity. I therefore turn to policies that might be effective in reducing these barriers.

From this perspective, at least three sets of forces influence social mobility, as enablers for some and as barriers for others, all of which have changed in the decades since the 1970s:

- Family. Family instability and insecurity create barriers for many disadvantaged families, while good parenting skills and abundant resources give upper-income and wealthy families a large advantage. We are increasingly seeing a *parenting gap* or *diverging destinies*, where parents at the top are able to spend both more and better time and more money on activities to promote their child's educational and social development, buy into safe neighborhoods with good schools, and so on, than lower-income parents.

- Markets, especially labor markets. Individuals deploy their skills in markets to improve family economic resources, but the returns to the skilled and the educated have blossomed, whereas those to the unskilled and undereducated have fallen. Both income and wealth matter, because they limit consumption and education spending on children's enrichment and school opportunities for the disadvantaged while enhancing the chances of the rich and well educated.

- Public policy and social institutions. Policy and social institutions are important forces because they create opportunities for some children and reduce them for others. We need to know how to reduce growing class gaps, especially in family formation, family resources, health, education, and neighborhoods.

The family income package (Rainwater and Smeeding 2003) is determined by these three institutions, all of which play a role in IGM. Family, markets, and policy and social institutions interact with one another and together determine both opportunity and mobility. They serve as resources that can play especially large roles at strategic transfer points in the life course (that is, places where more investments from parents or institutions make a big difference in child outcomes). Some come early, such as parent-child interactions and the development of cognitive skills and character (social competency, perseverance, and good habits) at home and in preschool. Some come from schooling choices, and some come later on through paying for college, providing funding for a child to experience an unpaid internship, direct job provision in family firms (nepotism), or helping children enter the housing market.

Of course, stagnant earnings and incomes in the 2000s suggest that the barriers we identify are a worry for the absolute mobility of the strapped middle classes, not just poor families with children. The difference between a poverty budget that allots just enough to feed, clothe, and shelter one's children, and a budget that allows for the higher cost of a "well-raised" child is substantial. Consideration is due as well to the important issue of the sharing of child-rearing costs between parents/families and the public sector. Hence mobility is a middle-class issue as well as a poor family issue.

Finally, the belief in the opportunity to reach the American Dream is in question today. It once was a strongly and widely held view that if you worked hard and played by the rules, you could get ahead in America. But this has changed. Today, only 42 percent of Americans agree that if you work hard you will get ahead. Also, notably, fewer than 33 percent of African Americans believe that hard work gets you ahead today, and one in seven (14 percent) never believed it (Jones, Cox, and Navarro-Rivera 2014). More to the point for IGM analyses, half of Americans believe that their own generation is better off financially than their children's generation will be. Most Americans (55 percent) believe that one of the biggest problems in the country is that not everyone is given an equal chance to succeed in life. Other recent surveys have shown the same result—parents' confidence in their children being better off than they are is at or near the lowest point ever recorded.[1] Overall, we must conclude that Americans are expressing significant concerns about the economic future for themselves and their children, and about their beliefs in America being an equal opportunity society. This is especially the case for the vulnerable groups we focus on here.

LIFE CYCLE MODEL AND VULNERABLE POPULATIONS

A recent pair of cross-national research volumes took the life cycle approach to studying the influence of parental education and income on child outcomes from birth to age thirty (Smeeding, Erikson, and Jäntti 2011; Ermisch, Jäntti, and Smeeding 2012). Figure 1 summarizes our model of the life course process from birth to adulthood for one generation, moving from origin (parental social economic status, or SES) to destination (children's adulthood SES) across six life stages. Parental investments, income, wealth, and social institutions affect each step of the life course, where intermediate gains or losses are measured in multiple domains.

This structure allowed us to observe different cohorts at different times, with every outcome in every country ranked by adult educational differences. Taken as a whole, these cross-national studies reveal a powerful effect of parental SES on child outcomes in health, cognitive testing, sociobehavioral outcomes, school achievement, and adult social and economic outcomes. Examination of standardized

---

1. William Galston (2014) documents at least five recent (mid-2014) surveys that show the same result.

Figure 1. A Model of Intergenerational Transmission of Advantage by Life Stage

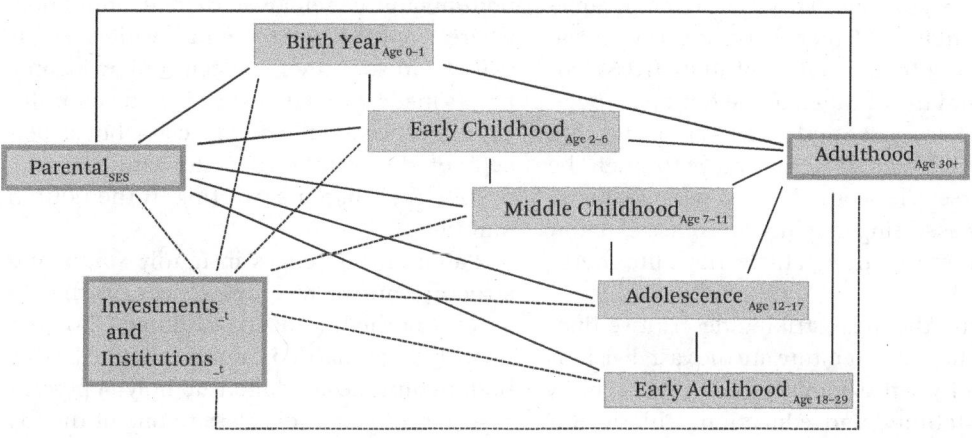

Source: Ermisch, Jäntti, and Smeeding 2012, figure 1.2.

outputs across eleven countries found a definite and universal pattern that the higher the adult SES as measured by educational attainment, the larger the positive effect on children's outcomes, and vice versa. These effects were observed from birth onward and they did not diminish as children matured into adulthood. Moreover, the slopes of the relationships between parental SES and child outcomes were steepest in the United States. But not all the steps were filled in for any one country, save Sweden (see Mood, Jonsson, and Bihagen 2012), and most outcomes were measured for only one cohort. This method proved a useful way to assess cross-national differences in IGM, and the same structure is also a useful way to assess how various cohorts of younger generation U.S. children will be affected by growing gaps in parental SES (education, earnings, wealth, and income) in our own nation.

Another domestic project approaching this question in the same way began at just about the same time the international work was published. The objective was to ask what one needs to accomplish at various life stages to achieve the American Dream. The Brookings-Urban Institute-Child Trends Social Genome Model (SGM) has now estimated a set of factors for assessing progress toward reaching the American Dream.[2] That is, the model maps out the steps one needs to take across the life course to progress to become a family with incomes at three times the poverty line in middle age, which is more or less making it well into the middle-income quintile or higher.

Both of these models and steps provide a framework to examine the parental-investment and institutional forces that boost life chances for some and provide barriers for others across the life cycle. The steps might be thought of as hurdles to overcome or descriptive markers of life progress and processes. One can still succeed if one stumbles at any one stage, but momentum and cumulative forces propel one along given courses. Richard Reeves and Isabel Sawhill (2015) review the overall patterns and contours of the SGM and how progress or lack thereof in each of these stages has affected recent generations. Here we use a similar framework to assess the characteristics of the most disadvantaged and vulnerable populations who have an especially hard time negotiating the life cycle process.

Reeves and Sawhill (2015) argue that overall social mobility is unacceptably low in the United States today: between 36 and 40 percent of those born into the bottom quintile remain there as adults, versus 30 to 34 percent of those

---

2. For more on SGM, see the Social Genome Project (http://www.social-genome.org/), the Brookings guide to the model (http://www.brookings.edu/~/media/Centers/ccf/sgm_guide.pdf), and Reeves and Sawhill 2015.

born into the top quintile staying at the top when they grow up.[3] They define the parameters of their SGM model using the 1979 National Longitudinal Survey of Youth (NLSY) for adults and the Children of the National Longitudinal Survey of Youth (CNLSY) for the children of these adults as they move through the life course. These are the best parameters we have for assessing mobility outcomes and how children move through the various life course steps.[4]

Among the most striking descriptive findings in the SGM literature are the vast divisions in mobility across family types by race, family status/stability, and education. This article dwells on vulnerable families and children differentiated by race, family status, and education, and I limit my interest to the most vulnerable and disadvantaged among these. In particular, I focus on adult outcomes for black children, children coming from families with low levels of adult education, and children growing up in single-parent and complex families, all of whose absolute and relative mobility out of the bottom quintile is the most pressing matter for IGM policy.

Table 1 is based on the Social Genome Model.[5] It presents the stark differences among the most disadvantaged children (those coming from the bottom income quintile) in the income status they have achieved when they are observed as adults. Although the results are mainly about the mobility of the adult generation today, I argue that the circumstances of children in these groups suggest even lower mobility for the current generation born into these same circumstances. Some low-income groups are obviously more successful than others in reaching the middle class (third quintile) or above. Half the black children born into the bottom quintile remained there in adulthood, whereas fewer than one in four whites in this cohort did so. Only 10 percent of low-income blacks made it to the top two income quintiles as adults, beyond the middle class, but 35 percent of disadvantaged white children did, despite their parents' starting in the bottom quintile.

Parental differences in family status and structure mirror race differences, in that 50 percent of the low-income children who grew up with never-married parents remained in the bottom quintile as adults, and only 14 percent rose above the middle class to one of the top two quintiles as adults. Those from the bottom who were in married-parent families at some point do a little better, but these children still had a 56 percent chance of ending up in the bottom two quintiles when they grow up. Poor children who grew up with continuously married parents did much better, though marriage is now rapidly shrinking in this group for those with less than a college education (Cherlin 2014). A general pattern of greater upward mobility is seen as we move up the family status scale to the continuously married.

Failure of an adult to graduate high school, even with a GED (general educational development) certificate, greatly depresses upward mobility rates (Murnane 2013). Bottom income quintile children in table 1 who were raised by a parent without a high school diploma had a 54 percent chance of remaining in the bottom quintile as adults, and only 6 percent made it to the top two quintiles in this cohort. Among low-income children whose parents achieved high school degrees by adulthood, 54 percent ended up in the bottom 40 percent of their

---

3. The ranges depend on the exact specifications, but combining NLSY and Panel Study of Income Dynamics results, the range delineates the stickiness in the tails (see Reeves and Sawhill 2015; Jäntti et al. 2006).

4. The CNLSY is used in the Social Genome Model to estimate patterns of mobility for children as they move through the life course. The CNLSY sample currently ranges in age from under five to over thirty-five and these parameters are closer to the current generation than are those in the NLSY. The oldest of the CNLSY's economic mobility sample can be traditionally measured in about five to ten years, when their incomes and earnings are best observed (Auten, Gee, and Turner 2013). The data in table 1 refer to the NLSY parents and their experiences growing up because it is summarizing adult outcomes of the IGM process.

5. Thanks to Emily Cuddy at Brookings who provided the Social Genome matrices underlying table 1. The parameters are taken from the 1979 NLSY panel and thus are based on the experiences of this particular cohort.

Table 1. Distribution of Adult Outcomes (Income Quintile as an Adult) for Children Born into Bottom Quintile

Characteristics	Percent in Each Adult Income Quintile*:			
	Bottom	Next	Middle	Top Two
Race:	20	20	20	40
Black	51	27	12	10
(White)	(23)	(19)	(23)	(35)
Family status of mother				
Never-married	50	24	13	14
Discontinuously married	32	24	20	24
(Continuously married)	(17)	(23)	(20)	(40)
Educational status of parent				
Less than high school	54	26	13	6
High school degree and some college	30	24	18	26
(College graduate)	(16)	(17)	(26)	(41)

Source: Author's calculations.

Notes: The graph shows standard deviation differences in skills and behavior for children in the lowest income quintile and the highest SES quintile based on estimates in table 1. ECLSK refers to the Early Childhood Longitudinal Study Kindergarten Cohort studies, which were fielded in 1998 and 2010. Approaches to Learning is the ECLS-K measure of attention and school engagement.

*Each row adds to 100 percent (except for rounding); under equal opportunity a full 20 percent of each group would be in each quintile.

adult income distribution. The bottom-quintile children who grew up in households headed by a college graduate had only a 30 percent chance of ending up in the bottom two quintiles when they reached adulthood, and a 41 percent chance of making it into the top quintile in their cohort as adults. Higher levels of education and degree completion among low-income parents are clearly associated with higher rates of upward mobility for their children when they reach adulthood.

Summarizing table 1, in the end, what do we have? At least half of all bottom-quintile children who were African American, whose parents did not finish high school, or who grew up with a never-married mother, remained in the bottom quintile as adults. Three-quarters or more (74, 78, and 80 percent, respectively) ended up in the bottom 40 percent of the income distribution as adults, thereby failing to realize the American Dream.[6] Moreover, the three groups in table 1 overlap, making it difficult to separate effects by race, family status, or parental education. In fact, future research needs to move beyond these bivariate associations and stratify by more than one disadvantage to understand mobility for those with multiple disadvantages. For instance, being born to a black unwed mother who grew up in a low-income family and who did not complete high school, and being born to an upper-income class married, white, college-graduate mother are the opposite ends of the "diverging destinies" for children in this cohort (McLanahan 2004; McLanahan and Jacobsen 2014).

---

6. In fact, in terms of current policy interest in absolute mobility, the living standards of the bottom 40 percent are precisely the key foci for those who want "growth with equity" (Cingano 2014), "shared prosperity" (Jolliffe and Lanjouw 2014), and "inclusive prosperity" (Summers and Balls 2015).

THE ROLE OF MONEY: INCOME, WEALTH, AND CONSUMPTION

Money matters for opportunity and mobility, especially in America. Low incomes as a child and as an adult are one key element of vulnerability, as seen in table 1. For those children living in the bottom quintile, especially when very young or for an extended period, low incomes have a well-established negative impact on brain development, social-emotional development, and lifelong outcomes. The effects range all the way from negative impacts on educational success and employment to longer-term health effects, such as heart disease and stress-related diseases showing up in adulthood that can be tracked to extended experiences of (economic) deprivation, trauma, and stress as a child (Smeeding 2016).

At the same time, a little more money makes a big difference to children on the bottom rungs of the ladder. A host of recent studies have shown that refundable tax credits—the Earned Income Tax Credit (EITC), the refundable portion of the Child Tax Credit (CTC), and the Additional Child Tax Credit (ACTC)—improve child outcomes in health, including birth outcomes for mothers, and the learning of young children (Evans and Garthwaite 2014; Hoynes, Miller, and Simon 2015; Dahl and Lochner 2012; Milligan and Stabile 2009). Supplemental Nutrition Assistance Program (SNAP) receipt during childhood is also shown to improve child health and learning outcomes, and to foster significant reduction in the incidence of metabolic syndrome (obesity, high blood pressure, and diabetes) and, for women, an increase in economic self-sufficiency (Almond, Hoynes, and Schanzenbach 2011; Hoynes, Schanzenbach, and Almond 2014; Hoynes, Miller, and Simon 2015). More generally, in childhood, higher incomes for low-income families have a large number of positive effects (for summaries, see Duncan, Morris, and Rodrigues 2011; Duncan, Magnuson, and Votruba-Drzal 2014; Cooper and Stewart 2013). The simple summary is that higher benefits from the EITC, CTC/ACTC, and SNAP lead to better outcomes for children and parents, especially positive longer-term developmental effects on low-income children.

Mobility also depends on how far apart the incomes of parents are. Because absolute differences between the top and bottom incomes of parents have changed a great deal since 1979, the stakes for remaining at the bottom or the top of the distribution are now much larger. Congressional Budget Office estimates of after-tax and transfer incomes show that the gap in incomes between the richest and poorest quintiles of families with children rose by almost $112,000 or 115 percent from 1979 to 2010 (see Smeeding 2016; Congressional Budget Office 2013). This is a huge difference across a fairly short time span. The main basis of income for parents and their children is employment and earnings. If anything, the Great Recession has made differences in economic status much worse, as we see increasingly stark differences in employment and wages by education and age, with earnings gains mainly above the bachelor's degree level where the IGM correlation of parents' and children's education is highest (Torche 2011). Cross-national research suggests that the premiums in pay for the highest educated are largest in the United States as well, meaning that the minority who reach college graduation and beyond do better in the U.S. labor market than their less-educated countrymen (Autor 2014; Blanden et al. 2014; Ermisch, Jäntti, and Smeeding 2012).

Money matters, but it is not just about income; consumption and wealth also matter. In figure 2 we document how the demography of income, consumption, and wealth differs among various age groups. This figure ranks distributions so that 20 percent of all people are in each quintile by each measure, and then focuses on where adults, elders, and children (as measured by their family variables) are located in each distribution (equivalence-scale adjusted) in 2010. In other words, if we were to look at the overall distribution of all people by any one of these measures, exactly 20 percent would be in each quintile. Those who are less likely to be well off are overrepresented in the bottom quintiles, and those who are better off are more heavily represented in the top quintiles. The takeaway is that children and elders in particular are located in very different parts of the distribution in terms of wealth and consumption compared to income. The position of children in the lowest 40 percent of each

Figure 2. Demography of Inequality by Age, 2010

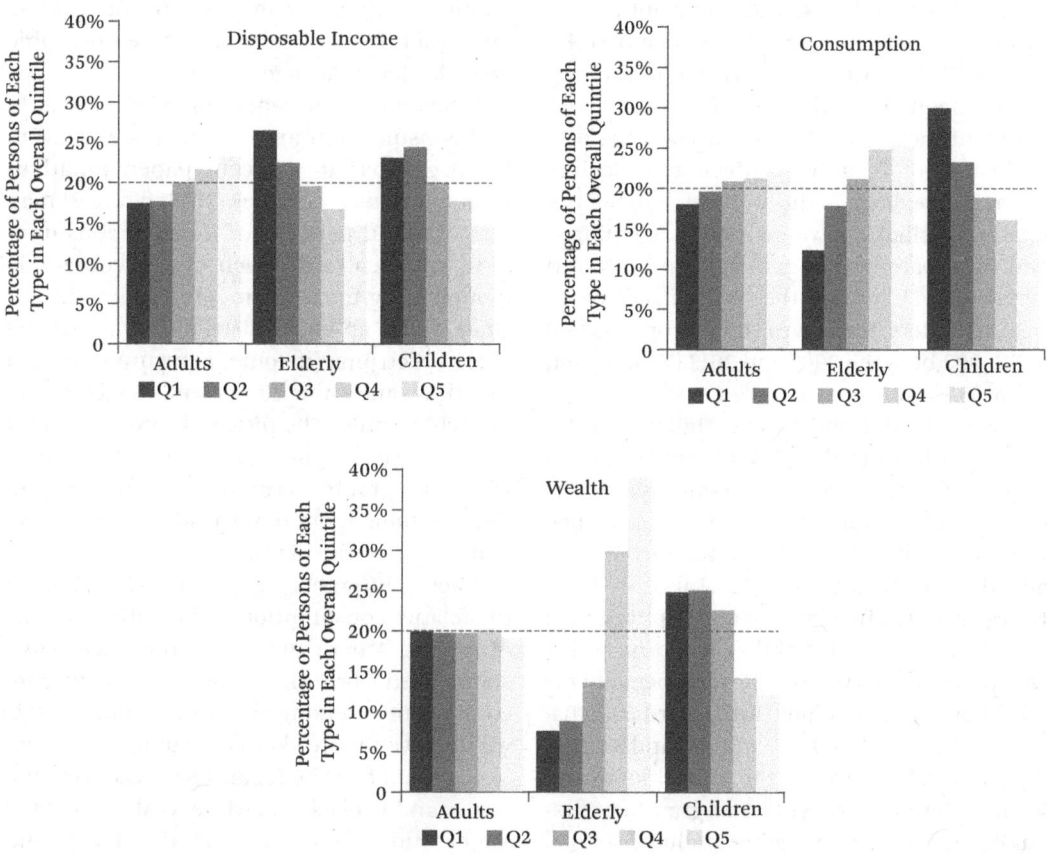

Source: Fisher et al. 2015.
Note: The data are for number of persons by age: children (under age eighteen); elders (age sixty-five and over), so person weighted. Overall inequality is not shown, but if so, it would be at 20 percent of the population overall in each quintile. Each quintile is ranked by its own measure (income, consumption, or wealth) with an equivalence scale adjustment using the square root of household size. Adults include those currently living with elders or children under age eighteen, as well as childless adults.

distribution, especially the consumption and wealth distributions, should cause concern about their upward mobility compared with that of the minority of advantaged children who are at the top of the wealth and consumption scales and whose grandparents as well as parents can help them overcome financial obstacles to upward mobility. Indeed, Janet Yellen (2014, figure 8) shows that the mean net worth of the top 5 percent of families with children was greater than $3 million in 2013, versus $500 or less for the bottom half of all families with children. And those children at the very bottom of the income distribution today are in large part the sons and daughters of the adults seen in the first two columns (first two quintiles) in table 1.

None of the current analyses of inequality have yet captured the full effect of net worth (assets, debt, and wealth) on consumption or income by considering all three measures of well-being simultaneously for the same households, though we know that each gives a different and important perspective on the distribution of economic well-being, and likely a different outcome when considering the effects of inequality on IGM.[7] Wealth is the most elusive, because it is a stock and not a flow. Evidence from the Survey of Consumer Finances (Yellen 2014, figure 3) suggests rising wealth inequality in the United States, the top 5 percent increasing their shares and the others losing out, including a precipitous decline in mean wealth for the bottom half of the wealth distribution, where most U.S. children and their parents increasingly can be found (see figure 2). Among the bottom half of all wealth holders, mean wealth fell from $32,000 to $12,000 between 2007 and 2013 (Yellen 2014, figure 4).

Fabian Pfeffer and Martin Hällsten (2012) and Timothy Smeeding (2016) argue that the impact of parental wealth on children works through its insurance effects (think of a "private family safety net"). High family wealth creates the ability to finance 529s and pre-fund college with tax-free interest and capital gains; as well as the greater ability to do more for well-timed intervivos transfers, especially for the following generations (Kirkegaard 2015; Banerjee 2015). Richard Reeves (2014) and Smeeding (2014) refer to this as the glass floor effect. Wealthy families (parents and grandparents) pay college tuition, including graduate school, leaving their graduating children and grandchildren debt-free after graduation. They subsidize rent and provide apprenticeship funds for children to move to high income-growth areas without jobs. Often they can and do provide jobs directly in family-run businesses (Bingley, Corak, and Westergard-Nielson 2012; Corak and Piraino 2011; Stinson and Wignall 2014; Yellen 2014). And they pass on homeownership subsidies to capture upswings in real estate by cosigning low-interest mortgages for children who do not qualify for the best rates. Of course, they also provide other glass floor advantages, such as good lawyers, subsidized travel for children's human capital building, good schools, and safe neighborhoods. Moreover, if we omit wealth or lack of it from our mobility analyses, we may be attributing some important true wealth effects to demographic variables like marriage or to race.

What about differences in income, wealth, and consumption among our key disadvantaged groups? In a recent paper, Jonathan Fisher and his colleagues (2015, figure 3) map rankings and patterns of income, consumption, and wealth for each of our vulnerable groups using the same method as in figure 2. Once again, an equal distribution across the three spectrums (income, consumption, and wealth) would show 20 percent of each group in each quintile. The picture is quite different in each case in figure 2, however. The income and demographic groupings correspond to those in table 1, but now we add consumption and wealth to the picture.[8]

Racial differences are stark. Considering the relative consumption and wealth positions of African Americans makes their economic status even worse than when we consider income alone. Ranking children's family status, we find even more skewed results. Tom Shapiro, Tatjana Meschede, and Sam Osoro (2013) also examine black and white wealth using the Panel Study of Income Dynamics (PSID), and find that the total wealth gap between white and black families nearly tripled in twenty-five years, from $85,000 in 1984 to $236,500 in 2009. The Great Recession was particularly devastating to the young black middle class because they were the ones who bought homes at the top of the market, between 2000 and 2006, often with subprime loans. Differences in housing wealth and homeownership, but also income, unemployment, inheritance, and financial transfers, all help explain this gap.

Fisher and his colleagues (2015) are unable to differentiate between never-married mothers and their discontinuously married counterparts, but it is clear that children being raised by single parents in 2010 were predominately

---

7. For instance, recent work shows that since 2001, with wealth measured in early 2013, wealth inequality has increased and income inequality with it (Yellen 2014; Pfeffer, Danziger, and Schoeni 2014; Bricker et al. 2014). And financial wealth has increased by 20 percent since the time of both surveys. Indeed, Fabian Pfeffer (2011) argues that wealth is more important than income for IGM.

8. Table 1 looks at single mothers but figure 3 includes single fathers (who make up about 10 percent of all single parents).

in the bottom 40 percent in each distribution (see also Painter, Frech, and Williams 2015). Perhaps the most differential rankings have to do with the educational status of adults, where high school dropouts are most heavily clustered in the bottom 40 percent of each distribution.

These snapshots of economic status allow us to look at the three dimensions of economic inequality for our three vulnerable parental groups whose experiences and achievements when growing up in the bottom quintiles are shown in table 1 and whose children we are most concerned about here. For the most part, net worth and consumption differences reinforce income differences, suggesting that the disadvantaged groups in whom we are most interested—blacks, nonmarried parents, and those with a high school education or less—find themselves in very poor economic positions by each index. Although a small proportion of children do well in terms of income, wealth, and consumption (figure 2), mostly they live with college-educated white families. The most vulnerable children are found near the bottom end of each distribution by each characteristic. Obviously the poor and lower middle-income groups are at risk simply because they have too little income (consumption and wealth) to afford the neighborhoods, schools, lifestyles, and other elements of raising a child well. Hence, lack of economic resources is correlated with many other disadvantages for these adults and their children.

THE TRULY DISADVANTAGED AND VULNERABLE

Most of our knowledge of group-specific mobility comes from the panel datasets and models based on them, and which have been part and parcel of economic and social research on mobility. Although these data cannot be used directly as policy guides, they have helped identify groups who have been historically likely to be vulnerable and in need of help to create and seize opportunities for their children (see table 1 and figure 3). As shown, vulnerabilities come in clumps, as do advantages, making it hard to apportion the influence of separate factors, despite the fact that each separate grouping has important negative consequences for opportunity and mobility (for an attempt to separate the effects of race from SES, see VanderWeele and Robinson 2014).

Race and Incarceration

African Americans are much less likely to succeed even holding multiple parental status variables constant. Research on differences in mobility between blacks and whites reveals stark variances. On average, blacks experience less upward mobility and whites less downward mobility, corroborating the Social Genome and economic rankings shown above. In fact, whites are on average 20 to 30 percentage points more likely to experience upward mobility than blacks are (Mazumder 2014). Studies of older cohorts find that almost 50 percent of black children born into the bottom 20 percent of the income distribution were in the same position as adults, but that only 23 percent of white children born in that quintile were (see table 1; see also Mazumder 2014; Sawhill, Winship, and Grannis 2012; Isaacs, Sawhill, and Haskins 2008; Acs 2011; Hertz 2005).[9] A range of personal and background characteristics—such as parental occupational status, individual educational attainment, and marital status—help explain this race gap. But, taking into account differences in Armed Forces Qualification Test (AFQT) scores between white and black men explains most of the variation in results, giving us some hope that educational treatments might improve black mobility outcomes in general if they can raise AFQT scores and college graduation rates (Mazumder 2014).[10]

Although family structure, parental and

---

9. Gregory Acs also finds that black men raised in middle-class families are 17 percentage points more likely to be downwardly mobile than white men raised in the middle class are: 38 percent of black men fall out, compared with 21 percent of white men (2011).

10. The AFQT is a measure of aptitude used mainly by the armed forces and by researchers who want to measure aptitudes in young adults. Scores are computed using the standard scores from four subtests: arithmetic reasoning, mathematics knowledge, paragraph comprehension, and word knowledge.

Figure 3. Vulnerable Groups in 2010

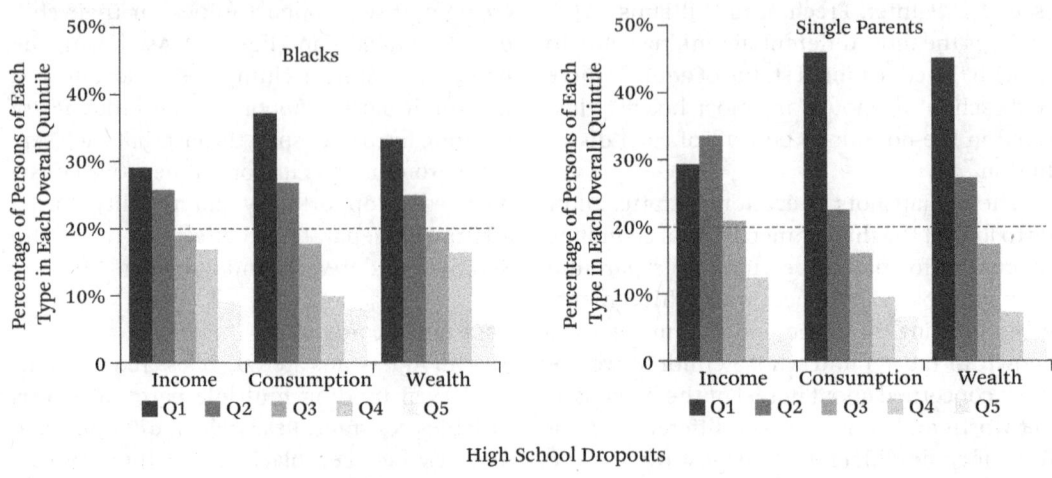
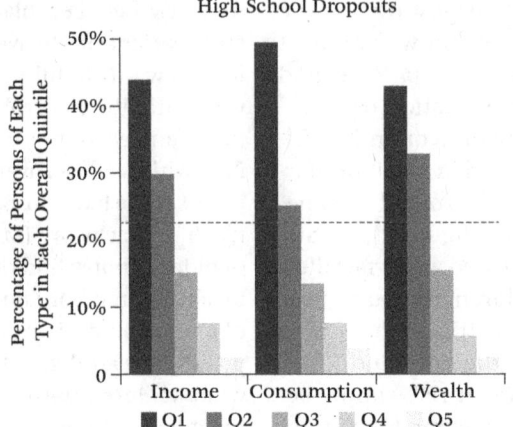

Source: Fisher et al. 2015.
Note: The data are for number of persons by race, all blacks; all children and adults who are single parents with children under age eighteen; and all adults (age twenty-one and over) who did not finish high school. Each quintile is ranked by its own measure (income, consumption, or wealth) for the whole population with an equivalence scale adjustment using the square root of household size. Hence, the figure shows where each group is located in the overall distributions of income, consumption, and wealth.

personal education, family background, income, and neighborhood all played a role in these disturbing findings, one important source of downward mobility for black men remains largely unaccounted for. Much of low black mobility, which is not yet fully recorded because of the age of the individuals involved, is affected by the spectacular rise in imprisonment in America between 1970 and 2010, and its negative long-term economic consequences for less-educated black men and their families, who are now mainly young or middle-aged adults (Pettit 2012; Pager 2003; Western and Pettit 2010; Pew Charitable Trusts 2010).

A thorough National Academy of Sciences report (Travis, Western, and Redburn 2014) concluded that among recent cohorts of black men, about one in five who have never been to college have served time in state or federal prison at some point in their lives. Among black male high school dropouts, about two-thirds have a prison record by age thirty—more than twice the rate for their white counterparts. IGM is most severely limited for those who have been in the prison system. In 2012, the overall correctional population—those incarcerated in prison, jail, or being supervised on parole—was about seven million persons, mainly originating from the most disadvantaged segments of the population. In 2007, before the onset of the Great Recession, only half of the ex-incarcerated were able to find jobs (Schmitt and Ware 2010).

Those most affected by incarceration are mainly minority (especially black) men under age forty who are poorly educated, often have mental illness issues, and lack formal work preparation or experience. These coincidental conditions and attributes make it difficult to precisely estimate effects of incarceration, as these conditions are each liable to reduce mobility for this population, while negatively affecting their communities and families. But even given these other barriers to progress, an incarceration history adds to the negative effects of poor schooling and race in ways we have just begun to explore. In fact, the growth of incarceration rates among black men in recent decades combined with the sharp drop in black employment rates during the Great Recession have left most black men in an economic position relative to white men that is really no better than in 1970 (Neal and Rick 2014). This of course affects intragenerational mobility as well: among former inmates in the bottom quarter of the earnings distribution in 1986, two-thirds remained there in 2006, twice the rate of nonincarcerated men. Further, only 2 percent of previously incarcerated men who started in the bottom fifth of the earnings distribution made it to the top fifth twenty years later, against 15 percent of all men who started at the bottom but were never incarcerated (Pew Charitable Trusts 2010).

Most of the men and women in prison have children. Nationally, about 53 percent of men and 61 percent of women in the U.S. prison population are parents (Maruschak, Glaze, and Mumola 2010). Christopher Wildeman (2009) and Becky Pettit (2012) calculate the probability that a child would experience a parent's being sent to prison by the child's teenage years. Among black children, parental imprisonment in the 1990 birth cohort was about 25 percent.

Further, although 15 percent of white children whose parents had not completed high school had had a parent sent to prison by age seventeen, 62 percent of their African American counterparts experienced some time with one parent in jail or prison (Wakefield and Wildeman 2013). Of course, these recent cohorts are too young to fully capture the effect of parental imprisonment, but the numbers are stunningly large and new evidence on the effects of parental incarceration on children is beginning to emerge (Lee, Fang, and Luo 2013; Hagan and Foster 2012).

Incarceration is highly correlated with family hardship, including housing insecurity and behavioral problems in children, especially boys. Prison stresses relationships within families and reduces child involvement postrelease. Studies that focus exclusively on incarcerated men have found that partners and children of male prisoners are particularly likely to experience adverse outcomes if the men were positively involved with their families prior to incarceration. But only about four in ten men reported living with their children before incarceration and studies are mixed on the effects of child separation from incarcerated parents, because, for example, being away from violent men can improve children's life chances (Travis, Western, and Redburn 2014, chapter 9). Many of these differences are hard to assess because of difficulty in following young men in and out of prison, especially among recent cohorts. Any new research on IGM ought to make such study a priority, because very few formerly incarcerated individuals are tracked by our datasets.

Declining manufacturing sector employment in inner cities accompanied the prison boom, as Wilson classically describes (1987, 1996), where the outmigration of whites and the rising black middle class left behind pockets of concentrated disadvantage. These poor, racially segregated neighborhoods are characterized not just by high rates of poverty and crime but also high rates of unemployment, single parenthood, and multiple-partner fertility (adults living with children from two or more partners). These neighborhoods were heavily populated by blacks, but Charles Murray (2012) shows similar effects appearing in former white middle-class neighborhoods as well.

FAMILY STATUS, STABILITY, AND PARENTING

Family status and stability as well as parenting practices may matter even more than incomes for equality of opportunity and IGM. As Sara McLanahan and Wade Jacobsen have established (McLanahan 2004; McLanahan and Jacobsen 2014), we are seeing a growing class divide in America— in income, in education, and in family formation. Children born into continuously married families have much better economic mobility than those in single-parent families, especially unmarried mothers, or families where the parents break up (see table 1). Indeed, family differences begin at birth. It is often useful to illustrate the middle ground of an issue by looking at its endpoints. If we examine both what is considered to be the best process by which to become a parent and the worst process, we can better understand the point of diverging destinies. The "best" way to become a parent for men and women alike is through living the American Dream: finish your schooling, find a decent job, find a partner you can rely on, make plans for a future together including marriage as a commitment device (see Lundberg and Pollak 2013), and then have a baby. Following this process will likely mean that parents are middle class or better and close to the age of thirty when a first child is born.[11] Parents who follow this process are (in some ways by definition) older, more educated, and more likely to have a stable marriage. They have better parenting skills, smaller families, and more income, benefits, and assets to support their children. These characteristics translate almost directly into more opportunities for their children.

At the other end of the spectrum, the "worst" way to become a parent is to have a baby as an adolescent or young adult between the ages of sixteen and twenty-two, preceding all the other steps. These parents typically have not finished schooling, do not have a steady or well-paying job, do not have a stable marriage or steady partnership, and likely never had a life plan for raising their children. They have less education (high school or less), are younger and less skilled, have lower wages and fewer benefits, have far less partnership experience, and will have more multiple-partner fertility. The result is less social and economic stability and fewer resources and opportunities for their children (Smeeding, Garfinkel, and Mincy 2011; Smeeding 2016).

More than 40 percent of all births in 2013 were out of wedlock, up from 19 percent in 1980. For those under age thirty, half of all births were to unmarried mothers (Hamilton et al. 2014). For these single women under thirty, almost 70 percent of births are unplanned as young adults "drift" into parenthood because of failed contraception or ambivalence about school and life goals (Sawhill 2014). Black out-of-wedlock births have risen from 57 percent in 1980 to more than 70 percent in 2013 (Hamilton et al. 2014). Marriage rates have never been high for blacks but are now falling, as they are for noncollege graduate whites (Murray 2012; Cherlin 2014). The fraction of never-married mothers with children under age eighteen is more than 20 percent for those who did not graduate secondary school and 15 percent for high school graduates, as compared to 3 percent for those with a bachelor's degree or more (Smeeding 2016). Not only is out-of-wedlock childbearing highest among the least educated, but these births occur mainly to younger mothers, most of whom are poor or near poor and have unstable living conditions in terms of both partners and housing (Edin, DeLuca, and Owens 2012; Tach 2015). Moreover, these mothers have more children per woman than the average mother over her lifetime (Smeeding, Garfinkel, and Mincy 2011). In contrast, well-educated parents have fewer children later (in marriage) under much better economic circumstances (McLanahan and Jacobsen 2014; Sawhill 2014).

Family complexity and instability are detrimental to upward mobility, but are also high among unmarried parents. In 2010, 20 percent of all births and roughly half of all births to

---

11. Indeed, findings are that the median age of first birth for women who are college graduates is twenty-nine (Smeeding, Garfinkel, and Mincy 2011).

unmarried mothers were to cohabiting couples at the time of a focal child's birth (Perelli-Harris et al. 2010). These families are highly unstable, however, almost 80 percent having a different partner by the time the child reaches age fifteen (Andersson 2002). Additionally, 67 percent of all unmarried cohabiting parents had found another partner within five years of the breakup (Andersson 2002). Multiple-partner fertility also comes into play here (Carlson and Furstenberg 2006). The Fragile Families data, from a sample of urban births, mainly among the vulnerable groups we emphasize here, finds that 79 percent of unmarried parents of the focal child have had a child with another partner within nine years of the focal birth. Among the married births, 25 percent had another child with another partner over this period (Carlson et al. 2013). Being raised by continuously married parents has a strong correlation with upward mobility for black children, but far too few of them grow up in such circumstances (Mazumder 2012).

Parenting is also highly unequal and parental endowments of skills are also important in determining life opportunities. More-educated, higher-income parents often have more parenting skills than their lower-income, less-educated counterparts. Hence, some types of skills training may offer overlapping benefits for parenting and the labor soft skills such as conflict resolution or knowing how to respond to setbacks, which also are better taught by highly educated parents (Heckman and Mosso 2014). High-skill parents not only realize the value of education, but also make every effort to make sure their children succeed in reaching a high level of educational attainment. In contrast, in the face of low education, family instability, complexity, and low income, most unmarried mothers live stressful lives that are not good for themselves or their children (Aizer and Currie 2014). For instance, hours spent reading to a young child or talking with a young child is where large differences in early language development begin and which also make a big difference in mobility outcomes.

Various studies document that time spent with young children in reading and personal interaction is much more developmentally oriented in older and more educated married-couple families than in younger, single, unmarried-mother families (Kalil, Ryan, and Corey 2012; Phillips 2011). Using a measure of parenting quality, Richard Reeves and Kimberly Howard (2013) establish that the children of lowest quartile parents do worse at every stage of the Social Genome Model compared with highest quartile parents, with differences in success rates between these groups on the order of 30 to 45 percent at each life stage.

EDUCATION

The final at-risk groups are those without a normal high school diploma, including those with a GED degree or less, by age thirty.[12] Formal schooling is the major vehicle for a child's upward mobility; but those who have not done well in school themselves will have a much harder time navigating school choices and embracing the elements of school success for their own children. The Organization for Economic Cooperation and Development (2014) has singled out the United States as being particularly deficient in one measure: the chances are greater than 70 percent that an American will not attend a four-year college if his or her parents do not have a college degree. The structure of our education system, not just secondary schools and colleges, but also early childhood education (ECE) and preschools and career and technical education (CTE) systems, has a large effect on who succeeds and who does not.

The correlation between parental and child education has been studied at least back through Gary Becker and Nigel Tomes (1986). Their model, and subsequent tests by others, establish that intergenerational correlations in socioeconomic status can arise from the greater ability of richer parents to invest in their children's human capital, from genetic or cultural inheritance, or from all of the above (Solon 2014). Because these different sources

---

12. These include high school dropouts but also high school graduates as the literature on educational mobility tends to favor the latter. Table 1 suggests that those with high school only do better than those who dropped out, but much worse than those who graduate college.

of intergenerational status transmission produce similar empirical results, distinguishing those processes from each other is a difficult task. The literature has established that large gaps exist in early childhood education and in school readiness by parental education and income, which are more pronounced in the United States than in other Anglo nations (Waldfogel and Washbrook 2011).

We also know that these gaps are larger now than in the past, in part because a good share of consumption among parents at the top end of the distribution is related to developmentally oriented goods and activities; indeed almost seven times as much is spent per child in the top than at the bottom (Kaushal, Magnuson, and Waldfogel 2011).[13] We also know that high-quality ECE programs are critical for disadvantaged children. Good preschools offer children productive teacher-child interactions, encouragement from teachers, and opportunities to engage with varied materials. Teacher quality and retention are also key ingredients for producing better outcomes for disadvantaged children. But these conditions are hard to establish or maintain in low-income areas (Magnuson and Duncan 2015).

Cross-national research in Denmark and France, where universal ECE is the norm, shows that effective high-quality preschools do reduce the gaps in achievement between children from high- and low-education backgrounds. But the remaining differences in both cognitive and behavioral outcomes are still significant when outcomes are ranked by parental education and income (Bingley, Corak, and Westergaard-Nielsen 2012; Dumas and Lefranc 2012). This significance suggests that though ECE can improve opportunity and mobility from the bottom, it is not by itself a magic bullet for desirable levels of IGM.

We also know that a child should accumulate human capital in elementary and middle school such that reading, math, and social-emotional skills are at acceptable levels to take full advantage of secondary school. Evidence from the Brookings Institution, however, reveals that 38 percent of children cannot cross this adequacy bar by fifth grade (Sawhill, Winship, and Grannis 2012). Sean Reardon (2011) has shown that differences in skills—such as test skills and reading attainment—by parents' education and income have increased over the past forty years. Moreover, gaps are substantial in self-regulation and externalizing behavior by income and education dating back to the 1980s or earlier (Cunha and Heckman 2008). Given that richer and better-educated parents buy into better schools and that poorer parents often are forced to send their children to inferior schools, the rise in incomes and wealth at the top of the distribution has propelled the children of the highest income parents still higher, increasing the achievement gap between children at the 90th percentile of parental income and the middle children at the 50th percentile (Reardon 2013; Reardon and Owens 2014).

College attendance and graduation clearly matter for mobility and especially for those born poor (table 1). Not everyone needs a four-year degree to reach the middle class, but some sort of credential is increasingly needed in today's labor market. Community colleges and CTE offer some hope of job advancement to noncollege goers, but the evidence of its success is limited at this time (Heinrich and Smeeding 2014b, 2014a). On the other hand, we know that most college-going and college-attainment gains have gone to upper-income classes. The gap in the fraction of children entering college and graduating college by income quartile has steadily expanded (Bailey and Dynarski 2011). Indeed, the children of the richest parents are increasingly likely to graduate within five years of starting college, most likely to attend and graduate from a high-quality college or university, receive family support while attending college, and graduate without college debt (Reardon, Baker, and Klasik 2012; Smeeding, Erikson, and Jäntti 2011). At the same time, evidence indicates that equally well-qualified lower-income children consistently choose lesser institutions than those for which they are qualified (Hoxby and Avery 2012). Reasons for not seizing the best opportunity are many and varied, including

---

13. The amounts spent on developmental goods and services by top and bottom quintile parents in 2006 were $8,872 and $1,315, respectively.

poor college counseling in urban high schools and inability to correctly gauge the actual cost of college-going.

These differences are also magnified by race. Postsecondary attendance among high school graduates at two-year and four-year postsecondary institutions is now 65 percent for blacks to 69 percent for whites (Casselman 2013). But college completion rates differ markedly: 62 percent of whites and only 40 percent of blacks receiving diplomas within six years of first attendance. Moreover, graduation rates among blacks differ substantially by gender, 48 percent of black women but only 35 percent of black men graduating.[14] Antidiscrimination acts, civil rights legislation, and school desegregation led to improved educational conditions and outcomes for African Americans and other minorities beginning in the late 1960s. But low-income students of all colors and races have always lagged behind wealthy students. As a result, Reardon reports the gap today between white and black children is 40 percent smaller than it was in the 1970s, but only about half the size of that between rich and poor children (2011, 2013). Reardon, Rachel Baker, and Daniel Klasik (2012) also find that while 15 percent of high-income students from the 2004 graduating class of high school enrolled in a highly selective college or university, only 5 percent of middle-income graduates and 2 percent of low-income graduates did so.

Bhashkar Mazumder (2014) shows that education can make a difference for all races. According to his calculations, almost 90 percent of whites with a college degree escape the bottom quintile, compared with 75 percent of whites with a terminal high school degree. For blacks, rates of upward mobility rise sharply for those who attain more than a high school education. He shows that only 28 percent of blacks with a high school degree will move up from the bottom quintile, compared with 69 percent of blacks with fourteen years of schooling. For college graduates, the rate of upward mobility from the bottom quintile of parental income is just about the same for blacks and whites. The problem is that only about 15 percent of all blacks have attained a college degree in the NLSY data Mazumder analyzes.

ETHNICITY

We do not yet know enough about a number of other subpopulations to fully assess their progress or regress in IGM terms. For example, we know far less about the mobility of ethnic minorities, especially immigrants, because they are not part of older panel datasets. For instance, the PSID and various NLS and NLSY surveys help assess IGM, but are constrained by study and sample designs that begin with the original adult samples in the 1960s or 1970s and follow their children, hence excluding all immigrants arriving in the United States after the survey sample was drawn, except for those who have "married into" the dataset. We can still learn some things from these data, for instance, the NLSY79 oversampled Hispanics whose children are now reaching adulthood, but used small samples as they attained adulthood (Acs 2011).[15] Further, cross-cohort studies of minorities, such as those Brian Duncan and Stephen

---

14. Ben Casselman (2013) and the *Journal of Blacks in Higher Education* (2014) also establish that blacks are more likely than whites to attend two-year institutions, to go part time and not full time, and to need remedial classes.

15. For instance, the one study we know of that uses the NLSY 1979 cohort for this purpose (Acs 2011) focuses on downward mobility from the middle class for youth who were age fourteen to seventeen in 1979 and who lived in their parents' homes in 1979 and 1980. Their adult economic status was then assessed in 2004 and 2006, when they were between thirty-nine and forty-four. The Acs study covers white, black, and the NLSY sample of Hispanic youth from middle-class families (parents' incomes in 1979 between 30th and 70th percentiles) who appear in the NLSY as adults in the 2004 to 2006 period. The Hispanic sample in adulthood then is only 201, despite the fact that originally 1,783 Hispanics-Latinos (encompassing at least seven national origins) were interviewed in 1979. Differences in follow-up are due to sample attrition as well as the study age and income selections. Acs found about 20 to 29 percent of Hispanics were, using three measures of downward mobility, in a worse economic position than their parents. In each case, the mobility was less than that of blacks but more than that of whites when they became adults.

Trejo mention (2015), are plagued by "ethnic sample attrition," whereby children reclassify themselves as something other than Hispanic as they age. What we know about Latino IGM, then, is sparse and again includes only those who emigrated before 1980. Hence data are limited about economic mobility among Hispanic families, who tend to have lower incomes than non-Hispanic blacks and whites, but more stable family structures than blacks.[16]

The importance of ethnicity looms large in America's future as the racial and ethnic makeup of today's children is changing rapidly. In 2011, for the first time, fewer than half of the children born in America were to two Anglo American partners. Soon, all children will be "minority" children—the traditional racial and ethnic minorities, who will be in the majority by the numbers, and Anglo children, who will become the new minority. By 2050, Anglo Americans will make up less than 50 percent of the population. Hispanics, Asians, and multiracial populations are expected to double over the next forty years as the result of immigration, higher birth rates among minority populations already here, and more interracial marriages. These changes will challenge the nation's legal, political, and economic systems, but are already beginning to affect the youngest of the emerging ethnic groups just now entering our school systems. Indeed, one should not forget that the children whose mobility we are trying to improve early on are unlikely to be white and Anglo-Saxon by heritage (Frey 2014). The combination of this explosion with the diminishing numbers of Anglo baby boomers will produce generational competition in future decades over resources and governmental priorities (see Brownstein and Taylor 2014; Brownstein 2015).

SUMMARY, CONCLUSION, AND POLICY IMPLICATIONS

This brief summary of vulnerable populations suggests many barriers to mobility, especially for black men and their children, those who grow up in unmarried-parent households, and the less educated. It also suggests that vulnerability comes in batches, and that low income, unstable family status, and especially lack of money inhibit upward IGM for the children of especially vulnerable groups. Changes in fertility and marriage, cohabitation and divorce, and education are also reinforcing differences in income inequality and further reducing economic mobility among disadvantaged children. The added effects of incarceration on black male mobility are largely unknown and underestimated.

Evidence is ample of diverging opportunities in the economic, sociological, social policy, demography, child well-being, and education literatures (Duncan and Murnane 2011; Ermisch, Jäntti, and Smeeding 2012; Smeeding, Garfinkel, and Mincy 2011). A widening gap in income, wealth, and consumption inequality is also likely to result in a decline in economic mobility (Corak 2013; Kenworthy 2012; Kenworthy and Smeeding 2014; Fisher et al. 2015). Parental earnings, adult skills, family structure, and neighborhood segregation all affect IGM. Higher returns to education encourage more investment in education, which affects opportunities, incentives, and degrees of mobility for rich versus poor children. However, not everyone has the capacity to make their own investments. Families with greater human capital, income, and wealth can invest more in their children and provide social connections to jobs and the labor market. Parents with higher incomes tend to provide supports and safety nets for their children. Less-educated, low-income, low-wealth, and unmarried parents do not enjoy these advantages and must rely on the public sector to provide education and health care for their children. Hence a set of social and economic factors can both boost opportunities for some and make upward mobility difficult for other, more vulnerable groups.

---

16. One more promising approach is for future studies to begin with the current population and trace back to find their parental heritage instead of the other way around (Grusky, Smeeding, and Snipp 2015). In fact, Duncan and Trejo (2015) mention that the 1997 NLSY has in its tenth round begun to collect grandparent's country of origin to attempt to measure immigrant assimilation and mobility, hence starting with a more recent cohort and moving back to trace parental and grandparental origin.

Policy

The two most important preventive measures that will increase family stability and child quality, as well as increase IGM, are, first, to improve the economic and social prospects of the bottom half in terms of job stability, income, and wage growth; and, second, to provide the means to reduce unplanned pregnancies and births. America's policy efforts to date have not increased much-needed skills among young men who do not have them. Without improved efforts in building human capital, it may take the better part of a decade to reach a point where demand for workers helps raise wages and increase job quality among younger low-skill workers, especially men (Heinrich and Smeeding 2014a). The solution for the hardest to employ should involve a stronger EITC (including one for single adults), larger refundable child tax credits, and a higher minimum wage (Sawhill and Karpilow 2014) so that low-skill parents who work have higher incomes. Although such a package would continue to help mitigate poverty, the labor market solution has to involve more than targeted programs alone for the poor if we are to provide greater chances for lower-middle-class children to succeed.

Changes in incarceration policy are in their infancy. For a long time, researchers have known about the effects of prison on earnings outcomes (Pager 2003), and more recently on the effects of imprisonment of parents on their children in terms of health (Wilbur et al. 2007; Lee, Fang, and Luo 2013) and education (Hagan and Foster 2012). Although we can begin to change sentencing guidelines and penalties for first-time offenders to reduce the effects of criminal behavior on the next generation, the best studies of the "de-carceration" initiative suggest that the dismantling of the prison state will take some time, and much damage has already been done to those currently imprisoned. Policies to reduce effects of imprisonment on the incarcerated and on their children, including more visitation while in prison and added employment and family reunification support after release, can help (Carter and McCarthy 2015). Reduction in legal exclusions for ex-inmates will also help them reintegrate into the community and workplace (Waters and Kasinitz 2015). However, most prisoners come from low-income backgrounds to begin with, suggesting that although changes in incarceration policy are important, they are not a panacea for social and economic mobility issues for disadvantaged adults and their children in and of themselves (Dolan and Carr 2015).

Despite this article's gloomy reports, we are making some limited progress in improving child mobility and life chances for the next generation. For example, United States fertility is at an all-time low, reaching a rate of 1.86 children per woman of childbearing age in 2013. More important, the way that American fertility has reached its record low is by falling birthrates among teens and women in their early twenties. This is indeed good news for improving the upward mobility of children, keeping young women who are having children too early out of poverty, and bringing the U.S. teen pregnancy rate closer to rates in other rich countries (Hamilton et al. 2014). Much of this success has come because of the spread of effective long-acting reverse contraceptives, which are much more effective than conventional birth control in preventing unplanned pregnancies (Sawhill 2014).

But prevention is only half of the policy package. We must at the same time do everything we can to improve the chances of today's disadvantaged children. Labor market and child outcomes suggest that soft skills such as conflict resolution and how to respond to setbacks should be emphasized more in preschools and in parenting classes (Heckman and Mosso 2014). And because parents are so important for child outcomes, we should try to make better parents, too. Although in the new policy realm of parental improvement, ideas and efforts so far outstrip evidence of success, with a few exceptions (King, Coffey, and Smith 2013), some parenting interventions, effective preschool programs, and successful K–12 programs have been shown to greatly improve mobility if each program is implemented and has the same success it had in experimental evaluations. The effect of a set of these programs simulated by the Social Genome team has been shown to reduce income gaps in the life course stages from 6 to 24 percentage points and racial gaps by a significant amount, 6 to 13 percentage points, depending on life stage. If all three treatments were applied successfully and continuously, the fraction of all children who start and remain in the bottom income quintile would be reduced by 11 percentage points, from 34 to 23 percent (Sawhill and Venator 2014).

We must be modest in our expectations because we will never achieve full equality of opportunity or mobility. The role of parents is important no matter where on the family SES spectrum a family lies (Duncan and Murnane 2011; Ermisch, Jäntii, and Smeeding 2012; Smeeding 2016). It is very difficult for society to directly interfere with parental access to resources and opportunities—in effect to limit what rich parents can do for their children. For example, promoting integrated schools with low-SES and high-SES children being instructed together might lead the rich to set up their own system of private and exclusive schools, as in the United Kingdom and to a lesser extent in the United States, thus perpetuating inequality of life chances (Blanden et al. 2014; Ermisch, Jäntti, and Smeeding 2012).

Taken altogether, these trends suggest that increasing social and economic inequality has a large tangible cost—that of diverging destinies for children as witnessed by trends toward less-equal life chances and lower social mobility for vulnerable children. Further, no single policy will by itself correct this inequity. Although evidence-based policy can make a difference and can ostensibly increase upward mobility for the truly disadvantaged, as Isabel Sawhill and Joanne Venator (2014) suggest, unless we add these proven and cost-effective programs to our policy arsenal and maintain them for a considerable period, opportunity and mobility will not increase for the most disadvantaged. In a society that falsely prides itself on equality of opportunity, this is indeed discouraging news.

REFERENCES

Acs, Gregory. 2011. "Downward Mobility from the Middle Class: Waking Up from the American Dream." Economic Mobility Project report, September. Washington, D.C.: Pew Charitable Trusts.

Aizer, Anna, and Janet Currie. 2014. "The Intergenerational Transmission of Inequality: Maternal Disadvantage and Health at Birth." Science 344(6186): 856–61.

Almond, Douglas, Hilary W. Hoynes, and Diane W. Schanzenbach. 2011. "Inside the War on Poverty: The Impact of Food Stamps on Birth Outcomes." Review of Economics and Statistics 93(2): 387–403.

Andersson, Gunnar. 2002. "Children's Experience of Family Disruption and Family Formation: Evidence from 16 FFS Countries." Demographic Research 7(7): 343–64.

Auten, Gerald, Geoffrey Gee, and Nicholas Turner. 2013. "Income Inequality, Mobility and Turnover at the Top in the U.S., 1987–2009." American Economic Review 103(3): 168–72.

Autor, David H. 2014. "Skills, Education, and the Rise of Earnings Inequality among the other 99 Percent." Science 344(6186): 843–51.

Bailey, Martha J., and Susan M. Dynarski. 2011. "Gains and Gaps: A Historical Perspective on Inequality in College Entry and Completion." In Whither Opportunity?: Rising Inequality, Schools, and Children's Life Chances, edited by Greg Duncan and Richard Murnane. New York: Russell Sage Foundation.

Banerjee, Sudipto. 2015. Intra-Family Cash Transfers in Older American Households. Issue Brief #415. Washington, D.C.: Employee Benefit Research Institute. Accessed April 7, 2016. http://www.ebri.org/pdf/EBRI_IB_415.June15.Transfers.pdf

Becker, Gary S., and Nigel Tomes. 1986. "Human Capital and the Rise and Fall of Families." Journal of Labor Economics 4(July): S1–S39.

Bingley, Paul, Miles Corak, and Neils Westergaard-Nielsen. 2012. "Equality of Opportunity and Intergenerational Transmission of Employers." In From Parents to Children: The Intergenerational Transmission of Advantage, edited by John Ermisch, Markus Jäntti, and Timothy Smeeding. New York: Russell Sage Foundation.

Blanden, Jo, Robert Haveman, Timothy Smeeding, and Kathryn Wilson. 2014. "Intergenerational Mobility in the United States and Great Britain: A Comparative Study of Parent-Child Pathways." Review of Income and Wealth 60(3): 425–49.

Bricker, Jesse, Lisa J. Dettling, Alice Henriques, Joanne W. Hsu, Kevin B. Moore, John Sabelhaus, Jeffrey Thompson, and Richard A. Windle. 2014. "Changes in U.S. Family Finances from 2010 to 2013: Evidence from the Survey of Consumer Finances." *Federal Reserve Bulletin* 100(4)(September): 1–40. Accessed December 5, 2015. http://www.federalreserve.gov/pubs/bulletin/2014/pdf/scf14.pdf.

Brownstein, Ronald. 2015. "The States that Will Pick the President: The Sunbelt." *National Journal*, February 4, 2015. Accessed December 5, 2015. http://www.nationaljournal.com/next-america/newsdesk/the-states-that-will-pick-the-president-the-sunbelt-20150204.

Brownstein, Ronald, and Paul Taylor. 2014. *The Next America: Boomers, Millennials, and the Looming Generational Showdown.* Philadelphia, Pa.: Perseus Books.

Carlson, Marcia J., and Frank F. Furstenberg. 2006. "The Prevalence and Correlates of Multipartnered Fertility among Urban U.S. Parents." *Journal of Marriage and Family* 68(3): 718–32.

Carlson, Marcia J., Frank F. Furstenberg, Sara S. McLahanan, and Alicia G. VanOrman. 2013. "Multi-Partnered Fertility and Child Well-Being Among Urban U.S. Families." Paper presented at the annual meetings of the Association for Public Policy Analysis and Management, Washington, D.C. (November 8, 2013).

Carter, Angela, and Bill McCarthy. 2015. "Reducing the Effects of Incarceration on Children and Families." *Policy Brief* 3, no. 10. Davis, Calif.: Center for Poverty Research.

Casselman, Ben. 2013. "Race Gap Narrows in College Enrollment, But Not in Graduation." FiveThirtyEight Economics Blog. Last modified April 30, 2014. Accessed December 5, 2015. http://fivethirtyeight.com/features/race-gap-narrows-in-college-enrollment-but-not-in-graduation/.

Cherlin, Andrew J. 2014. *Labor's Love Lost: The Rise and Fall of the Working-Class Family in America.* New York: Russell Sage Foundation.

Cingano, Federico. 2014. "Trends in Income Inequality and Its Impact on Economic Growth." Social, Employment and Migration Working Papers no. 163. Paris: OECD Publishing. Accessed December 5, 2015. http://www.oecd.org/els/soc/trends-in-income-inequality-and-its-impact-on-economic-growth-SEM-WP163.pdf.

Congressional Budget Office. 2013. "Trends in the Distribution of Household Income Between 1979 and 2010." Washington: U.S. Government Printing Office. Accessed December 5, 2015. http://www.cbo.gov/sites/default/files/113th-congress-2013-2014/reports/44604-AverageTaxRates.pdf.

Cooper, Kerris, and Kitty Stewart. 2013. "Does Money Affect Children's Outcomes? A Systematic Review." October 2013. Yokr, UK: Joseph Rowntree Foundation. Accessed December 5, 2015. http://sticerd.lse.ac.uk/dps/case/cr/casereport80.pdf.

Corak, Miles. 2013. "Income Inequality, Equality of Opportunity, and Intergenerational Mobility." *Journal of Economic Perspectives* 27(3): 79–102.

Corak, Miles, and Patrizio Piraino. 2011. "The Intergenerational Transmission of Employers." *Journal of Labor Economics* 29(1): 37–68.

Cunha, Flavio, and James J. Heckman. 2008. "Formulating, Identifying and Estimating the Technology of Cognitive and Noncognitive Skill Formation." *Journal of Human Resources* 43(4): 738–82.

Dahl, Gregory B., and Lance Lochner. 2012. "The Impact of Family Income on Child Achievement: Evidence from the Earned Income Tax Credit." *American Economic Review* 102(5): 1927–56.

Dolan, Karen, and Jodi L. Carr. 2015. "The Poor Get Prison: The Alarming Spread of the Criminalization of Poverty." Washington, D.C.: Institute for Policy Studies. Accessed December 5, 2015. http://www.ips-dc.org/wp-content/uploads/2015/03/IPS-The-Poor-Get-Prison-Final.pdf.

Dumas, Christelle, and Arnaud Lefranc. 2012. "Early Schooling and Later Outcomes." In *From Parents to Children: The Intergenerational Transmission of Advantage*, edited by John Ermisch, Markus Jäntti, and Timothy Smeeding. New York: Russell Sage Foundation.

Duncan, Greg J., Katherine Magnuson, and Elizabeth Votruba-Drzal. 2014. "Boosting Family Income to Promote Child Development." *Future of Children* 24(1): 99–120.

Duncan, Greg J., Pamela Morris, and Chris Rodrigues. 2011. "Does Money Really Matter? Estimating Impacts of Family Income on Young Children's Achievement with Data from Random-Assignment Experiments." *Developmental Psychology* 47(5): 1263–79. doi: 10.1037/a0023875.

Duncan, Greg J., and Richard Murnane, eds. 2011. *Whither Opportunity: Rising Inequality, School, and Children's Life Chances.* New York: Russell Sage Foundation.

Duncan, Brian, and Stephen J. Trejo. 2015. "Assessing the Socioeconomic Mobility and Integration of U.S. Immigrants and Their Descendants." *Annals of the American Academy of Political and Social Science* 657 (January): 108–35.

Edin, Kathryn, Stefanie DeLuca, and Ann Owens. 2012. "Constrained Compliance: Solving the Mystery of MTO Lease-Up Rates and Why Mobility Matters." *Cityscape* 14(2): 181–94.

Ermisch, John, Markus Jäntti, and Timothy Smeeding, eds. 2012. *From Parents to Children: The Intergenerational Transmission of Advantage.* New York: Russell Sage Foundation.

Evans, William N., and Craig L. Garthwaite. 2014. "Giving Mom a Break: The Impact of Higher EITC Payments on Maternal Health." *American Economic Journal: Economic Policy* 6(2): 258–90.

Fisher, Jonathan, David Johnson, Timothy Smeeding, and Jeffrey Thompson. 2015. "The Demography of Inequality: Income, Wealth and Consumption, 1989–2010." Working Paper, January 20. Madison: University of Wisconsin–Madison, Institute for Research on Poverty.

Frey, William H. 2014. *Diversity Explosion: How New Racial Demographics Are Remaking America.* Washington, D.C.: Brookings Institution Press.

Galston, William A. 2014. "Declining Optimism Among the Obama Coalition." Brookings Institution. Last modified September 23, 2014. Accessed December 5, 2015. http://www.brookings.edu/blogs/fixgov/posts/2014/09/23-american-values-survey-american-dream-galston.

Grusky, David, Timothy Smeeding, and Matthew Snipp. 2015. "Monitoring Social Mobility in the 21st Century." *Annals of the American Academy of Political and Social Science* 657 (January): 63–82.

Hagan, John, and Holly Foster. 2012. "Intergenerational Educational Effects of Mass Imprisonment in America." *Sociology of Education* 85(3): 259–86.

Hamilton, Brady E., Joyce A. Martin, Michelle J. K. Osterman, and Sally C. Curtin. 2014. "Births: Preliminary Data for 2013." *National Vital Statistics Reports* 63, no. 2. Hyattsville, Md.: National Center for Health Statistics. Accessed December 5, 2015. http://www.cdc.gov/nchs/data/nvsr/nvsr63/nvsr63_02.pdf.

Heckman, James, and Stefano Mosso. 2014. "The Economics of Human Development and Social Mobility." *Annual Review of Economics* 6(1): 689–733.

Heinrich, Carolyn, and Timothy Smeeding. 2014a. "Building Economic Self-Sufficiency." *Focus on Policy* No. 2 (September). Institute for Research on Poverty, University of Wisconsin–Madison. Accessed December 5, 2015. http://www.irp.wisc.edu/publications/policybriefs/pdfs/PB2-SelfSufficiency.pdf.

———. 2014b. "Building Human Capital and Economic Potential." *Fast Focus* no. 21–2014 (September). Institute for Research on Poverty, University of Wisconsin–Madison. Accessed December 5, 2015. http://www.irp.wisc.edu/publications/fastfocus/pdfs/FF21-2014.pdf.

Hertz, Tom. 2005. "Rags, Riches, and Race: The Intergenerational Economic Mobility of Black and White Families in the United States." In *Unequal Chances: Family Background and Economic Success*, edited by Samuel Bowles, Herbert Gintis, and Melissa Osborne Groves. Princeton, N.J.: Princeton University Press.

Hoxby, Caroline, and Christopher Avery. 2012. "The Missing 'One-Offs': The Hidden Supply of High-Achieving, Low Income Students." *NBER* working paper no. 18586. Cambridge, Mass.: National Bureau of Economic Research.

Hoynes, Hilary, Doug Miller, and David Simon. 2015. "Income, the Earned Income Tax Credit, and Infant Health." *American Economic Journal: Economic Policy* 7(1): 172–211. Accessed December 5, 2015. http://dx.doi.org/10.1257/pol.20120179.

Hoynes, Hilary, Diane Whitmore Schanzenbach, and Douglas Almond. 2014. "Long-Run Impacts of Childhood Access to the Safety Net." Unpublished paper. University of California, Berkeley.

Isaacs, Julia B., Isabel V. Sawhill, and Ron Haskins. 2008. *Getting Ahead or Losing Ground: Economic Mobility in America.* Washington, D.C.: The Brookings Institution. Accessed December 5, 2015, http://www.brookings.edu/~/media/research/files/reports/2008/2/economic-mobility-sawhill/02_economic_mobility_sawhill.pdf.

Jäntti, Markus, Brent Bratsberg, Knut Reed, Oddbjørn Raaum, Robin Naylor, Eva Österbacka, Anders Björklund, and Tor Eriksson. 2006. "American Exceptionalism in a New Light: A Comparison of Intergenerational Earnings Mobility in the Nordic Countries, the United Kingdom and the United States." *IZA* discussion paper no. 1938. Bonn: Institute for the Study of Labor.

Jencks, Christopher, and Laura Tach. 2006. "Would

Equal Opportunity Mean More Mobility?" In *Mobility and Inequality: Frontiers of Research from Sociology and Economics*, edited by Stephen B. Morgan, David L. Grusky, and Gary S. Fields. Redwood City, Calif.: Stanford University Press.

Jolliffe, Dean, and Peter Lanjouw. 2014. *A Measured Approach to Ending Poverty and Boosting Shared Prosperity: Concepts, Data, and the Twin Goals*. Washington, D.C.: World Bank Group. Accessed December 5, 2015. https://openknowledge.worldbank.org/bitstream/handle/10986/20384/9781464803611.pdf.

Jones, Robert P., Daniel Cox, and Juhem Navarro-Rivera. 2014. "Economic Insecurity Rising Inequality and Doubts about the Future: Findings from the 2014 American Values Survey." Washington, D.C.: Public Religion Research Institute. Accessed December 5, 2015. http://publicreligion.org/site/wp-content/uploads/2014/09/AVS-web.pdf.

Journal of Blacks in Higher Education. 2014. "Black Student College Graduation Rates Remain Low, But Modest Progress Begins to Show." Accessed December 5, 2015. http://www.jbhe.com/features/50_blackstudent_gradrates.html.

Kalil, Ariel, Rebecca Ryan, and Michake R. Corey. 2012. "Diverging Destinies: Maternal Education and the Developmental Gradient in Time with Children." *Demography* 49(4): 1361–83.

Kaushal, Nerraj, Katherine Magnuson, and Jane Waldfogel. 2011. "How Is Family Income Related to Investments in Children's Learning?" In *Whither Opportunity: Rising Inequality, School, and Children's Life Chances*, edited by Greg J. Duncan and Richard J. Murnane. New York: Russell Sage Foundation.

Kenworthy, Lane. 2012. "It's Hard to Make It in America: How the United States Stopped Being the Land of Opportunity." *Foreign Affairs* 91(6): 97–109.

Kenworthy, Lane, and Timothy Smeeding. 2014. "The United States: High and Rapidly-Rising Inequality." In *Inequality and Its Impacts*, vol. 2, edited by Brian Nolan and Wiemer Salverda. Oxford: Oxford University Press.

King, Chrisopher, Rheagan Coffey, and Tara C. Smith. 2013. "Promoting Two-Generation Strategies: A Getting Started Guide for State and Local Policy Makers." Austin: Ray Marshall Center, LBJ School of Public Affairs, University of Texas at Austin. Accessed December 5, 2015. http://fcd-us.org/resources/promoting-two-generation-strategies-getting-started-guide-state-and-local-policy-makers.

Kirkegaard, Jacob F. 2015. "The True Levels of Government and Social Expenditures in Advanced Economies." Policy Brief no. 15-4. Washington, D.C.: Peterson Institute for Advanced Economics. Accessed December 5, 2015. http://www.piie.com/publications/pb/pb15-4.pdf.

Lee, Rosalyn D., Xiangming Fang, and F. Luo. 2013. "The Impact of Parental Incarceration on the Physical and Mental Health of Young Adults." *Pediatrics* 131(4): e1188–95.

Lundberg, Shelley, and Robert Pollak. 2013. "Cohabitation and the Uneven Retreat from Marriage in the United States: 1950–2010." *NBER* working paper no. 19413. Cambridge, Mass.: National Bureau of Economic Research. Accessed December 5, 2015. http://www.nber.org/papers/w19413.

Magnuson, Katherine, and Greg J. Duncan. 2015. "Can Early Childhood Interventions Reduce Inequality of Opportunity?" Paper presented to the Conference on Economic Opportunity and Inequality, Federal Reserve Bank of Boston. Boston, Mass. (October 17, 2015).

Maruschak, Christopher, Leo E. Glaze, and Christopher J. Mumola. 2010. "Incarcerated Parents and Their Children." In *Children of Incarcerated Parents: A Handbook for Researchers and Practitioners*, edited by J. Mark Eddy and Julie Poehlmann. Washington, D.C.: Urban Institute Press.

Mazumder, Bhashkar. 2012. "Upward Intergenerational Economic Mobility in the United States." Washington, D.C.: The Pew Charitable Trusts.

———. 2014. "Black-White Differences in Intergenerational Economic Mobility in the United States." Working Paper. Chicago: Federal Reserve Bank of Chicago. Accessed December 5, 2015. https://www.chicagofed.org/digital_assets/publications/economic_perspectives/2014/1Q2014_part1_mazumder.pdf.

McLanahan, Sara. 2004. "Diverging Destinies: How Children Are Faring Under the Second Demographic Transition." *Demography* 41(4): 607–27.

McLanahan, Sara, and Wade Jacobsen. 2014. "Diverging Destinies Revisited." Draft prepared for the "Annual Symposium on Family Issues," The Pennsylvania State University. University Park (October 6, 2014).

Milligan, Kevin, and Mark Stabile. 2009. "Child Benefits, Maternal Employment, and Children's

Health: Evidence from Canadian Child Benefit Expansions." *American Economic Review* 99(2): 128–32.

Mood, Carina, Jan O. Jonsson, and Erik Bihagen. 2012. "Socioeconomic Persistence Across Generations: Cognitive and Noncognitive Processes." In *From Parents to Children: The Intergenerational Transmission of Advantage*, edited by John Ermisch, Markus Jäntti, and Timothy Smeeding. New York: Russell Sage Foundation.

Murnane, Richard J. 2013. "U.S. High School Graduation Rates: Patterns and Explanations." *Journal of Economic Literature* 51(2): 370–422.

Murray, Charles. 2012. *Coming Apart: The State of White America, 1960–2010*. New York: Crown Publishing.

Neal, Derek, and Armin Rick. 2014. "The Prison Boom and the Lack of Black Progress after Smith and Welch." *NBER* working paper no. 20283. Cambridge, Mass.: National Bureau of Economic Research. Accessed December 5, 2015. http://www.nber.org/papers/w20283.

Organization for Economic Cooperation and Development. 2014. *Education at a Glance, 2014: OECD Indicators*. Paris: OECD Publishing. Accessed December 5, 2015. http://www.oecd.org/edu/Education-at-a-Glance-2014.pdf.

Pager, Devah. 2003. "The Mark of a Criminal Record." *American Journal of Sociology* 108(5) (March): 937–75.

Painter, Matthew, Adrianna Frech, and Kristi Williams. 2015. "Nonmarital Fertility, Union History, and Women's Wealth." *Demography* 52(1): 153–82.

Perelli-Harris, Brienna, Wendy Sigle-Rushton, Trude Lappegard, Renske Keizer, Michaela Kreyenfeld, and Caroline Berghammer.2010. "The Educational Gradient of Childbearing within Cohabitation in Europe." *Population and Development Review* 36(4): 775–801. doi:10.1111/j.1728-4457.2010.00357.x.

Pettit, Becky. 2012. *Invisible Men: Mass Incarceration and the Myth of Black Progress*. New York: Russell Sage Foundation.

The Pew Charitable Trusts. 2010. *Collateral Costs: Incarceration's Effects on Economic Mobility*. Washington, D.C.: The Pew Charitable Trusts. Accessed December 5, 2015. http://www.pewtrusts.org/~/media/legacy/uploadedfiles/pcs_assets/2010/CollateralCosts1pdf.pdf.

Pfeffer, Fabian T. 2011. "Status Attainment and Wealth in the United States and Germany." In *Persistence, Privilege, and Parenting: The Comparative Study of Intergenerational Mobility* edited by Timothy M. Smeeding, Robert Erikson, and Markus Jäntti. New York: Russell Sage Foundation.

Pfeffer, Fabian T., Sheldon H. Danziger, and Robert F. Schoeni. 2014. "Wealth Levels, Wealth Inequality and the Great Recession." Research Summary. New York: Russell Sage Foundation. Accessed December 5, 2015. http://web.stanford.edu/group/scspi/_media/working_papers/pfeffer-danziger-schoeni_wealth-levels.pdf.

Pfeffer, Fabian T., and Martin Hällsten. 2012. "Mobility Regimes and Parental Wealth: The United States, Germany, and Sweden in Comparison." Population Studies Center Research Report no. 12-766. Ann Arbor: University of Michigan. Accessed December 5, 2015. http://www.psc.isr.umich.edu/pubs/abs/7676.

Phillips, Meredith. 2011. "Parenting, Time Use, and Disparities in Academic Outcomes." In *Whither Opportunity: Rising Inequality, Schools, and Children's Life Chances*, edited by Greg J. Duncan and Richard R. Murnane. New York: Russell Sage Foundation.

Rainwater, Lee, and Timothy Smeeding. 2003. *Poor Kids in a Rich Country*. New York: Russell Sage Foundation.

Reardon, Sean F. 2011. "The Widening Academic Achievement Gap between the Rich and the Poor: New Evidence and Possible Explanations." In *Whither Opportunity: Rising Inequality, Schools, and Children's Life Chances*, edited by Greg J. Duncan and Richard R. Murnane. New York: Russell Sage Foundation.

——. 2013. "The Great Divide: No Rich Child Left Behind." *Opinionator* (blog). *New York Times*, April 27, 2013. Accessed December 5, 2015. http://opinionator.blogs.nytimes.com/2013/04/27/no-rich-child-left-behind/.

Reardon, Sean F., Rachel Baker, and Daniel Klasik. 2012. *Race, Income, and Enrollment Patterns Highly Selective Colleges, 1982–2004*. Stanford, Calif.: Center for Education Policy Analysis.

Reardon, Sean F., and Ann Owens. 2014. "60 Years After Brown: Trends and Consequences of School Segregation." *Annual Review of Sociology* 40: 199–218.

Reeves, Richard. 2014. "The Science of Power: Billionaires, Elites, and Social Mobility." *Social Mo-*

bility Memos (blog), September 22. Washington, D.C.: Brookings Institution. Accessed December 5, 2015. http://www.brookings.edu/blogs/social-mobility-memos/posts/2014/09/22-science-of-power-billionaires-elite-social-mobility.

Reeves, Richard, and Kimberly Howard. 2013. "The Glass Floor: Education, Downward Mobility, and Opportunity Hoarding." Washington, D.C.: Brookings Institution. Accessed December 5, 2015. http://www.brookings.edu/~/media/research/files/papers/2013/11/glass-floor-downward-mobility-equality-opportunity-hoarding-reeves-howard/glass-floor-downward-mobility-equality-opportunity-hoarding-reeves-howard.pdf.

Reeves, Richard, and Isabel V. Sawhill. 2015. "Equality of Opportunity: Definitions, Trends, and Interventions." Paper presented to the Conference on Economic Opportunity and Inequality, Federal Reserve Bank of Boston. Boston, Mass. (October 17, 2015).

Sawhill, Isabel. 2014. *Generation Unbound: Drifting into Sex and Parenthood Without Marriage.* Washington, D.C.: Brookings Institution Press.

Sawhill, Isabel V., and Quentin Karpilow. 2014. "Raising the Minimum Wage and Redesigning the EITC." Washington, D.C.: The Brookings Institution. Accessed December 5, 2015. http://www.brookings.edu/research/papers/2014/01/30-raising-minimum-wage-redesigning-eitc-sawhill.

Sawhill, Isabel V., and Joanne Venator. 2014. "Three Policies to Close the Class Divide in Family Formation." *Social Mobility Memos* (blog), January 21. Washington, D.C.: The Brookings Institution. Accessed December 5, 2015. http://www.brookings.edu/blogs/social-mobility-memos/posts/2014/01/21-3-policies-to-close-family-formation-class-divide-sawhill.

Sawhill, Isabel V., Scott Winship, and Kelly Grannis. 2012. "Pathways to the Middle Class: Balancing Personal and Public Responsibilities." Washington, D.C.: The Brookings Institution. Accessed December 5, 2015. http://www.brookings.edu/research/papers/2012/09/20-pathways-middle-class-sawhill-winship.

Schmitt, John, and Kris Ware. 2010. "Ex-Offenders and the Labor Market." Washington, D.C.: Center for Economic and Policy Research. Accessed December 5, 2015. http://www.cepr.net/documents/publications/ex-offenders-2010-11.pdf.

Schwartz, Christine R. 2013. "Trends and Variation in Assortative Mating: Causes and Consequences." *Annual Review of Sociology* 39: 451–70.

Shapiro, Tom, Tatjana Meschede, and Sam Osoro. 2013. "The Roots of the Widening Racial Wealth Gap: Explaining the Black White Economic Divide." IASP research and policy brief, February. Waltham, Mass.: Brandeis University. Accessed December 5, 2015. http://iasp.brandeis.edu/pdfs/Author/shapiro-thomas-m/racialwealthgapbrief.pdf.

Smeeding, Timothy. 2014. "Social Mobility: Three Reasons To Worry About the Future." *Social Mobility Memos* (blog), February 26. Washington, D.C.: The Brookings Institution. Accessed December 5, 2015. http://www.brookings.edu/blogs/social-mobility-memos/posts/2014/02/26-3-reasons-to-worry-about-the-future.

———. 2016. "Gates, Gaps, and Inter-Generational Mobility (IGM): The Importance of an Even Start." In *The Dynamics of Opportunity in America*, edited by Irwin Kirsch and Henry Braun. New York: Springer.

Smeeding, Timothy M., Robert Erikson, and Markus Jäntti, eds. 2011. *Persistence, Privilege and Parenting: The Comparative Study of Intergenerational Mobility.* New York: Russell Sage Foundation.

Smeeding, Timothy M., Irwin Garfinkel, and Ron Mincy, eds. 2011. "Young Disadvantaged Men: Fathers, Families, Poverty, and Policy." *Annals of the American Academy of Political and Social Science* 635(1): 6–21.

Solon, Gary. 2014. "Theoretical Models of Inequality Transmission Across Multiple Generations." *Research in Social Stratification and Mobility* 35 (March): 13–18.

Stinson, Martha, and Christopher Wignall. 2014. "Fathers, Children, and the Intergenerational Transmission of Employers." *SIPP* working paper no. 265. Washington, D.C.: U.S. Census Bureau. Accessed December 5, 2015. https://www.census.gov/content/dam/Census/library/working-papers/2014/demo/SIPP-WP-265.pdf.

Summers, Lawrence H., and Ed Balls. 2015. *Report of the Commission on Inclusive Prosperity.* Washington, D.C.: Center for American Progress. Accessed December 5, 2015. https://cdn.americanprogress.org/wp-content/uploads/2015/01/IPC-PDF-full.pdf.

Tach, Laura. 2015. "Social Mobility in an Era of Family Instability and Complexity." *Annals of the*

American Academy of Political and Social Science 657(1): 83–96.

Torche, Florencia. 2011. "Is a College Degree Still the Great Equalizer? Intergenerational Mobility Across Levels of Schooling in the U.S." *American Journal of Sociology* 117(3): 763–807.

Travis, Jeremy, Bruce Western, and Steve Redburn, eds. 2014. *The Growth of Incarceration in the United States: Exploring Causes and Consequences.* Washington, D.C.: National Academies Press.

VanderWeele, Tyler J., and Whitney R. Robinson. 2014. "On the Causal Interpretation of Race in Regressions Adjusting for Confounding and Mediating Variables." *Epidemiology* 25(4): 473–84.

Wakefield, Sara, and Christopher Wildeman. 2013. *Children of the Prison Boom: Mass Incarceration and the Future of American Inequality.* New York: Oxford University Press.

Waldfogel, Jane, and Elizabeth Washbrook. 2011. "Income-Related Gaps in School Readiness in the United States and United Kingdom." In *Persistence, Privilege, and Parenting: The Comparative Study of Intergenerational Mobility*, edited by Timothy Smeeding, Robert Erikson, and Markus Jäntti. New York: Russell Sage Foundation.

Waters, Mary C., and Philip Kasinitz. 2015. "The War on Crime and the War on Immigrants: Racial and Legal Exclusion in 21st Century United States." In *Fear, Anxiety and National Identity: Immigration and Belonging in North America and Europe*, edited by Nancy Foner and Patrick Simon. New York: Russell Sage Foundation.

Western, Bruce, and Becky Pettit. 2010. "Incarceration & Social Inequality." *Daedalus* 139(3): 8–19.

Wilbur, MaryAnn B., Jodi E. Marani, Danielle Appugliese, Ryan Woods, Jane A. Siegel, Howard J. Cabral, and Deborah A. Frank. 2007. "Socioemotional Effects of Fathers' Incarceration on Low-Income, Urban, School-Aged Children." *Pediatrics* 120(3): e678–85.

Wildeman, Christopher. 2009. "Parental Imprisonment, the Prison Boom, and the Concentration of Childhood Disadvantage." *Demography* 46(2): 265–80.

Wilson, William Julius. 1987. *The Truly Disadvantaged.* Cambridge, Mass.: Harvard Press.

———. 1996. *When Work Disappears.* New York: Alfred A. Knopf.

Yellen, Janet L. 2014. "Perspectives on Inequality and Opportunity from the Survey of Consumer Finances." Presentation to the Conference on Economic Opportunity and Inequality, Federal Reserve Bank of Boston. Boston, Mass. (October 17, 2014). Accessed December 5, 2015. http://federalreserve.gov/newsevents/speech/yellen20141017a.htm.

Can Early Childhood Interventions Decrease Inequality of Economic Opportunity?

KATHERINE MAGNUSON AND GREG J. DUNCAN

This paper considers whether expanding access to center-based early childhood education (ECE) will reduce economic inequality later in life. A strong evidence base indicates that ECE is effective at improving young children's academic skills and human capital development. We review evidence that children from low-income families have lower rates of preschool enrollment than their more affluent peers. Our analysis indicates that increasing enrollments for preschoolers in the year before school entry is likely to be a worthy investment that will yield economic payoffs in the form of increased adult earnings. The benefits of even a moderately effective ECE program are likely to be sufficient to offset the costs of program expansion, and increased enrollment among low-income children may reduce later economic inequality.

Keywords: early childhood education, preschool, economic inequality

Early childhood has emerged as a "frontier" in economic research related to the production of human capital. It is an important stage for the human capital production function, and the only period of childhood and adolescence with relatively little public investment. But, as the frontier metaphor suggests, early childhood is a contested field of research. Some scholars interpret the early childhood intervention evidence as showing promising opportunities for remediating inequities in human capital and thus argue for significant expansions in public investments. Others come to more cautious or even negative conclusions, worrying about the uncertainty in the evidence base regarding the long-term payoffs to early childhood investments that might be made today.

MODELS OF CHILD INVESTMENTS AND DEVELOPMENT

Both human and animal studies point to the critical importance of the earliest years of life to establishing the brain architecture and other biological systems that will shape future cognitive, social, and emotional development, as well as physical and mental health (Blair and Raver 2012; Knudsen al. 2006). Infants, toddlers, and preschoolers benefit from environments that provide sensitive, responsive caregiving and a variety of language-rich learning opportunities. Research on the malleability (plasticity) of cognitive and language abilities shows these skills to be highly responsive to both positive and negative influences (Fox, Levitt, and Nelson 2010; Shonkoff 2010). Environmental enrichment can promote cognitive

Katherine Magnuson is a professor of social work at the University of Wisconsin–Madison. **Greg J. Duncan** is Distinguished Professor in the School of Education at the University of California, Irvine.

Direct correspondence to: Katherine Magnuson at kmagnuson@wisc.edu, School of Social Work, University of Wisconsin–Madison, 1350 University Ave., Madison, WI 53711; and Greg J. Duncan at gduncan@uci.edu, School of Education, University of California, Irvine, 2001 Education, Irvine, CA 92697.

development, whereas a variety of adverse experiences may shape cognitive development in ways that limit later learning (Shonkoff 2010).

Economic models of human development formalize thinking about the human capital production function, and emphasize how investments and child endowments interact to create a child's stock of human capital. Flavio Cunha and James Heckman (2007) describe a cumulative model of the production of human capital that allows for the possibility of differing childhood investment stages as well as roles for the past effects and future development of both cognitive and socioemotional ("noncognitive") skills. Their model highlights the interactive nature of skill building and investments from families, preschools and schools, and other agents. It posits that human capital accumulation results from *self-productivity*—skills developed in earlier stages bolster the development of skills in later stages—as well as the dynamic complementarity that results from the assumption that skills acquired prior to a given investment increase the productivity of that investment. Taken together, these two principles undergird their hypothesis that skill begets skill.

An important strength of Cunha and Heckman-type models is that they generate clear and testable hypotheses. Although widely described and endorsed, the hypothesis of dynamic complementarity in early childhood currently rests on a thin empirical base. The most direct evidence comes from work by Anna Aizer and Flavio Cunha (2012) who use data from a longitudinal study begun in the 1960s that spans the period surrounding the introduction of Head Start, the largest preschool intervention for low-income children, and finds larger impacts of the program on children with higher scores on a measure of infant cognitive development. However, evidence using more recent data from an experimental evaluation of Head Start does not find that significantly larger gains accrue to students who enter the program with higher skills at program entry (Purtell and Gershoff 2013).

Developmental psychologists, like economists, describe children's development as the result of the dynamic interplay between an individual child and his or her environment. Recent developmental theory and research on how early environments affect learning and later outcomes have two foci. The first centers on how particular contexts, especially interpersonal relationships and interactions, affect children's acquisition of specific skills. These studies are focused on discovering which types of experiences, on average, lead to learning specific knowledge or skills. They typically generate their estimates by exploiting naturally occurring variation in developmental processes in population-based samples (Sameroff 2010). For example, several studies have documented considerable variability in the amount of speech directed at children by caregivers during the course of a typical day (Hoff 2003; Rowe 2012). In turn, this variability in experience of speech is strongly linked to the child's later language expression and vocabulary (Rowe 2012; Weisleder and Fernald 2013). Similarly, studies of parenting and children's self-regulation point to associations between parents' early support of their children's autonomy with later assessments of children's executive function (Bernier, Carlson, and Whipple 2010).

A second and newer body of developmental res dowments are largely invariant during development, changes in the epigenome—the biochemical system that regulates gene expression—are not. Moreover, the epigenome is found to be particularly responsive to environmental conditions (Champagne and Mashoodh 2009). For example, animal studies have shown that experimental manipulation of the amount and timing of a rat grooming her pups is related to the pups' gene expression and subsequent developmental trajectories (Meaney 2010). Although much of this work began with studies of adverse events and animal models, increasingly such studies are extending to humans. For example, Marilyn Essex and her colleagues (2013) find that early maternal stressors were related to epigenetic changes in their children during adolescence, with implications for their mental health.

Economists' and developmentalists' differing models of development generate contrasting predictions regarding the effects of preschool investments. If focused on the preschool period, defined roughly as ages three to five, the Cunha and Heckman model implies that school readiness is a product of the child's cognitive and socioemotional skills on entry into the preschool period plus preschool period investments from parents and possible ECE programs. Their hypothesis of dynamic complementarity implies that impacts of parental and ECE investments on child outcomes will be largest for children who enter the preschool period with the highest levels of cognitive and socioemotional skills. Indeed, this is the very evidence that Aizer and Cunha (2012) provide.

Developmental theories link productivity to the quality of the match between what a program offers and the kinds of developmental supports needed by a child (Blair and Raver 2012). Specifically, "compensatory" models are based on the premise that preschool investments can function effectively as a substitute for, rather than as a complement to, sensitive or enriched home environments (Ramey and Ramey 1998). Thus, children whose skill development may be hindered by economic disadvantage or low-quality home environments are predicted to benefit more from high-quality ECE programs than more advantaged children. In particular, if preschool settings expose children to sensitive caregiving environments, developmental theory would suggest that they would increase children's socioemotional skills most among children with less sensitive parental caregivers. Recent evidence supports these compensatory patterns of association (Watamura et al. 2011). This compensatory or protective model of high-quality early childhood care and education argues for understanding specific qualities and nature of investments, as they pertain to differing domains of development.

WHICH EARLY SKILLS MATTER FOR HUMAN CAPITAL ACCUMULATION?

If early childhood programs seek to build skills that will generate lasting changes in adults' human capital, which skills should they target? Economists tend to lump IQ and achievement into a cognitive category and everything else into a noncognitive or soft-skills category. This is unhelpful for a variety of reasons. First, the cognitive category mixes general cognitive ability with concrete academic skills such as literacy and numeracy. Although scores on tests of cognitive ability and achievement tend to be highly correlated, the conceptual difference between cognitive ability as a relatively stable trait and the concrete achievement skills that develop in response to schooling and other human capital investments, including ECE, is an important one. Second, noncognitive skills such as the ability to sustain attention when performing tasks, plan ahead, and control emotions involve many of the same elements of brain circuitry as learning concrete skills, and are therefore inherently cognitive. Third, conceptualizing and measuring distinct components of noncognitive skills might be important for understanding why ECE and other human capital inventions affect so many outcomes in the long run.

Our recent review classifies competencies into four groups: achievement, attention, externalizing behavior problems, and mental health (Duncan and Magnuson 2011). Attention refers to the ability to control impulses and focus on tasks (see, for example, Raver 2004). Externalizing behavior refers to a cluster of related behavioral problems that include antisocial behavior, conduct disorders, and more general aggression (Campbell, Shaw, and Gilliom 2000). Mental health constructs include anxiety and depression as well as somatic complaints and withdrawn behavior (Bongers et al. 2003). All of these skills and behaviors might both respond to ECE investments and contribute to subsequent educational attainment, skill development, and labor market participation.

The evidence base on how early skills link to later earnings in adulthood is thin. Longitudinal datasets that have collected multiple domains of early childhood data and followed subjects through adulthood are rare, and often made up of convenience samples. In addition, drawing causal conclusions from these nonexperimental studies is difficult because of confounding characteristics and contexts and the likely bidirectional nature of developmental processes. Nevertheless, analysis of the British cohort studies and recent data from U.S. studies suggest that early achievement skills directly predict later earnings (Chetty et al. 2011; Currie and Thomas 1999).

More evidence is found linking early skills to later childhood and adolescent outcomes. Data from several large studies of young children find that when a constellation of skills and behavior are taken into account and differences in family background are held constant, early achievement skills (reading and math) best predict achievement later in childhood, followed by attention skills (sometimes measured by the lack of attention and hyperactivity) (Duncan et al. 2007). Somewhat surprising is that early problem behavior such as aggression or even prosocial behaviors did not predict later achievement (Grimm et al. 2010).

A somewhat different picture of the role of early behavior is found, however, if the outcomes considered are educational attainment, later criminal activity, and earnings, rather than achievement skills. In the case of high school graduation, as would be expected, concrete achievement skills play an important role. However, early problem behavior, and more specifically persistent antisocial behavior during middle childhood, also predicts high school completion, college attendance, and years of educational attainment (Magnuson et al., forthcoming). Follow-up evaluations of high-quality early childhood interventions that had sizable impacts on multiple developmental domains also suggest the importance of early skills and behavior for long-term criminal activity and higher earnings (Heckman, Pinto, and Savelyev 2013).

Decisions about which skills to make the target of early childhood education efforts should be guided not only by which skills are important for later outcomes, but also be guided by where socioeconomic status (SES) differences in development are largest. The data are very clear on this point. Differences in development between more and less advantaged children are found early in life, recent data pointing to differences by poverty status as early as nine months of age (Halle et al. 2009). By school entry, family SES much more sharply differentiates children's early achievement skills than their early behavior. Table 1 provides data from the Early Childhood Longitudinal Study Kindergarten Cohorts of 1998 and 2010. Twelve years apart, the studies collected similar data from nationally representative samples of U.S. children and thus provide a useful comparison. They include one-on-one achievement skill assessments, as well as teacher and parent surveys, first gathered in the fall of the kindergarten year. These data provide a snapshot of skills and behavior that children have at the start of formal schooling.

In table 1, we provide two estimates of the differences across groups of children. The first *unadjusted* estimates describe mean differences for all children, and the second estimates from teacher fixed-effect models, which are based on the comparison of children within the same kindergarten classrooms. This second strategy provides an indication of how these differences are manifest among children sitting in the same schools and classrooms.

Disparities in children's skills are evident along a number of demographic dimensions in both the unadjusted and teacher fixed-effect estimates. Girls outperform boys in reading and are reported by teachers to be better behaved. White children outperform African American and Hispanic children in terms of reading and math and are rated as having better approaches to learning. Yet, the magnitude of these differences is dwarfed by those related to family SES (as measured by a composite of parental education and family income). Figure 1 shows differences in these early school entry skills by SES quintiles. The lowest SES quintile corresponds to an average family income of about $15,500 (in 1998) and the highest to incomes over $100,000 (in 1998). The differences between children in the top SES quintile and the bottom quintile are large. The difference in math and reading skills was 1.2 to 1.3 standard deviations for reading and math in 1998, and only slightly less in 2010. It is also notable from the fixed effects columns that differences of nearly these magnitudes are found among children in the same classroom.

Turning to children's attention skills, as measured by their teachers' response to questions forming the "approaches to learning" scale, bottom-to-top quintile differences across the SES spectrum are about half the size of

Table 1. Gaps in Children's Academic and Behavior Skills in the Fall of Kindergarten

	Reading		Math		Approaches to Learning		Externalizing Behavior		Lack of Internalizing Behavior	
	Unadj.	Teacher FE	Unadj.	Teacher FE	Unadj.	Teacher FE	Unadj.	Teacher FE	Unadj.	Teacher FE
ECLSK-10										
Boys/girls	0.11	0.11	−0.03	−0.03	0.43	0.44	0.42	0.42	0.07	0.06
Black/white	0.30	0.23	0.57	0.36	0.25	0.32	0.29	0.29	0.08	0.06
Hispanic/white	0.52	0.31	0.64	0.35	0.12	0.12	0.02	0.10	0.01	−0.02
SES: 1st quintile/5th quintile	1.14	0.95	1.23	0.87	0.50	0.72	0.30	0.39	0.28	0.39
SES: 1st quintile/3rd quintile	0.52	0.39	0.61	0.39	0.25	0.22	0.12	0.09	0.15	0.16
SES: 3rd quintile/5th quintile	0.62	0.49	0.62	0.43	0.26	0.34	0.17	0.16	0.13	0.12
ECLSK-98										
Boys/girls	0.17	0.15	0.03	0.01	0.40	0.39	0.41	0.39	0.06	0.05
Black/white	0.43	0.30	0.62	0.40	0.36	0.30	0.31	0.28	0.06	0.04
Hispanic/white	0.53	0.29	0.77	0.36	0.22	0.14	−0.01	−0.07	0.05	0.03
SES: 1st quintile/5th quintile	1.26	0.85	1.34	0.85	0.63	0.63	0.26	0.17	0.30	0.31
SES: 1st quintile/3rd quintile	0.59	0.45	0.72	0.46	0.36	0.35	0.14	0.08	0.21	0.23
SES: 3rd quintile/5th quintile	0.67	0.47	0.62	0.40	0.27	0.27	0.12	0.13	0.09	0.08

Source: Authors' calculations.

Notes: In this table, all positive numbers represent gaps in reference to the advantaged group indicated on the right-hand side of the first column. Unadj. refers to unadjusted comparisons across groups and Teacher FE provides estimates from teacher fixed effect models in which children are compared to other children in the same classroom. Negative numbers indicate that the left-hand group has better scores, on average. For both externalizing and internalizing behaviors, a positive gap indicates better behavior (less externalizing and internalizing) for the advantaged group. Approaches to Learning is the ECLS-K measure of attention and school engagement. Calculations done by Sharon Wolf, National Poverty Postdoctoral Fellow at UW–Madison, Institute for Research on Poverty.

Figure 1. Differences in School Readiness by Family Socioeconomic Status

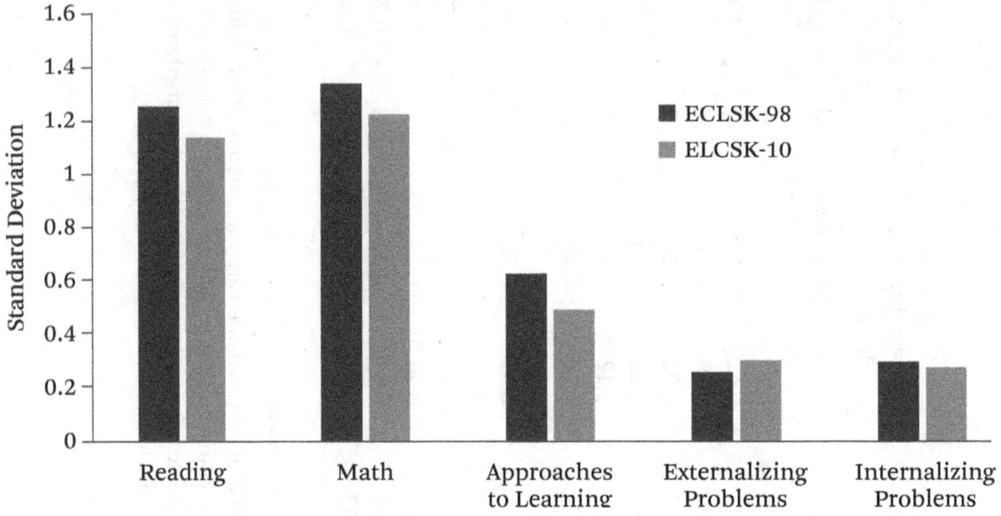

[Bar chart showing standard deviation differences between lowest income quintile and highest SES quintile for ECLSK-98 and ELCSK-10 cohorts across five measures: Reading (~1.25, ~1.15), Math (~1.35, ~1.23), Approaches to Learning (~0.62, ~0.48), Externalizing Problems (~0.25, ~0.30), Internalizing Problems (~0.29, ~0.27).]

Source: Authors' calculations.
Notes: The graph shows standard deviation differences in skills and behavior for children in the lowest income quintile and the highest SES quintile based on estimates in table 1. ECLSK refers to the Early Childhood Longitudinal Study Kindergarten Cohort studies, which were fielded in 1998 and 2010. Approaches to Learning is the ECLS-K measure of attention and school engagement.

concrete achievement skills, though still sizable—about 0.60 standard deviations in 1998 and 0.50 standard deviations in 2010. For externalizing and internalizing behaviors, although SES differences are apparent, they are a quarter of the size of the SES-related reading and math skill gaps. All in all, SES-based differences in concrete achievement skills are by far the largest.

It might be hoped that schools would be able to ameliorate some of the skill and behavior differences across the SES spectrum. For the 1998 cohort, the ECLS-K study followed the same children over the course of elementary school and into middle school. For reading and math skills, the magnitude of the gaps in standardized scores are largely similar over time—the gaps in eighth grade are of a magnitude similar to those in kindergarten. For teacher reports of problem behaviors, despite no evident change over time for internalizing behaviors, the gap in externalizing behavior over the course of elementary school is increasing (Magnuson, Waldfogel, and Washbrook 2012).

Turning to other national data to explore SES differences in adult outcomes, Duncan and Magnuson (2011) report that, compared with children in the top SES quintile, children in the lowest SES quintile subsequently have arrest rates 15 percentage points higher, high school completion rates 31 percentage points lower, and college attendance rates 40 percentage points lower. In sum, large SES-related differences in early skills and moderate differences in aspects of behavior forecast later disparities in schooling and criminal involvement that have important implications for youth's experiences in the labor market.

CURRENT PRESCHOOL INVESTMENTS

The large and enduring SES differences in early skills, as well as their consequences for later learning, have not gone unnoticed by educators and policymakers. Indeed these differences helped motivate the creation of Head Start, the expansion of state and local prekindergarten programs, and most recently President Obama's proposed expansion of enrollment in high-quality early learning programs. Despite advocates' and critics' focus on the findings from just a handful of programs, it is important to understand that preschool comprises a very heterogeneous set of programs, many of which have been evaluated and studied over time.

The rubric of *preschool* includes three broad types of programs serving children two years prior to kindergarten (ages three to five): private preschool programs (which may be publicly paid for with child-care subsidies), Head Start, and prekindergarten programs supported by state and local education funds. About 75 percent of U.S. children attended a center-based preschool program the year before kindergarten and just over half attended a center-based program the year before that (at age three) (Federal Interagency Forum on Child and Family Statistics 2011).

Despite the similarities among preschool programs, some differ in important ways from others. The oldest, largest, and best known federally funded preschool program is Head Start. Conceived as part of the Johnson administration's War on Poverty, Head Start has served more than thirty-one million children since its inception in 1965 (Head Start 2013). Federal guidelines require that at least 90 percent of the families served in each Head Start program be poor (incomes below the federal poverty threshold), and that 10 percent of children served by Head Start have developmental disabilities.

Head Start's 2013 federal budget was just under $7.6 billion, and funds were distributed to 1,591 local private and public nonprofit grantees serving just over nine hundred thousand children. Nearly half of Head Start programs provide full-week, full-time center care (Hamm 2006). Head Start programs are designed to enhance the development of economically disadvantaged children using a holistic approach, including the provision of educational services, parenting education, and providing families support to achieve parents' educational and employment goals. Head Start also provides services to identify health concerns and increase access to a full range of health care services including dental and mental health care (Puma et al. 2005). All Head Start centers are required to adopt a "whole-child" curriculum. A high priority is placed on parents' involvement in their children's education and the local administration of Head Start programs.

Public prekindergarten (pre-K) programs are a second form of publicly provided preschool and funded by states or local school districts. Funding and enrollment in state pre-K programs have increased dramatically over the past several years. As of 2012 to 2013, forty states (including the District of Columbia) had pre-K initiatives serving approximately 28 percent of four-year-olds and 4 percent of three-year-olds (Barnett et al. 2013). Most pre-K programs are targeted to low-income children (thirty-one state programs have income eligibility requirements); however, a small but growing number of states either offer, or are currently considering funding, universal access for all four-year-olds and, in some cases, three-year-olds (Barnett et al. 2013). Pre-K initiatives are intended to complement, rather than supplant, existing sources of ECE funding such as Head Start.

State prekindergarten programs vary substantially in terms of funding levels, program design, and quality. A majority of pre-K programs are either part time or have locally determined hours. Some programs offer an extensive set of support services, such as transportation and health screenings and referrals, others very few of these kinds of services. Most states use a mixed service delivery system that provides pre-K programming in schools as well as community-based settings, by contracting with privately run preschools and federally funded Head Start programs. Approximately one-third of children receiving pre-K services in 2011 were served outside public schools (Barnett et al. 2013).

Despite expansions in Head Start and pre-K programs, a large proportion of children still attend a private preschool the year before they enter kindergarten. These programs are typically licensed or regulated by states as child-care providers, and include both for-profit and not-for-profit entities. Steven Barnett and Milagros Nores's (2012) analysis of the National Higher Education Survey data finds, as would be expected, that participation in private preschool is most common among higher-income families, who are less likely to qualify for public programs.

META-ANALYSIS OF SHORT-TERM PRESCHOOL PROGRAM EFFECTS

What do we know about how children's preschool attendance affects their school readiness?

Despite the hundreds of evaluation studies of early childhood education programs that have been published over the past fifty years, only a handful of programs have been prominently discussed in policy circles by advocates and critics: Perry Preschool, the Abecedarian program, Head Start, and more recently some state and local prekindergarten programs. These programs provide a selective view of the impact of early education programs. Given the range of diverse programs that children experience, attention to the broader set of impacts and averages across programs seem most relevant and important. In a collaborative research project, we have focused on evaluations of preschool programs conducted over the course of the last half-century that used strong experimental or quasi-experimental methods and provided impact estimates for cognitive or achievement-related outcomes.[1]

Figure 2 shows the distribution of eighty-four program-average treatment effect sizes for cognitive and achievement outcomes, measured at the end of each program's treatment period, by the calendar year in which the program began. Reflecting their approximate contributions to weighted results, bubble sizes are proportional to the inverse of the squared standard error of the estimated program impact. The figure differentiates between evaluations of Head Start and other ECE programs and also includes a weighted regression line of effect size by calendar year.

Taken as a whole, the simple average effect size for early childhood education on cognitive and achievement scores was 0.28 standard deviations at the end of the program treatment periods, an amount equal to nearly half of race differences in the kindergarten achievement gap found in the Early Childhood Longitudinal Program, Kindergarten (ECLSK) data, but less than a quarter of the top-to-bottom quintile SES-related gaps (see table 1). However, as can be seen from figure 2, average effect sizes vary substantially and studies with the largest effect sizes tended to have the fewest subjects. When weighted by the inverse of the squared standard errors of the estimates, the average drops to 0.23 standard deviations (Leak et al. 2014).

STUDIES OF PRESCHOOL'S LONG-TERM EFFECTS

What do we know about the long-term effects of these programs? A key motivation for investing in early childhood education programs is that they will generate important long-term benefits. Indeed, any discussion of preschool's potential to equalize opportunity and mitigate economic inequality hinges on these programs' long-term effects on low-income children's later education, employment, and earnings. The evidence is fairly clear on two issues. First is that short-term impacts on achievement skills dissipate over time. Estimates from our meta-analysis suggest that for each year after program impact on average the effects decline by 0.02 standard deviations (Leak et al. 2014). That suggests that if the average program impact at the end of the program was 0.23 standard deviations, the treatment effect would be entirely gone ten years after the program ended. However, we also find support for the conclusion that impacts decline more quickly in the years right after program completion than in later years. Our results align with those of other researchers who have sought to answer similar questions (Aos et al. 2004).

Despite the frequent convergence between preschool attendees and comparison-group children's IQ scores or achievement skills, studies that have followed early education participants beyond adolescence typically find a range of substantial program impacts on measures of young adult and adult human capital,

---

1. Programs selected for our analysis had both treatment and control comparison groups, included at least ten participants in each condition, incurred less than 50 percent attrition, and measured children's outcomes close to end of their programs. Studies had to have used random assignment or a rigorous quasi-experimental design that established baseline equivalence of groups.

Figure 2. Average Cognitive and Achievement Skill Impact at the End of Program Treament

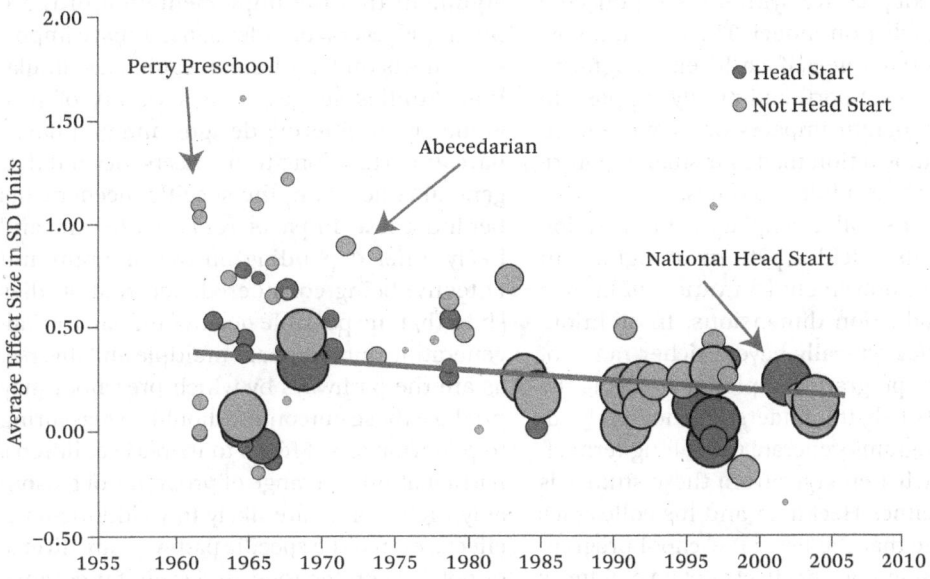

Source: Authors' compilation.

including increases in educational attainment, reductions in criminal activity, and greater earnings (Currie and Almond 2011). Studying the long-term effects of large, public programs, primarily Head Start, has required different methods than have been used for model demonstration programs, because of the dearth of experimental studies with long-term followups (Garces, Thomas, and Currie 2002; Johnson and Jackson 2015; Ludwig and Miller 2007). Head Start is the most examined public program because of its large size and scope. Long-term studies of Head Start have used a variety of econometric methods to construct appropriate comparison groups for preschool attendees, with particular concern that the same level of disadvantage is found among preschool attendees and non-attendees. For example, Eliana Garces and her colleagues' (2002) find in their sibling fixed-effect study using data from of the Panel Study of Income Dynamics that among white children, attending Head Start was linked with additional 22 percentage points higher rates of high school graduation and 19 percentage points higher rates of college attendance. Among African American children, attending Head Start was linked with lower likelihoods of being charged or convicted of a crime (12 percentage points lower). Similarly, David Deming (2009) finds that Head Start is associated with a 0.23 standard deviation increase in this adult outcome index (a mix of education, employment and parental outcomes). Although the pattern of results from the long-term studies is consistent in term of positive effects on human capital, that these studies lack measures other than early achievement test scores means that the processes that produce these long-term effects are essentially a "black box."

An evaluation study of the Chicago Child Parent Centers (CPC) provides the only longitudinal evaluation of a large, public program other than Head Start (Reynolds and Temple 1998). It follows a cohort of children who attended the Chicago Public School prekindergarten program and a matched comparison group. Age twenty-eight results showed positive impacts on participants' educational attainment and income, and negative impacts on their criminal involvement, substance and drug abuse. Arthur Reynolds, Judy Temple, and Suh-Ruu Ou's (2010) efforts to understand the early foundation of the program's later effects on occupational prestige and reduced crime and depressive symptoms produced a complex mediation model. Their work points to substantial roles of children's cognitive skills, school support, and family support. In contrast, program impacts on social adjustment and motivation made far smaller contributions to these adult outcomes.

Studies of small, exemplary demonstration programs also yield a pattern of significant long-term improvement in a variety of human capital production dimensions. In addition, these studies typically have a richer range of measures at program completion, offering the opportunity to better understand how early education programs generate these long-term effects. Yet, what emerges from these studies is puzzling. James Heckman and his colleagues (2010) argue that the Perry Preschool program had its most important effects not on children's academic skills, but on their character. Indeed, reductions in criminal activity in adulthood for male participants were the largest contribution to the program's positive long-term effects, and appear to have been most closely linked to changes in children's earlier behavior. The importance of behavior may constitute a significant part of the economic case for Perry Preschool, but it does not appear to generalize more broadly to other preschool studies.

Abecedarian—an intensive, high-quality early education program that began in the first year of life and lasted through school entry—demonstrated positive effects on adult human capital outcomes, but both the range of outcomes affected and the possible explanatory pathways appear to differ in important ways from those found among Perry Preschool attendees. For example, by age twenty-eight, children who attended the Abecedarian program were more likely to be college graduates than the control group and to have substantially higher earnings, though these did not rise to the level of statistical significance (Campbell et al. 2012). However, there was no apparent treatment difference in measures of criminal conviction, which may have been foreshadowed by early study findings that indicated no reductions in problem behavior for program participants (Clarke and Campbell 1998).

Taken together, these studies support the argument that the implementation of these programs several decades ago may have important effects on later human capital accumulation. Studies suggest that a variety of programs, with differing designs and emphasis, have important long-term effects. Beyond that general conclusion, the specific mechanisms behind these impacts remain unclear, and likely differ depending on the program and outcome being considered. Yet, that studies show that the possible positive human capital-generating outcomes are multiple and diverse, as are the pathways by which preschool may produce these outcomes, should be reassuring to policymakers. Efforts to increase children's participation in a range of programs of reasonably high quality are likely to yield long-term effects, even if the specific pathways are diverse or not fully understood, and even if programs' boosts to achievement do not persist. However, if policy goals are broader than increasing access to quality programs—for example, increasing the magnitude of long-term effects—then it would seem that more information about the potential pathways and mechanisms by which early skills and behaviors turn into longer-term outcomes is needed. Specifically, we need to know which skills and program design features to improve in order to yield larger long-term effects, and efforts that would boost early academic skills might differ from those that might more directly target socioemotional skills, behavior, or self-regulation.

COSTS OF EXPANDING PRESCHOOL ACCESS

Recent trends have suggested that through the late 1990s rates of preschool attendance were climbing among all SES groups, although rates of attendance continue to lag for lower-income children. In figure 3, we present enrollment trends for three- and four-year-olds from 1968 to 2010 using nationally representative data from the October Current Population Survey and dividing families into five groups based on income quintiles. Enrollment in preschool has grown for three- and four-year-olds from all income groups over time, but rates are consistently higher for the top two income groups than for the middle and lower two (figure 3).

Figure 3. Children Enrolled in Preschool, Three- and Four-Year-Olds

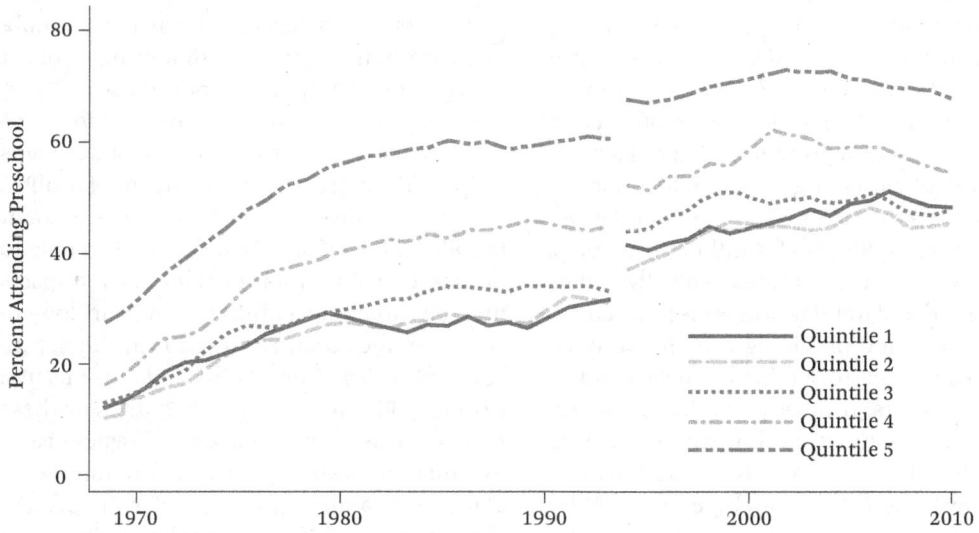

Source: Authors' calculations.
Notes: Data are taken from the October CPS, and represent three-year moving averages. The break in 1994 is due to a change in the wording of the question. Quintile 1 refers to lowest and quintile 5 to the highest income families.

Looking more closely at the year before children enter school, recent estimates indicate that about 75 percent of children have attended a preschool-like program. As would be expected, ECE participation is higher among the top income quintiles, nearly 90 percent, and lower among the three bottom quintiles, 64 percent to 69 percent (Barnett and Nores 2012).

Public investments have clearly played a role in boosting enrollment among low-income children. The cost of early education programs is typically expensive, with the median state average cost of full-time private preschool (center-based care) at about $8,000 per year (ChildCare Aware 2011). Without public investments to offset the price, the expense of private preschools is often prohibitive for many low-income and even middle-income families. Although expansions have no doubt been important to boosting preschool enrollments for low-income children, they have not been generous enough for all low-income children to benefit (Magnuson, Meyers, and Waldfogel 2007).

Other demographic groups have comparatively low levels of preschool enrollment—Hispanic children and children of immigrants. No doubt part of the lower rates of enrollment can be attributed to these groups' lower incomes, but African American children, in contrast, are if anything more likely than comparable white children to be enrolled in school- or center-based care (Magnuson, Lahaie, and Waldfogel 2006; Magnuson and Waldfogel 2005). Indeed, both language barriers and cultural factors are also likely influences that play a role in the lower levels of enrollment among Hispanic children and children of immigrants (Takanishi 2004). Rural communities with their transportation impediments are a final, and often overlooked dimension of under-enrollment. Indeed, less than half of four-year-olds in rural communities attend preschool, compared with nearly 80 percent of their urban or suburban peers (Nores and Barnett 2014).

Could we reach near universal enrollment in prekindergarten or preschool programs? The answer is almost certainly yes. In a relatively short period of time, kindergarten was introduced and became universal. Other countries, most notably France, have near universal attendance in public programs, even among immigrant minorities. What would it cost to do this in the United States? There are roughly four million four-year-olds, three-quarters of whom attend some form of preschool already. The cost of providing public education per child could range from $5,000 for half-day programs to about $10,000 for full-day programs.[2] Currently four-year olds are evenly divided between part- and full-day programs (Barnett and Nores 2012), and providing this mix of hours seems important to serving the needs and desires of parents. If we assume that those who are not currently attending would have the same distribution across full- and part-time programs, this yields an average cost of $7,500 per newly attending child. With these assumptions, the added cost for reaching 100 percent enrollment would be $7.5 billion ($7,500 for one million four-year-olds).

But, of course, we cannot devise a policy that would pay only for those children whose parents did not otherwise enroll in them. When public programs are available, some children whose parents are currently paying for care will shift to a publicly provided program (Cascio and Schanzenbach 2013). If the public program paid costs for all four-year-olds, the price tag would be $30 billion ($7,500 for four million four-year-olds). More than $5.12 billion is already being spent on state pre-kindergarten and $8.5 billion on Head Start, therefore the marginal new public investment would amount to $16.35 billion for a mix of full- and part-day program slots. We expect that once the cost of child-care subsidies was taken into account, this price would fall by possibly $1 billion. It is also certain that, as is the case for public education, some proportion of families would prefer to pay for a private preschool than participate in public programs. If a similar proportion chose private preschools as choose private K–12 schools (10 percent), that would suggest a total price tag of $27 billion and a marginal public investment of $13.35 billion.

A key question, however, is whether the public investment should be attempting to offset the costs for all families, or only those in lower-income families. With limited public resources, there are compelling reasons to focus on providing access for low-income families, rather than offsetting costs for more affluent families. Low-income families are less able to purchase ECE on their own and ECE impacts may be larger for children reared in low-income families than for those from higher-income families (Duncan and Sojourner 2013; Gormley, Phillips, and Gayer 2008). For these reasons, it is worth considering residence in low-income communities or low family income (or a combination of similar characteristics) as the basis for categorical eligibility. In particular, the bottom three income quintiles (60 percent) all share similarly low rates of enrollment, compared with the upper two income quintiles (figure 3). Combined, roughly 52 percent of these income groups are either not enrolled or enrolled in private programs (Barnett and Nores 2012). Thus, the cost for publicly providing for all these children who are currently not enrolled in publicly funded programs would require new public investments on the order of $9.36 billion ($7,500 per child for 1.248 million children). This amounts to a little more than currently being spent on Head Start, and a little less than twice what is being spent on state pre-K programs.

Quantifying the costs of expanding preschool access is important not only in terms of approximating how much more public money would be needed to increase enrollments, but also because it is a necessary step in considering whether such efforts would generate more social benefits than costs. Cost-benefit perspective offers an accounting of whether spending for a program yields societal benefits. Although one might endorse a policy or program that redistributes educational or economic opportunity because it produces

---

2. These price points are meant to reflect the real costs of providing high-quality programs. But $10,000 is less than the average per pupil cost for K–12 schooling and Perry Preschool. It is a midpoint between the costs of the recently studied Tulsa Pre-K program ($4,403 for part-day and $8,803 for full-day) and the Boston preschool program ($12,000 for full-day).

outcomes that generate the desired benefit, regardless of cost. Given the many ways in which such outcomes could be achieved as well as the tight budgets and strong arguments for fiscal austerity, cost-benefit comparisons provide one way to consider and compare the economic efficiency of programs and policies.

WHAT ARE THE LIKELY BENEFITS OF INCREASING PRESCHOOL ENROLLMENT?

Documenting the economic benefits of preschool participation is an important part of a cost-benefit comparison. These efforts are obviously most complete and useful when children are followed by researchers well into their adulthood and many types of outcome data are collected. By and large, studies of this type are based on expensive program models in operation decades ago. We adopt an alternative approach in which we ask what magnitude of test score impacts, expressed in standard deviation units, would a pre-K program expansion need to generate long-term benefits that exceed program costs. We believe that this approach is instructive because the field knows more about the magnitude of impacts generated by the existing variety of program models than it does about specific benefits accrued much later in life for the vast majority of these models. Our effort is thus an exercise that seeks to roughly consider whether a public investment in preschool might also be economically productive. Of course, for any specific program model, a more careful and detailed full accounting of costs and benefits would yield a more precise estimate of the benefits, costs and the implied internal rate of return (the discount rate applied to future benefits that would yield a $0 present value cost).

Research efforts to quantify the benefits of early childhood education are accumulating. We adopt methods used by Timothy Bartik, William Gormley, and Shirley Adelstein (2012) to project benefits for the Tulsa pre-K program.

A first needed piece of information is the association between end-of-kindergarten test scores and adult earnings. We use estimates from Raj Chetty and his colleagues' (2011) analysis of the Tennessee Star experiment, which finds that at the end of kindergarten a 1 percentile increase in test scores is associated with approximately 0.5 percent increase in adult earnings. Bartik and his colleagues (2012) compare predicted earnings impacts based on Chetty and his colleagues' (2011) estimates to measured earnings impacts for available long-term follow-up studies, and find that prediction model seems to do reasonably well thus indicating that this approach seems to provide a good approximation for the effects of test scores at the end of a preschool program.[3]

Second, we need to know likely earnings of future cohorts. In prior work, we have used the 2013 March Current Population Survey data to estimate the present value of lifetime earnings for adult high school graduates and adults with some college (ages twenty to sixty-five, including zero earnings for nonworkers, we think a reasonable group for this exercise) (Magnuson, Brooks-Gunn, and Waldfogel 2014). Predicting lifetime earnings requires numerous assumptions. Here, we offer a low and high estimate of lifetime earnings. For the low estimate, we assume no wage growth over time, and 3 percent discount to age five; the resulting present value of lifetime earnings for workers with a high school degree or some college is about $382,392.

Now suppose we assume an expenditure of $7,500 per child to fund a fifty-fifty mix of part-day and full-day program expansion. How much of a program impact, expressed as a fraction of a kindergarten test score standard deviation, would the ECE program expansion need to generate more benefits than costs? At $7,500 per child, the preschool investment would represent 2 percent of lifetime earnings, suggesting that the program would need to result in an on average 4 percentile point in-

---

3. For example, based on the prediction model earnings would increase by about 16 percent, 10 percent, and 8 percent for Perry Preschool, Abecedarian, and the CPC, respectively. The actual earnings effects in these programs were 19 percent, 14 percent, and 7 percent. However, it is unclear whether these associations would hold when moving from a small-scale intervention to a large-scale intervention, in which the entire distribution shifted upward.

crease in test scores (given the 0.5 percent association between test score percentile and earnings). Translating from test score percentiles to effect sizes suggests that this would be an effect size of 0.095 standard deviations for someone who was at the 50th percentile, but closer to 0.15 standard deviation effect size for those scoring at just the 25th (or 75th) test score percentile.

For the high estimate of lifetime earnings, we assume that earnings make up 80 percent of total compensation (the remainder consisting of fringe benefits such as health insurance and retirement contributions), wages grow by 1 percent wage per year, but that the discount rate to age five is still 3 percent. This results in a much larger estimate of lifetime earnings—$681,544. Under these assumptions, $7,500 amounts to just 1.1 percent of earnings. Based on the Chetty (Chetty et al. 2011) estimates, this suggests that impacts of just 2.5 percentile points are needed to equalize costs and these earnings benefits. This translates into an effect size of 0.035 standard deviations at the 50th percentile and of a 0.07 standard deviation effect size for 25th (or 75th) percentile test scores. These projections should be interpreted as rough approximations, and with the appropriate warning that any projection into the future involves significant uncertainty. Yet, most effect sizes shown in figure 2 are comfortably above those levels.

Taken together, these admittedly rough benefit estimates seem to suggest that even if expansions to preschool programs yield relatively small effect sizes in improvements in academic skills, the spending and expected returns are likely in the very least to break even, and to bring increased income and economic opportunity. As has been found in long-term evaluations and in recent projections, a program that yields substantial impacts on academic skills will have earnings benefits that well exceed the program costs (Heckman et al. 2010).

Even if program impacts on later earnings were the only benefit to be considered, the exercise indicates that increasing enrollments in preschool programs is likely to be a wise investment. Earnings represent only a proportion of total ECE benefits. In the benefit-cost evaluations of model preschool programs earnings have amounted to from one-third to one-half of estimated program benefits in prior cost-benefit studies. Reductions in spending for special education, grade repetition, child protection services, public welfare benefits, and crime are important documented benefits, with large payoffs (Barnett and Masse 2007; Heckman et al. 2010; Temple and Reynolds 2007). Yet, each study has identified in a slightly different set of non-earnings benefits. In Perry Preschool, a large category was reductions in crime. For CPC, both reductions in crime and reductions in participation in the child welfare system were important. For Abecedarian, benefits were counted from increased maternal employment early in life and later improvements in the children's adult health. All of this suggests that estimating the specifics of likely benefits is hard to do without long-term data, and requires a careful understanding of the populations that will be served by expanded funding and the specifics of the programs being funded. Nonetheless, if prior studies are a useful guide, then other benefits are likely to amount to an important return on the investment.

If the focus of policy attention is on improving inequality in economic fortunes, then it is important that our calculations of increased earnings do not differentiate between the magnitudes of earnings gains for children from differing economic backgrounds. The extent to which both short- and long-term program impacts differ by family background along a number of relevant demographic characteristics is not fully understood. Some evidence suggests that effect sizes might be slightly larger for children from more disadvantaged backgrounds, but the differences are often relatively small and not always significantly different (Burchinal et al. 2015). Thus, although preschool may increase later economic productivity, it is likely to do so for all participating children. It is therefore likely to result in a modest reduction in the inequality of economic opportunity between disadvantaged and affluent children, the magnitude of the reduction contingent on the extent to which policies close the gap in preschool enrollment rates between low-income and higher-income children.

WHAT OTHER TYPES OF INVESTMENTS SHOULD BE CONSIDERED?

Low-income children's preschool enrollment in the year prior to kindergarten is only one margin for improving young children's development and building human capital. Several other types of investments need greater development, evaluation, and policy attention. First, improving the effectiveness of preschool instruction may be an important way to improve children's skills. Increasingly, evidence suggests that one of the most important opportunities to increase children's learning is by selecting good curricula and supporting teachers as they implement it. Curricula and related professional development that are intensive, focused, developmentally appropriate, and sequential can have especially positive impacts on early childhood instruction and on children's learning (Burchinal et al. 2015).

A comparative evaluation of preschool curricula was conducted by the Preschool Curriculum Evaluation Research initiative. The impact of fourteen curricula implemented in early childhood classrooms serving primarily low-income children was assessed using experimental methods (PCERC 2008). Unfortunately, inference from the individual studies was weakened by their cluster design and small sample sizes, which generated low statistical power for analyzing impacts. During the pre-K year, eight of the fourteen curricula had a positive impact on teacher instruction, but only two had statistically significantly positive effects on child outcomes (effect sizes of 0.32 to 0.96 standard deviations). A recent reanalysis of these data by Duncan and his colleagues (2014), which pools across curricula based on their content in order to better detect significant small to moderate effects, concludes that content-specific curricula focused on literacy and math are better able to promote academic skills, compared with more general whole-child curricula.

The Building Blocks math program illustrates a recently developed content-specific curriculum. Developed by Julie Sarama and Douglas Clements (2004), the curriculum includes large- and small-group instruction focused on teaching math skills in a focused and sequential manner, and hands-on and computer activities that promote children's active involvement in solving problems and explaining their solutions. An experimental evaluation found that the curriculum resulted in large improvements in children's math knowledge when compared with a different math curriculum (effect size of 0.47 standard deviations) and a business-as-usual control group (effect size of 1.07 standard deviations) (Clements and Sarama 2008).

An example of a public preschool program that has taken seriously the need to identify exemplary curricula and implement them well is the Boston Pre-Kindergarten Program. The program developed their curriculum by integrating proven literacy, math, and social skills interventions. The academic component combined two curricula, Building Blocks for math instruction and Opening the World of Learning for language and literacy. Extensive teacher training and coaching was provided. The rigorous evaluation indicated large impacts on vocabulary, math, and reading (effect sizes of 0.45 to 0.62) and somewhat smaller impacts on executive functions (effect sizes of 0.21 to 0.28) (Duncan and Murnane 2013; Weiland and Yoshikawa 2013).

While evidence is accumulating, much more research related to preschool curriculum development, implementation, and evaluation is needed. This work is critical, but not easy for several reasons. First, the costs associated with successful implementation are not negligible, often requiring substantial investments in materials and teacher training time. Second, there are often nonpecuniary obstacles to overcome. In general, the early childhood education workforce often works long hours for low salaries, which often results in workers with low levels of education and high rates of job turnover. Sometimes, these circumstances can make implementation challenging, especially in community-based settings. Finally, the associated research costs are often quite high because multisite experimental evaluations that include individual child assessments are expensive.

All the discussion of preschool leaves out infants and toddlers. These earliest years of life are also an important period of development and warrant greater policy and programmatic attention. The developmentally appropriate model early learning programs for preschoolers cannot be simply extended downward for younger children at the same cost for the same effect. Some model home visiting programs and parenting programs for mothers of infants have also demonstrated the potential to have important impacts on children's trajectories, with potential implications for human capital accumulation (Olds, Sadler, and Kitzman 2007). Yet, at this time what is needed most are continued efforts to innovate and evaluate the feasibility and effectiveness of theoretically informed interventions for very young children.

CONCLUSIONS

Development during early childhood is an important foundation for human capital development, and has substantial long-term links to economic earnings and opportunity later in life. The accumulated evidence suggests multiple aspects of early skills—achievement, behavior, and mental health—if improved early in life can improve children's life chances. Moreover, evidence is accumulating that attending good quality preschools for a year or two results in long-lasting improvements in educational attainment and earnings, even when short-term improvements in concrete achievement skills fade during the elementary school years. The process by which these changes occur, however, seem to vary depending on the populations being served and the emphasis of the programs. Taken together, this argues for the importance of early childhood investments as a way to increase economic opportunity.

Currently, about 25 percent of children do not attend preschool before they enter kindergarten. Because low-income children are least likely to be enrolled compared with higher-income children, and because income gaps in early development forecast lower levels of human capital accumulation, improving attendance should be a first priority for policy. Efforts to expand enrollment will also need to consider other potential barriers such as language and program location. We estimate the costs of providing publicly funded preschool, a mix of part- and full-day programs, for all children in the bottom three income quintiles. We estimate that this would cost an additional $9.6 billion.

Our consideration of the potential benefits finds that programs that have relatively small effects on children's achievement are projected to "break even" (our low estimate of income, which is more conservative, would require a 0.09 to 0.15 standard deviation impact on achievement to do so). Prior studies of preschool programs that produce larger end of program effects on achievement have been shown to yield larger returns on investments than we project. Although all efforts to forecast years in the future involve uncertainty, we read the evidence to point toward the importance of increased investments in public preschool programs. Other targets for investment include improving learning through research-based preschool curricula and programs for infants and toddlers.

REFERENCES

Aizer, Anna, and Flavio Cunha. 2012. "The Production of Human Capital: Endowments, Investments and Fertility." *NBER* working paper no. w18429. Cambridge, Mass.: National Bureau of Economic Research.

Aos, Steve, Roxanne Lieb, Jim Mayfield, Marna Miller, and Annie Pennucci. 2004. "Benefits and Costs of Prevention and Early Intervention Programs for Youth." Report no. 04-07-3901. Olympia, Wash.: Washington State Institute for Public Policy.

Barnett, W. Steven, Megan E. Carolan, James H. Squires, and Kristy C. Brown. 2013. *The State of Preschool 2011: State Preschool Yearbook*. New Brunswick, N.J.: National Institute for Early Education Research.

Barnett, W. Steven, and Leonard N. Masse. 2007. "Comparative Cost-Benefit Analysis of the Abecedarian Program and Its Policy Implications." *Economics of Education Review* 26(1): 113–25.

Barnett, W. Steven, and Milagros Nores. 2012. "Estimated Participation and Hours in Early Care and Education by Type of Arrangement and Income at Ages 2 to 4 in 2010." *NIEER* working paper. New Brunswick, N.J.: National Institute for Early Education Research.

Bartik, Timothy, William Gormley, and Shirley Adelstein. 2012. "Earnings Benefits of Tulsa's Pre-K Program for Different Income Groups." *Economics of Education Review* 31(6): 1143–61.

Bernier, Annie, Stephanie M. Carlson, and Natasha

Whipple. 2010. "From External Regulation to Self-Regulation: Early Parenting Precursors of Young Children's Executive Functioning." *Child Development* 81(1): 326–39.

Blair, Clancy, and Cybele C. Raver. 2012. "Child Development in the Context of Adversity Experiential Canalization of Brain and Behavior." *American Psychologist* 67(4): 309–18.

Bongers, Ilja L., Hans M. Koot, Jan Van der Ende, and Frank C. Verhulst. 2003. "The Normative Development of Child and Adolescent Problem Behavior." *Journal of Abnormal Psychology* 112(5): 179–92.

Burchinal, Margaret, Katherine Magnuson, Douglas Powell, and Sandra Soliday Hong. 2015. "Children in Early Care and Education" In *Handbook of Child Psychology and Developmental Science, Volume 4, Ecological Settings and Processes in Developmental Systems*, edited by Richard M. Lerner, Marc H. Bornstein, and Tama Leventhal. Hoboken, N.J.: John Wiley & Sons.

Campbell, Frances A., Elizabeth Pungello, Margaret Burchinal, Kirsten Kainz, Yi Pan, Barbara Wasik, Oscar Barbarin, Joseph Sparling, and Craig Ramey. 2012. "Adult Outcomes as a Function of an Early Childhood Educational Program: An Abecedarian Project Follow-Up." *Developmental Psychology* 48(4): 1033–43.

Campbell, Susan B., Daniel S. Shaw, and Miles Gilliom. 2000. "Early Externalizing Behavior Problems: Toddlers and Preschoolers at Risk for Later Maladjustment." *Development and Psychopathology* 12(3): 467–88.

Cascio, Elizabeth U., and Diane W. Schanzenbach. 2013. "The Impacts of Expanding Access to High-Quality Preschool Education." *NBER* working paper no. w19735. Cambridge, Mass.: National Bureau of Economic Research.

Champagne, Frances A., and Rahia Mashoodh. 2009. "Genes in Context Gene–Environment Interplay and the Origins of Individual Differences in Behavior." *Current Directions in Psychological Science* 18(3): 127–31.

Chetty, Raj, John Friedman, Nathaniel Hilger, Emmanuel Saez, Diane Schanzenbach, and Danny Yagan. 2011. "How Does Your Kindergarten Classroom Affect Your Earnings? Evidence from Project STAR." *Quarterly Journal of Economics* 126(4): 1593–660.

ChildCare Aware. 2011. *Parents and the High Cost of Child Care*. Arlington, Va.: ChildCare Aware of America. Accessed December 8, 2015. https://www.ncsl.org/documents/cyf/2014_Parents_and_the_High_Cost_of_Child_Care.pdf.

Clarke, Stevens H., and Frances A. Campbell. 1998. "Can Intervention Early Prevent Crime Later? The Abecedarian Project Compared with Other Programs." *Early Childhood Research Quarterly* 13(2): 319–43.

Clements, Douglas H., and Julie Sarama. 2008. "Experimental Evaluation of the Effects of a Research-Based Preschool Mathematics Curriculum." *American Educational Research Journal* 45(2): 443–94.

Cunha, Flavio, and James J. Heckman. 2007. "The Technology of Skill Formation." *American Economic Review* 97(2): 31–47.

Currie, Janet, and Douglas Almond. 2011. "Human Capital Development Before Age Five." In *Handbook of Labor Economics*, edited by Orley Ashenfelter and David Card, vol. 4. Philadelphia, Pa.: Elsevier.

Currie, Janet, and Duncan Thomas. 1999. "Early Test Scores, Socioeconomic Status and Future Outcomes." *NBER* working paper no. w6943. Cambridge, Mass.: National Bureau of Economic Research.

Deming, David. 2009. "Early Childhood Intervention and Life-Cycle Skill Development: Evidence from Head Start." *American Economic Journal-Applied Economics* 1(3): 111–34.

Duncan, Greg J., Chantelle J. Dowsett, Amy Claessens, Katherine Magnuson, Aletha C. Huston, Pamela Klebanov, Linda Pagani, Leon Feinstein, Mimi Engel, Jeanne Brooks-Gunn, Holly Sexton, Kathryn Duckworth, and Crista Japel. 2007. "School Readiness and Later Achievement." *Developmental Psychology* 43(6): 1428–46.

Duncan, Greg J., Jade M. Jenkins, Anamarie Auger, Margaret Burchinal, Thurston Domina, and Marianne Bitler. 2014. "Boosting School Readiness with Preschool Curricula and Quality." Unpublished paper. University of California, Irvine.

Duncan, Greg J., and Katherine Magnuson. 2011. "The Nature and Impact of Early Achievement Skills, Attention and Behavior Problems." In *Whither Opportunity: Rising Inequality, Schools, and Children's Life Chances*, edited by Greg J. Duncan and Richard J. Murnane. New York: Russell Sage Foundation.

Duncan, Greg J., and Richard J. Murnane. 2013. *Restoring Opportunity: The Crisis of Inequality and* the Challenge for American Education. Cambridge, Mass.: Harvard Education Press.

Duncan, Greg J., and Aaron J. Sojourner. 2013. "Can Intensive Early Childhood Intervention Programs Eliminate Income-based Cognitive and Achievement Gaps?" Journal of Human Resources 48(4): 945–68.

Essex, Marilyn J., W. Thomas Boyce, Clyde Hertzman, Lucia L. Lam, Jeffrey M. Armstrong, Sarah M. A. Newman, and Michael S. Kobor. 2013. "Epigenetic Vestiges of Early Developmental Adversity: Childhood Stress Exposure and DNA Methylation in Adolescence." Child Development 84(1): 58–75.

Federal Interagency Forum on Child and Family Statistics. 2011. "America's Children: Key National Indicators of Well-Being, 2011." Washington: U.S. Government Printing Office.

Fox, Sharon E., Pat Levitt, and Charles A. Nelson III. 2010. "How the Timing and Quality of Early Experiences Influence the Development of Brain Architecture." Child Development 81(1): 28–40. Doi: 10.1111/j.1467-8624.2009.01380.x.

Garces, Eliana, Duncan Thomas, and Janet Currie. 2002. "Longer-Term Effects of Head Start." American Economic Review 92(4): 999–1012.

Gormley, Willian T., Deborah Phillips, and Ted Gayer. 2008. "Preschool Programs Can Boost School Readiness." Science 320(5884): 1723–24.

Grimm, Kevin J., Joel S. Steele, Andrew J. Mashburn, Margaret Burchinal, and Robert C. Pianta. 2010. "Early Behavioral Associations of Achievement Trajectories." Developmental Psychology 46(5): 976–83.

Halle, Tamara, Nicole Forry, Elizabeth Hair, Kate Perper, Laura Wandner, Julia Wessel, and Jessica Vick. 2009. "Disparities in Early Learning and Development: Lessons from the Early Childhood Longitudinal Study–Birth Cohort (ECLS-B)." Washington, D.C.: Child Trends.

Hamm, Katie. 2006. "More Than Meets the Eye: Head Start Programs, Participants, Families, and Staff in 2005." Policy Brief no. 8. Washington, D.C.: Center for Law and Social Policy.

Head Start. 2013. "Head Start Program Facts: Fiscal Year 2013." Fact Sheet. Washington: U.S. Department of Health and Human Services, Administration for Children and Families. Accessed December 28, 2015. http://eclkc.ohs.acf.hhs.gov/hslc/data/factsheets/docs/hs-program-fact-sheet-2013.pdf.

Heckman, James J., Seong H. Moon, Rodrigo Pinto, Peter A. Savelyev, and Adam Yavitz. 2010. "The Rate of Return to the High Scope Perry Preschool Program." Journal of Public Economics 94(1–2): 114–28.

Heckman, James J., Rodrigo Pinto, and Peter A. Savelyev. 2013. "Understanding the Mechanisms Through Which an Influential Early Childhood Program Boosted Adult Outcomes." American Economic Review 103(6): 2052–86.

Hoff, Erika. 2003. "The Specificity of Environmental Influence: Socioeconomic Status Affects Early Vocabulary Development Via Maternal Speech." Child Development 74(5): 1368–78.

Johnson, Rucker C., and C. Kirabo Jackson. 2015. "School Spending and the Long-Run Effects of Head Start." Unpublished paper. University of California, Berkeley.

Knudsen, Eric I., James J. Heckman, Judy L. Cameron, and Jack P. Shonkoff. 2006. "Economic, Neurobiological, and Behavioral Perspectives on Building America's Future Workforce." Proceedings of the National Academy of Sciences of the United States of America 103(27): 10155–62.

Leak, James, Greg J. Duncan, Weilin Li, Katherine Magnuson, Holly Schindler, and Hirokazu Yoshikawa. 2014. "Is Timing Everything? How Early Childhood Education Program Cognitive and Achievement Impacts Vary by Starting Age, Program Duration and Time Since the End of the Program." Unpublished paper. University of California, Irvine.

Ludwig, Jens, and Douglas L. Miller. 2007. "Does Head Start Improve Children's Life Chances? Evidence from a Regression Discontinuity Design." Quarterly Journal of Economics 122(1): 159–208.

Magnuson, Katherine, Jeanne Brooks-Gunn, and Jane Waldfogel. 2014. "Projecting the Long-Run Economic Effects of Early Childhood Programs." Unpublished paper. University of Wisconsin–Madison.

Magnuson, Katherine, Greg J. Duncan, You-Geon Lee, and Molly Metzger. Forthcoming. "Elementary School Adjustment and Educational Attainment?" American Education Research Journal.

Magnuson, Katherine, Claudia Lahaie, and Jane Waldfogel. 2006. "Preschool and School Readiness of Children of Immigrants." Social Science Quarterly 87(5): 1241–62.

Magnuson, Katherine, Marcia Meyers, and Jane Waldfogel. 2007. "Public Funding and Enrollment in Formal Child Care in the 1990s." *Social Service Review* 81(1): 47–83.

Magnuson, Katherine, and Jane Waldfogel. 2005. "Early Childhood Care and Education: Effects on Ethnic and Racial Gaps in School Readiness." *Future of Children* 15(1): 169–96.

Magnuson, Katherine, Jane Waldfogel, and Elizabeth Washbrook. 2012. "The Development of SES Gradients in Skills During the School Years: Evidence from the US and UK." In *From Parents to Children: The Intergenerational Transmission of Advantage*, edited by John Ermisch, Markus Jantti, and Timothy Smeeding, New York: Russell Sage Foundation.

Meaney, Michael J. 2010. "Epigenetics and the Biological Definition of Gene × Environment Interactions." *Child Development* 81(1): 41–79.

Nores, Milagros, and Steven Barnett. 2014. "Access to High Quality Early Care and Education: Readiness and Opportunity Gaps in America." National Institute for Early Education and Center on Enhancing Early Learning Policy report. New Brunswick, N.J.: Center on Enhancing Early Learning Outcomes. Accessed February 13, 2015. http://ceelo.org/wp-content/uploads/2014/05/ceelo_policy_report_access_quality_ece.pdf.

Olds, David L., Lois Sadler, and Harriet Kitzman. 2007. "Programs for Infants and Toddlers: Recent Evidence from Randomized Trials." *Journal of Child Psychology and Psychiatry* 48(3–4): 355–91.

Preschool Curriculum Evaluation Research Consortium (PCERC). 2008. *Effects of Preschool Curriculum Programs on School Readiness: Report from the Preschool Curriculum Evaluation Research Initiative*. Washington, D.C.: National Center for Education Research.

Puma, Michael, Stephen Bell, Ronna Cook, Camilla Heid, and Michael Lopez. 2005. *Head Start Impact Study: First Year Findings*. Washington: U.S. Department of Health and Human Services, Administration for Children and Families.

Purtell, Kelly M., and Elizabeth T. Gershoff. 2013. "The 'Skill Begets Skill' Hypothesis and the Experimental Effects of Head Start on Children's Academic Skills and Social Behaviors." Paper presented at the Association for Public Policy Analysis and Management Annual Meeting. Washington, D.C. (November 7–9, 2013).

Ramey, Craig T., and Sharon L. Ramey. 1998. "Early Intervention and Early Experience." *American Psychologist* 53(2): 109–20.

Raver, C. Cybele. 2004. "Placing Emotional Self-Regulation in Sociocultural and Socioeconomic Contexts." *Child Development* 75(2): 346–53.

Reynolds, Arthur J., and Judy A. Temple. 1998. "Extended Early Childhood Intervention and School Achievement: Age Thirteen Findings from the Chicago Longitudinal Study." *Child Development* 69(1): 231–46.

Reynolds, Arthur J., Judy A. Temple, and Suh-Ruu Ou. 2010. "Preschool Education, Educational Attainment, and Crime Prevention: Contributions of Cognitive and Non-Cognitive Skills." *Children and Youth Services Review* 32(8): 1054–63.

Rowe, Meredith L. 2012. "A Longitudinal Investigation of the Role of Quantity and Quality of Child-Directed Speech in Vocabulary Development." *Child Development* 83(5): 1762–74.

Sameroff, Arnold. 2010. "A Unified Theory of Development: A Dialectic Integration of Nature and Nurture." *Child Development* 81(1): 6–22.

Sarama, Julie, and Douglas H. Clements. 2004. "Building Blocks for Early Childhood Mathematics." *Early Childhood Research Quarterly* 19(1): 181–89.

Shonkoff, Jack P. 2010. "Building a New Biodevelopmental Framework to Guide the Future of Early Childhood Policy." *Child Development* 81(1): 357–67.

Takanishi, Ruby. 2004. "Leveling the Playing Field: Supporting Immigrant Children from Birth to Eight." *Future of Children* 14(2): 61–79.

Temple, Judy A., and Arthur J. Reynolds. 2007. "Benefits and Costs of Investments in Preschool Education: Evidence from the Child-Parent Centers and Related Programs." *Economics of Education Review* 26(1): 126–44.

Watamura, Sarah E., Deborah A. Phillips, Taryn W. Morrissey, Kathleen McCartney, and Kristen Bub. 2011. "Double Jeopardy: Poorer Social Emotional Outcomes for Children in the NICHD SECCYD Experiencing Home and Child Care Environments that Confer Risk." *Child Development* 82(1): 48–65.

Weiland, Christina, and Hirokazu Yoshikawa. 2013. "Impacts of a Prekindergarten Program on Children's Mathematics, Language, Literacy, Executive Function, and Emotional Skills." *Child Development* 84(6): 2112–30.

Weisleder, Adriana, and Anne Fernald. 2013. "Talking to Children Matters: Early Language Experience Strengthens Processing and Builds Vocabulary." *Psychological Science* 24(11): 2143–52.

Rising Inequality in Family Incomes and Children's Educational Outcomes

GREG J. DUNCAN AND RICHARD J. MURNANE

Increases in family income inequality in the United States have translated into widening gaps in educational achievement and attainments between children from low- and high-income families. We describe the mechanisms that have produced this disturbing trend. We argue that the three dominant policy approaches states and the federal government have used to improve the education of the disadvantaged have had at best modest success in improving education for disadvantaged children. To conclude, we describe the building blocks for an American solution to the problem of growing inequality of educational outcomes.

Keywords: inequality, educational outcomes, accountability, school supports

America has always taken pride in being the land of opportunity, a country in which hard work and sacrifice result in a better life for one's children. In the quarter century following World War II, the pride was justified, as the benefits of substantial economic growth were shared by both high- and low-income families (Duncan and Murnane 2011). But, beginning in the 1970s, economic changes favoring highly educated workers, plus demographic shifts such as the rise of single-parent families, produced sharply growing income gaps between high- and low-income families.

Figure 1 shows the average annual cash income in a particular year (in 2012 dollars) for children at the 20th, 80th, and 95th percentiles of the nation's family income distribution.[1] Compared with 1970, the 2010 cash family income at the 20th percentile has fallen by more than 25 percent. In contrast, the incomes of families at the 80th percentile grew by 23 percent, to $125,000, and the incomes of the rich-

Greg J. Duncan is Distinguished Professor in the School of Education at the University of California, Irvine. **Richard J. Murnane** is Thompson Research Professor at the Harvard Graduate School of Education.

This chapter draws from the introductory chapter in *Whither Opportunity?* and from our 2014 book. We thank the Russell Sage Foundation and the Spencer Foundation for supporting the research and allowing us to summarize the lessons from our books here. Direct correspondence to: Greg J. Duncan at gduncan@uci.edu, School of Education, University of California, Irvine, 2001 Education, Irvine, CA 92697; and Richard J. Murnane at richard_murnane@harvard.edu, Gutman Library, Rm. 406B, Harvard University, 6 Appian Way, Cambridge, MA 02138.

1. All dollar figures in this paper are expressed in 2012 dollars, and consequently are net of inflation. The income figures are drawn from the Current Population Survey (for a description, see Duncan and Murnane 2014). We are grateful to Sean Reardon and Demetra Kalogrides for supplying these data. Note that they are weighted by children rather than families or households, which produces a somewhat different time series than one sees with published Census data on family incomes. This means the fact that the 20th percentile family income (in 2012 dollars) was $37,700 in 1970 in figure 1 means that 20 percent of the nation's children live in families with income below that level. Because lower-income families tend to have more children than higher-income families, fewer than 20 percent of the nation's families in 1970 had income lower than $37,700.

Figure 1. Children's Family Income over Time

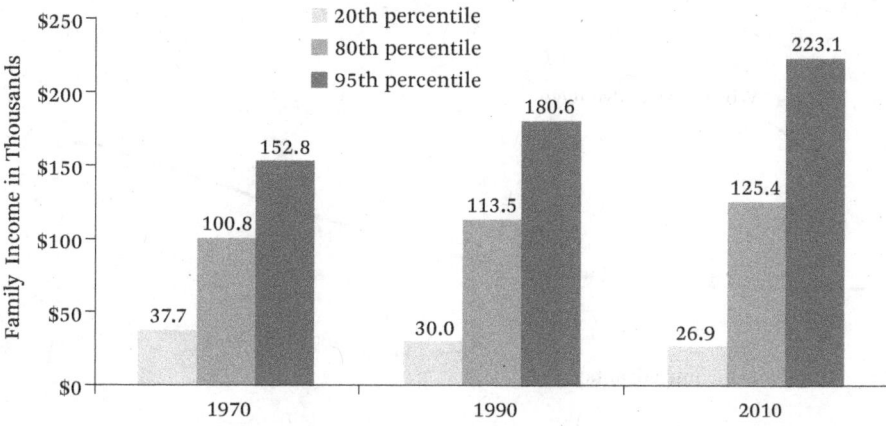

Source: Duncan and Murnane 2011. © Russell Sage Foundation.
Note: Chart shows 20th, 80th and 95th percentiles of the distribution of family incomes for all children ages five to seventeen. They are based on data from the U.S. Bureau of the Census and are adjusted for inflation. Amounts are in 2012 dollars.

est 5 percent of families rose even more. The stagnation of the incomes of families at the lower end of the spectrum is also reflected in the nation's child poverty rate, which increased by more than 6 percentage points between 1970 and 2011, but appears to have fallen modestly using a more comprehensive measure of poverty.[2] These growing income gaps translated into increased gaps between the academic achievement and educational attainments of children from high- and low-income families.

In this paper, we explain the mechanisms through which rising family income inequality result in growing inequality of educational outcomes between children growing up in low- and higher-income families. We then interpret the evidence on the consequences of several decades of attempts to improve the nation's schools and describe our view of the public policies needed to improve schooling for students from low-income families.

GROWING GAPS IN ACHIEVEMENT AND ATTAINMENT

Sean Reardon (2011) documents growth in the income-based gap in the reading skills of children over time (figure 2). Among children who were adolescents in the late 1960s, test scores in reading of low-income children lagged behind those of their better-off peers by four-fifths of a standard deviation—about 80 points on an SAT-type test. Forty years later, this gap was 50 percent larger, amounting to nearly 125 SAT-type points. Trends in mathematics skill gaps were similar (Reardon 2011). Growth in these income-based achievement gaps is surprising in light of the fact that racial gaps in test scores have diminished considerably in the fifty years since *Brown v. Board of Education* (Magnuson and Waldfogel 2008).

Growing achievement gaps mask an important fact: achievement levels of low-income children have increased over the past three decades. Most notably, the mathematics scores

---

2. Official poverty data are based on a measure of family economic resources using cash incomes and do not reflect the growing value of near-cash transfers such as food stamps and the Earned Income Tax Credit. Moreover, the thresholds used in the poverty calculations are not adjusted for changes in living standards. Liana Fox and her colleagues' (2014) calculation of poverty trends for children using a more comprehensive measure of poverty shows that it fell by about 3 percentage points between 1970 and 2011.

Figure 2. Race and Income-Based Gaps in Reading Achievement in SAT-Type Units

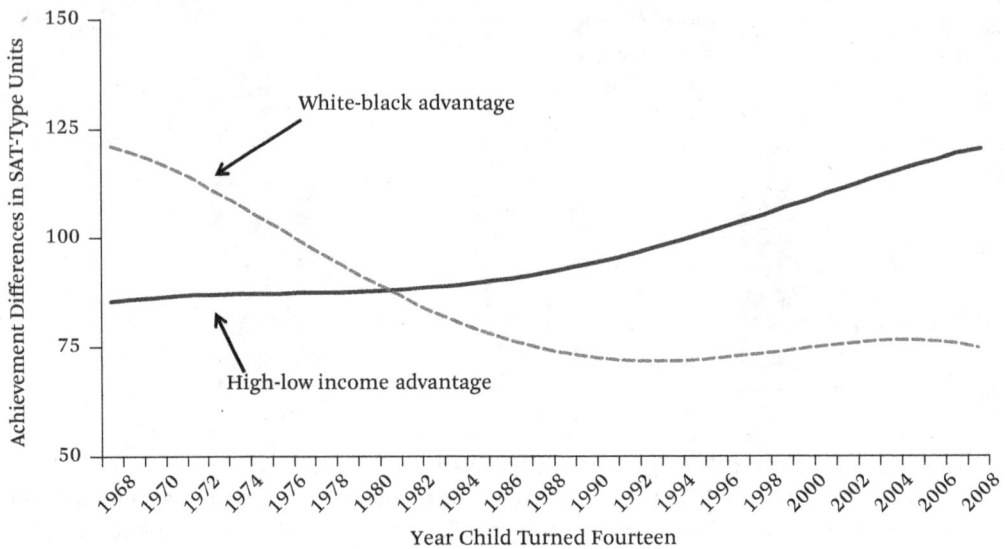

Source: Reardon 2011. © Russell Sage Foundation.

of low-income children increased by a substantial 40 points—0.40 standard deviations—over the thirty years between the late 1970s and late 2000s.[3] Achievement *gaps* increased because the scores of children at the top of the income distribution grew at a much faster rate—70 points, or 0.70 standard deviations.

Given the importance of academic preparation to success in postsecondary education, it should come as no surprise that growth in the income-based gaps in children's reading and mathematics achievement have contributed to a growing gap in the rate of college completion. As with test scores, college graduation rates for children from low-income (defined as the bottom quartile) families rose—from 5 percent for children who were teenagers in the late 1970s to 9 percent for those who were teenagers in the mid-1990s. But this 4 percentage point increase was dwarfed by the 18 percentage point jump for children with family income in the top quartile, from slightly more than one-third to more than one-half (Bailey and Dynarski 2011). Analysts differ in their assessments of the relative importance of college costs and academic preparation in explaining the increasing gulf between the college graduates rates of affluent and low-income children in our country (Heckman and Krueger 2005). However, both are rooted, at least in part, in the growth in family income inequality.

HOW RISING INEQUALITY INFLUENCES CHILDREN'S SKILLS AND ATTAINMENTS

To understand how rising inequality in family incomes contributed to rising inequality in educational outcomes between children from low- and high-income families, we need to understand the roles of families and schools. We consider these two important contexts for children's lives in turn.

Families

We begin by examining the skills and behaviors of children just as they enter kindergarten. Economists and developmental psychologists define school readiness in various ways, but nearly all definitions include elements of both

---

3. The average reading skills of low-income students also increased during this period, albeit at a slower and less stable rate.

cognitive skills and socioemotional behaviors, to use the term favored by developmental psychologists (Duncan and Magnuson 2011). In the cognitive category, we concentrate on concrete academic skills such as literacy (for example, for kindergarteners, decoding skills such as beginning to associate sounds with letters at the beginning and end of words) and basic mathematics (for example, ability to recognize numbers and shapes and to compare relative sizes). Socioemotional behaviors include the ability to control impulses and focus on tasks, and a cluster of related behaviors including antisocial behavior, conduct disorders, and more general aggression.

We used data on a nationally representative sample of children entering kindergarten in September 1998 (ECLS-K) to measure differences in school entry skills and behaviors for children whose parental incomes placed them in the top and bottom quintiles of the income distribution. Kindergarten teachers rated kindergarteners from high-income families more than half a standard deviation ahead of those from low-income families in their abilities to pay attention and engage in school work, and more than a quarter of a standard deviation higher in their abilities to get along with peers and teachers. Much more striking were differences in math and literacy skills. These patterns are present before children start formal schooling, and illustrate the importance of families.

None of these income-based gaps in academic skills and behaviors had declined by the time the children were in fifth grade. Part of the explanation concerns differences in the school experiences of children from low- and higher-income families, a topic we take up below. Another part concerns differences between the experiences of these groups of children outside of school, especially during the summer months, when school is not in session (Raudenbush and Eschmann 2015).

Identifying the extent to which gaps in the

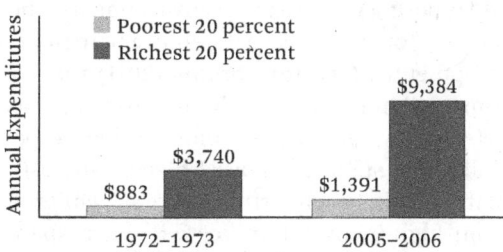

Figure 3. Family Enrichment Expenditures on Children

Source: Duncan and Murnane 2011. © Russell Sage Foundation.
Note: Amounts are in 2012 dollars.

skills and behaviors of children from low- and high-income families are caused by income itself as opposed to differences in innate capabilities or other family characteristics (such as two-parent family structure or parental education levels) is a challenge. An obvious advantage of a higher family income is that it provides more resources to buy books, computers, high-quality child care, summer camps, private schooling, and other enrichments. Figure 3 shows how spending, net of inflation, on child-enrichment goods and services increased to a far greater extent for families in the top quintile than for those in the bottom income quintile.[4] In the 1972–1973 survey, high-income families spent about $2,850 more per year per child on child enrichment than low-income families did. By the 2005–2006 school year, this gap had nearly tripled, to $8,000. Neeraj Kaushal, Katherine Magnuson, and Jane Waldfogel (2011) show that spending differences are largest for enrichment activities such as music lessons, travel, and summer camps. Differential access to such activities may explain the gaps in background knowledge and vocabulary between children from high-income families and those from low-income families that are so predictive of reading skills in the middle and high school years (Snow 2002).

---

4. All dollar amounts are expressed in 2012 price levels. We are very grateful to Sabino Kornich of Emery University for providing these data, which are based on four large consumer expenditure surveys conducted between the early 1970s and the mid-2000s. The figures reflect only out-of-pocket expenditures. They do not reflect transfer payments such as food stamps.

Parents also spend different amounts and quality of time interacting with their children and exposing them to novel environments, and these factors can make a difference in their development. Meredith Phillips (2011) reports some striking differences in time-use patterns between low- and high-income families, especially time spent in "novel" places. She estimates that between birth and age six, children from high-income families will have spent 1,300 more hours in novel contexts (that is, other than at home, school, or the care of another parent or a day-care provider) than children from low-income families. These experiences, financed by the higher incomes of more affluent families, contribute to the background knowledge that is so critical for comprehending science and social studies texts in the middle-school grades.

The money and time expended on behalf of children also differ markedly between single- and two-parent families. Megan Sweeney (2011) shows that increases in both marital disruption and births to unmarried women have fueled a large rise in the proportion of children living with only one biological parent. These trends are particularly pronounced among African American children. Numerous studies have established that children who grow up with two biological parents complete more schooling than children who do not. Income differences are a leading explanation for these effects, although characteristics of couples who divorce or separate also matter.

It is difficult to untangle the precise effects of all these family-related factors—income and expenditures, family structure, time and language use—on the disparities in children's school readiness and later academic success that have emerged over the past several decades. But evidence establishing causal links between family income and children's school achievement suggests that the sharp increase in income gaps between high- and low-income families since the 1970s and the concomitant increases in the gaps in children's school success by income are hardly coincidental (Maynard 1977; Maynard and Murnane 1979; Duncan, Ziol-Guest, and Kalil 2010; Dahl and Lochner 2012).[5] Some children have always enjoyed greater benefits and advantages than others, but the income gap has widened dramatically over the past four decades. The implication of these studies is that, partly in consequence, the gap in children's school success has widened as well.

Schools

Researchers have long known that children attending schools with mostly low-income classmates have lower academic achievement and graduation rates than those attending schools with more affluent student populations. Less well understood until recently is the extent to which increasing family income inequality contributed to the segregation of low-income children in particular schools (which we call high-poverty schools) and the mechanisms through which school segregation by income affects children's developmental trajectories and long-term outcomes.

One pathway through which the increase in income inequality contributed to increases in inequality in educational outcomes is increases in residential segregation by income and the school segregation by income it engendered. As high-income families became wealthier, they tended to move to neighborhoods in which high housing prices excluded all but the affluent. This left other neighborhoods populated by primarily low-income families. Sean Reardon and Kendra Bischoff (2011) and Bischoff and Reardon (2014) document that residential segregation by income increased dramatically between 1980 and 2009. Because most American children attend school close to home, it is not surprising that school segregation by income also increased during this pe-

---

5. The causal evidence comes from studies that have examined the consequences for children's achievement of changes in family incomes that stemmed from intentional experiments or natural experiments. For example, Rebecca Maynard and Richard Murnane (1979) examine the consequences for children of families being assigned to treatment or control groups in the federally funded Gary, Indiana Negative Income Tax Experiment. Gordon Dahl and Lance Lochner (2012) study the effects on children's achievement of large increases in family income stemming from changes in the Earned Income Tax Credit.

riod (Altonji and Mansfield 2011; Owens 2015; Owens, Reardon, and Jencks 2014). Duncan and Murnane (2011, 2014) explain three mechanisms through which the increased concentration of children from low-income families in high-poverty schools reduced their effectiveness.

From 1972 to 1988, schools became more economically segregated, and teenagers from affluent families were less and less likely to have classmates from low-income families. The result is that a child from a poor family is two to four times as likely as a child from an affluent family to have classmates in both elementary and high school with low skills and with behavior problems (Duncan and Murnane 2011). This sorting matters, because the weak cognitive skills and greater behavioral problems among low-income children have a negative effect on the learning of their classmates. Especially important is the concentration in high-poverty schools of children who exhibit severe behavioral problems as a result of witnessing or experiencing abuse at home, in their neighborhood, or in the violence-prone country from which their family emigrated. Scott Carrell and Mark Hoekstra (2010) show that the presence of such children in a classroom dramatically reduces the academic achievement of their classmates.

Student mobility is another mechanism through which the increasing concentration of low-income children in high-poverty schools reduces their achievement. Urban families living in poverty move frequently and, as a result of school sorting by socioeconomic status, children from poor families are especially likely to attend schools with relatively high rates of new students arriving during the school year. Stephen Raudenbush, Marshall Jean, and Emily Art (2011) document that children attending elementary schools with considerable student mobility make less progress in mathematics than children attending schools with low student mobility do. Moreover, the negative effects apply to students who themselves are residentially stable as well as to those who are not, and likely stem at least in part from the disruption of instruction caused by the entry of new students into a class.

Teacher quality is another factor contributing to the weak academic performance of students in high-poverty schools. A substantial body of research has shown that schools serving high concentrations of poor, nonwhite, and low-achieving students find it difficult to attract and retain skilled teachers. Susan Johnson, Matthew Kraft, and John Papay (2012) show that this does not stem from teachers' reluctance to teach students from low-income families and students of color. Instead, high staff turnover in high-poverty schools stems from a lack of the strong leadership, culture of collaboration and shared responsibility, and resources necessary for success in educating a high-needs student population.

In summary, the decades-long increase in family income inequality has contributed to increasing gaps in educational achievement and attainment between children growing up in low- and high-income families. Some of the mechanisms concern family life directly. Others concern growing isolation of low-income children in high-poverty schools.

IMPROVING THE EDUCATION OF LOW-INCOME CHILDREN

For most of its history, the United States has relied on its public schools to solve difficult social problems. In the nineteenth century, the country was a leader in providing universal primary schooling. During the first three-quarters of the twentieth century, schools successfully taught generations of students the basic reading and mathematical skills they needed to fill the large number of assembly-line and back-office clerical jobs that the economy was producing (Goldin and Katz 2008). Can the nation's schools meet the current challenge of providing all students with the skills they will need to thrive in the rapidly changing economy and society of the twenty-first century?

The Difficult Challenge

It will be extraordinarily difficult to reverse the striking growth in inequality in educational outcomes in the United States for three separate but interrelated reasons. First, high-income parents, most of whom have college degrees, can invest in their children's education by choosing where to live and which schools their children will attend, and by using

Figure 4. Questions Reflecting 6th Grade Math Standards

Early 1980s	Common Core State Standards 2015
Carol can ride her bike ten miles per hour	Mr. Ruiz is starting a marching band for his school. He first does research and finds the following data about other local marching bands.

Early 1980s:

Carol can ride her bike ten miles per hour

If Carol rides her bike to the store, how long will it take?

To solve this problem, you would need to know

A. How far it is to the store.

B. What kind of bike Carol has.

C. What time Carol will leave.

D. How much Carol has to spend.

Common Core State Standards 2015:

Mr. Ruiz is starting a marching band for his school. He first does research and finds the following data about other local marching bands.

	Band 1	Band 2	Band 3
Number of brass instrument players	123	42	150
Number of percussion instrument players	41	14	50

Mr. Ruiz realizes that there are ☐ brass instrument player(s) per percussion player.

Mr. Ruiz has 210 students who are interested in joining the marching band. He decides to have 80 percent of the band be made of percussion and brass instruments. Use the unit rate you found in Part A to determine how many students should play brass instruments. Show or explain all your steps.

PARCC sample grade 6 math item.

Source: Kidder 1989, 199; PARCC 2014.

their financial resources and knowledge to help their children acquire skills and knowledge beyond what is taught in school. In contrast, low-income parents, most of whom have no postsecondary education, lack the resources to provide for their children's education in the same ways.

A second factor challenging American education is the increase in the skills students are expected to master. The increase stems from the realization that computer-based technological changes and globalization have eliminated many repetitive jobs that paid good wages in the past and increased the demand for analytical problem-solving skills and communication skills (Levy and Murnane 2004). In response to these changes in the economy, almost all states introduced standards-based educational reforms aimed at assuring that all students master higher-order skills that only a modest minority of students learned in the past. Figure 4 illustrates the increase in standards by comparing a question from a mathematics test administered to Massachusetts sixth graders in the early 1980s (left column) and a sample question from a Common Core aligned mathematics examination that all Massachusetts eighth graders will take in 2016 (right column). Notice the differences between the two questions in reading level, in mathematical complexity, and in the type of answer required (multiple choice versus open-ended response with explanation required). Standards-based educational reforms make sense as a response to a changing economy. However, they increase the burden on high-poverty schools serving students who lack the vocabulary and background knowledge that are especially important in mastering complex skills.

A third factor hindering efforts of American educators to level the playing field is decentralization of governance. The U.S. Constitution delegates the governance of public education to the states, which in turn delegate decisions about curricula and teacher salaries to more than thirteen thousand local school districts. A consequence of this decentralization is that changes in national priorities for education pass through many levels of government, each of which provides its own interpretation of the change. The net result is that policy changes often have only modest effects on classroom instruction and the educational experiences of children (Cohen and Spillane 1992).

As we explain in the second part of our book *Restoring Opportunity*, the difficulty of improving classroom instruction and enriching the educational experiences of children, especially those attending high-poverty schools, is documented in research on the consequences of the three major policy initiatives designed to improve the education of disadvantage children over the last fifty years: more money, more accountability, new governance structures. We briefly summarize themes from this research.

More Money
As a result of successful suits filed in state courts on behalf of families in low-spending districts, many states substantially increased funding of public education during the 1970s and 1980s. The federal government has also contributed to the funding of high-poverty schools with the passage of the Elementary and Secondary Education Act (ESEA) of 1965. In fiscal year 2013, Title 1 of ESEA provided more than $14 billion dollars for compensatory education. Analysts disagree on some of the consequences of increased school funding, but few if any believe that it has been effective in closing income-based gaps in children's achievement.

One reason is that a substantial part of state and federal education funding replaced locally raised tax revenues for schooling (Gordon 2004). A second is that relatively few school leaders have successfully used extra funds to improve teaching, a process that requires opening up classrooms to frequent observation by supervisors and peers, and enlisting all teachers in collaborative efforts to make instruction more coherent and consistent. Instead, most have used Title I funds to purchase goods and services that have little impact on the work teachers do with students, and consequently, have little impact on student achievement.

Almost all research on the impact of additional school funding on student achievement antedates standards-based educational reforms. As we discuss in more detail, evidence suggests that, at least in some settings, money is a critical ingredient for producing sustained improvements in student achievement in environments in which school-based educators are under considerable pressure to increase the skills of all students.

Test-Based Accountability
Frustrated that simply increasing funding had yielded no dramatic improvement in public education, state policymakers turned to standards-based educational reforms in the late 1980s and 1990s. The basic idea was to specify the skills students should master at each grade level and develop assessments to measure the extent to which children mastered them. Over time, standards-based reforms morphed into test-based accountability, with the emphasis on holding schools accountable for children's mastery of the skills laid out in state standards. Passage of the No Child Left Behind Act in 2001 made this federal policy.

Educators' responses to test-based accountability pressures have not consistently improved educational quality (Dee and Jacob 2011). NCLB created incentives for states to choose relatively undemanding tests and set low proficiency thresholds. Moreover, some schools, particularly those with the least capacity to educate children well, responded to accountability pressures by narrowing the curriculum and focusing undue attention on students with scores just below proficiency, neglecting children with lower scores (Neal and Schanzenbach 2010). The basic problem is that many school faculties lack the knowledge to increase substantially the skills of their students.[6] Accountability without supports to succeed in the requisite work does not serve children well.

---

6. Inadequacies in teachers' skills have several causes. First, the United States has never developed a high-quality system of screening applicants for the teaching profession, preparing potential teachers well, and rewarding excellence. Second, today's teachers are expected to teach all students to master skills that only a modest percentage of the nation's children mastered in the past. Third, relatively few schools are organized in a way that promotes the ongoing improvement of teachers' skills.

New Governance Structures

Some analysts have argued that the reason why more money and test-based accountability have not produced markedly better education for low-income children is that a great many school districts, especially those in big cities, are dysfunctional (Chubb and Moe 1990). An implication is that changes in governance structures may be needed. This provides one of the arguments for charter schools, which are publicly funded schools typically governed by a group or organization under a legislative contract (or charter) with the state or jurisdiction. The charter exempts the school from certain state or local rules and regulations. In return for autonomy, the charter school must meet the accountability standards stated in its charter. Currently almost six thousand charter schools operate in the country, serving almost 5 percent of the nation's public school students. Some of these schools have produced dramatic improvement in their students' skills (see, for example, Abdulkadiroğlu et al. 2011; Dobbie and Fryer 2011). However, the best available evidence is that most charter schools are not more effective than conventional public schools at improving the skills of low-income children (CREDO 2013).

In summary, the three dominant reform strategies that the United States has used to improve the education of disadvantaged children in recent decades have had at best modest success. None has succeeded in closing the growing gaps in educational achievement and attainment between children from low- and high-income families. The attraction of these strategies is that they are actions that policymakers at the state and federal level can carry out. The limitation is that, in the American context, they have not resulted in consistent improvement in the instruction in high-poverty schools.

We do not intend to imply that funding, accountability, and governance structures are irrelevant to increasing the quality of education provided to American children from low-income families. Indeed, all are essential for making progress toward this goal. However, in the past, the complementary nature of these strategies has received too little attention in policy design, as has the need to remain focused on improving the quality, coherence, and consistency of instruction.

Building Blocks for an American Solution

It is easy to dwell on the characteristics of American education that make constructive change difficult. However, there are also strengths to build on. Of particular importance are educational interventions conducted at considerable scale in which rigorous evaluations show impacts on the skills of a substantial number of low-income children. In *Restoring Opportunity*, we feature three such programs—the Boston pre-K program, the campuses of the University of Chicago charter school, and New York City's small high schools of choice. These innovative, quite durable programs provide existence proofs that it is possible to improve the education of substantial numbers of low-income children.

All three of the interventions we highlight have been evaluated using cutting-edge methods. Christina Weiland and Hirokazu Yoshikawa (2013) use a regression-discontinuity strategy to compare the skills of children who, as a result of their birth dates, were just eligible or not eligible to participate in the Boston pre-K program. They find that the mathematics, literacy, and language skills of children who participated in the pre-K program were considerably more advanced than those of similarly-aged children who spent the year in other child-care settings. The size of the pre-K impacts was enough to close more than half of the gap at kindergarten entry between the academic skills of children from low-income families and those from relatively affluent ones.

A research team led by the sociologist Stephen Raudenbush conducted an evaluation of the impact of enrollment in a University of Chicago charter school campus on children's academic skills. The team found significantly higher average reading and mathematics scores for children who had enrolled in a University of Chicago charter school campus after winning an admissions lottery than for children who had lost the same lottery and subsequently enrolled in another public school. In both reading and mathematics achievement, the difference was thirty-six points on an SAT-type scoring scale, or about 40 percent of the overall gap between African-American and white children in the Chicago (Hassrick, Raudenbush, and Rosen, forthcoming).

MDRC, a research organization based in New York City, conducted an evaluation of the impact on students' educational attainments of enrollment in one of 123 New York City small high schools of choice that opened between 2002 and 2006. These schools were located in low-income neighborhoods of the city and served primarily educationally and economically disadvantaged students of color. The evaluation compared the educational outcomes of students who won and lost lotteries for entry to particular small high schools of choice. Of particular importance, the research team followed the students long enough to examine college enrollment patterns. It found that enrollment in a small high school of choice increased the probability of high school graduation by 9.5 percentage points (Bloom and Unterman 2012). It also found that enrollment in a small high school of choice boosted college enrollment by 8.4 percentage points (Unterman 2014). These gains represent about one-quarter of the gaps in high school graduation and college enrollment rates between children from low- and higher-income families. Operating independently of MDRC, a group of researchers from Duke and MIT conducted an evaluation of the NYC small schools of choice and reported strikingly similar impacts on high school graduation and college enrollment rates (Abdulkadiroğlu, Hu, and Pathak 2013).

These programs provide truly exceptional quality of education to the low-income children they serve. Importantly, they also share key characteristics that can help guide thinking about the broader changes needed to improve the education of a much greater number of low-income children. The characteristics include making use of *advances in knowledge* about the components of good pre-K, elementary school, and high school education; strong, sustained *school supports*; *sensible accountability*; and embrace of the quite demanding academic standards that are embodied in the Common Core State Standards. Together, these constitute the building blocks needed to bring about genuine improvement in the life chances of low-income children. We consider these in turn.

Advances in Knowledge

Increased understanding of the nature of children's and adolescents' cognitive and socioemotional development, of effective ways to make use of student assessment results, and of the design of effective professional development have expanded the knowledge available to educators about how to serve children well. For example, the designers of the Boston pre-K program made use of recent research on key elements of children's language, mathematics, and socioemotional skills in selecting curricula that allowed children to develop these skills through hands-on exploration and group interactions. Indeed, Boston was able to take advantage of lessons learned from the rigorous evaluations of a growing number of preschool curricula that have been supported by funding from several federal government agencies and private foundations.

The principals of the University of Chicago Charter School campuses were aware of research showing that a lack of vocabulary and background knowledge prevents many low-income children from comprehending texts in core subject areas such as science and social studies. This led them to adopt curricula and pedagogical strategies aimed at building children's knowledge and vocabulary from the start of kindergarten. They also took advantage of recent research on effective strategies for using student assessment results to track the progress of individual children and to guide instructional design. They also made use of research showing that effective professional development is a process, not an event; that it focuses on methods for teaching particular skills; that observing effective instruction should be part of the learning process; and that it is important for novices to observe effective instruction and receive detailed feedback on the strengths and weaknesses of their own teaching.

In preparing ninth graders to do high school work, the faculties of many of the New York small high schools took advantage of knowledge that the skills needed for science literacy are different from those needed for literacy in social studies. As a result, developing literacy skills was a critical element of the work of all faculty members, not just English teachers. The faculties of the small high schools we highlight also knew about the research on *summer melt*, the phenomenon that many low-income students graduate from high school intending to enroll in college the next fall, but do not follow through because of the complexity of the financial aid application process and fear of the unknown (Castleman and Page 2014). As a result, the schools developed strategies to support recent graduates during the period of transition to college.

Which of the elements of the interventions we highlight are most critical to their success? Unfortunately, we cannot answer this question because the design of the intervention among participating schools incorporated no planned variation. However, our intuition, as informed by the work of Roland Fryer, is that interaction effects are strong. For example, careful analysis of student assessment results would not result in improved student achievement without a long-enough school day to provide adequate time for remediation. A well-developed code for student behavior would not have produced the positive culture all the schools enjoyed without the time teachers spent in collaboratively working out a common way to implement the code. This interpretation is consistent with the positive results Fryer obtained when he convinced a set of conventional public schools in Houston, Texas, to adopt a set of practices that effective charter schools used. These practices included increased instructional time, more effective teachers and administrators, high-dosage tutoring, data-driven instruction, and a culture of high expectations (Fryer 2014). It seems highly unlikely that it would be possible to retain a culture of high expectations without the time and resources to build students' skills.

Supports and Support Organizations
Preparing large numbers of low-income children to meet demanding academic standards is extremely difficult work. Most schools serving low-income students lack the human resources and the knowledge to do it successfully without strong, sustained supports. Commonly needed supports include technical expertise and resources for developing curricula, planning and implementing effective professional development, dealing with emotionally troubled children, and learning to use student assessment results to guide instructional improvement. But even these supports are not enough.

The experiences of high-poverty schools that have made progress in educating low-income children—like many of those profiled in *Restoring Opportunity*—show that it takes more than simply providing good instruction for six hours per day (Dobbie and Fryer 2011). Typically, the school day starts early in these schools, usually with breakfast for the children. It continues until late in the afternoon, providing time for remediation of lagging skills and engagement in enrichment activities. Many of these schools offer instruction on Saturdays and well into the summer months. Unlike typical afterschool and summer programs that do not improve student outcomes because they are disconnected from the core instructional program, the extended-day and extended-year programs in effective high-poverty schools are well-integrated parts of a coherent strategy to continually build children's skills. Another benefit of such a comprehensive approach to schooling is that the school becomes the center of children's daily experiences, which reduces their exposure to the lures and dangers of the neighborhood. The argument that schools can, on a sustained basis, significantly improve life chances for large numbers of low-income children requires this broad definition of schooling. Implementing this broad and deep vision of schooling requires significant expertise and a variety of resources that most high-poverty schools lack.

The schools participating in the effective interventions we highlight had consistent access to strong school supports. In one case, they came from a district central office Department of Early Childhood Education; in a second, from a charter management organization; in a third, from nonprofit organizations that New York City schools contracted with to provide needed services.

Providing high-quality education on a consistent, long-term basis to low-income children requires institutions that provide consistently strong supports of the same high quality as those afforded to the schools participating in the effective programs we highlighted. The United States has not developed a network of institutions that do this effectively. A promising recent trend, however, is the growing number of organizations that offer supports to public schools. Some, such as the New York Leadership Academy and New Leaders for New Schools, prepare principals to create schools that are effective learning communities for both teachers and students. Others, such as the Boston Teachers Residency Program, recruit academically talented college graduates and support their work in high-poverty schools. Still others—such as New Visions for Public Schools, the Urban Assembly, and many charter management organizations—recruit leadership teams to start new schools and provide ongoing support for those teams. And then there are the comprehensive school reform design organizations such as Success for All and America's Choice that offer detailed guidance and tools to large numbers of high-poverty schools. The challenge is to devise organizational structures that provide high-poverty schools with the resources, knowledge, and freedom to choose the collection of supports they need, with the goal of increasing the coherence and quality of students' daily experiences.

Accountability

Over the last twenty years, it has come to be almost universally accepted that schools should be judged by their effectiveness in educating all students—an enormously important change in thinking. A well-designed accountability system promotes a willingness to use resources in new ways and encourages school faculties to work together to develop the skills of every student.

Our observations, research reviews, and interviews with leaders at the North Kenwood/Oakland (NKO) campus in Chicago and the Urban Assembly School for Law and Justice (SLJ) in Brooklyn revealed a strikingly consistent explanation for their success: strong supports and internal accountability pervade teachers' work lives (Duncan and Murnane 2014).[7]

Carrie Walsh, director of NKO, uses every opportunity to develop teachers' skills, including teacher evaluations. She videotapes and transcribes teachers' lessons, and points out particular areas where improvement is needed. "It could be something as simple as . . . you're just calling on boys all the time and girls actually are hesitant about raising their hand in your class."

Part of SLJ Principal Suzette Dyer's effort to be accountable to the teachers in her school is that she and her leadership team "sit together weekly and create the protocols that we want grade teams and departments to use when they're talking about student work, when they're talking about lesson plans, when they're thinking about end-of-the-year outcomes."

To help reduce the isolation that many teachers experience, both schools work at creating a culture in which accepting and offering criticism is a normal and positive part of a teacher's job. Tanika Island, chief academic officer for NKO, acknowledges that no one wants to hear that something they have put a lot of effort into is not quite right. "You have to train teacher leaders and teachers to be open-minded, to be willing to take feedback, and that takes time," she said. "You have to practice doing that together. And you have to model [that] for teachers."

As the mounting evidence on the weak effects of No Child Left Behind illustrates, it is extraordinarily difficult to design accountability systems that take into account the intense challenges of educating high concentrations of low-income children (Dee and Jacob 2011). Without downplaying the immense challenge of getting accountability right, it is important to remember the value of judging schools by their effectiveness in educating the students they serve rather than by their adherence to rules regarding the uses of resources. A litmus test of the promise of particular accountability systems is the extent to which they provide incentives for skilled teachers to work together in high-poverty schools.

Sensible accountability and sustained

---

7. Transcripts and videos describing their work are available at http://restoringopportunity.com/.

school supports are critical complements for improving schools, especially those serving high concentrations of low-income children. Accountability without supports does not do the job because most educators are already using the skills and energies they have to educate children. They need the supports that will allow them to be more successful. Supports without accountability do not work because most adults do not change their behaviors readily. Sensible accountability provides the push to embrace the opportunities provided by strong school supports and to redesign schools to make instruction more consistent and coherent and of higher quality.

Common Core State Standards
The Common Core Standards outline the skills in English language arts and mathematics that American students are expected to master at each grade level from kindergarten through twelfth grade. As of this writing, forty-five of the country's fifty states have adopted these standards, which set goals that are considerably higher than the accomplishments of most American students, especially those from low-income families.

Creating the Common Core Standards in English language arts and mathematics is an important step in preparing American students to thrive in a rapidly changing economy and society. Carefully designed to reflect the latest research, the standards can offer teachers and school leaders a fundamental school support: clarity about the conceptual and procedural skills children should master in each grade. And the assessments that two consortia of states are developing to measure students' mastery of the Common Core Standards can provide another critical school support: detailed information for teachers about children's mastery of essential skills and knowledge. These are remarkable accomplishments, reflecting a level of rigor and a degree of cooperation among states that few observers of American education would have thought possible thirty years ago.

Of course, common standards and high-quality assessments alone do not produce better teaching, nor do they enhance student learning. Indeed, the Common Core State Standards are only an early step down a long path leading to better education for all American children. Yet clarity about the specific skills students should master at each grade level makes it possible to improve teacher training programs and on-the-job professional development. The standards can also facilitate the development of curricula and assessments that are closely aligned with their content. Better teacher preparation and better curricula are essential elements for improving teaching and learning.

Support for the Common Core Standards is widespread but fragile. One reason for the fragility is that the introduction of student assessments aligned with the Common Core are starting to show that a great many students, especially those from low-income families, have not met the new standards.[8] We caution against letting high-stakes accountability get ahead of the difficult work of providing educators in high-poverty schools with the knowledge and extensive school supports they will need to help their students master the Common Core Standards. Only if consistent, strong supports are in place can accountability improve the education of low-income children. In other words, strong supports and well-designed accountability are essential comple-

---

8. Some of the resistance to the Common Core stems from the aggressive manner in which the Department of Education made adoption of the national standards a de facto condition for receiving some federal education funds states desperately needed in the midst of the Great Recession. The accompanying requirement that states implement teacher evaluation systems that incorporate students' test scores also weakened support for the Common Core among teachers. As the politics leading up to the 2016 U.S. elections intensify, some states are retreating from the Common Core Standards and assessments. However, several state legislatures that recently voted to withdraw their commitment to the Common Core, including Alaska, Florida, and Indiana, then adopted educational standards that are virtually identical to the Common Core Standards. Educators and politicians in these states seem to think that the content of the standards makes sense, even if association with the name Common Core does not.

ments, not substitutes. Moreover, accountability that improves education in high-poverty schools must encourage and not undercut the shared work that allowed the schools we highlight to serve low-income students much more effectively than most high-poverty schools do.

Meeting the Challenge
Relying on the heroic efforts of charismatic leaders who create schools that "beat the odds" will not solve the nation's most pressing education problem. These leaders produce results by devoting vast amounts of time to recruiting teachers who share their vision and are willing to work long hours creating curricula, offering extra instruction, and providing emotional support to students from troubled homes. The efforts of such educators are laudable and are the subjects of many heartwarming media stories. However, all too often, the successes of such schools are short lived, because leaders move on and teachers burn out (Harris 2007). Meeting the educational needs of low-income students must be done by creating the conditions for systems of effective schools rather than by relying on exceptions. Reasons why the central offices of public school districts, particularly those in big cities, do not provide schools with the combination of sustained supports and sensible accountability necessary for success are numerous. They include conflicting priorities of schoolboard members and other civic leaders, brief tenures of district superintendents, and bureaucracies with many noncoordinating silos. Changing this situation is a necessary condition for improving urban education.

Is it possible to improve the life chances of children from low-income families in a country in which inequality in family incomes is so large? Compelling evidence that it is comes from a comparison of educational outcomes for children from low- and higher-socioeconomic status families in four countries that have a common language and heritage, the United Kingdom, Australia, Canada, and the United States. Inequality increased in all these countries, but more so in the United States than elsewhere, and the levels of inequality remain lower in Canada and Australia than in the United States and the UK (OECD 2011). Bruce Bradbury and his colleagues (2015) show that the gap in educational outcomes between children from low- and higher-socioeconomic status families is much smaller in the UK, Australia, and Canada than it is in the United States, and that this stems to a large extent from differences in public policies toward families and schools.

The Boston Pre-K program, the University of Chicago charter school campuses, and the New York City small schools of choice provide evidence from the United States that it is possible to close income-based gaps in educational outcomes. All of these interventions created the conditions for networks of schools to educate low-income children and adolescents well. They share characteristics that could inform the design of other successful networks. However, at this time most high-poverty schools do not operate in environments that provide the combination of sustained supports and sensible accountability necessary for success.

Evidence from Montgomery County, Maryland; Long Beach, California; and Aldine, Texas, also shows that it is possible at considerable scale to improve educational outcomes for children from low-income families (see Childress, Doyle, and Thomas 2009; Childress, Grossman, and King 2011; Austin et al. 2006). So does evidence from Achievement First, an effective network of charter schools, which provides an alternative model for supporting schools and holding them accountable (see Education Resource Strategies 2013). It is not clear at this point which model or combination of models holds the most promise. However, it is clear that developing systems of supports and accountability is a necessary condition for improving the education of low-income students.

We want to be clear about the implications of our research for school funding levels. Evidence is ample that simply spending more money will not produce better education. Indeed, in many schools and districts, money can be used much more effectively. However, in many schools serving large numbers of disadvantaged children, implementing the effective strategies we describe in *Restoring Opportunity* will cost more money. These expenditures, appropriately targeted and carefully assessed, represent an essential investment in the nation's future.

Evidence that adequate funding is a key element of systemic improvement comes from Massachusetts, where a quite stringent accountability system was accompanied by more than $2 billion in increased state funding for education. One result has been dramatic improvement in the mathematics and reading scores of Massachusetts students on the National Assessment of Educational Progress and on international test score comparisons. Another is a 20 percent decline in the gap in four-year graduation rates between Massachusetts students from low- and higher-income families (Papay, Murnane, and Willett 2015).[9]

Can schools make a meaningful contribution to alleviating the growing inequality in educational outcomes between children from low- and high-income families? The answer will have a profound impact on the nation's future. The answer depends on the nation's commitment to supporting a broad and comprehensive definition of schooling, its recognition of the immense challenges high-poverty schools face, and its willingness to find ways to provide the consistently strong school supports and well-designed accountability necessary for lasting success.

REFERENCES

Abdulkadiroğlu, Atila, Joshua D. Angrist, Susan Dynarski, Thomas J. Kane, and Parag A. Pathak. 2011. "Accountability and Flexibility in Public Schools: Evidence from Boston's Charters and Pilots." *Quarterly Journal of Economics* 126(2) (May): 699–748.

Abdulkadiroğlu, Atila, Weiwei Hu, and Parag A. Pathak. 2013. "Small High Schools and Student Achievement: Lottery-Based Evidence from New York City." *NBER* working paper no. 19576. Cambridge, Mass.: National Bureau of Economic Research.

Altonji, Joseph G., and Richard Mansfield. 2011. "The Role of Family, School and Community Characteristics in Inequality in Education and Labor Market Outcomes." In *Whither Opportunity: Growing Inequality, Schools, and Children's Life Chances*, edited by Greg J. Duncan and Richard J. Murnane. New York: Russell Sage Foundation; Chicago: Spencer Foundation.

Austin, James E., Allen E. Grossman, Robert B. Schwartz, and Jennifer M. Suesse. 2006. "Long Beach Unified School District (A): Change That Leads to Improvement (1992–2002)." Cambridge Mass.: Public Education Leadership Project at Harvard University. Accessed December 27, 2015. http://pelp.fas.harvard.edu/files/hbs-test/files/pel006p2.pdf?m=1441050956.

Bailey, Martha J., and Susan M. Dynarski. 2011. "Inequality in Postsecondary Education." In *Whither Opportunity: Growing Inequality, Schools, and Children's Life Chances*, edited by Greg J. Duncan and Richard J. Murnane. New York: Russell Sage Foundation; Chicago: Spencer Foundation.

Bischoff, Kendra, and Sean F. Reardon. 2014. "Residential Segregation by Income, 1970–2009." In *Diversity and Disparities: America Enters a New Century*, edited by John R. Logan. New York: Russell Sage Foundation.

Bloom, Howard S., and Rebecca Unterman. 2012. "Sustained Positive Effects on Graduation Rates Produced by New York City's Small Public High Schools of Choice." New York: MDRC.

Bradbury, Bruce, Miles Corak, Jane Waldfogel, and Elizabeth Washbrook. 2015. *Too Many Children Left Behind*. New York: Russell Sage Foundation.

Carrell, Scott E., and Mark L. Hoekstra. 2010. "Externalities in the Classroom: How Children Exposed to Domestic Violence Affect Everyone's Kids." *American Economic Journal: Applied Economics* 2(1): 211–28.

Castleman, Benjamin L., and Lindsay C. Page. 2014. *Summer Melt: Supporting Low-Income Students Through the Transition to College*. Cambridge Mass.: Harvard Education Press.

Center for Research on Educational Outcomes (CREDO). 2013. *National Charter School Study 2013*. Stanford, Calif.: Stanford University.

Childress, Stacey M., Denis P. Doyle, and David A. Thomas. 2009. *Leading for Equity: The Pursuit of Excellence in Montgomery County Public Schools*. Cambridge, Mass.: Harvard Education Press.

Childress, Stacey M., Allen S. Grossman, and Caro-

---

9. In the dataset providing information on trends in academic outcomes for public school students in Massachusetts, the only indicator of family income is whether a child's family income is less than 1.85 times the poverty line, the limit for eligibility for a free- or reduced-price school lunch.

line King. 2011. *Meeting New Challenges at the Aldine Independent School District (A)*. Cambridge, Mass.: Public Education Leadership Project at Harvard University.

Chubb, John E., and Terry M. Moe. 1990. *Politics, Markets & America's Schools*. Washington, D.C.: Brookings Institution.

Cohen, David K., and James P. Spillane. 1992. "Policy and Practice: The Relations Between Governance and Instruction." In *Review of Research in Education*, vol. 18, edited by Gerald Grant. Washington, D.C.: American Educational Research Association.

Dahl, Gordon B., and Lance Lochner. 2012. "The Impact of Family Income on Child Achievement: Evidence from the Earned Income Tax Credit." *American Economic Review* 102(5): 1927–56.

Dee, Thomas S., and Brian Jacob. 2011. "The Impact of No Child Left Behind on Student Achievement." *Journal of Policy Analysis and Management* 30(3): 418–46.

Dobbie, Will, and Roland G. Fryer Jr. 2011. "Are High Quality Schools Enough to Close the Achievement Gap? Evidence from a Social Experiment in Harlem." *American Economic Journal: Applied Economics* 3(3): 158–87.

Duncan, Greg J., and Katherine Magnuson. 2011. "The Nature and Impact of Early Achievement Skills, Attention Skills, and Behavior Problems." In *Whither Opportunity: Growing Inequality, Schools, and Children's Life Chances*, edited by Greg J. Duncan and Richard J. Murnane. New York: Russell Sage Foundation; Chicago: Spencer Foundation.

Duncan, Greg J., and Richard J. Murnane. 2011. "Introduction: The American Dream, Then and Now." In *Whither Opportunity: Growing Inequality, Schools, and Children's Life Chances*, edited by Greg J. Duncan and Richard J. Murnane. New York: Russell Sage Foundation; Chicago: Spencer Foundation.

———. 2014. *Restoring Opportunity: The Crisis of Inequality and the Challenge for American Education*. Cambridge, Mass.: Harvard Education Press and the Russell Sage Foundation.

Duncan, Greg J., Kathleen M. Ziol-Guest, and Ariel Kalil. 2010. "Early-Childhood Poverty and Adult Attainment, Behavior, and Health." *Child Development* 81(1): 306–25.

Education Resource Strategies. 2013. *Promising Practices in Professional Growth & Support: Case Study of Achievement First*. Watertown, Mass.: Education Resource Strategies.

Fox, Liana, Irwin Garfield, Neeraj Kaushal, Jane Waldfogel, and Christopher Wimer. 2014. "Waging War on Poverty: Historical Trends in Poverty Using the Supplemental Poverty Measure." NBER working paper no. 19789. Cambridge, Mass.: National Bureau of Economic Research.

Fryer, Roland G., Jr. 2014. "Injecting Charter School Best Practices into Traditional Public Schools: Evidence from Field Experiments." *Quarterly Journal of Economics* 129(3): 1355–407.

Goldin, Claudia D., and Lawrence F. Katz. 2008. *The Race Between Education and Technology*. Cambridge, Mass.: Belknap Press of Harvard University Press.

Gordon, Nora. 2004. "Do Federal Grants Boost School Spending? Evidence from Title I." *Journal of Public Economics* 88(9–10): 1771–92.

Harris, Douglas N. 2007. "High Flying Schools, Student Disadvantage, and the Logic of NCLB." *American Journal of Education* 113(3): 367–94.

Hassrick, Elizabeth McGhee, Stephen W. Raudenbush, and Lisa Rosen. Forthcoming. *The Ambitious Elementary School: Its Conception, Design and Contribution to Educational Equity*. Chicago: University of Chicago.

Heckman, James J., and Alan B. Krueger. 2005. *Inequality in America: What Role for Human Capital Policies?* Cambridge, Mass.: MIT Press.

Johnson, Susan M., Matthew A. Kraft, and John P. Papay. 2012. "How Context Matters in High-Need Schools: The Effects of Teachers' Working Conditions on Their Professional Satisfaction and Their Students' Achievement." *Teachers College Record* 114(10): 1–39.

Kaushal, Neeraj, Katherine Magnuson, and Jane Waldfogel. 2011. "How Is Family Income Related to Investments in Children's Learning?" In *Whither Opportunity: Growing Inequality, Schools, and Children's Life Chances*, edited by Greg J. Duncan and Richard J. Murnane. New York: Russell Sage Foundation; Chicago: Spencer Foundation.

Kidder, Tracy. 1989. *Among Schoolchildren*. Boston, Mass.: Houghton Mifflin.

Levy, Frank, and Richard J. Murnane. 2004. *The New Division of Labor: How Computers Are Creating the Next Labor Market*. Princeton, N.J.: Princeton University Press.

Magnuson, Katherine A., and Jane Waldfogel. 2008.

Steady Gains and Stalled Progress: Inequality and the Black-White Test Score Gap. New York: Russell Sage Foundation.

Maynard, Rebecca A. 1977. "The Effects of the Rural Income Maintenance Experiment on the School Performance of Children." *American Economic Review* 67(1): 370–75.

Maynard, Rebecca A., and Richard J. Murnane. 1979. "The Effects of a Negative Income Tax on School Performance: Result of an Experiment." *Journal of Human Resources* 14(4): 463–76.

Neal, Derek, and Diane Whitmore Schanzenbach. 2010. "Left Behind by Design: Proficiency Counts and Test-Based Accountability." *Review of Economics and Statistics* 92(2): 263–83.

Organization for Economic Cooperation and Development (OECD). 2011. *Divided We Stand: Why Inequality Keeps Growing*. Paris: OECD Publishing.

Owens, Ann. 2015. "Inequality in Children's Contexts: The Economic Segregation of Households with and Without Children." Unpublished paper. Department of Sociology, University of Southern California.

Owens, Ann, Sean F. Reardon, and Christopher Jencks. 2014. "Trends in School Economic Segregation, 1970 to 2010." Stanford, Calif.: Stanford University, Center for Education Policy Analysis.

Papay, John P., Richard J. Murnane, and John B. Willett. 2015. "Inequality and Educational Attainment: Evidence from Massachusetts." *Educational Evaluation and Policy Analysis* 73(1S): 29–52.

Partnership for Assessment of Readiness for College and Careers (PARCC). 2014. "The PAARC Difference: Middle School." Accessed December 28, 2015. http://www.parcconline.org/images/Assessments/PracticeTests/oldvnew-middle_1.pdf.

Phillips, Meredith. 2011. "Parenting, Time Use, and Disparities in Academic Outcomes." In *Whither Opportunity: Growing Inequality, Schools, and Children's Life Chances*, edited by Greg J. Duncan and Richard J. Murnane. New York: Russell Sage Foundation; Chicago: Spencer Foundation.

Raudenbush, Stephen W., and Robert D. Eschmann. 2015. "Does Schooling Increase or Reduce Social Inequality?" *Annual Review of Sociology* 41(August): 443–70.

Raudenbush, Stephen W., Marshall Jean, and Emily Art. 2011. "Year-by-Year and Cumulative Impacts of Attending a High-Mobility Elementary School on Children's Mathematics Achievement in Chicago, 1995 to 2005." In *Whither Opportunity: Growing Inequality, Schools, and Children's Life Chances*, edited by Greg J. Duncan and Richard J. Murnane. New York: Russell Sage Foundation; Chicago: Spencer Foundation.

Reardon, Sean F. 2011. "The Widening Academic Achievement Gap Between the Rich and the Poor: New Evidence and Possible Explanations." In *Whither Opportunity: Growing Inequality, Schools, and Children's Life Chances*, edited by Greg J. Duncan and Richard J. Murnane. New York: Russell Sage Foundation; Chicago: Spencer Foundation.

Reardon, Sean F., and Kendra Bischoff. 2011. "Income Inequality and Income Segregation." *American Journal of Sociology* 116(4): 1092–153.

Snow, Catherine. 2002. *Reading for Understanding: Toward a Research and Development Program in Reading Comprehension*. Santa Monica, Calif.: RAND Corporation.

Sweeney, Megan M. 2011. "Family-Structure Instability and Adolescent Educational Outcomes: A Focus on Families and Stepfathers." In *Whither Opportunity: Growing Inequality, Schools, and Children's Life Chances*, edited by Greg J. Duncan and Richard J. Murnane. New York: Russell Sage Foundation; Chicago: Spencer Foundation.

Unterman, Rebecca. 2014. "Headed to College: The Effects of New York City's Small High Schools of Choice on Postsecondary Enrollment." Policy Brief. New York: MDRC. Accessed December 28, 2015. http://www.mdrc.org/sites/default/files/Headed_to_College_PB.pdf.

Weiland, Christina, and Hirokazu Yoshikawa. 2013. "Impacts of a Prekindergarten Program on Children's Mathematics, Language, Literacy, Executive Function, and Emotional Skills." *Child Development* 84(6): 2112–30.

Neighborhoods, Cities, and Economic Mobility

PATRICK SHARKEY

Most of the research literature explaining the level of economic mobility in the United States focuses on characteristics of individuals or families. This article expands the focus beyond the individual and the family to consider features of communities and cities. Although evidence is strong that features of neighborhoods and cities have causal effects on individual economic mobility, there is much less evidence on the most relevant mechanisms. The article reviews the available evidence at both levels of analysis before concluding with a discussion of the implications for social policy.

Keywords: neighborhood effects, economic mobility, economic segregation, urban policy

Although the literature on intergenerational economic mobility in the United States has advanced considerably over time, less progress has been made in explaining the mechanisms leading to the persistence of economic status across generations. Empirical research designed to explain why economic advantage and disadvantage tend to be transmitted from parents to children has focused on characteristics of individuals or families. This article expands the focus to consider features of communities and cities.

This focus on the spatial foundations of economic mobility in the United States is based on two basic claims (Sharkey and Faber 2014). The first is that systems of stratification are organized, in part, along spatial lines. This claim is uncontroversial. The spatial organization of American social, economic, and political life is reflected in patterns of discrimination and segregation, zoning decisions, the establishment of boundaries for political districts, school catchment areas, and police precincts, the siting of environmental hazards, and the location decisions of public institutions and private firms (Dreier, Mollenkopf, and Swanstrom 2001). The second claim is that the spatial organization of America's stratification system affects the life chances and the economic trajectories of different segments of the population in ways that maintain, and reinforce, inequality. This claim has been the subject of more vigorous debate, and the empirical evidence that has been generated to support or refute this claim is the focus of this article.

The article is guided by three questions: How do residential contexts affect prospects for mobility? How do cities and metropolitan areas affect economic mobility? What are the implications for social policy?

Patrick Sharkey is associate professor of sociology at New York University.

I thank Katharine Bradbury, Nathaniel Hendren, Robert Putnam, and Robert Triest for insightful feedback and ideas for the article. I would also like to thank Jacob Faber and Bryan Graham, respectively, for their collaborative work on projects related to neighborhoods and economic mobility. Much of this collaborative research has informed the argument in this article. Direct correspondence to: Patrick Sharkey at patrick.sharkey@nyu.edu, New York University, 295 Lafayette St., New York, NY 10012.

HOW DO RESIDENTIAL CONTEXTS AFFECT PROSPECTS FOR MOBILITY?

Only a few studies have analyzed the relationship between childhood neighborhood conditions and adult economic outcomes, primarily because there are few datasets that follow sample members across multiple generations. Most of the observational studies that allow for cross-generational analysis draw on data from the Panel Study of Income Dynamics (PSID) and find an association between measures of neighborhood economic status during childhood and adult economic status after adjusting for observed individual and family characteristics, although the strength of the association varies widely depending on the methods used, the specific neighborhood measures considered in the analysis, the outcome under study, and the subpopulations examined. Studies conducted by Linda Datcher (1982), Mary Corcoran and Terry Adams (1999), Corcoran and her colleagues (1992), Steven Holloway and Stephen Mulherin (2004), and Thomas Vartanian (1999) report conditional associations between neighborhood economic status and adult outcomes related to employment and income.

Taking a different approach, Daniel Aaronson (1998) and Vartanian and Page Buck (2005) exploit variation in childhood neighborhood conditions experienced by siblings within families and find significant effects of neighborhood economic status on adult educational and economic outcomes. However, Robert Plotnick and Saul Hoffman (1999) conduct a similar analysis with a sample of sisters in the PSID to study outcomes related to welfare receipt and fertility, and find null effects of childhood neighborhood conditions when using family fixed-effects specifications.

A much larger literature examines how neighborhoods affect some of the key mechanisms influencing later economic outcomes such as academic success, cognitive skills, and educational attainment. Several of these studies have found a strong association between different compositional characteristics of children's neighborhoods, such as the level of neighborhood poverty, the presence of affluent neighbors, and rates of residential mobility, and individual outcomes like dropping out of high school or scores on assessments of cognitive skills (Leventhal and Brooks-Gunn 2000; Sastry 2012). David Harding's (2003) study of the effect of neighborhood poverty on high school dropout is one example of a carefully designed observational study that analyzed matched pairs of children who look extremely similar in every aspect of their lives but their neighborhood. Harding estimated that living in a high-poverty neighborhood during adolescence doubles the likelihood that a child will drop out of high school relative to living in a low-poverty neighborhood among both blacks and whites. His findings were found to be robust to a conservative sensitivity analysis.

Harding's study also is unique because he measured neighborhood conditions of children over an extended duration of childhood. Several descriptive studies have documented the persistence of neighborhood advantage and disadvantage over long periods and across generations, suggesting the need for a greater focus on the temporal dimensions of exposure to neighborhood poverty (Briggs and Keys 2009; Quillian 2003; Sharkey 2008; Timberlake 2007).

A set of recent studies has used methods that adjust for time-varying confounders to estimate the cumulative consequences of exposure to neighborhood disadvantage on academic and cognitive outcomes. Robert Sampson, Patrick Sharkey, and Stephen Raudenbush (2008) find that exposure to concentrated disadvantage altered the development of cognitive skills of African American children in Chicago, with consequences that persist years after exposure to neighborhood disadvantage. Geoffrey Wodtke, David Harding, and Felix Elwert (2011) find that exposure to concentrated disadvantage over the course of childhood reduces the probability of high school graduation by 20 percentage points for black youth and by 10 percentage points for all other youth. Sharkey and Elwert (2011) use a similar approach but look further back into families' histories, and find that exposure to neighborhood poverty over consecutive generations reduces children's performance on tests of cognitive skills by between 8 and 9 points, more than half of a standard deviation. A formal sensitivity analysis demonstrated that the effect of multigenerational neighborhood poverty is robust to high levels of potential bias arising from unobserved selection processes. The common conclusion reached by these studies is that the effect of neighborhood disadvantage on cognitive and academic outcomes is more severe if disadvantage is persistent, experienced over long periods of a family's history.

Evidence from Housing Mobility Programs

A second strand of evidence comes from studies that exploit quasi-experimental or experimental changes in families' neighborhoods and schools arising from low-income housing assistance programs (Briggs 1997; DeLuca and Dayton 2009). Among the many residential mobility programs that have been studied in the literature, the two most prominent examples are the Gautreaux Assisted Housing Program in Chicago and the Moving to Opportunity program, which was conducted in five U.S. cities.

Gautreaux was the result of a desegregation settlement that required the Chicago Housing Authority to provide housing to eligible families in neighborhoods across the Chicago metropolitan area. Specific units were identified across a range of neighborhoods that included the affluent and predominantly white suburbs surrounding Chicago, and families were offered specific units at least partly on the basis of their position on the waitlist for housing. Early studies based on samples of families that moved in the Gautreaux program found that families moving outside Chicago's city limits experienced substantial changes in adults' economic outcomes and children's educational attainment (Kaufman and Rosenbaum 1992; Rosenbaum and Popkin 1991; Rubinowitz and Rosenbaum 2000). For instance, 54 percent of children in families who moved to the suburbs attended any college, against 21 percent of children in families who remained in the suburbs (Rubinowitz and Rosenbaum 2000).

However, subsequent research has questioned whether the changes in neighborhood conditions induced by the program should be thought of as exogenous. Mark Votruba and Jeffrey Kling (2009) document a correlation between the characteristics of Gautreaux families' origin neighborhoods and their destination neighborhoods, suggesting that families' preferences played at least some role in determining the neighborhoods to which they were assigned. Subsequent research on families in the Gautreaux program adjusts for observed differences between families and finds that caregivers were more likely to remain in the labor force and and earn higher wages when they left the deeply segregated, high-poverty neighborhoods of Chicago and moved to more integrated, less-poor communities across the metropolitan area (Mendenhall, DeLuca, and Duncan 2006).

Motivated in part by the strong findings from Gautreaux, the Moving to Opportunity Program (MTO) was a social experiment conducted in five cities—Baltimore, Boston, Chicago, Los Angeles, and New York—to test whether moving into low-poverty neighborhoods affected the social and economic outcomes of families living in areas of concentrated poverty (Briggs, Popkin, and Goering 2010; Goering and Feins 2003; Sanbonmatsu et al. 2011). In each of the cities, families in designated public housing developments who volunteered for the program were randomized into one of three groups: an experimental group that received housing vouchers that could only be used to rent in low-poverty neighborhoods; a Section 8 group that received standard Section 8 vouchers without requirements on where the voucher could be used; and a control group that received no voucher at all.

The results from MTO are complex and difficult to summarize. The most recent reports have found that ten to fifteen years after the initial random assignment, adults in the experimental group experienced substantial improvements in mental and physical health and overall subjective well-being, but no improvements in economic outcomes related to labor force participation or income (Ludwig et al. 2012). The impact of the program on children appeared to vary by gender. Girls in the experimental group experienced improved mental health and were less likely to participate in some risky behaviors, but boys showed few changes in their lives as a result of the program but increases in some risky behaviors (Clampet-Lundquist et al. 2011; Sanbonmatsu et al. 2011).

This crude summary of results from MTO obscures an even more complex set of findings that has emerged in the five sites at different times following the implementation of the program. A review of studies that report outcomes related to cognitive and academic skills reveals an erratic set of findings that vary across the five cities and across subgroups within the cities. To begin with, analyses that pooled all children across the five cities found no effects on cognitive skills either four to seven years after the program began or ten to fifteen years after (Sanbonmatsu et al. 2006; Sanbonmatsu et al. 2011). However, African American children in the experimental group scored 0.08 standard deviations higher than African American children in the control group on an assessment of broad reading skills conducted four to seven years after random assignment (Sanbonmatsu et al. 2006). Further, among families who remained in low-poverty neighborhoods for a longer time, Margery Turner and her colleagues (2012) find positive effects of moving to low-poverty neighborhoods on both reading and math scores for boys and girls. Raj Chetty, Nathan Hendren, and Larry Katz (2015) find that younger children in the experimental group may have fared much better than children whose families moved at an older age. Children who were younger than thirteen when their families received vouchers were 2.5 percentage points were more likely to attend college than children in the control group and made roughly $1,600 more per year in income in their mid-twenties.

Studies focusing attention on samples of families from specific cities have generated even more divergent findings. In the New York site, Tama Leventhal and Jeanne Brooks-Gunn (2004) find no overall effects of the program after three years following implementation, but positive effects on assessments of cognitive skills for boys. Subsequent research on the New York City sample finds negative effects of moving to low-poverty neighborhoods ten to fifteen years after the program implementation (Sanbonmatsu et al. 2011). Research on the Baltimore sample finds strong effects on children's test scores four to seven years after random assignment that were no longer present ten to fifteen years after the program was implemented (Burdick-Will et al. 2011; Ludwig, Ladd, and Duncan 2001; Sanbonmatsu et al. 2011). Research on the Chicago site, on the other hand, documents similarly strong effects on children's test scores four to seven years after random assignment, and smaller effects that persisted through the latter follow-up ten to fifteen years after the program was implemented (Burdick-Will et al. 2011; Sanbonmatsu et al. 2011).

Making sense of these conflicting findings is challenging because of the nature of the MTO experiment and the variation in its implementation and impact across the five cities (Briggs, Popkin, and Goering 2010). Research examining where families moved demonstrates that in some cities families in the experimental group moved into areas of the city in proximity to communities of families who received no vouchers and were in the control groups (Sampson 2008). In other cities, families assigned to the experimental group experienced much more substantial changes in their residential environments, but these changes were short lived (Clark 2008). In the latest follow-up, conducted ten to fifteen years after random assignment, families in the experimental group lived in neighborhoods with poverty rates just 3 percentage points lower, on average, than families in the control group (Ludwig et al. 2012).

Making general conclusions from MTO becomes even more difficult when one considers the changes taking place in major U.S. cities at the same time as the experiment. The intervention was implemented at a time when employment opportunities were expanding rapidly in high-poverty communities, welfare reform was being implemented, public housing was being demolished in many cities around the country, and violent crime was just beginning to decline after several decades of rising violence in central cities (Sharkey 2013). None of these observations make MTO any less useful for understanding the effects of a policy designed to move families into lower-poverty communities. However, it is important to consider MTO in the context of its time, and to consider results from MTO alongside those from Gautreaux and the many other housing mobility programs that have been implemented and studied over time.

Many of these other housing mobility programs have generated evidence suggesting that moving out of highly disadvantaged communities can lead to positive effects on children's academic trajectories and economic outcomes. George Galster, Anna Santiago, and Jessica Lucero (2015a, 2015b) analyze data from Denver County's "Dispersed Housing Program," in which low-income families were offered specific housing units based on the family type and what was available when the family reached the top of the list. The authors argue that the unique nature of this housing assignment process created exogenous variation in the locations of units offered to families. They find that children from families moving to neighborhoods with higher crime, greater social problems in the community, and lower average socioeconomic status have worse developmental, health, education, and early labor market outcomes.

Jens Ludwig and his colleagues (2010) analyze data from housing assistance recipients in Chicago who were randomly assigned a position on a wait list when the local housing authority opened this wait list for the first time in years. Exploiting variation in the timing of when families were offered housing in lower-poverty neighborhoods, the researchers found that children offered housing vouchers scored 0.05 standard deviations higher on reading scores and 0.08 standard deviations higher on math scores than children in the control group. Because most families offered a voucher did not actually move, the estimated effects of moving into lower-poverty neighborhoods among those families that moved are substantially larger.

Douglas Massey and a team of researchers analyze the outcomes of families who were able to move into a new housing development in the Philadelphia suburb of Mt. Laurel, New Jersey (2013). Matching families that moved into the new housing development with families on the waiting list who were not offered housing, Massey and his colleagues find that those who moved had higher earnings and employment rates than those who did not, but that moving had no effect on welfare receipt. Children in families that moved to the new development attended higher quality schools and their parents were more involved with their schools, although children's grades did not change as a result of their moves.

Whereas these studies focus on variation in neighborhood conditions, other research has exploited exogenous variation in school quality arising from natural experiments in order to identify how the school setting affects academic success. Heather Schwartz (2010) analyzes data on test performance among low-income students in Montgomery County, Maryland, one of the wealthiest urban school districts in the nation. Montgomery County is unique not only because of the quality of its public schools, but also because it has the nation's oldest and most extensive inclusionary zoning program. As part of this zoning policy, the county's housing authority is able to purchase up to one-third of the units set aside by developers to be rented or sold at below market rates. The housing authority randomly assigns families selected for housing assistance to these units, which are scattered across all neighborhoods and school attendance zones throughout the county.

Exploiting the random assignment of low-income families to housing units, Schwartz estimated the effect of attending elementary schools with relatively low levels of student poverty versus moderate or high levels of poverty. The study tracked academic performance among 850 low-income students over five to seven years, and found that students in low-poverty elementary schools performed 0.4 standard deviations higher in math and 0.2 standard deviations higher in reading than similar students assigned to schools with 20 percent or higher poverty rates. By the end of elementary school, the gap between low-income students assigned to low-poverty schools and their peers in the larger student body had been cut by half in math and by a third in English.

Will Dobbie and Roland Fryer (2011) analyze the effect on academic performance of attending a charter school run by the Harlem Children's Zone (HCZ). The HCZ is a well-known community organization targeting a roughly hundred-block area of Harlem with high-quality social services, schools, and programs for youth and families. To identify the effect of attending a HCZ school, Dobbie and Fryer exploit the fact that attendance at the HCZ Promise Academy Schools was based on a lottery among all applicants. As a second identification strategy, the researchers used variation in the probability of attending HCZ schools derived from the interaction of the student's address and birth cohort. The study found that both older and younger students who were able to attend a Promise Academy experienced substantial improvements in English and math performance, and were less likely to be absent from school. Effect sizes ranged from one-quarter to four-fifths of a standard deviation improvement in standardized test performance, with larger gains in the math assessments.

In considering this evidence, it is important to be clear about what it reveals and what it does not. The studies by Schwartz (2010) and Dobbie and Fryer (2011) both focus on school composition and school quality, but do not indicate that schools are the sole mechanism underlying neighborhood effects, nor that simply offering alternatives to poor-performing public schools will sever the link between neighborhood disadvantage and academic inequality. Analyzing data on student performance derived from thirty-six charter schools that used attendance lotteries, Philip Gleason and his colleagues (2010) find that, overall, attending a charter school had no detectable effects on on academic or behavioral outcomes. Some schools showed strong positive impacts on student performance, particularly those that served more disadvantaged student populations. Other schools produced null or negative impacts. These results suggest that the findings from a specific program or school, such as the Promise Academies within the Harlem Children's Zone or other programs that offer their own unique and effective approaches,[1] do not necessarily generalize to other schools or programs that may differ in quality, approach, or in the skill of teachers and administrators.

The evidence from the studies of school quality does reveal that when low-income students living in highly disadvantaged residential settings are able to attend high-quality schools, their academic performance improves substantially.[2] This research provides tangible evidence that the explanations for persistence at the bottom of the academic distribution do not lie fully within low-income individuals or families. Instead, aspects of the residential environment surrounding such families, such as schools, can play an important role in influencing their academic trajectories and, in turn, their prospects for economic mobility.

Evidence on the Effects of Community Change

A third strand of evidence analyzes how change in the neighborhood or local labor market that occurs around individuals affects individual economic trajectories. Sharkey (2012a) compares matched pairs of African American children who lived in neighborhoods that had similar economic and demographic composition but began to change in different ways as they aged into early adulthood. Conditional on initial neighborhood conditions and the trajectory of change in the past, Sharkey argues that it is plausible to think of subsequent neighborhood change as exogenous and to assume any impacts of neighborhood change are causal. The study found that African American children in neighborhoods where the level of concentrated disadvantage declined by one standard deviation had roughly $4,000 higher annual earnings and $6,000 higher annual family income in adulthood. This finding appears to have been driven by economic opportunities because the effect was null on other outcomes, such as educational attainment and marital status.

Other studies have exploited local economic

---

1. Vilsa Curto and Roland Fryer's (2011) evaluation of the SEED charter school program, for example, is the only charter school that provides boarding for low-income students.

2. The large literature on early childhood education programs is also highly relevant here (see, for example, Heckman, Pinto, and Svelyev 2013; Morris et al. 2014).

shocks to identify the effect of changes in economic opportunities around individuals and families. For example, Elizabeth Ananat, Anna Gassman-Pines, and Christina Gibson-Davis (2011) use factory plant closings in North Carolina counties to identify the effect of local job losses on aggregate measures of children's academic performance. Changes in local economic conditions arising from plant closings were found to have large effects on children's reading and math scores in the state, and impacts were larger for eighth graders than fourth graders. Statewide job losses of 1 percent of the working-age population were estimated to reduce eighth grade math scores by 0.076 standard deviations.[3]

Another example comes from the experience of American Indian tribes in the aftermath of the 1988 law that allowed for the development of large-scale gaming facilities on reservation land (Wolfe et al. 2012). Several researchers have used variation in the timing at which gaming facilities have opened on reservation land to identify the effect of an influx of income and economic opportunities into highly disadvantaged areas. These studies have found substantial effects on educational attainment, on median income and employment, and on physical and mental health, including mortality (Copeland and Costello 2010; Costello et al. 2003; Wolfe et al. 2012). Although the establishment of casino gaming is a unique form of change in the local economic environment and one that may come with serious social consequences, the evidence from American Indian reservations does indicate that large-scale transformations of local economic opportunities can generate substantial economic benefits for the residents of the area (on the impact of the Tennessee Valley Authority, see Kline and Moretti 2013).

Summary and Next Steps
Several conclusions can be made from the range of empirical work summarized, some of which stand on firmer ground than others. First, evidence from observational studies typically documents an association between child neighborhood conditions and adult economic outcomes, although this relationship is not found in all studies that have been conducted. A much larger literature has examined the relationship between neighborhood conditions and local school quality and outcomes related to educational attainment and academic performance. This strand of research has generated consistent evidence that growing up in disadvantaged residential environments and attending low-quality schools impedes children's academic trajectories and development of cognitive skills. Recent contributions to this literature have made improvements in modeling selection into high-poverty neighborhoods over time, and have shown that the consequences of long-term exposure to disadvantaged environments appear to be cumulative, more harmful effects arising from sustained or multigenerational exposure to neighborhood disadvantage.

Evidence derived from housing mobility programs is more difficult to interpret. Research from several quasi-experimental and experimental studies has yielded strong evidence that moving out of concentrated disadvantage can have substantial benefits for the developmental trajectories of youth and for parents' well-being, but these findings depend on the nature of the housing mobility program and the types of moves that families make. This evidence is more useful for evaluating the impact of specific policies implemented in unique locations and times, than for making general conclusions about the relationship between neighborhoods and social and economic mobility.

Last, several studies focusing on shocks in local labor market opportunities have documented strong impacts on adults' labor market outcomes and children's academic outcomes. These studies confirm the intuitive idea that the presence or absence of opportunities in the residential environment can play important roles in affecting prospects for economic suc-

---

3. Phillip Levine (2011) analyzes the effect of parental job loss by any means (voluntary and involuntary) and does not find similar negative effects on children's academic performance, suggesting that the reason for job loss may be central to understanding the consequences for children.

cess, with impacts that extend across generations.

The research reviewed here focuses primarily on economic opportunities and schools as key pathways linking neighborhoods with economic mobility. However, the literature on neighborhood effects has developed much more extensive theoretical models focusing on how the residential environments surrounding children may affect their developmental trajectories and ultimately influence their prospects for economic mobility (Harding et al. 2011; Galster 2012). Patrick Sharkey and Jacob Faber (2014) argue that greater attention should be devoted to the full range of mechanisms linking residential settings with children's outcomes, including environmental exposures such as air pollution, lead, and violence; the quality and quantity of local institutions such as day-care centers, nonprofits, and churches; and peer groups, networks, and role models. Although a large literature documents the effect of these various dimensions of children's lives on health, education, and cognitive skill development during childhood, very few studies have attempted to make the connection to economic mobility. Moving beyond schools and jobs to provide evidence on the full range of mechanisms linking neighborhoods with economic mobility is a clear next step for this literature.

HOW DO CITIES AND METROPOLITAN AREAS AFFECT ECONOMIC MOBILITY?

Virtually all of the research on intergenerational economic mobility in the United States describes the level of mobility in the nation as a whole. Whereas early estimates suggested only a weak relationship between the economic status of parents and their children, more recent research that corrects for methodological problems in the original studies finds much lower levels of economic mobility (Mazumder 2005a, 2005b; Solon 1992). Recent estimates of the intergenerational elasticity of family income in the United States, measured as the strength of the relationship between the natural logarithm of total family income measured at the same age across successive generations, range from around 0.40 up to as high as 0.60. The former estimate, which represents a rough lower bound of the estimated intergenerational elasticity in the United States, can be interpreted to mean that if a parent's income is roughly twice as high as the national average, then the child's adult income would be expected to be about 40 percent higher.

This estimate indicates much greater persistence of economic status across generations in the United States than in European nations or Canada (Corak 2006; Smeeding, Erikson, and Jantii 2011; Solon 2002). Recent research has looked to national policy as a way of explaining the relatively low level of economic mobility in the United States, but this approach overlooks the potential to explore variation within the nation to begin to understand what drives intergenerational economic mobility. Considering the tremendous diversity in population characteristics, regional and local economies, politics, and culture within the United States, there are good reasons to expect substantial variation across U.S. states and cities in levels of economic mobility. Several recent studies confirm this expectation.

An analysis by Bhashkar Mazumder and published by the Pew Charitable Trusts Economic Mobility Project (Economic Mobility Project 2012) offers estimates of intergenerational economic mobility across the states, identifying a pocket of northeastern states with high levels of economic mobility, and another pocket of southern states with much lower levels. Bryan Graham and Sharkey (2013) use data from three national surveys and document substantial variation in levels of economic mobility across urban areas. Chetty and his colleagues (2014) use data from the Internal Revenue Service to create several measures of relative and absolute income mobility across the nation's commuting zones, which are sets of contiguous counties that surround central cities and cover the entire nation. These authors find substantial variation in levels of economic mobility, and that some commuting zones have mobility levels equal to those of the most mobile nations in Western Europe and others with lower levels of mobility than any of the developed nations.

All of these studies indicate that national measures of intergenerational economic mobility obscure substantial geographic variation in levels of mobility across urban areas, commuting zones, states, and regions of the country. Recent evidence suggests that this variation is a function of places themselves, rather than the people within them. Chetty and Hendren (2015) use data from the Internal Revenue Service to analyze the relationship between time spent in low- and high-mobility areas and economic outcomes later in life. The authors exploit variation across siblings and other "exogenous displacement shocks" and find that "spending more of one's childhood in an area with higher rates of upward mobility . . . leads to higher earnings in adulthood" (Chetty 2015, 25). In other words, something about high-mobility areas seems to affect the chances for economic mobility among residents. Although this evidence suggests a causal effect of places on economic mobility, less progress has been made in explaining what it is about those places that increases or reduces the chances for residents to move upward in the income distribution.

Mechanisms Explaining Variation
Chetty and his colleagues (2014) analyze the correlations between a range of social, demographic, and economic characteristics of commuting zones and the level of economic mobility, focusing primary attention on the probability of upward mobility from the bottom of the income distribution. The level of upward mobility in a commuting zone was found to be most strongly associated with the degree of racial and economic segregation in the commuting zone, with the rate of high school dropouts and single parents, with the level of violent crime and measures of social capital, and with the level of economic inequality in the commuting zone. This descriptive analysis provides several suggestive conclusions about the types of commuting zones with high and low levels of economic mobility, but the analysis is exploratory and not designed to generate convincing causal evidence.

Graham and Sharkey (2013) focus on the connection between economic segregation, defined as the proportion of overall variance in income within a metropolitan area that lies between neighborhoods, and levels of economic mobility. This focus is motivated by a theoretical model in which transmission of parents' economic status is driven by both family-level mechanisms and place-based mechanisms such as the quality of local schools and other institutions, property values, crime, and other aspects of the residential environment. This model predicts that in urban areas where the rich live in separate neighborhoods from the poor, the benefits of economic resources and the costs of poverty are exacerbated because of the tight connection between family economic status and neighborhood economic status. As a result, family economic status is transmitted more easily to the next generation (for similar propositions, see Loury 1977; Durlauf 1996). An association between economic segregation and economic mobility was found in three different datasets, and also was found in analyses that examine change in economic segregation and change in mobility within urban areas. Similar to that of Chetty and his colleagues (2014), the analysis by Graham and Sharkey (2013) provides suggestive evidence linking economic segregation with variation in levels of mobility, but not evidence that allows for strong causal claims.

Summary and Next Steps
Two summary conclusions are possible on the basis of these studies. First, geographic variation in levels of economic mobility within the United States is substantial. This observation means that national estimates of income mobility, though informative, pool data from places that have widely divergent patterns of both absolute and relative mobility. Perhaps the most notable geographic pattern is found in maps Chetty and his colleagues (2014) present, which document a large swath of the southeastern part of the country featuring extremely low levels of mobility. This striking pattern reveals a large section of the country where upward mobility is rare, and suggests the need for more empirical research to explain regional variation in economic mobility.

Second, new evidence from Chetty and Hendren (2015) suggests that geographic variation in levels of economic mobility reflects the causal effects of places, rather than the selection of more or less mobile people into areas. This evidence is based on the empirical finding that children who spend more time in areas with greater levels of mobility have a higher probability of upward economic mobility relative to other children who spend less time in the high-mobility area.

Third, some evidence has been generated on the characteristics of places that are associated with economic mobility, but minimal progress has been made in providing evidence that allows for causal claims. Graham and Sharkey (2013) provide a strong theoretical motivation for the focus on economic segregation, and Chetty and his colleagues (2014) document conditional associations between economic mobility and a range of characteristics of commuting zones. As a whole, however, the research explaining geographic variation in economic mobility remains at a very early stage. Generating causal evidence on the mechanisms explaining variation in economic mobility is the most pressing challenge for researchers in this area.

WHAT ARE THE IMPLICATIONS FOR SOCIAL POLICY?

Two broad approaches are commonly proposed to reduce neighborhood inequality and its consequences. The first confronts neighborhood inequality with investments in communities, or families within them, designed to weaken the link between growing up in a disadvantaged neighborhood and its consequences for children's economic trajectories. The second confronts neighborhood inequality more directly by attempting to alter the distribution of neighborhoods occupied by different segments of the population. The most common policy tool used to implement the second approach is residential mobility or housing assistance programs for low-income populations. In addition to such mobility programs, however, a set of more basic changes in housing and urban policy represent alternative approaches to compressing the distribution of neighborhood advantage and disadvantage.

Place-Based Investment

Several examples of investments and initiatives have been designed to target disadvantaged places or the individuals and families within them. The New Hope program, implemented in Milwaukee in the mid-1990s, offered extensive work supports, wage supplements, and temporary guaranteed jobs for individuals willing to work at least thirty hours per week (Duncan, Huston, and Weisner 2009). Certain features of the program distinguished it from many other welfare-to-work programs implemented in the same period, one of which was to target low-income individuals living in low-income neighborhoods. New Hope is thus an example of a "place-conscious" program that directed resources and supports toward individuals and families within disadvantaged areas (Pastor and Turner 2010).

Applicants to the program were randomly assigned to a treatment and control group, and several studies have tracked the outcomes of participants over an extended period. Results show that the treatment group had higher rates of employment and earnings while the program was in operation, a finding that was driven, in part, by the guarantee of community service employment for participants unable to find a job in the private market (Huston et al. 2003). The program reduced family poverty from 60 percent among control group members to 52 percent among program group members; and multiple studies have documented improvements in academic performance and behavior among the children of families in the program's treatment group (Duncan, Huston, and Weisner 2009; Huston et al. 2001; Huston et al. 2003). Children in the program group scored 0.12 standard deviations higher than their counterparts in the control group on an assessment of reading and language skills several years after the program began (Huston et al. 2003). The program costs totaled roughly $16,000 per individual over three years, or $5,300 per person per year (Huston et al. 2003).

Another place-conscious intervention focusing on individuals' prospects in the labor market was the Jobs-Plus program implemented in the 1990s by the federal Department of Housing and Urban Development in five very different cities: Baltimore, Chattanooga, Dayton, Los Angeles, and St. Paul. Jobs-Plus saturated public housing developments both with services designed to enhance individuals' capacity to obtain and retain employment over time, and with rent incentives designed to encourage work. Over the course of the program, resident employment and income rose steadily in three of the sites that implemented the full package of services and incentives offered through the program (Bloom et al. 2005). In these three sites, the program was estimated to increase employment by roughly 10 percent and to increase annual earnings of participants by between 8 and 19 percent (Bloom et al. 2005). The full costs of the rent incentives and on-site services were roughly $1,800 per individual per year (in 2003 dollars), although if public housing agencies are already administering some of the services offered through Jobs-Plus then the incremental costs of this program would be lower (Bloom et al. 2005).

Whereas New Hope and Jobs-Plus targeted individuals within high-poverty areas, an alternative set of interventions attempt to create greater demand for labor through incentives designed to encourage firms to invest and to hire local residents. The most notable example is the Empowerment Zones/Enterprise Communities (EZ/EC) program that began in the mid-1990s.[4] This federal program provided firms, in dozens of communities, tax incentives designed to encourage expansion, investment, and employment of local residents. The most persuasive evidence demonstrating positive effects of the designation as Empowerment Zones comes from Matias Busso, Jesse Gregory, and Patrick Kline (2013), who estimate the effect of the program by comparing the six selected sites with others that applied and were rejected or that applied and were later accepted. The researchers estimate that the program increased the number of jobs for residents within the zone boundaries by 15 percent, and increased wages of workers within the zone by 8 percent (in addition to benefits for workers not living in the zone). The authors' best estimates of program costs indicate that the federal government spent roughly $850 per resident on grants and wage credits, though the various sources of funding that went into the Empowerment Zones were difficult to measure and all of the point estimates from the analysis are imprecise (Busso et al. 2013).

This study's findings stand in contrast to other empirical findings of minimal effects of the program in different sites (see Elvery 2009; Oakley and Tsao 2006). Further, several commentators have raised doubts, from both theoretical and empirical perspectives, that any spatially targeted economic development program can generate cost-effective, positive effects on residents in the absence of supplemental investments (Glaeser and Gottlieb 2008; Ladd 1994).

The interventions discussed to this point focus on reducing poverty, improving prospects in the labor market, and creating job opportunities for individuals in disadvantaged neighborhoods. However, the presence or absence of economic opportunities is only one of several mechanisms through which neighborhood inequality may be linked with economic mobility. A range of interventions targeted toward disadvantaged areas have been conducted over time to improve the quality of schooling, reduce violent crime, or improve community health (see, for instance, Braga 2005; Cook et al. 2015; Dobbie and Fryer 2011; Heller 2014; Heller et al. 2013; Papachristos et al. 2007; Schwartz 2010). These types of place-based or place-conscious interventions may indirectly affect levels of economic mobility through exposure to violence, school quality, health, or the many additional mechanisms by which neighborhood advantage and disadvantage are linked with economic mobility.

The recognition that economic disadvantage tends to be concentrated in areas that face a range of associated challenges is the motivation for a set of interventions that have come to be identified as Community Change Initiatives (CCIs). CCIs focus on comprehensive neighborhood revitalization designed to flood an area with resources focused on economic development, institutional support, physical infrastructure, and social services (Kubisch et al. 2010). As Anne Kubisch notes in a report describing how CCIs have been implemented over time, most Community Change Initiatives have in practice not received the level of sustained resources necessary to generate trans-

---

4. My reading of this literature was influenced by a review of the literature conducted by Christopher Wimer (2013).

formative community change. Reviews of the field have identified other challenges faced by any effort to implement comprehensive community change, including the coordination of services and supports, building institutional capacity, and engaging residents and other important local actors in the effort (Chaskin, Joseph, and Chipenda-Dansokho 1997; Kubisch et al. 2010). Like many other efforts to revitalize communities through place-based investment, the impact of CCIs is difficult to assess because programs rarely have been designed in ways that allow for a clear assessment of program impact, and because these types of programs typically are not implemented at a scale that could generate tangible change that is sustained over time (O'Connor 1995, 1999; Sharkey 2013).

Although interventions designed to generate neighborhood change have not demonstrated a clear track record of success, empirical work on large-scale changes in local economic opportunities provide proof-of-concept evidence suggesting that major investments that alter the local economic environment in a fundamental way can have substantial, long-term effects on residents. Research on federal investments in the Tennessee Valley Authority and the introduction of casino gaming to American Indian reservations provides suggestive evidence that large-scale transformations of local economic opportunities can generate substantial economic benefits for the residents of the area (Kline and Moretti 2013; Copeland and Costello 2010; Wolfe et al. 2012). For example, Barbara Wolfe and her colleagues (2012) estimate that the introduction of casino gaming increased average household income by 5.3 percent, leading to indirect declines in smoking (9.6 percent), anxiety (7.3 percent decline in days of anxiety), heavy drinking (5.2 percent), and health outcomes related to obesity (2 to 4 percent). These estimates do not consider any larger costs associated with casino gaming, of course, and are included here only as an illustration of the potential gains that arise from large-scale economic transformation of a clearly defined area or zone. How to turn these examples into effective policies or programs targeting disadvantaged communities is a much more challenging question.

Expanding Mobility and Reducing Inequality

The alternative approach to confronting neighborhood inequality is to implement new policies or revise existing policies specifically to alter directly, or compress, the distribution of neighborhood advantage and disadvantage. One method of moving toward this goal is residential mobility programs for recipients of housing assistance.

I have already discussed results from various housing mobility programs that have been implemented and evaluated over time. A more basic consideration is whether such programs are effective mechanisms to generate meaningful changes in families' residential environments. Research from the most well-known residential mobility program, the Moving to Opportunity experiment, has demonstrated that families in the experimental groups from several sites did experience changes in exposure to neighborhood poverty but were highly likely to move into communities that were both near and similar in racial-ethnic composition and school quality to their origin neighborhoods (Clark 2008; Sampson 2008). Over time, the change in neighborhood poverty induced by the program faded away (Ludwig et al. 2012).

This pattern of findings reflects the challenges families face in navigating a highly stratified urban landscape, but it also reflects the "psychological constraints" (Shroder 2002) that condition the choices made by different groups of families in urban housing markets. For example, one of the primary predictors of whether families in the MTO experiment were able to "lease up" in a new apartment was their uncertainty about whether they would like their new neighborhood if they were to move (Shroder 2002). This type of uncertainty arises from unfamiliarity with communities around an urban area (Krysan and Bader 2009), from concerns about how families would be treated in new communities (Thompson 2001), and from a very real historical legacy of discrimination and violence. As a result, residential moves made by families receiving housing assistance and navigating the private rental market often are found to reinforce, rather than disrupt, patterns of urban inequality (Sharkey 2012b).

A few housing assistance programs have been more successful in generating transformative changes in families' neighborhood contexts. One common feature of these programs is that they take a more active role in expanding the choice set of families deciding where to relocate. For example, many housing experts call for more intensive counseling for recipients of housing assistance; and some argue for efforts to alter the choice architecture of families as they begin their search for housing. Xavier de Souza Briggs, Susan Popkin, and John Goering (2010) suggest providing families with a "default" set of two or three units that are available in different communities within the city. An extreme version of this approach is the Gautreaux Assisted Housing Program in Chicago, where participating families were offered specific units located throughout the Chicago metropolitan area based on their position on a waitlist (Rubinowitz and Rosenbaum 2000). Unlike in most residential mobility programs, the Gautreaux moves took families across the entire Chicago metropolitan area and brought about a change in families' neighborhood environments that persisted over time (Keels et al. 2005).

A few current housing assistance programs follow a similar approach by providing extensive information, support, and resources necessary to allow families to make the kind of residential moves that bring them into entirely new sections of their metropolitan areas. The Baltimore Housing Mobility Program also arose from a settlement with the federal Department of Housing and Urban Development, and features intensive counseling designed to bring families into new, racially diverse communities with low rates of poverty and abundant economic opportunities (Darrah and DeLuca 2014). This active approach is necessary to allow families to make the kinds of moves that disrupt the structure of residential stratification within the metropolitan area, and that are rare among low-income families navigating the rental market on their own.

However, providing vouchers that allow low-income families to move is not the sole mechanism to expand residential options for low-income families or members of racial and ethnic minority groups. An alternative approach involves taking active steps to break down barriers that limit housing choice. Manuel Pastor and Margery Turner (2010) review an extensive list of options that include expanding the supply of affordable housing, confronting exclusionary zoning policies, promoting and enforcing fair-share housing plans, taking active steps to reduce residential discrimination by race and ethnicity, and developing coordinated metropolitan-wide plans for transportation, housing, education, and economic development (see also Goering 2006; Katz and Turner 2001; Katz 1999, 2000; Rusk 1999; Quigley 2011; Quigley and Raphael 2004; Turner and Ross 2005).

These proposed policy shifts reinforce the point that to weaken the connection between neighborhood inequality and economic mobility it may not be necessary to implement new interventions, programs, or initiatives with substantial costs attached to them. Altering or ending several existing housing and land use policies that exacerbate inequality, and instead implementing programs that confront inequality, would be an initial step in an urban policy agenda designed to reduce neighborhood inequality.

One example is the home mortgage interest deduction. In 2012, the estimated costs of the mortgage interest deduction were $70 billion, most of which went to homeowners making $100,000 or more in annual income (Fischer and Huang 2013; Turner et al. 2013). Various proposals to reform this deduction have been put forth in an effort to make it less regressive, more efficient, and less expensive while limiting any potential negative impacts of the reforms on the housing market. To confront neighborhood inequality, one could argue for shifting federal tax expenditures forfeited to the mortgage interest deduction toward programs designed to provide affordable housing or to expand housing options in high-opportunity neighborhoods. For example, Barbara Sard and Will Fischer (2012) argue for reforming the mortgage interest deduction and instituting a renter's tax credit as part of an effort to create a more balanced approach toward housing policy. In advocating for this type of approach, it is important to acknowledge the dearth of research on the impact of the mortgage interest deduction. With the exception of research focusing on the mortgage interest deduction and home ownership (Hilber and Turner 2014), little empirical work has been conducted that would inform our understanding of the likely consequences of these proposed reforms on economic or racial-ethnic segregation or on neighborhood inequality.

It is certainly true that promising new programs and reforms of existing housing assistance programs can be effective in reducing the consequences of neighborhood disadvantage. However, it is also true that neighborhood inequality is in part the result of active intervention into the housing market through law and public policy. A basic approach to confront neighborhood inequality is to change the way that the federal and state governments invest in places. This can be done with new programs or investments, but it can also be done by altering existing policies in basic ways designed to compress the distribution of neighborhood economic status and to reduce the consequences of neighborhood disadvantage.

REFERENCES

Aaronson, Daniel. 1998. "Using Sibling Data to Estimate the Impact of Neighborhoods on Children's Educational Outcomes." *Journal of Human Resources* 33(4): 915–46.

Ananat, Elizabeth O., Anna Gassman-Pines, and Christina M. Gibson-Davis. 2011. "The Effects of Local Employment Losses on Children's Educational Achievement." In *Whither Opportunity: Rising Inequality, Schools, and Children's Life Chances*, edited by Greg J. Duncan and Richard J. Murnane. New York: Russell Sage Foundation.

Bloom, Howard S., James A. Riccio, Nandita Verma, and Johanna Walter. 2005. "Promoting Work in Public Housing. The Effectiveness of Jobs-Plus." New York: Manpower Demonstration Research Corporation.

Braga, Anthony A. 2005. "Hot Spots Policing and Crime Prevention: A Systematic Review of Randomized Controlled Trials." *Journal of Experimental Criminology* 1(3): 317–42.

Briggs, Xavier de Souza. 1997. "Moving Up Versus Moving Out: Neighborhood Effects in Housing Mobility Programs." *Housing Policy Debate* 8(1): 195–234.

Briggs, Xavier de Souza, and Benjamin Keys. 2009. "Has Exposure to Poor Neighbourhoods Changed in America? Race, Risk and Housing Locations in Two Decades." *Urban Studies* 46(2): 429–58.

Briggs, Xavier de Souza, Susan J. Popkin, and John Goering. 2010. *Moving to Opportunity: The Story of an American Experiment to Fight Ghetto Poverty*. New York: Oxford University Press.

Burdick-Will Judith, Jens Ludwig, Stephen W. Raudenbush, Robert J. Sampson, Lisa Sanbonmatsu, and Patrick Sharkey. 2011. "Converging Evidence for Neighborhood Effects on Children's Test Scores: An Experimental, Quasi-experimental, and Observational Comparison." In *Whither Opportunity: Rising Inequality, Schools, and Children's Life Chances*, edited by Greg J. Duncan and Richard J. Murnane. New York: Russell Sage Foundation.

Busso, Matias, Jesse Gregory, and Patrick Kline. 2013. "Assessing the Incidence and Efficiency of a Prominent Place Based Policy." *American Economic Review* 103(2): 897–947.

Chaskin, Robert J., Mark L. Joseph, and Selma Chipenda-Dansokho. 1997. "Implementing Comprehensive Community Development: Possibilities and Limitations." *Social Work* 42(5): 435–44.

Chetty, Raj. 2015. "Behavioral Economics and Public Policy: A Pragmatic Perspective." *American Economic Review Papers and Proceedings* 105(5): 1–33.

Chetty, Raj, and Nathan Hendren. 2015. "The Effects of Neighborhoods on Children's Long-Term Outcomes: Quasi-Experimental Estimates for the United States." *Equality of Opportunity Project* working paper. Cambridge, Mass.: Harvard University.

Chetty, Raj, Nathan Hendren, and Larry Katz. 2015. "The Effects of Exposure to Better Neighborhoods on Children: New Evidence from the Moving to Opportunity Experiment." *NBER* working paper no. 21156. Cambridge, Mass.: National Bureau of Economic Research.

Chetty, Raj, Nathaniel Hendren, Patrick Kline, and Emmanuel Saez. 2014. "Where Is the Land of Opportunity? The Geography of Intergenerational Mobility in the US." *Quarterly Journal of Economics* 129(4): 1553–623.

Clampet-Lundquist, Susan, Kathy Edin, Jeff Kling, Greg Duncan. 2011. "Moving Teenagers Out of High-Risk Neighborhoods: How Girls Fare Better Than Boys." *American Journal of Sociology* 116(4): 1154–89.

Clark, William A. V. 2008. "Reexamining the Moving to Opportunity Study and Its Contribution to Changing the Distribution of Poverty and Ethnic Concentration." *Demography* 45(3): 515–35.

Cook, Philip J., Kenneth Dodge, George Farkas, Roland G. Fryer, Jr., Jonathan Guryan, Jens Ludwig, Susan Mayer, Harold Pollack, and Laurence Steinberg. 2015. "Not Too Late: Improving Academic Outcomes for Disadvantaged Youth." *IPR* working paper no. 15–01. Chicago: Northwestern University.

Copeland, William, and Elizabeth J. Costello. 2010. "Parents' Incomes and Children's Outcomes: A Quasi-Experiment." *American Economic Journal: Applied Economics* 2(1): 86–115.

Corak, Miles. 2006. "Do Poor Children Become Poor Adults? Lessons from a Cross Country Comparison of Generational Earnings Mobility." *IZA* discussion paper no. 1993. Bonn: Institute for the Study of Labor.

Corcoran, Mary, and Terry Adams. 1999. "Race, Sex, and the Intergenerational Transmission of Poverty." In *The Consequences of Growing up Poor*, edited by Greg J. Duncan and Jeanne Brooks-Gunn. New York: Russell Sage Foundation.

Corcoran, Mary, Roger Gordon, Deborah Laren, and Gary Solon. 1992. "The Association Between Men's Economic Status and Their Family and Community Origins." *Journal of Human Resources* 27(4): 575–601.

Costello, E. Jane, Scott N. Compton, Gordon Keeler, and Adrian Angold. 2003. "Relationships Between Poverty and Psychopathology: A Natural Experiment." *Journal of the American Medical Association* 290(15): 2023–29.

Curto, Vilsa E., and Roland G. Fryer Jr. 2011. "Estimating the Returns to Urban Boarding Schools: Evidence from SEED." *NBER* working paper no. w16746. Cambridge, Mass.: National Bureau of Economic Research.

Darrah, Jennifer, and Stefanie DeLuca. 2014. "Living Here Has Changed My Whole Perspective: How Escaping Inner-City Poverty Shapes Neighborhood and Housing Choice." *Journal of Policy Analysis and Management* 33(2): 350–84.

Datcher, Linda. 1982. "Effects of Community and Family Background on Achievement." *Review of Economics and Statistics* 64(1): 32–41.

DeLuca, Stefanie, and Elizabeth Dayton. 2009. "Switching Social Contexts: The Effects of Housing Mobility and School Choice Programs on Youth Outcomes." *Annual Review of Sociology* 35: 457–491.

Dobbie, Will, and Roland G. Fryer Jr. 2011. "Are High-Quality Schools Enough to Increase Achievement Among the Poor? Evidence from the Harlem Children's Zone." *American Economic Journal: Applied Economics* 3(3): 158–87.

Dreier, Peter, John Mollenkopf, and Todd Swanstrom. 2001. *Place matters: Metropolitics for the 21st Century*. Lawrence, Kansas: University Press of Kansas.

Duncan, Greg J., Aletha C. Huston, and Thomas S. Weisner. 2009. *Higher Ground: New Hope for the Working Poor and Their Children*. New York: Russell Sage Foundation.

Durlauf, Steven N. 1996. "A Theory of Persistent Income Inequality." *Journal of Economic Growth* 1(1): 75–93.

Economic Mobility Project. 2012. "Economic Mobility of the States." Washington, D.C.: Pew Center on the States. Accessed December 28, 2015. http://www.pewtrusts.org/en/multimedia/data-visualizations/2012/economic-mobility-of-the-states.

Elvery, Joel A. 2009. "The Impact of Enterprise Zones on Resident Employment: An Evaluation of the Enterprise Zone Programs in California and Florida." *Economic Development Quarterly* 23(1): 44–59.

Fischer, Will, and Chye-Ching Huang. 2013. "Mortgage Interest Deduction Is Ripe for Reform." Washington, D.C.: Center on Budget and Policy Priorities.

Galster, George. 2012. "The Mechanism(s) of Neighbourhood Effects: Theory, Evidence, and Policy Implications." In *Neighbourhood Effects Research: New Perspectives*, edited by M. van Ham, D. Manley, N. Bailey, L. Simpson, and D. Maclennan. Dordrecht: Springer.

Galster, George, Anna Santiago, and Jessica Lucero. 2015a. "Adrift at the Margins of Urban Society: What Role Does Neighborhood Play?" *Urban Affairs Review* 51(1): 10–45.

———. 2015b. "Employment of Low-Income African American and Latino Teens: Does Neighborhood Social Mix Matter?" *Housing Studies* 30(2): 192–227.

Glaeser, Edward L., and Joshua D. Gottlieb. 2008. "The Economics of Place-Making Policies." *NBER* working paper no. w14373. Cambridge, Mass: National Bureau of Economic Research.

Gleason, Philip, Melissa Clark, Christina Clark Tuttle,

and Emily Dwoyer. 2010. *The Evaluation of Charter School Impacts: Final Report*. NCEE 2010-4029. Washington: U.S. Department of Education.

Goering, John. 2006. "The Effectiveness of Fair Housing Programs and Policy Options." In *Fragile Rights Within Cities: Government, Housing, and Fairness*, edited by John Goering. Lanham, Md.: Rowman and Littlefield.

Goering, John M., and Judith D. Feins. 2003. *Choosing a Better Life? Evaluating the Moving to Opportunity Social Experiment*. Washington, D.C.: Urban Institute Press.

Graham, Bryan, and Patrick Sharkey. 2013. "Mobility and the Metropolis: The Relationship Between Inequality in Urban Communities and Economic Mobility." Washington, D.C.: Pew Charitable Trusts.

Harding, David J. 2003. "Counterfactual Models of Neighborhood Effects: The Effect of Neighborhood Poverty on High School Dropout and Teenage Pregnancy." *American Journal of Sociology* 109(3): 676-719.

Harding David J., Lisa Gennetian, Christopher Winship, Lisa Sanbonmatsu, and Jeffrey Kling. 2011. "Unpacking Neighborhood Influences on Education Outcomes: Setting the Stage for Future Research." In *Whither Opportunity: Rising Inequality, Schools, and Children's Life Chances*, edited by Greg J. Duncan and Richard J. Murnane. New York: Russell Sage Foundation.

Heckman, James, Rodrigo Pinto, and Peter Savelyev. 2013. "Understanding the Mechanisms Through Which an Influential Early Childhood Program Boosted Adult Outcomes." *American Economic Review* 103(6): 2052-86.

Heller, Sara B. 2014. "Summer Jobs Reduce Violence Among Disadvantaged Youth." *Science* 346(6214): 1219-23.

Heller, Sara, Harold Pollack, Roseanna Ander, and Jens Ludwig. 2013. "Preventing Youth Violence and Dropout: A Randomized Field Experiment." *NBER* working paper no. 19014. Cambridge, Mass.: National Bureau of Economic Research.

Hilber, Christian A. L., and Tracy M. Turner. 2014. "The Mortgage Interest Deduction and Its Impact on Homeownership Decisions." *Review of Economics and Statistics* 96(4): 618-37.

Holloway Steven R., and Stephen Mulherin. 2004. "The Effect of Adolescent Neighborhood Poverty on Adult Employment." *Journal of Urban Affairs* 26(4): 427-54.

Huston, Aletha C., Greg J. Duncan, Robert Granger, Johannes Bos, Vonnie McLoyd, Rashmita Mistry, and Danielle Crosby. 2001. "Work-Based Antipoverty Programs for Parents Can Enhance the School Performance and Social Behavior of Children." *Child Development* 72(1): 318-36.

Huston, Aletha C., Cynthia Miller, Lashawn Richburg-Hayes, Greg J. Duncan, Carolyn A. Eldred, Thomas S. Weisner, Edward Lowe, Danielle A. Crosby, Marika N. Ripke, and Cindy Redcross. 2003. "New Hope for Families and Children: Five-Year Results of a Program to Reduce Poverty and Reform Welfare." New York: Manpower Demonstration Research Corporation.

Kaufman, Julie E., and James E. Rosenbaum. 1992. "The Education and Employment of Low-Income Black Youth in White Suburbs." *Educational Evaluation and Policy Analysis* 14(3): 229-40.

Keels, Micere, Greg J. Duncan, Stefanie DeLuca, Ruby Mendenhall, and James Rosenbaum. 2005. "Fifteen Years Later: Can Residential Mobility Programs Provide a Long-Term Escape from Neighborhood Segregation, Crime, and Poverty?" *Demography* 42(1): 51-73.

Katz, Bruce J. 1999. "Beyond City Limits: A New Metropolitan Agenda." In *Setting National Priorities: The 2000 Elections and Beyond*, edited by Henry J. Aaron and Robert D. Reischauer. Washington, D.C.: Brookings Institution.

———. 2000. *Reflections on Regionalism*. Washington, D.C.: Brookings Institution.

Katz, Bruce J., and Margery Austin Turner. 2001. "Who Should Run the Housing Voucher Program? A Reform Proposal." *Housing Policy Debate* 12(2): 239-62.

Kline, Patrick M., and Enrico Moretti. 2013. "Local Economic Development, Agglomeration Economies, and the Big Push: 100 Years of Evidence from the Tennessee Valley Authority." *NBER* working paper no. w19293. Cambridge, Mass.: National Bureau of Economic Research.

Krysan, Maria, and Michael D. M. Bader. 2009. "Racial Blind Spots: Black-White-Latino Differences in Community Knowledge." *Social Problems* 56(4): 677-701.

Kubisch, Anne C., Patricia Auspos, Prudence Brown, and Tom Dewar. 2010. *Voices from the Field III: Lessons and Challenges from Two Decades of*

Community Change Efforts. Washington, D.C.: Aspen Institute.

Ladd, Helen. 1994. "Spatially Targeted Economic Development Strategies: Do They Work?" *Cityscape* 1(1): 193–218.

Leventhal, Tama, and Jeanne Brooks-Gunn. 2000. "The Neighborhoods They Live in: The Effects of Neighborhood Residence on Child and Adolescent Outcomes." *Psychological Bulletin* 126(20): 309–37.

———. 2004. "A Randomized Study of Neighborhood Effects on Low-Income Children's Educational Outcomes." *Developmental Psychology* 40(4): 488–507.

Levine, Phillip B. 2011. "How Does Parental Unemployment Affect Children's Educational Performance." In *Whither Opportunity: Rising Inequality, Schools, and Children's Life Chances*, edited by Greg J. Duncan and Richard J. Murnane. New York: Russell Sage Foundation.

Loury, Glenn C. 1977. "A Dynamic Theory of Racial Income Differences." In *Women, Minorities and Employment Discrimination*, edited by Phyllis A. Wallace and Annette M. LaMond. Lexington, Mass.: Lexington Books.

Ludwig, Jens, Greg J. Duncan, Lisa A. Gennetian, Lawrence F. Katz, Ronald C. Kessler, Jeffrey R. Kling, and Lisa Sanbonmatsu. 2012. "Neighborhood Effects on the Long-Term Well-Being of Low-Income Adults." *Science* 337(6101): 1505–10.

Ludwig, Jens, Brian Jacob, Greg J. Duncan, James Rosenbaum, and Michael Johnson. 2010. "Neighborhood Effects on Low-Income Families: Evidence from a Housing-Voucher Lottery in Chicago." Chicago: University of Chicago.

Ludwig, Jens, Helen Ladd, and Greg J. Duncan. 2001. "The Effects of Urban Poverty on Educational Outcomes: Evidence from a Randomized Experiment." *Brookings-Wharton Papers on Urban Affairs* 2: 147–201.

Massey, Douglas S., Len Albright, Rebecca Casciano, Elizabeth Derickson, and David N. Kinsey. 2013. *Climbing Mount Laurel: The Struggle for Affordable Housing and Social Mobility in an American Suburb*. Princeton, N.J.: Princeton University Press.

Mazumder, Bhashkar. 2005a. "Fortunate Sons: New Estimates of Intergenerational Mobility in the United States Using Social Security Earnings Data." *Review of Economics & Statistics* 87(2): 235–55.

———. 2005b. "The Apple Falls Even Closer to the Tree Than We Thought." In *Unequal Chances: Family Background and Economic Success*, edited by Samuel Bowles, Herbert Gintis, and Melissa Osborne Groves. New York: Russell Sage Foundation.

Mendenhall, Ruby, Stefanie DeLuca, and Greg J. Duncan. 2006. "Neighborhood Resources, Racial Segregation, and Economic Mobility: Results from the Gautreaux Program." *Social Science Research* 35(4): 892–923.

Morris, Pamela, Shira K. Mattera, Nina Castells, Michael Bangser, Karen Bierman, and Cybele Raver. 2014. "Impact Findings from the Head Start CARES Demonstration: National Evaluation of Three Approaches to Improving Preschoolers' Social and Emotional Competence." *OPRE* report no. 2014-44. Washington: U.S. Department of Health and Human Services.

Oakley, Deirdre, and Hui-Shien Tsao. 2006. "A New Way of Revitalizing Distressed Urban Communities? Assessing the Impact of the Federal Empowerment Zone Program." *Journal of Urban Affairs* 28(5): 443–71.

O'Connor, Alice. 1995. "Evaluating Comprehensive Community Initiatives: A View from History." In *New Approaches to Evaluating Community Initiatives: Concepts, Methods, and Contexts*, edited by James P. Connel, Anne C. Kubish, Lisbeth B. Schorr, and Carol H. Weiss. Washington, D.C.: Aspen Institute.

———. 1999. "Swimming Against the Tide: A Brief History of Federal Policy in Poor Communities." In *Urban Problems and Community Development*, edited by Ronald F. Ferguson and William T. Dickens. Washington, D.C.: Brookings Institution.

Papachristos, Andrew, Tracey Meares, and Jeffrey Fagan. 2007. "Attention Felons: Evaluating Project Safe Neighborhoods in Chicago." *Journal of Empirical Legal Studies* 4(2): 223–72.

Pastor, Manuel, and Margery Austin Turner. 2010. "Reducing Poverty and Economic Distress After ARRA: Potential Roles for Place-Conscious Strategies." Washington, D.C.: Urban Institute.

Plotnick, Robert D., and Saul Hoffman. 1999. "The Effect of Neighborhood Characteristics on Young Adult Outcomes: Alternative Estimates." *Social Science Quarterly* 80(1): 1–8.

Quigley, John M. 2011. "Rental Housing Assistance." *Cityscape* 13(2): 157–69.

Quigley, John M., and Steven Raphael. 2004. "Is Housing Unaffordable?" *Brookings Papers on Urban Affairs* 5(1): 149–205.

Quillian, Lincoln. 2003. "How Long Are Exposures to Poor Neighborhoods? The Long-Term Dynamics of Entry and Exit into Poor Neighborhoods." *Population Research and Policy Review* 22(3): 221–49.

Rosenbaum, James E., and Susan J. Popkin. 1991. "Employment and Earnings of Low-Income Blacks Who Move to Middle-Class Suburbs." In *The Urban Underclass*, edited by Christopher Jencks and Paul E. Peterson. Washington, D.C.: Brookings Institution.

Rubinowitz, Leonard S., and James E. Rosenbaum. 2000. *Crossing the Class and Color Lines: From Public Housing to White Suburbia*. Chicago: University of Chicago Press.

Rusk, David. 1999. *Inside Game/Outside Game: Winning Strategies for Saving Urban America*. Washington, D.C.: Brookings Institution.

Sampson, Robert J. 2008. "Moving to Inequality: Neighborhood Effects and Experiments Meet Social Structure." *American Journal of Sociology* 114(1): 189–231.

Sampson, Robert J., Patrick Sharkey, and Stephen W. Raudenbush. 2008. "Durable Effects of Concentrated Disadvantage on Verbal Ability Among African-American Children." *Proceedings of the National Academy of Sciences* 105(3): 845–52.

Sanbonmatsu, Lisa, Jeffrey R. Kling, Greg J. Duncan, and Jeanne Brooks-Gunn. 2006. "Neighborhoods and Academic Achievement Results from the Moving to Opportunity Experiment." *Journal of Human Resources* 41(4): 649–91.

Sanbonmatsu, Lisa, Jens Ludwig, Lawrence F. Katz, Lisa A. Gennetian, Greg J. Duncan, Ronald C. Kessler, Emma Adam, Thomas W. McDade, and Stacy Tessler Lindau. 2011. "Moving to Opportunity for Fair Housing Demonstration Program—Final Impacts Evaluation." Washington: U.S. Department of Housing & Urban Development.

Sard, Barbara, and Will Fischer. 2012. "Renters' Tax Credit Would Promote Equity and Advance Balanced Housing Policy." Washington, D.C.: Center on Budget and Policy Priorities.

Sastry, Narayan. 2012. "Neighborhood Effects on Children's Achievement: A Review of Recent Research." In *Oxford Handbook on Child Development and Poverty*, edited by Rosalind B. King and Valerie Maholmes. New York: Oxford University Press.

Schwartz, Heather. 2010. "Housing Policy Is School Policy: Economically Integrative Housing Promotes Academic Success in Montgomery County, MD." New York: The Century Foundation.

Sharkey, Patrick. 2008. "The Intergenerational Transmission of Context." *American Journal of Sociology* 113(4): 931–69.

———. 2012a. "An Alternative Approach to Addressing Selection into and out of Social Settings: Neighborhood Change and African American Children's Economic Outcomes." *Sociological Methods & Research* 41(2): 251–93.

———. 2012b. "Residential Mobility and the Reproduction of Unequal Neighborhoods." *Cityscape* 114(1): 9–32.

———. 2013. *Stuck in Place: Urban Neighborhoods and the End of Progress Toward Racial Equality*. Chicago: University of Chicago Press.

Sharkey, Patrick, and Felix Elwert. 2011. "The Legacy of Disadvantage: Multigenerational Neighborhood Effects on Cognitive Ability." *American Journal of Sociology* 116(6): 1934–81.

Sharkey, Patrick, and Jacob Faber. 2014. "Where, When, Why, and for Whom Do Residential Contexts Matter? Moving Away from the Dichotomous Understanding of Neighborhood Effects." *Annual Review of Sociology* 40: 559–79.

Shroder, Mark. 2002. "Locational Constraint, Housing Counseling, and Successful Lease-Up in a Randomized Housing Voucher Experiment." *Journal of Urban Economics* 51(2): 315–38.

Smeeding, Timothy M., Robert Erikson, and Markus Jantti, eds. 2011. *Persistence, Privilege, and Parenting: The Comparative Study of Intergenerational Mobility*. New York: Russell Sage Foundation.

Solon, Gary. 1992. "Intergenerational Income Mobility in the United States." *American Economic Review* 82(3): 393–408.

———. 2002. "Cross-Country Differences in Intergenerational Earnings Mobility." *Journal of Economic Perspectives* 16(3): 59–66.

Thompson, Mark A. 2001. "Black-White Residential Segregation in Atlanta." In *The Atlanta Paradox*, edited by David L. Sjoquist. New York: Russell Sage Foundation.

Timberlake, Jeffrey M. 2007. "Racial and Ethnic Inequality in the Duration of Children's Exposure to

Neighborhood Poverty and Affluence." *Social Problems* 54(3): 319–42.

Turner, Margery Austin, Jennifer Comey, Daniel Kuehn, and Austin Nichols. 2012. "Residential Mobility, High-Opportunity Neighborhoods, and Outcomes for Low-Income Families: Insights from the Moving to Opportunity Demonstration." Washington: U.S. Department of Housing and Urban Development.

Turner, Margery A., and Stephen L. Ross. 2005. "How Racial Discrimination Affects the Search for Housing." In *The Geography of Opportunity: Race and Housing Choice in Metropolitan America*, edited by Xavier de Souza Briggs. Washington, D.C.: Brookings Institution.

Turner, Margery A., Eric Toder, Rolf Pendall, and Claudia Sharygin. 2013. "How Would Reforming the Mortgage Interest Deduction Affect the Housing Market?" Washington, D.C.: Urban Institute.

Vartanian, Thomas P. 1999. "Adolescent Neighborhood Effects on Labor Market and Economic Outcomes." *Social Service Review* 73(2): 142–67.

Vartanian, Thomas P., and Page W. Buck. 2005. "Childhood and Adolescent Neighborhood Effects on Adult Income: Using Siblings to Examine Differences in Ordinary Least Squares and Fixed-Effect Models." *Social Service Review* 79(1): 60–94.

Votruba, Mark E., and Jeffrey Kling. 2009. "Effects of Neighborhood Characteristics on the Mortality of Black Male Youth: Evidence from Gautreaux, Chicago." *Social Science & Medicine* 68(5): 814–23.

Wimer, Christopher. 2013. "Place Based Policies: Evidence and Mechanisms." Washington: U.S. Department of Health and Human Services.

Wodtke, Geoffrey T, David J. Harding, and Felix Elwert. 2011. "Neighborhood Effects in Temporal Perspective The Impact of Long-Term Exposure to Concentrated Disadvantage on High School Graduation." *American Sociological Review* 76(5): 713–36.

Wolfe, Barbara, Jessica Jakubowski, Robert Haveman, and Marissa Courey. 2012. "The Income and Health Effects of Tribal Casino Gaming on American Indians." *Demography* 49(2): 499–524.

Inequality of Opportunity and Aggregate Economic Performance

KATHARINE BRADBURY AND ROBERT K. TRIEST

Economists have developed an extensive literature examining the relationships between inequality of outcomes and growth, but few research papers have investigated the relationship between inequality of opportunity and growth. That extensive literature finds both positive and negative effects of inequality on growth, as theory predicts. By contrast, inequality of opportunity should be a drag on growth, as it represents less than full utilization of potential resources. Using recently released data on intergenerational mobility in commuting zones within the United States, this paper investigates the relationship between intergenerational mobility measures (as indicators of inequality of opportunity) and economic growth and finds that local areas with higher intergenerational mobility display faster economic growth over the 2000–2013 and 2007–2013 periods. This is true when intergenerational mobility is measured in both relative and, especially, absolute terms. In the reverse direction, the paper provides suggestive evidence that faster growth enhances economic opportunity.

Keywords: intergenerational mobility, economic growth, inequality of opportunity

Income inequality has grown dramatically within many countries in recent decades, raising the question of whether inequality is an integral part of the economic growth process. Paralleling the growth of inequality, as well as the growth of research on inequality and economic growth, has been the emergence of a substantial research literature on inequality of opportunity. Although inequality of opportunity has long been a subject of concern to policymakers and commentators, it is only relatively recently that a formal conceptual and empirical research literature on this topic has developed, and few research papers have explicitly addressed the relationship between inequality of opportunity and economic growth. Despite this, one can see elements of the nexus between inequality of opportunity and economic performance implicit in many analyses of inequality and economic growth, even in some of the earliest related research.

The modern economic literature on the relationship between economic growth and income inequality starts with Simon Kuznets's

Katharine Bradbury is senior economist and policy advisor at the Federal Reserve Bank of Boston. **Robert K. Triest** is vice president and economist at the Federal Reserve Bank of Boston.

The views expressed are those of the authors and do not necessarily represent the positions of the Federal Reserve Bank of Boston or the Federal Reserve System. The authors thank Jared Bernstein, Larry Mishel, participants at the Boston Fed/RSF conference on Inequality of Economic Opportunity, and two anonymous reviewers for helpful comments, and Stephanie Bonds and Sam Richardson for expert research assistance. Direct correspondence to: Katharine Bradbury at katharine.bradbury@bos.frb.org, Research Department, Federal Reserve Bank of Boston, 600 Atlantic Ave., Boston, MA 02210; and Robert K. Triest at robert.triest@bos.frb.org, Research Department, Federal Reserve Bank of Boston, 600 Atlantic Ave., Boston, MA 02210.

1954 American Economic Association Presidential address, in which he not only described the relationship, but also proposed explanations for the patterns he uncovered in the data (Kuznets 1955). He argued that inequality tends to rise in a country's early stages of economic development and observed that it then appears to stabilize and decline as developed nations' economies continue to grow and mature (giving rise to what is now known as the Kuznets curve). Kuznets discussed two major factors involved in the evolution of incomes in developed nations—the cumulative effects of a concentration of savings among high earners and the industrial shift from agriculture to industrial urban settings—both of which would lead to continued widening of the income distribution. However, finding no such widening—indeed documenting declines in inequality in the United States and United Kingdom from the 1920s through 1950—he argued that the inequality-worsening factors were counteracted by other forces embodied in "the dynamism of a *growing* and free economic society" (11, emphasis added).

Among the factors Kuznets cited as contributing to reduced income inequality as growth progresses is the greater ability of people born into an urban industrial economy to "take advantage of opportunities of city life" (15) relative to those who migrated from rural agricultural areas, suggesting that growth might lead to a reduction in what we would now call inequality of opportunity, with a consequent decrease in inequality of outcomes. Kuznets also posited a role for an endogenous policy shift that led to reduced income inequality: "in democratic societies the growing political power of the urban lower-income groups led to a variety of protective and supporting legislation, much of it aimed to counteract the worst effects of rapid industrialization and urbanization and to support the claims of the broad masses for more adequate shares of the growing income of the country" (15). Kuznets saw the "long swing" he observed in inequality as part of the wider process of economic growth and development, with causation running from growth (development) to inequality.

In the sixty years since Kuznets's path-breaking address, a voluminous research literature has developed on the relationship between growth and inequality, and the debate is ongoing regarding the extent to which the Kuznets curve pattern describes the relationship between growth and inequality as a country develops. Even if the Kuznets curve arguably describes how inequality evolves as an economy progresses from a low level of development to an industrial economy, it is clear that a quite different relationship describes the relationship between growth and inequality in high-income countries in recent decades. The pattern of declining inequality in pre-tax pre-transfer family incomes that Kuznets described in 1954 continued in the United States through the 1970s, but has reversed markedly since then, the distribution of U.S. family and household incomes becoming more unequal in the 1980s, 1990s, and 2000s even as average real incomes have continued to rise.

On a theoretical level, inequality might be either positively or negatively related to growth, causality running in either direction, for a number of reasons. Inequality may be associated with incentives for work, risk-taking, and savings, leading to greater economic growth. Or inequality may be associated with loss of social capital and diminished capacity for efficient investment among the poor, leading to diminished economic growth. Given that some mechanisms point to a trade-off between greater equality and growth and others to a complementary relationship, the nature of the relationship is fundamentally a question that must be answered empirically, and may vary over time and space depending on the economic and institutional context. Not surprisingly, researchers in this area have not yet reached a consensus. However, the range of mechanisms through which inequality *of opportunity* may be related to economic growth is more limited, and we argue in this paper—both theoretically and empirically—that inequality of opportunity has a negative effect on economic growth. Because social justice motivations are involved in seeking greater equality of opportunity, it is useful to quantify and distinguish its (positive) role in growth from the mixed role of broader inequality (of outcomes).

In this paper, we review the research literature on the relationship between inequality of opportunity and economic growth and provide new empirical evidence.[1]

ECONOMIC GROWTH AND INEQUALITY (OF OUTCOMES)

We first highlight some of the themes and findings in the research literature on growth and inequality of outcomes that are most pertinent to understanding the relationship between aggregate economic performance and inequality of opportunity, particularly in the recent era (post-Kuznets) of growth accompanying increased inequality of outcomes in advanced economies. We turn to the literature that explicitly focuses on the relationship between inequality of opportunity and aggregate economic performance in the subsequent section. Our review of the literature is by no means comprehensive; readers are referred to the articles and books cited here for additional references.

The main driving forces behind economic growth are increases in the factors of production, including human capital, and changes in technology, operating within an institutional context. To the extent that growth causes changes in income inequality, this causal relationship is likely to come about from inequality being affected by technological change or by factor accumulation and investment. The causality may also run in the opposite direction, with inequality affecting technological change or factor investment. We first consider causal mechanisms from growth to inequality, and then examine mechanisms in the opposite direction.

How Does Economic Growth Affect Inequality of Outcomes?

The increase in inequality that accompanies industrialization in Kuznets' theory is essentially due to technological change. Agreement is widespread that the surge in earnings inequality over the past few decades is due, at least in part, to another technological revolution: changes in information technology that have generated increases in educational and technical skill premiums. Like industrialization, the revolution in information technology has benefited entrepreneurs and investors in sectors related to information technology and in sectors that exploit the new technology in production, as well as workers whose skills complement the new technologies. Something like the mechanism posited by Kuznets with respect to the shift from rural farm to industrial city seems to be in effect, but occurring at an advanced stage of development. In this case, it is not growth per se, but the specific source of economic growth, skill-biased technical change, that generates inequality.

Skill-biased technical change does not necessarily result in an increase in income inequality. Claudia Goldin and Lawrence Katz (2008) depict relative wages in the United States over the course of the twentieth century as being determined by the outcome of a race between technological change and increases in educational attainment. Skill-biased technological change increases demand for and hence the wages of highly educated workers relative to their less educated counterparts, leading toward an increase in earnings inequality. Increased educational attainment raises the supply of highly educated workers relative to less educated workers and leads toward a compression of relative wages across educational groups. Goldin and Katz argue that during roughly the first three-quarters of the century, increases in educational attainment outpaced the increase in demand for highly educated workers in the United States, leading to a decrease in inequality. However, in recent decades, at least through the 1990s, the demand for highly educated workers generated by technological change has dominated the increase in educational attainment, leading to an increase in the educational wage premium and a consequent increase in earnings inequality.

Both technological change and increases in educational attainment generate economic growth. That growth, however, increases in-

---

[1]. Research on the relationship between inequality and growth at a business cycle frequency is beyond the scope of the paper. Earlier research documented an empirical regularity: inequality rose during recessions and tended to fall during expansions; this empirical regularity broke down after the 1980s, as inequality rose during expansions as well as recessions.

equality only if increases in educational attainment do not keep up with the increase in demand for highly educated workers that accompanies skill-biased technological change, or if other aspects of the growth process generate higher inequality.

In addition to industrialization, Kuznets' conception of growth also involved the accumulation of savings to fund investment; he saw such accumulation as an additional force elevating inequality as development proceeded. Growth allowed high-income individuals to save, and savings concentrations both raised investment levels, augmenting growth, and fed back to widen inequality as investment returns accrued to the high-income investors. By contrast, Thomas Piketty's (2014) hypothesis that inequality among wealth holders rises whenever the rate of return on financial capital exceeds the rate of economic growth implies that strong growth can *reduce* inequality, other things (including the financial rate of return) equal.

Kuznets and other researchers suggest another path through which growth can affect inequality: as economic growth raises incomes in a democracy, expanding political power of lower-income groups can bring about a shift in policy toward "sharing the wealth," either directly through taxes and transfers or indirectly through public financing of investments in both physical and human capital. More generally, the growth process itself may bring about institutional changes that can alter the distribution of economic rewards. Frank Levy and Peter Temin (2007) attribute much of the increase in American inequality since 1980 to policy changes that occurred in the 1970s and 1980s, including a falling real minimum wage and a weakening of unions. They attribute the policy changes, in turn, to the post-1973 productivity slowdown and stagflation of the 1970s. In their model, slow growth led to policy changes that increased inequality.

How Does Inequality Affect Economic Growth?

Skill-biased technical change appears to be a key driving force behind growth and recent increases in inequality, but inequality in turn may affect the investment response to the incentives created by skill-biased technical change. Philippe Aghion, Eve Caroli, and Cecilia Garcia-Penalosa (1999) present a growth model in which they assume away opportunities for borrowing and lending. The lack of a borrowing and lending market results in wealthy individuals facing a lower marginal return on investment (because of decreasing returns) than poor individuals, who by definition have limited funds to invest. In this model—and another in which the authors examine capital market "imperfections"—inequality reduces aggregate productivity and growth because it results in an inefficient allocation of investment; in this context, they note that redistribution can create investment opportunities and enhance growth. The form of inequality that matters here is essentially inequality of opportunity. Inequality, combined with imperfect capital markets or frictions, may interfere with efficient investment in areas such as schooling, health, and entrepreneurship. The friction that prevents the poor from taking advantage of investment opportunities may literally be a borrowing constraint, or it may be a related factor such as lack of information about investment opportunities, greater perceived level of risk associated with the investment, or insufficient availability of family resources to insure against possible downside risks of the investment. When inequality prevents efficient investments from being undertaken, growth is reduced relative to what it would otherwise be.

Educational attainment provides an example of such missed investment opportunities. College-going and completion result from decisions made by students and their families, the opportunities for schooling that they encounter, and public policies that shape those opportunities. The increase in the educational wage premium provides an incentive for people to invest in more years of schooling, but recent research, often based on a comparison across cohorts in the National Longitudinal Survey of Youth, suggests that students from relatively disadvantaged backgrounds are not able to take full advantage of the high expected rate of return to educational attainment because family background is playing an increasingly important role in educational attainment in the United States. Martha Bailey and Susan Dynarski (2011) find that college completion rates are higher for the U.S. cohort born around 1980 than those for the cohort born in the early 1960s, but that the increase is much greater for children born in high-income families than for their low-income counterparts. Philippe Belley and Lance Lochner (2007) find a similar empirical pattern, and develop a model that allows for borrowing constraints to play a role in college attendance. They conclude that their data are consistent with borrowing constraints having become more widespread over time. Gonzalo Castex and Evgenia Dechter (2014) find that although the economic return to formal education increased between the two cohorts, the return to cognitive ability (measured by aptitude test scores) decreased, suggesting that barriers to formal educational attainment are now more costly to students who confront them. Mary Anne Fox, Brooke Connolly, and Thomas Snyder (2005) report NCES data indicating that only 29 percent of low-SES children with eighth grade test scores in the top quartile in 1988 attained a bachelor's degree (BA) by 2000, but that 74 percent of high-SES high test-score children did so; indeed, the low-SES children with high test scores were less likely to attain a BA than high-SES children with test scores in the lowest quartile (30 percent). The inefficiencies represented by such wasted resources are a drag on growth.

One of the key pathways through which economists hypothesize that inequality positively affects growth is its role in creating incentives for effort and risk-taking. That is, when an economy's reward structure provides greater returns to those who work hard or to those who take risk than to those who do not, inequality is higher and the induced extra effort or risk-taking helps propel the economy forward. Arthur Okun (1975) wrote of "the big tradeoff" between equality and efficiency: "The contrasts between American families in living standards and in material wealth reflect a system of rewards and penalties that is intended to encourage effort and channel it into socially productive activity" (1).

In addition to inefficient investment on the downside and growth-promoting incentives on the upside, inequality may influence growth via its effects on volatility. Aghion, Caroli, and Garcia-Penalosa (1999) model the way in which unequal access to investment opportunities and credit market imperfections can lead to persistent credit cycles and macroeconomic volatility. Joseph Stiglitz argues that "inequality is associated with more frequent and more severe boom-and-bust cycles that make our economy more volatile and vulnerable" (2013). Michael Kumhof and Romain Ranciere (2010) and Barry Cynamon and Steven Fazzari (2013) put forward models of this process. The degree to which this volatility manifests itself solely in more frequent or wider-swinging business cycles is beyond the scope of this paper, but several of these authors argue that such volatility also reduces long-term growth at the least by slowing the recovery after downturns.

A fourth channel is via inequality's effect on demand. Sarah Voitchovsky's 2009 *Handbook* overview says that lower inequality in the form of a strong middle class (in terms of numbers and income levels) supports demand for a nation's output, necessary to maintain growth. Stiglitz (2012) argues that the weakness of the U.S. middle class led to soft consumer demand and held back the recovery from the Great Recession. To the degree that inequality takes the form of larger increases in income among the rich, these theories build on the rich's having a lower marginal propensity to consume than those further down the income ladder (see Dynan, Skinner, and Zeldes 2004). Laura Carvalho and Armon Rezai (2015) document that "lowering wage income inequality always increases aggregate demand."

Another channel through which inequality may affect growth is through increasing the demand for policies that attenuate inequality. Kuznets (1955) saw this as one of the mechanisms that would eventually lead to reduced inequality as economies develop. Voitchovsky (2009) provides a thoughtful review of the literature, and notes that the relationship between inequality and growth through the redistribution channel is ambiguous. Although high marginal tax rates may discourage capital investment, risk-taking, and labor supply (reducing growth), some redistributive spending may be growth enhancing. For example, spending on subsidized education for low-income families may reduce inefficiencies arising from inequality of opportunity. Moreover, increased inequality may not result in increased political pressure for redistribution. Indeed, among some commentators in the United States in recent years, concern has focused on the opposite outcome: they ask whether inequality has risen so high that the rich have been able to take over political institutions and shift policymaking in their favor to such a degree that it contributes to greater inequality. Daron Acemoglu and James Robinson (2012) emphasize the importance of institutions in the growth process, contrasting the generally negative effect on growth of "extractive" institutions that mainly benefit the small, closed group that controls them with the positive effect on growth of "inclusive" institutions that are controlled by and benefit a large open group. Increases in high-end inequality might result in the concentration of political power among a fairly small group controlling a large share of income and wealth, with the potential for the creation and control of extractive economic and political institutions by this group. Along these lines, Stiglitz (2012) argues that pressure for tax cuts for corporations and wealthy individuals has undermined the ability of the government to fund public infrastructure as well as income-support programs, the lack of which harms growth.

Whether redistributive policies and institutions arise in response to increased inequality, they may nonetheless affect the relationship between growth and inequality. Gary Burtless (2003) maintains that the relatively modest transfer system and labor market regulations in the United States compared with other G7 countries likely both boosted U.S. employment growth relative to the other countries and also resulted in a greater increase in inequality in the United States. Burtless notes that, for the most part, U.S. labor market policies and institutions did not directly cause the increase in inequality. Instead, the U.S. policies resulted in the economic forces pushing toward greater inequality having a greater impact in the United States than they did in other countries with more generous transfer systems and more restrictive regulations and institutions. In his view, U.S. policies resulted in a more positive correlation between growth and inequality than existed in other advanced economies. A recent Organization for Economic Cooperation and Development report (2012) attempts to identify policy changes that can "yield a double dividend in terms of boosting the gross domestic product (GDP) per capita and reducing income inequality" (181).

Finally, inequality is part of the economic setting in which growth occurs. In addition to the potential for high inequality to result in redistributive policies that could hinder growth by reducing incentives to make effort and take risk, high inequality might result in other changes to the economic environment that are not conducive to growth. Among the factors Voitchovsky (2009) discusses as being potentially exacerbated by increased inequality are political instability, loss of social capital, corruption, and crime rates.

WHAT ARE THE EMPIRICAL RELATIONSHIPS?

The conceptual and theoretical literature provides explanations for why growth and inequality may be either positively or negatively related, with the sign possibly varying over countries or over time for any given country. As discussed, the causal direction between growth and inequality may run either or both ways. Given the theoretical ambiguity regarding the relationship, the lack of a clear consensus on the empirical relationship between growth and inequality is not surprising.

Most of the empirical literature attempts to identify the causal effect of inequality on growth. Abhijit Banerjee and Esther Duflo (2003) review many of the econometric specifications used by previous researchers, and find them all wanting. Their most basic criticism is that researchers have generally estimated linear specifications, but the theories that Banerjee and Duflo review lead to nonlinear and possibly nonmonotonic relationships. Banerjee and Duflo present results from nonparametric estimation of the relationship, showing that growth is an inverted U-shaped function of changes (rather than levels) in inequality, with the peak of the curve at close to the point with no change in inequality. This implies that either increases or decreases in inequality will result in lower growth. Banerjee and Duflo caution against giving a causal interpretation to this empirical relationship due to identification problems.

Voitchovsky (2005) explores whether the effect of inequality on growth varies by the type of inequality. She finds that inequality at the top of the distribution, which might reflect incentives for investment and risk-taking, is positively associated with growth. In contrast, inequality lower in the distribution is negatively associated with growth. This might reflect lack of opportunities for educational investment by the poor and possible social or political unrest associated with inequality. Federico Cingano argues that "what matters most [for the negative effect of income inequality on growth] is the gap between low-income households and the rest of the population"; he finds evidence that "increased income disparities depress skills development among individuals with poorer parental education background, both in terms of the quantity of education attained (for example, years of schooling), and in terms of its quality (that is, skill proficiency)" (2014, 6). Era Dabla-Norris and her colleagues (2015) similarly find that an increase in the income share of the bottom 20 percent of the income distribution (the poor) is associated with higher GDP growth in a cross section of nations, and that growth in the top income share reduces it.

In a recent working paper, Jonathan Ostry, Andrew Berg, and Charalambos Tsangarides (2014) investigate the empirical relationship between inequality and growth using a dataset that allows them to separate inequality in market (pre-tax and transfer) income from the redistribution that occurs through the tax and transfer system. They find that net (after tax and transfer) inequality is negatively related to economic growth. Redistribution through the tax and transfer system is found to be positively related to growth for most of the range of distribution observed in the data, but is negatively related for the most strongly redistributive countries. This suggests that the effect of redistribution on enhanced opportunities for lower-income families and on social and political stability outweighs any negative effects on growth by damping incentives.

Although most of the research on the effect of inequality on growth uses cross-country data, a small number of papers estimate the relationship based on intranational comparisons. Using a panel of data on U.S. states, Ugo Panizza (2002) finds some evidence of a negative association between inequality and growth. However, he notes that the results are not robust to changes in specification. Also using U.S. state-level panel data, Mark Frank (2009) estimates a positive effect of inequality on growth. Frank's finding is driven by inequality in the upper end of the income distribution, and data limitations prevent him from investigating the effect of low-end inequality. Citing Voitchovsky (2005), Frank acknowledges that inequality in the lower end of the income distribution might have the opposite effect. In a similar vein, Roy van der Wiede and Branko Milanovic (2014) investigate how inequality affects growth, but broaden the focus to examine growth at a range of income percentiles, using state-level measures within the United States. They find that high overall inequality hurts income growth among the poor and, in most specifications, helps income growth among the rich. When they disaggregate inequality into top-half and bottom-half inequality (measured over the richest and poorest 40 percent, respectively), they find it is mostly inequality among the rich that is holding back income growth among the poor.

In addition to academic papers that estimate empirical relationships, two recent policy-oriented literature reviews offer frameworks within which to interpret much of the literature discussed above. Heather Boushey and Carter Price (2014) note that a great deal of research lines up behind the empirical regularity that long-term economic growth is harmed by inequality, but that this is not the case for short-term growth.

Jared Bernstein (2013) posits four classes of causal mechanisms to categorize the forces discussed that link inequality and growth: supply side (how inequality affects the quality and quantity of inputs and hence growth), demand side (lower marginal propensity to consume among the rich slows growth as inequality rises), political economy (rising inequality augments the political and economic power of the rich who reduce investment in shared prosperity), and credit bubbles and busts (inequality leads the poor to borrow to maintain consumption, making them vulnerable to downturns and the economy more volatile).

One would expect the causal channels relating intranational inequality to intranational growth to differ somewhat from those relating inequality and growth across nations. A key reason for this difference is that trade of goods and services, and flows of financial capital and workers, are much greater at the intranational level than they are across countries. One implication is that the savings channel is likely to be less important at the intranational level. This is also true of the demand channel, though perhaps to a somewhat lesser extent. Endogeneity of inequality may also be more of a problem in intranational data than at the national level. The easy geographic mobility of workers within countries provides another potential channel relating inequality and growth, though this seems most likely to be in the growth to inequality direction. If high growth attracts relatively low-income migrants seeking economic opportunity, this might lead to a positive relationship between growth and inequality of outcomes. However, the enhanced labor market prospects associated with growth might be associated with reduced inequality of opportunity.

RELATIONSHIP BETWEEN INEQUALITY OF OPPORTUNITY AND GROWTH

Virtually all of the empirical work relating inequality of opportunity and macroeconomic growth examines causation running from inequality of opportunity to growth.

How Does Inequality of Opportunity Affect Growth?

The underlying causal mechanism for inequality of opportunity to influence growth is that inequality of opportunity prevents some potential workers or entrepreneurs in the economy from developing their full capacity, generating wasted resources and hence lower-than-possible output. As discussed, for example, the inefficiencies represented by unequal access to education constitute a drag on growth. By improving the efficiency of resource use, increased equality of opportunity increases steady state output in the economy, and increases the economy's growth rate during the transition to the higher steady state. To the extent that opening up opportunities for individuals to develop and use their talents also affects the rate of technological change or generates externalities, as Robert Lucas (1988) finds, then a sustained higher rate of growth may result. Although various mechanisms suggest both positive and negative effects of inequality of outcomes on growth, the arguments for how inequality might increase growth are not applicable to inequality of opportunity. Theory suggests that inequality of opportunity will have a negative effect on economic growth.

Three recent papers attempt to quantify the effect of inequality of opportunity on economic performance. One aims to measure directly the output added via the increased opportunity gained by women and blacks over the period since 1960 in the United States. The other two grew out of the much larger literature (discussed earlier) examining the effect of inequality (of outcomes) on growth. The authors of both of these latter papers decompose total inequality into two components—one of which measures inequality of opportunity—and investigate their effects on growth.

Voitchovsky's (2009) *Handbook* review includes a discussion of how inequality at the bottom of the distribution is often associated with inequality of opportunity, which in turn keeps the poor from contributing fully to the nation's accumulation process and thereby stunts growth. In addition to credit constraints, which might prevent investment in education and also stunt entrepreneurship, those at the bottom of the distribution may face diminished incentives and opportunities to engage in productive economic activity. Voitchovsky cites relatively high rates of criminal activity and childbearing as resulting from the poor facing a diminished opportunity cost of forgoing market work. More generally, inequality of opportunity may be detrimental to the functioning of a market economy by diluting social capital and the sense of trust and fair dealing that is necessary for well-functioning markets.

One way in which inequality of opportunity may arise is through unequal access to advantageous professions. Chang-Tai Hsieh and his colleagues (2013) measure the macroeconomic consequences of the "remarkable" convergence in the occupational distribution between 1960 and 2008. They start from the premise that innate talent for different types of work cannot possibly be so differentially distributed across race and gender as to explain the very unbalanced occupational distributions in 1960 of white women, black women, and black men, compared with white men. They note, for example, that 94 percent of doctors and lawyers were men in 1960. Therefore, they argue, these nonwhite or nonmale groups were not able to contribute their full potential to the economy, held back by occupational barriers. These barriers may reflect differences in access (geographic or social) to high quality K–12 schools, social forces steering some individuals into particular occupations, differential early-life investments in health or other important inputs into human capital, workers' preferences, or discrimination in either education or hiring.

The authors estimate how much occupational barriers declined over the almost fifty years they study and what that decline contributed to productivity. They find that changes in occupational barriers facing blacks and women "account for 15 to 20 percent of growth in aggregate output per worker since 1960" (Hsieh et al. 2013, 1).[2] They go on to note that three-quarters of the gain reflects the movement of white women into high-skilled occupations, largely because white women make up a much larger proportion of the population than blacks. They indicate that these productivity gains can come from reducing misallocation across occupations and from boosting average human capital investments, and go on to estimate that most of the gains come from reduced misallocation. In concluding, they say that though the paper focuses on the gains from reducing barriers facing women and blacks, they "suspect that barriers facing children from less affluent families and regions have worsened in the last few decades," leaving the issue for future work (2013, 43).

Gustavo Marrero and Juan Rodriguez (2013) and Francisco Ferreira and his colleagues (2014) take a very different approach from Hsieh and his colleagues (2013) in estimating the impact of inequality of opportunity on growth. These two papers have similar methodologies, the former applying it to panel data on selected U.S. states, the latter to panel data on nations around the globe. The growth models in these papers posit that growth in any period is influenced by many beginning-of-period characteristics and conditions, including the degree of inequality in the economy.

In these papers, the inequality of opportunity concept builds on a literature (especially Roemer 1993) that distinguishes individual circumstances—such as race and parental socioeconomic status—which are not in an individual's control, and individual "effort," which stands in for the range of factors influencing economic success that an individual can make decisions about, including occupational choice and hours of work.[3] Inequality resulting from differential effort (as described in the earlier discussion of inequality of outcomes and growth) is seen as providing incentives for people to work hard, take risks, and invest in education, and hence is expected to promote growth.

Following much of the literature on inequality of opportunity (as discussed in the introduction to this issue), the authors decompose total inequality into a component associated with inequality of opportunity and a residual component that is labeled inequality of effort. The measure of inequality of opportunity used in these studies is based on determining how much of overall inequality is due to a set of measured circumstances beyond the individual's control; both papers take the ex ante type-compensation approach to measuring inequality of opportunity (see Roemer and

---

2. They also note that reducing barriers to zero would provide further productivity gains.

3. Hsieh and colleagues build their paper on the idea that occupational choice may be constrained by circumstances. However, because *effort* is measured as a residual component of inequality, this apparent disagreement is irrelevant in the current context.

Trannoy, forthcoming). Marrero and Rodriguez (2013) use father's education and race as the circumstances they use to compute their measure of inequality of opportunity; Ferreira and his colleagues (2014) use gender, race or ethnicity, the language spoken at home, religion, caste, nationality of origin, immigration status, and region of birth or of residence (with two to five of these indicators available for each nation). As the authors acknowledge, the inequality associated with a limited set of circumstances will tend to underestimate true inequality of opportunity, leaving "too much" inequality for the residual.

Once they decompose total inequality into components associated with opportunity and effort, the authors expect inequality of opportunity to exert a negative influence on growth and inequality of effort to add positively to growth. Measured inequality of opportunity is likely to reflect factors that are associated with reduced growth, such as market imperfections that lead to too little investment in the human capital of low-circumstance children (such as children with low-education parents or children of disadvantaged minority parents) relative to children with more positive circumstances. The association between measured inequality of effort and growth is less clear. Measured inequality of effort will partly reflect the incentives to work hard and take risks, which will be positively correlated with economic activity. However, because it is a residual category, it will also reflect unmeasured aspects of inequality of opportunity (circumstances), the effects of institutions and policies that affect income, luck, and other factors not associated with effort, so its overall correlation with economic activity is not clear.

Marrero and Rodriguez, using data from the Panel Study of Income Dynamics for a subset of U.S. states with adequate numbers of observations, find "robust support for a negative relationship between inequality of opportunity and growth and a positive relationship between inequality of effort and growth." They interpret their findings as follows: "returns to effort may encourage people to invest in education and to exert an effort, while inequality of opportunity may not favor human and physical capital accumulation in the more talented individuals." Marrero and Rodriguez further argue that their results are consistent with "prediction of [theoretical] models with multiple steady states and borrowing constraints. . . . people with initial adverse circumstances would be likely exposed to barriers for accessing credit or education, independently of their talent or effort, which would undermine subsequent economic growth" (2013, 120).[4]

Marrero and Rodriguez say that their results call for proper design of policy, in the sense that improving equality of opportunity has positive benefits and that policies that interfere with incentives on the effort side may have negative consequences. They note that affirmative action, which is an attempt to reduce inequality of opportunity, is seen by some as reverse discrimination which may have negative effects on effort across the board. But, as Voitchovsky observes, a highly unequal playing field also discourages effort among the disadvantaged, contributing to inefficiency.

Ferreira and his colleagues (2014) characterize the literature as having two basic foci, one in which the effects of inequality operate through markets and the other in which they operate through the political process. But once they decompose total inequality into "a component associated with inequality of opportunity and a residual component (notionally related to inequality arising from effort differences)" they expect, like Marrero and Rodriguez, to find the former has a negative effect on growth and the latter a positive effect (2014, 2). Their failure to find support for either of these hypothesized relationships in two panels of nations may reflect the spotty set of circumstance variables they eke out of their income and expenditure survey sample and their demographic and health survey sample. Or it may be that the estimated relationships do not apply across nations with different institutional backdrops.

With these papers as background, we exam-

---

4. Marrero and Rodriguez note that Barro's result of negative relationship between growth and inequality in less developed nations might reflect a bigger role of inequality of opportunity there.

ine the relationship between inequality of opportunity and growth in a cross section of U.S. commuting zones (CZs), geographic areas representing aggregations of counties that coincide with metropolitan areas where they exist, and exhaust U.S. territory by also including rural areas.[5] This level of geography is one the earlier research has not examined. In addition, we use measures of inequality of opportunity new to this literature. Using rich and extensive tax return data for thirty-year-old "children" in 2011–2012 matched to their parents' tax returns when they were growing up, Raj Chetty and his colleagues (2014a) calculate various measures of intergenerational mobility, indicating how the thirty-year-olds have fared economically, compared with their parents' place in the U.S. income distribution during their childhood. Intergenerational mobility is strongly related to equality of opportunity, with the income of an individual's parents when she or he was growing up taken as the measure of circumstances. That is, intergenerational mobility quantifies the differences in adult outcomes between children of rich and poor parents, just as a between-group measure of inequality of opportunity would for circumstance groups defined by parental income.[6] However, as discussed in the introduction, measures of intergenerational mobility and indices of inequality of opportunity, such as those both Marrero and Rodriguez and Ferreira and his colleagues use, capture somewhat different concepts. Measures of inequality of opportunity depend on inequality of circumstances as well as the relationship between circumstances and outcomes; only the latter is captured by measures of intergenerational mobility. Nonetheless, Miles Corak reviews the literature and concludes that "indices of inequality of opportunity are in fact strongly correlated with indicators of intergenerational mobility, be it in earnings or education" (2013, 85).

We focus on Chetty and colleagues' (2014a) preferred measure of "absolute upward mobility," which indicates the rank in the national children's income distribution (around age thirty) expected for a child growing up in a specific CZ whose parent was at the 25th percentile of the national parent distribution. Because it measures absolute mobility, it captures the effects of both the rate of income growth within a CZ compared with the nation (because parent and child ranks are measured in the national distributions) and the degree of reranking of children's income relative to the ordering of their parents' income.

We also present results using the Chetty and colleagues' measure of relative mobility, which is based on the difference in outcomes between children from the top of the income distribution within a CZ and those at the bottom of the distribution. As Chetty and his colleagues point out, this measure may be driven by high levels of absolute (downward) mobility among the rich as well as by high degrees of absolute (upward) mobility among the poor. Following Jo Blanden, Paul Gregg, and Lindsey Macmillan (2007), we rescale Chetty and colleagues' relative measure so that it is higher when intergenerational mobility is greater.[7]

We combine economic data from the U.S. Bureau of Economic Analysis (2014) and demographic data from decennial censuses (U.S. Census Bureau 2014), in both cases aggregated to CZs from the county level, with mobility and inequality measures from Chetty and his colleagues (2014c). Table A1 reports the sample characteristics of the variables included in the analysis. Because the mobility measures refer to one cohort (children born in the early 1980s

---

5. Our analysis includes only 709 of 741 CZs nationwide, because it is limited to the CZs for which Chetty and his colleagues (2014c) publish measures of mobility, which they do only for CZs with at least 250 observations on children matched to parents' tax forms. These 709 CZs contain 99.96 percent of the U.S. population in 2000.

6. Paolo Brunori, Francisco Ferreira, and Vito Peragine (2013) note that the intergenerational elasticity is "very closely related to" between-group inequality when the groups are defined in terms of parental income.

7. Chetty and colleagues' (2014a) relative measure is the elasticity of child rank with respect to parent rank (in their corresponding national income distributions) and hence is higher when children's and parents' situations are more closely tied, that is, when intergenerational mobility is lower.

who are about age thirty in 2011–2012), we estimate a growth model in the cross section.

Table 1 reports selected coefficient estimates from a simplified growth model. Following Marrero and Rodriguez and Ferreira and colleagues, the dependent variable is growth in per capita income; in panel A, growth is measured from 2000 to 2013; in panel B, the period is shortened, from 2007 to 2013. The first explanatory variable is the mobility measure, proxying inequality of opportunity. The other explanatory variables represent conditions in the CZ at the beginning of the growth period; for inequality, it is the Gini measure of overall inequality measured across the parental generation in the CZ and hence the inequality experienced by the children's generation when they were growing up with their parents. Like other authors, we include beginning-of-period per capita income in the growth regressions to allow for convergence. We include the lagged dependent variable to control for persistent unmeasured CZ-specific influences on growth because we lack the ability to estimate panel regressions. To control for exogenous (to the CZ) factors related to the CZ's industry mix, we include a variable equal to the pace of employment growth that would occur if each industry in the CZ grew at its U.S. pace.[8] For estimated coefficients, see table 1.

In all the regressions, we include regional fixed effects for the nine census divisions. The regressions in columns 2 and 4 for both periods also include a set of demographic control variables: the age mix of the CZ population, the mix of educational attainments in the CZ population, and the labor force participation rates of men and women in the CZ, all as of the beginning of the period in 2000 (or before the beginning of the period in the case of the 2007 to 2013 regressions). Because inequality of opportunity is hypothesized to affect economic growth through its negative effect on human capital accumulation, especially among the poor (those with limited opportunities), it is important to control for such human capital characteristics in the CZ at the start of the growth period.[9] The complete regression results, including the estimated coefficients on these demographic variables, are available from the authors on request.

The estimates in columns 1 and 2 show a statistically significant positive coefficient on absolute mobility in explaining economic growth in either period, indicating a strongly negative effect of inequality of opportunity on growth. Columns 1 and 2 also document a modest positive effect on 2000 to 2013 growth of overall inequality (Gini), but not for 2007 to 2013 growth (panel B). Relative mobility (columns 3 and 4) obtains moderately positive estimated coefficients in the growth equations, except in column 4 of panel B—for growth from 2007 to 2013 and including demographic controls—where the estimated coefficient is indistinguishable from zero. Unexpectedly, the estimated coefficient on the Gini (overall inequality) is negative when controlling for relative rather than absolute mobility (columns 3 and 4).

The effect of both relative and absolute mobility on growth is what the literature hypothesizes; the effect of overall inequality, however, does not consistently match the hypothesized positive incentive effects of inequality on growth. Predicted employment growth obtains a positive coefficient (significantly different from zero in both periods), suggesting that industry mix (and the national performance of each industry) has a strong influence on area per capita income growth. The beginning-of-period per capita income level is negatively as-

---

8. That is, predicted employment growth is equal to the weighted average of U.S. industry growth rates, where the weights are the fraction of CZ employment in each industry. Industries for which a CZ's data are missing are assumed to grow at the overall U.S. pace. The U.S. growth rates refer to the 2001 to 2010 span and CZ industry mix refers to 2001 in the 2000 to 2010 regression because the Bureau of Economic Analysis shifted from the Standard Industrial Classification (SIC) system to the North American Industry Classification System (NAICS) in 2001; the U.S. growth rates are between 2007 and 2012 for the 2007 to 2012 growth period.

9. Note also that the 2000 educational composition data do not reflect the educational attainment of the child generation whose mobility is being measured, because the census reports education data for population age twenty-five and older (the child generation is age eighteen or nineteen in 2000).

Table 1. Regressions of Growth on Mobility

	(1)	(2)	(3)	(4)
Panel A	\multicolumn{4}{c}{Per capita income growth, 2000–2013}			
Absolute mobility	2.353***	2.498***		
	(0.188)	(0.212)		
Relative mobility			0.529***	0.338*
			(0.159)	(0.161)
Gini (inequality) of parental income	23.502+	31.384*	−31.070*	−16.086
	(13.338)	(14.509)	(13.797)	(15.273)
Per capita income, 2000	−1.664***	−1.228***	−1.425***	−0.734*
	(0.178)	(0.304)	(0.195)	(0.330)
Per capita income growth, 1990–2000	−0.310***	−0.266***	−0.400***	−0.369***
	(0.080)	(0.077)	(0.088)	(0.084)
Predicted employment growth, 2001–2013	1.057***	0.882***	1.301***	1.275***
	(0.196)	(0.204)	(0.216)	(0.220)
Constant	2.519	−17.287	85.198***	44.712
	(12.505)	(36.576)	(14.146)	(40.639)
2000 demographics[a]	No	Yes	No	Yes
Regional fixed effects	Yes	Yes	Yes	Yes
Observations	709	709	709	709
R^2	0.500	0.548	0.397	0.460
Panel B	\multicolumn{4}{c}{Per capita income growth, 2007–2013}			
Absolute mobility	1.145***	1.145***		
	(0.105)	(0.118)		
Relative mobility			0.215*	0.124
			(0.084)	(0.084)
Gini (inequality) of parental income	−8.324	−0.934	−38.064***	−25.666**
	(7.250)	(8.027)	(7.199)	(8.121)
Per capita income, 2007	−0.641***	−0.386**	−0.516***	−0.220+
	(0.070)	(0.117)	(0.075)	(0.123)
Per capita income growth, 2000–2007	0.279***	0.161**	0.398***	0.250***
	(0.051)	(0.055)	(0.054)	(0.058)
Predicted employment growth, 2007–2013	0.757***	0.690***	0.767***	0.873***
	(0.179)	(0.179)	(0.193)	(0.190)
Constant	−12.561+	−17.312	25.152***	10.652
	(6.466)	(19.256)	(7.437)	(20.939)
2000 demographics[a]	No	Yes	No	Yes
Regional fixed effects	Yes	Yes	Yes	Yes
Observations	709	709	709	709
R^2	0.485	0.535	0.403	0.473

Source: Authors' calculations based on U.S. Census Bureau 2014, U.S. Bureau of Economic Analysis 2014, and Chetty, Hendren, Kline, and Saez 2014c.

[a] 2000 demographics include proportion of population with less than and more than a high school degree, proportion of population under age fifteen, age fifteen to twenty-four, and over age fifty-four, male and female labor force participation rates, and logarithm of population. For the 2007–2013 growth regressions (panel B), the population measure refers to 2007.

+$p < 0.10$; *$p < 0.05$; **$p < 0.01$; ***$p < 0.001$

sociated with subsequent growth in both periods, suggesting income convergence over time among the CZs, other things equal. The lagged dependent variable obtains a negative coefficient in the 2000 to 2013 period and a positive coefficient for growth between 2007 and 2013; the latter period is only six years, starts at the pre-recession peak, and covers the Great Recession and several years of recovery, so the estimates may reflect cyclical responses as well as (or instead of) the longer term relationships likely to be captured in the 2000 to 2013 period. The additional growth regressions that follow analyze only the longer 2000 to 2013 period because previous research suggests that it is in the longer term that inequality (in our case, inequality of opportunity proxied by mobility) affects growth. Indeed, even the 2000 to 2013 period might be construed as only medium term, but we are constrained by the timing of our mobility measures and beginning in 2000 allows the growth period to be, to some degree, later than the mobility period (mid-1990s to 2011).

Building on Sarah Voitchovsky's (2009) insight that the effect of inequality on growth differs depending on the part of the income distribution on which the inequality measure focuses, table 2 displays regression results when we explore alternative measures of inequality, focused on different parts of the income distribution. That is, rather than controlling only for overall inequality (Gini) and mobility in the growth regressions, we examine also the impact on growth of inequality measured at the bottom, middle, or top of the distribution. A simple bottom- and top-inequality measure is the ratio of 90th to 50th percentile (parent) income and the ratio of 50th to 10th percentile income in the CZ. Alternatively, a middle-class variable measures the proportion of the CZ (parental generation) population with incomes between the 25th and 75th percentiles of the nationwide parental distribution. A measure of very-top-income tallies the fraction of CZ income held by the richest 1 percent of parents.

Both the middle-class proportion and the top 1 percent share of income obtain negative coefficients when controlling for absolute mobility (column 1), but coefficients indistinguishable from zero when relative mobility is included (column 3). Voitchovsky cites reasons for either positive or negative effects on growth of a concentration of income at the top, and the negative estimated coefficient provides support for her political-economy story of co-option of government tax and transfer policy by the rich to the detriment of investments in both human and physical capital (infrastructure) that might benefit middle class and lower-income residents and thereby foster growth.

The negative sign on the middle class is the opposite of what would be expected based on Voitchovsky's "channels," which posit that the size and income level of the middle class should be positively associated with growth for both political economy reasons and via the strength of consumer demand. However, a demand-based argument is much weaker for relatively small, open-economy areas like commuting zones (versus nations), where the strength of local demand is not likely to have a direct influence on growth by stimulating local production. Furthermore, while the Gini and the top 1 percent measures reflect the income distribution within the CZ, the proportion middle class tallies the proportion of CZ residents in the middle range of the *national* parental income distribution, which reflects the degree to which the central tendency of the CZ distribution differs from the national as well as how bunched CZ residents are in the local middle.

Greater inequality in both the top and bottom of the income distribution enhances growth when controlling also for absolute mobility (column 3) but has effects indistinguishable from zero when relative mobility is included (column 4). Any of these alternative inequality measures leave the estimated coefficients on relative or absolute mobility positive and significantly different from zero.

As noted earlier, the absolute mobility measure includes changes in ranks of CZ children relative to their parents, which will partially reflect faster or slower growth of incomes in a CZ relative to the nation. To test whether the positive relationship between absolute mobility and growth documented in table 1 is due solely to the undoubted correlation between

Table 2. Regressions of Growth on Mobility and Alternative Inequality Measures

	Dependent Variable: Per Capita Income Growth, 2000–2013				
	(1)	(2)	(3)	(4)	(5)
Absolute mobility	2.886***		2.934***		
	(0.233)		(0.223)		
Relative mobility		0.288+		0.380*	
		(0.172)		(0.168)	
Residuals (see text)					1.892***
					(0.350)
Gini (inequality) of parental income	55.014*	−10.219			14.960
	(26.139)	(28.431)			(16.252)
Parental middle class	−51.486**	18.887			
	(19.784)	(21.235)			
Top 1 percent income share	−0.523+	−0.001			
	(0.287)	(0.316)			
Parent income ratio 90th percentile to 50th			17.295***	2.236	
			(3.312)	(3.515)	
Parent income ratio 50th percentile to 10th			9.083***	−0.531	
			(2.416)	(2.605)	
Per capita income, 2000	−1.151***	−0.721*	−1.408***	−0.819*	−1.294***
	(0.321)	(0.354)	(0.299)	(0.329)	(0.338)
Per capita income growth, 1990–2000	−0.260***	−0.361***	−0.280***	−0.392***	−0.309***
	(0.077)	(0.085)	(0.076)	(0.084)	(0.083)
Predicted employment growth, 2001–2013	0.792***	1.283***	0.789***	1.302***	1.194***
	(0.203)	(0.221)	(0.205)	(0.226)	(0.216)
Constant	2.943	33.724	−108.468**	46.050	55.939
	(39.011)	(43.686)	(41.912)	(46.822)	(38.562)
2000 demographics[a]	Yes	Yes	Yes	Yes	Yes
Regional fixed effects	Yes	Yes	Yes	Yes	Yes
Observations	709	709	709	709	709
R^2	0.557	0.461	0.565	0.460	0.479

Source: Authors' calculations based on U.S. Census Bureau 2014, U.S. Bureau of Economic Analysis 2014, and Chetty, Hendren, Kline, and Saez 2014c.
[a] 2000 demographics include proportion of population with less than and more than a high school degree, proportion of population under age fifteen, age fifteen to twenty-four, and over age fifty-four, male and female labor force participation rates, and logarithm of population.
+$p < 0.10$; *$p < 0.05$; **$p < 0.01$; ***$p < 0.001$

that component of the mobility measure and income growth in the CZ (the dependent variable), we reestimate the regression in table 2 column 2, including the ratio of child median income to parent median income in the CZ. In these estimates (not shown), the estimated coefficient on absolute mobility is smaller than in table 1, but still significantly different from zero at the 0.1 percent confidence level. The ratio of median incomes also obtains a positive coefficient estimate that is significantly different from zero.[10] Another indicator that the par-

10. The ratio of medians is not an exogenous variable, since the period between when the parent and child incomes are observed (late 1990s to between 2011 and 2012) overlaps the growth period (2000 to 2013) and hence directly measures some of what the dependent variable measures. That relationship should bias upward the

tially endogenous increase in income of children relative to parents in the CZ is not wholly responsible for absolute mobility's significant positive effect on CZ income growth between 2000 and 2013 is provided by substituting the residuals from a regression of absolute mobility on the ratio of child to parent median income for the absolute mobility measure in the growth regression. Those estimated coefficients are shown in table 2 column 5 and indicate a positive effect of growth-purged absolute mobility on economic growth that is significantly different from zero with better than 99.9 percent confidence.

A more comprehensive approach addresses these concerns as well as the overlap in timing of the mobility and growth measures by treating the mobility measures as endogenous in the growth equation. As instruments for mobility, we include measures of family structure, segregation, and earlier foreign immigration. Although we hypothesize that these variables influence mobility but not growth (other than indirectly via mobility), it is also possible that the instrumental variables are correlated with a latent factor, such as social capital, that also affects growth. Selected estimated coefficients from these two-stage least squares regressions are shown in table 3. The estimated coefficient on the endogenous absolute mobility variable is positive and significantly different from zero, but the coefficient on relative mobility is statistically indistinguishable from zero when the variable is treated as endogenous.

The equations reported in tables 1 through 3 suffer from various robustness issues. One key issue arises because the equations are estimated in the cross section. When cross-section studies omit some time-invariant characteristics that are associated with both inequality and growth, it can bias the inequality coefficients downward. Voitchovsky points out that "the negative effect [of inequality on growth] reported in cross-section studies is usually found to be sensitive to the inclusion of regional dummies, of other explanatory variables, or to sample composition" (2009, 565). Some of these concerns, at least regarding mobility results, should be assuaged by the fact that the estimates are largely invariant to inclusion of a variety of demographic control variables and regional fixed effects. Furthermore, we address the concern of Banerjee and Duflo (2003) regarding an assumption of linearity of inequality's effects on growth by including several measures of inequality at different points in the income distribution; Voitchovsky makes the same claim.

That said, caution in interpreting the estimates is important. The mobility coefficients are likely driven by a host of factors associated with inequality of opportunity, such as the quality of schools available to poor children, access to higher education and training, and low barriers of entry into desirable occupations and employment. Most of these factors are temporally predetermined, but some concern remains that unobserved (by us) determinants of growth may be correlated with unobserved determinants of inequality of opportunity. For example, persistent positive shocks to a CZ's competitiveness may lead to both enhanced labor market opportunities for young workers and increased per capita income growth, leading to upward bias in the estimator of the mobility coefficient in a growth regression. We address this concern to some extent in the next section, where we empirically examine whether past growth (or endogenous current growth) is associated with mobility.

All in, the estimates in tables 1 through 3 provide some confirmation of the results in Marrero and Rodriguez, indicating that inequality of opportunity may hinder growth.[11] At least across commuting zones, the positive relationship between absolute upward mobility and growth in the 2000s (both 2000 to 2013 and 2007 to 2013) is quite robust to inclusion

---

estimated coefficient of the ratio of medians on CZ income growth. The point of reporting these results is to make clear that even controlling for shifts in the central tendency of children's income relative to parents' income, absolute mobility still contributes positively to growth.

11. The results are also consistent, in a more indirect way, with Hsieh and colleagues' findings of significant negative effects on output of inequality of opportunity in occupational choice.

Table 3. Two-Stage Least Squares Regressions of Growth on Mobility

	Dependent Variable: Per Capita Income Growth, 2000–2013	
	(1)	(2)
Absolute mobility[a]	0.882*	
	(0.397)	
Relative mobility[a]		0.156
		(0.284)
Gini (inequality) of parental income	−2.544	−18.762
	(16.425)	(15.439)
Per capita income, 2000	−0.924**	−0.747*
	(0.318)	(0.325)
Per capita income growth, 1990–2000	−0.325***	−0.363***
	(0.080)	(0.083)
Predicted employment growth, 2001–2013	1.170***	1.303***
	(0.217)	(0.220)
Constant	37.422	56.874
	(39.143)	(43.001)
2000 demographics[b]	Yes	Yes
Regional fixed effects	Yes	Yes
Observations	709	709
R^2	0.510	0.459

Source: Authors' calculations based on U.S. Census Bureau 2014, U.S. Bureau of Economic Analysis 2014, and Chetty, Hendren, Kline, and Saez 2014c.
[a] Absolute mobility and relative mobility are treated as endogenous variables in two-stage least squares estimation. Instruments for both measures include 1990 and 1980 proportion foreign-born, proportion commuting less than fifteen minutes, and proportion of households with children that have female head and no spouse present.
[b] 2000 demographics include proportion of population with less than and more than a high school degree, proportion of population under age fifteen, age fifteen to twenty-four, and over age fifty-four, male and female labor force participation rates, and logarithm of population.
+$p < 0.10$; *$p < 0.05$; **$p < 0.01$; ***$p < 0.001$

of other CZ characteristics. The relative mobility results are somewhat less conclusive, but generally also find a positive relationship between relative mobility and growth.

How Does Growth Affect Inequality of Opportunity?

We next turn briefly to the reverse direction of causation: the effects of growth on inequality of opportunity.[12] The only paper we have found that directly investigates this topic is that of Marrero and Rodriguez (2012), who use U.S. time series data to model the macroeconomic determinants of both inequality of opportunity and inequality of effort (the residual category). After statistically adjusting their data to extract the trend-cycle components, they find that the change in lagged real GDP has a statistically significant negative coefficient in regressions for both the change in inequality of opportu-

---

12. To the degree that growth affects overall inequality (inequality of outcomes) as discussed above, and inequality of outcomes in turn affects inequality of opportunity, as discussed in the introduction, growth could have indirect effects on inequality of opportunity as well as the direct effects discussed immediately below. For ex-

nity and the change in inequality of effort, implying that growth reduces both components of inequality.

Chetty and his colleagues (2014a) discuss correlations of their absolute mobility measure with a variety of other CZ characteristics. But they do not look at economic growth except as a possible measurement problem.[13] One class of variables they include in their correlation analysis (Chetty et al. 2014b) is local (CZ) labor market conditions, but none of these variables—labor force participation rate, fraction working in manufacturing, growth in Chinese imports, and young teen (ages fourteen to fifteen) participation rate—are indicators of economic growth.

The channels through which economic growth might enhance or weaken equality of opportunity include the political sphere: a fast-growing area might have more resources to share, via the public sector, with all residents. That is, faster economic growth might lead to greater public investments, including investment in the human capital of low-income residents who, as discussed, are less able to make those investments privately.[14] Fast-growing areas might also provide better labor market opportunities to disadvantaged groups that extend beyond the effect on human capital investments. Tight labor markets may induce firms to offer jobs or promotions to employees who would be passed over in slower growing localities, effectively reducing the role of circumstances.

Table 4 reports estimated coefficients from regressions of absolute or relative mobility on per capita income growth in an earlier period (earlier than the mid-1990s to 2012 period in which the mobility is occurring) or contemporaneous growth treated endogenously, plus selected control variables that might influence mobility. However, we are not able to control for welfare and health expenditure or availability of consumer credit at the CZ level, two macro factors that Marrero and Rodriguez (2013) find are associated with lower inequality of opportunity.

In columns 1 and 2, earlier-period growth has a positive estimated coefficient when explaining mobility (absolute or relative); however, the estimated coefficient is significantly different from zero when 1980 demographics are controlled for (and the earlier period is 1970 to 1980) but not when 1990 demographics are controlled for and the earlier period is 1980 to 1990 (that is, panel B, not panel A). When we also include per capita income growth between 2000 and 2013 treated as an endogenous variable in columns 3 and 4, early-period growth remains important in explaining mobility, but contemporaneous growth adds a further positive effect only when controlling for 1990 demographics (panel A).[15]

All in all, we find that earlier economic growth (and in some cases contemporaneous economic growth) is positively associated with mobility, suggesting that faster growth enhances economic opportunity. However, lack-

---

ample, some see signs of a negative reinforcing cycle in recent years along the following lines: as the rich benefit disproportionately from growth (growth leads to increased inequality of outcomes), it augments their degree of control over the political process. This increased control, in turn, allows them to induce policy changes that cut back on (equalizing) redistribution via taxes and spending, which makes it more difficult for the poor to gain access to education, preventive health care, and so on (increasing inequality of opportunity). Stiglitz, for example, says "the rich, needing few public services and worried that a strong government might redistribute income, use their political influence to cut taxes and curtail government spending. This leads to underinvestment in infrastructure, education, and technology, impeding the engines of growth" (Stiglitz 2012).

13. They are concerned that economic growth differentials may be responsible for the spatial variation in upward mobility. But they check on income growth, residuals from a mobility-on-growth regression, and cost-of-living differences and find that none of the adjustments substantially alter absolute mobility's spatial patterns.

14. As discussed earlier, this is one of the arguments made by Kuznets as to why inequality did not continue expanding indefinitely as growth proceeded in an advanced economy.

15. We instrument for the endogenous growth variable with variables expected to influence growth but not mobility, including predicted employment growth, per capita income at the beginning of the growth period (2000), and the age mix of the CZ population.

Table 4. Coefficients on Economic Growth in Mobility Regressions

	OLS		2SLS	
	(1)	(2)	(3)	(4)
	Absolute Mobility	Relative Mobility	Absolute Mobility	Relative Mobility
Panel A				
Per capita income growth, 1980–1990	0.011+	0.010	0.027***	0.020+
	(0.006)	(0.009)	(0.007)	(0.011)
Per capita income growth, 2000–2013[a]			0.087***	0.056+
			(0.018)	(0.029)
Constant	33.224***	79.590***	34.444***	80.374***
	(4.558)	(6.723)	(4.077)	(6.706)
Parental inequality measures[b]	Yes	Yes	Yes	Yes
1990 demographics[c]	Yes	Yes	Yes	Yes
Regional fixed effects	Yes	Yes	Yes	Yes
Observations	709	709	709	709
R^2	0.792	0.652	0.829	0.644
Panel B				
Per capita income growth, 1970–1980	0.017***	0.028***	0.016**	0.030**
	(0.004)	(0.007)	(0.006)	(0.009)
Per capita income growth, 2000–2013[a]			0.005	−0.012
			(0.023)	(0.037)
Constant	27.994***	68.971***	28.386***	68.024***
	(4.095)	(6.524)	(4.360)	(7.064)
Parental inequality measures[b]	Yes	Yes	Yes	Yes
1980 demographics[c]	Yes	Yes	Yes	Yes
Regional fixed effects	Yes	Yes	Yes	Yes
Observations	709	709	709	709
R^2	0.823	0.655	0.828	0.653

Source: Authors' calculations based on U.S. Census Bureau 2014, U.S. Bureau of Economic Analysis 2014, and Chetty, Hendren, Kline, and Saez 2014c.

[a] Per capita income growth 2000–2013 is treated as an endogenous variable in two-stage least squares estimation. Instruments include predicted employment growth, per capita income, and age mix of the population at beginning of growth period (2000).

[b] Parental inequality measures are Gini coefficient, proportion middle class, and top 1 percent income share.

[c] Demographic variables (1980 or 1990) include per capita income, proportion foreign born, proportion commuting less than fifteen minutes, proportion of households with children that have female head and no spouse present, proportion population with education less than high school, proportion population with greater than high school education, male labor force participation rate, female labor force participation rate, log of population size.

+$p < 0.10$; *$p < 0.05$; **$p < 0.01$; ***$p < 0.001$

ing any direct measures of redistribution and tightness of local labor markets, through which faster growth might translate into more equal opportunity, these estimates are only weakly suggestive and might better be viewed as partial correlations, rather than being given a causal interpretation.

DISCUSSION AND CONCLUSION

Although a rich literature has developed on the relationship between inequality of outcomes and economic growth, a consensus has not yet emerged from this literature. Theory suggests that the relationship is complex and empirical results on this relationship are notoriously mixed. By contrast, inequality of opportunity is generally theorized to be a drag on growth. The limited empirical literature investigating this relationship is also somewhat mixed, though two of the three existing papers we cite find a negative effect. This paper adds to that literature, also finding a negative effect of low mobility (high inequality of opportunity) on growth. In addition, we provide suggestive evidence that faster growth boosts intergenerational mobility.

Unequal opportunity represents inefficiency because barriers prevent the most productive use of human and other resources. It has long been recognized that, at a microeconomic level, policies that relax barriers to opportunity will also enhance economic efficiency. The interesting result that appears to be emerging from the nascent research literature on inequality of opportunity and economic growth is that the strength of the efficiency effect is strong enough to be picked up at an aggregate level. The finding that inequality of opportunity has a negative effect on growth suggests that relaxing barriers to opportunity may be a viable strategy for promoting economic growth.

An important unanswered question is to what extent does the increased economic growth that results from reduced inequality of opportunity accrue to those who directly benefit from enhanced opportunities, and to what extent does it spill over to other economic actors? One obvious source of positive spillovers is through fiscal externalities. The improved economic outcomes of those facing enhanced opportunities would result in their paying higher taxes and receiving fewer public transfers and services. However, externalities from increased equality of opportunity may also operate in more subtle ways. Complementarities between the human capital investments made by those with enhanced opportunities and the productivity of other workers (and capital) may be another potential source of positive spillovers. Thinking more broadly, positive externalities may also be generated by the improved operation of market mechanisms resulting from higher levels of trust and sense of fairness in an economy with fewer barriers to opportunity. An interesting task for future research will be to unravel the source of the effect of increased equality of opportunity on growth, separately identifying the direct effects and the spillovers.

Another important area for further investigation is which aspects of inequality of opportunity are most detrimental to economic growth. This insight is needed to give policymakers a guide to which set of opportunity-enhancing policies is likely to be most effective in boosting growth. The existing research we summarize and our own analysis do not shed light on specific policy tools that enhance both equal opportunity and growth. Understanding which aspects of enhanced opportunities are likely to generate the greatest spillovers would also be an important input into the policy process.

Equality of opportunity is almost universally viewed as a desirable goal on ethical and moral grounds. The finding that reduced inequality of opportunity is associated with increased economic growth suggests that pursuing this goal may have a lower cost than one might otherwise have calculated. As Federico Cingano notes, "policies that help limiting or—ideally—reversing the long-run rise in inequality would not only make societies less unfair, but also richer" (2014, 28). However, the moral and ethical dimension of the policy goal is important to remember. On close inspection, some barriers to opportunity may turn out to be more closely associated with growth than are others, but relaxing barriers to opportunity may still be very desirable on ethical grounds even when the resulting effect on economic growth is minor or nonexistent.

APPENDIX

Table A1. Summary Statistics

	Mean	SD
Absolute mobility	43.94	5.681
Relative mobility	67.49	6.479
Gini (inequality) of parental income	0.410	0.0792
Parental middle class	0.550	0.0786
Top 1 percent income share	10.84	5.049
Parent income ratio 90th percentile to 50th	2.283	0.378
Parent income ratio 50th percentile to 10th	3.276	0.424
Per capita income, 1980	8.538	1.777
Per capita income, 1990	15.88	2.989
Per capita income, 2000	24.43	4.766
Per capita income, 2007	32.52	6.491
Per capita income growth, 1970–1980	149.2	26.42
Per capita income growth, 1980–1990	87.68	20.83
Per capita income growth, 1990–2000	54.14	9.944
Per capita income growth, 2000–2007	33.42	9.304
Per capita income growth, 2000–2013	63.09	26.16
Per capita income growth, 2007–2013	21.94	13.94
Predicted employment growth, 2001–2013	8.676	4.200
Predicted employment growth, 2007–2013	0.694	2.407
Residuals (see text)	0.000	4.214
Foreign born, 1980	0.0252	0.0318
Foreign born, 1990	0.0275	0.0391
Workers with commute < fifteen minutes, 1980	0.508	0.142
Workers with commute < fifteen minutes, 1990	0.489	0.139
Households with kids headed by single mom, 1980	0.0491	0.0168
Households with kids headed by single mom, 1990	0.0582	0.0194
Less than high school, 1980	0.381	0.110
Less than high school, 1990	0.287	0.0907
Less than high school, 2000	0.215	0.0760
More than high school, 1980	0.399	0.0809
More than high school, 1990	0.441	0.0912
More than high school, 2000	0.452	0.0946
Age less than fifteen, 2000	0.210	0.0268
Age fifteen to twenty-four, 2000	0.143	0.0282
Age greater than fifty-four, 2000	0.238	0.0485
Male labor force participation rate, 1980	72.27	6.050
Male labor force participation rate, 1990	70.62	5.787
Male labor force participation rate, 2000	67.82	6.573
Female labor force participation rate, 1980	46.07	5.966
Female labor force participation rate, 1990	52.87	6.206
Female labor force participation rate, 2000	55.65	5.786
Logarithm of population, 1980	11.57	1.406
Logarithm of population, 1990	11.60	1.454
Logarithm of population, 2000	11.69	1.488
Logarithm of population, 2007	11.72	1.525
Observations	709	

Source: Authors' calculations based on U.S. Census Bureau 2014, U.S. Bureau of Economic Analysis 2014, and Chetty, Hendren, Kline, and Saez 2014c.

REFERENCES

Acemoglu, Daron, and James A. Robinson. 2012. *Why Nations Fail: The Origins of Power, Prosperity, and Poverty.* New York: Crown Publishing.

Aghion, Philippe, Eve Caroli, and Cecilia Garcia-Penalosa. 1999. "Inequality and Economic Growth: The Perspective of the New Growth Theories." *Journal of Economic Literature* 37(4): 1615-60.

Bailey, Martha J., and Susan M. Dynarski. 2011. "Gains and Gaps: Changing Inequality in U.S. College Entry and Completion." *NBER* working paper no. 17633. Cambridge, Mass.: National Bureau of Economic Research.

Banerjee, Abhijit V., and Esther Duflo. 2003. "Inequality and Growth: What Can the Data Say?" *Journal of Economic Growth* 8(3): 267-99.

Belley, Philippe, and Lance Lochner. 2007. "The Changing Role of Family Income and Ability in Determining Educational Achievement." *NBER* working paper no. 13527. Cambridge, Mass.: National Bureau of Economic Research.

Bernstein, Jared. 2013. "The Impact of Inequality on Growth." Washington, D.C.: Center for American Progress. Accessed December 29, 2015. https://www.americanprogress.org/wp-content/uploads/2013/12/BerensteinInequality.pdf.

Blanden, Jo, Paul Gregg, and Lindsey Macmillan. 2007. "Accounting for Intergenerational Income Persistence: Noncognitive Skills, Ability and Education." *Economic Journal* 117(519): C43-60.

Boushey, Heather, and Carter C. Price. 2014. "How Are Economic Inequality and Growth Connected? A Review of Recent Research." Washington, D.C.: Washington Center for Equitable Growth.

Brunori, Paolo, Francisco H. G. Ferreira, and Vito Peragine. 2013. "Inequality of Opportunity, Income Inequality and Economic Mobility: Some International Comparisons." *Policy Research* working paper no. 6304. Washington, D.C.: The World Bank.

Burtless, Gary. 2003. "Has Widening Inequality Promoted or Retarded US Growth?" *Canadian Public Policy/Analyse de Politiques* 29 (Supplement): S185-201.

Carvalho, Laura, and Armon Rezai. 2015. "Personal Income Inequality and Aggregate Demand." *Cambridge Journal of Economics.* Online: March 20, 2015. Accessed December 28, 2015. doi: 10.1093/cje/beu085.

Castex, Gonzalo, and Evgenia Kogan Dechter. 2014. "The Changing Role of Education and Ability in Wage Determination." *Journal of Labor Economics* 32(4): 685-710.

Chetty, Raj, Nathaniel Hendren, Patrick Kline, and Emmanuel Saez. 2014a. "Where Is the Land of Opportunity? The Geography of Intergenerational Mobility in the United States." *Quarterly Journal of Economics* 129(4): 1553-623.

———. 2014b. "Online Appendices for 'Where Is the Land of the Opportunity? The Geography of Intergenerational Mobility in the United States.'" *Quarterly Journal of Economics* 129(4). Accessed December 28, 2015. http://qje.oxfordjournals.org/content/suppl/2014/09/14/qju022.DC1/QJEC12904_CHETTY_ONLINE_appendix.pdf.

———. 2014c. "Data from Chetty, Hendren, Kline, and Saez (2014): Descriptive Statistics by County and Commuting Zone." Data downloaded from the Equality of Opportunity Project. Accessed February 2, 2016. http://equality-of-opportunity.org/index.php/data.

Cingano, Federico. 2014. "Trends in Income Inequality and Its Impact on Economic Growth." *OECD Social, Employment and Migration* working paper no. 163. Paris: OECD.

Corak, Miles. 2013. "Income Inequality, Equality of Opportunity, and Intergenerational Mobility." *Journal of Economic Perspectives* 27(3): 79-102.

Cynamon, Barry Z., and Steven M. Fazzari. 2013. "Inequality and Household Finance During the Consumer Age." *SSRN* working paper no. 752. Rochester, N.Y.: Social Science Research Network.

Dabla-Norris, Era, Kalpana Kochhar, Nujin Suphaphiphat, Frantisek Ricka, and Evridiki Tsounta. 2015. "Causes and Consequences of Income Inequality: A Global Perspective." *IMF* staff discussion note no. SDN/15/13. Washington, D.C.: International Monetary Fund. Accessed December 28, 2015. https://www.imf.org/external/pubs/ft/sdn/2015/sdn1513.pdf.

Dynan, Karen E., Jonathan Skinner, and Stephen P. Zeldes. 2004. "Do the Rich Save More?" *Journal of Political Economy* 112(2): 397-444.

Ferreira, Francisco H. G., Christoph Lakner, Maria Ana Lugo, and Berk Ozler. 2014. "Inequality of Opportunity and Economic Growth: A Cross-Country Analysis." *Policy Research* working paper no. WPS6915. Washington, D.C.: World Bank. Accessed December 28, 2015. http://documents.worldbank.org/curated/en/2014/06/19646107

/inequality-opportunity-economic-growth-cross-country-analysis.

Fox, Mary Anne, Brooke A. Connolly, and Thomas D. Snyder. 2005. *Youth Indicators 2005: Trends in the Well-Being of American Youth*. NCES 2005-050. Washington: U.S. Department of Education.

Frank, Mark W. 2009. "Inequality and Growth in the United States: Evidence from a New State-Level Panel of Income Inequality Measures." *Economic Inquiry* 47(1): 55-68.

Goldin, Claudia, and Lawrence F. Katz. 2008. *The Race Between Education and Technology*. Cambridge, Mass.: Harvard University Press.

Hsieh, Chang-Tai, Eric Hurst, Charles I. Jones, and Peter J. Klenow. 2013. "The Allocation of Talent and U.S. Economic Growth." NBER working paper no. 18693. Cambridge, Mass.: National Bureau of Economic Research.

Kumhof, Michael, and Romain Ranciere. 2010. "Inequality, Leverage and Crises." IMF working paper no. 268. Washington, D.C.: International Monetary Fund. Accessed December 28, 2015. https://www.imf.org/external/pubs/ft/wp/2013/wp13249.pdf.

Kuznets, Simon. 1955. "Economic Growth and Income Inequality." *American Economic Review* 45(1): 1-28.

Levy, Frank, and Peter Temin. 2007. "Inequality and Institutions in 20th Century America." NBER working paper no. 13106. Cambridge, Mass.: National Bureau of Economic Research.

Lucas, Robert R., Jr. 1988. "On the Mechanics of Economic Development." *Journal of Monetary Economics* 22(1): 3-42.

Marrero, Gustavo A., and Juan G. Rodriguez. 2012. "Macroeconomic Determinants of Inequality of Opportunity and Effort in the US: 1970-2009." ECINEQ working paper no. 249. Verona: Society for the Study of Economic Inequality.

———. 2013. "Inequality of Opportunity and Growth." *Journal of Development Economics* 104 (September): 107-22.

Okun, Arthur M. 1975. *Equality and Efficiency: The Big Tradeoff*. Washington, D.C.: Brookings Institution.

Organization for Economic Cooperation and Development. 2012. "Reducing Income Inequality While Boosting Economic Growth: Can It Be Done?" In *Economic Policy Reforms 2012: Going for Growth*. Paris: OECD.

Ostry, Jonathan D., Andrew Berg, and Charalambos G. Tsangarides. 2014. "Redistribution, Inequality, and Growth." *IMF* staff discussion note SDN/14/02. Washington, D.C.: International Monetary Fund. Accessed December 28, 2015. https://www.imf.org/external/pubs/ft/sdn/2014/sdn1402.pdf.

Panizza, Ugo. 2002. "Income Inequality and Economic Growth: Evidence from American Data." *Journal of Economic Growth* 7(1): 25-41.

Piketty, Thomas. 2014. *Capital in the Twenty-First Century*. Translated by Arthur Goldhammer. Cambridge, Mass.: The Belknap Press of Harvard University Press.

Roemer, John E. 1993. "A Pragmatic Theory of Responsibility for the Egalitarian Planner." *Philosophy and Public Affairs* 22(2): 144-66.

Roemer, John E., and Alain Trannoy. Forthcoming. "Equality of Opportunity: Theory and Measurement." *Journal of Economic Literature*.

Stiglitz, Joseph. 2012. *The Price of Inequality: How Today's Divided Society Endangers Our Future*. New York: W. W. Norton.

———. 2013. "Inequality Is Holding Back the Recovery." *New York Times Opinionator*, January 19. Accessed December 28, 2015. http://opinionator.blogs.nytimes.com/2013/01/19/inequality-is-holding-back-the-recovery.

U.S. Bureau of Economic Analysis. 2014. "Regional Data: GDP and Personal Income," tables CA1–3 (Personal income summary), CA4 (Personal income and employment summary), CA25 (Total full-time and part-time employment by SIC industry), and CA25N (Total full-time and part-time employment by NAICS industry). Washington: U.S. Government Printing Office. Accessed September 17, 2014. http://bea.gov/itable/iTable.cfm?ReqID=70&step=1#reqid=70&step=1&isuri=1.

U.S. Census Bureau. 2014. Data from decennial censuses accessed via Minnesota Population Center. *National Historical Geographic Information System: Version 2.0*. Minneapolis, Minn.: University of Minnesota. Accessed August 27, 2014. https://nhgis.org/.

Van der Wiede, Roy, and Branko Milanovic. 2014. "Inequality Is Bad for Growth of the Poor (But Not for That of the Rich)." *Policy Research* working paper no. 6963. Washington, D.C.: World Bank.

Voitchovsky, Sarah. 2005. "Does the Profile of Income Inequality Matter for Economic Growth?: Distinguishing Between the Effects of Inequality in Different Parts of the Income Distribution." *Journal of Economic Growth* 10(3): 273–96.

———. 2009. "Inequality and Economic Growth." In *The Oxford Handbook of Economic Inequality*, edited by Wiemer Salverda, Brian Nolan, and Timothy Smeeding. Oxford: Oxford University Press.